ATLANTIC

OCEAN

Berry
Islands

Spanish Wells

Current
Eleuthera Island

Governor's Harbour

New Providence

Nicholls'
Town

Nassau

Behring
Point

Wemyss
Bight

Arthur's
Town

Little
San Salvador

Cat Island

Andros
Island

Kemps
Bay

Devil's
Point

San Salvador

Cockburn
Town

BAHAMAS

Great
Guana
Cay

Stella
Maris

Rum Cay

Rolleville

George
Town

Great
Exuma

Long Island

Samana
Cay

Clarence Town

page 216

page 268

Crooked Island

French
Cays

Cayo
Coco

Archipiélago de Camagüey

Long
Cay

Snug
Corner

Mayaguana

Betsy Bay

Abraham's
Bay

Ragged Island

Acklins
Island

Cayo
Romano

Loma de
Cunagua
338

Morón

Esmeralda

Cayo
Sabinal

Ciego de
Ávila

San
Pablo

Little
Inagua

Florida

San
Antonio

Nuevitas

Puerto
Manatí

Playa
Uvero

Great
Inagua

Northeast Pt

page 271

Camagüey

Camalote

Carretera Central

Lake
Rosa

Golfo de
Ana María

Vertientes

Guáimaro

Macedonio

Puerto
Padre

Gibara

Punta
de Mulas

Southeast Pt

La Lima

301

Sierra del Chorrillo

Las
Tunas

Banes

Matthew
Town

page 278

La Jagua

Amancio
Rodríguez

Jobabo

Buenaventura

Holguín

Cueto

La Chiva

Santa Cruz
del Sur

Llanura del
Cauto

Guacanayabo

Mayari

Sagua de
Tánamo

Moa

Reina

Golfo de
Guacanayabo

Manzanillo

Cauto

Pico del Cristal
1231

Pico del
Tolde
1175

Baracoa

Campechuela

Bayamo

Contramaestre

Alturas de Baracoa

Maisí

Barrancas

page 294

Palma
Soriano

Punta
de Maisí

Niquero

Sierra Maestra

1128

San
Antonio
del Sur

Manguicito

Cajobabo

Île de la Tortue

Pico
Turquino
1972

Loma el Jobo

Santiago
de Cuba

Gran
Piedra
1214

Baconao

Guantánamo

Port-de-Paix

Cabo
Cruz

Pilón

St-Nicolas

Gros-
Morne

Île de la Gonâve

Gonaïves

Windward

Golfe de la
Gonâve

St-Marc

HAITI

Trench

Montego
Bay

St Ann's
Bay

JAMAICA

Navassa
(USA)

Île de la Gonâve

Lucea

Jérémie

Massif de la Hotte

Savanna
la Mar

1030

Spanish
Town

Port Antonio

Jamaica Channel

Anse
d'Hainault

Les
Cayes

Petit-
Goâve

Mandeville

May
Pen

Kingston

Morant
Point

Port-à-
Piment

Pointe-
à-Gravois

Portland Point

INSIGHT GUIDES

CUBA

APA PUBLICATIONS

Part of the Langenscheidt Publishing Group

2

※ INSIGHT GUIDE

CUBA

Editorial
Project Editor
Pam Barrett
Managing Editor
Lesley Gordon
Editorial Director
Brian Bell

Distribution

UK & Ireland
GeoCenter International Ltd
Meridian House, Churchill Way West
Basingstoke, Hampshire RG21 6YR
Fax: (44) 1256 817988

United States
Langenscheidt Publishers, Inc.
36–36 33rd Street 4th Floor
Long Island City, NY 11106
Fax: 1 (718) 784 0640

Australia
Universal Publishers
1 Waterloo Road
Macquarie Park, NSW 2113
Fax: (61) 2 9888 9074

New Zealand
Hema Maps New Zealand Ltd (HNZ)
Unit D, 24 Ra ORA Drive
East Tamaki, Auckland
Fax: (64) 9 273 6479

Worldwide
Apa Publications GmbH & Co.
Verlag KG (Singapore branch)
38 Joo Koon Road, Singapore 628990
Tel: (65) 6865 1600. Fax: (65) 6861 6438

Printing

Insight Print Services (Pte) Ltd
38 Joo Koon Road, Singapore 628990
Tel: (65) 6865 1600. Fax: (65) 6861 6438

©2008 Apa Publications GmbH & Co.
Verlag KG (Singapore branch)
All Rights Reserved

Fourth Edition 2008

ABOUT THIS BOOK

The first Insight Guide pioneered the use of creative full-color photography in travel guides in 1970. Since then, we have expanded our range to cater for our readers' need not only for reliable information about their chosen destination but also for a real understanding of the culture and workings of that destination and its people. Now, when the internet can supply inexhaustible (but not always reliable) facts, our books marry text and pictures to provide those much more elusive qualities: knowledge and discernment. To achieve this, they rely heavily on the authority of locally based writers and photographers.

Insight Guide: Cuba is structured to convey an understanding of the country and its people as well as to guide readers through its attractions:
♦ The **Features** section, indicated by a yellow bar at the top of each page, covers the political, social and cultural history of Cuba as well as the country's arts, music and sporting scenes, in a series of informative essays.
♦ The main **Places** section, indicated by a blue bar, is a complete guide to all the sights and areas worth visiting. Places of special interest are coordinated by number with the maps, and the chapters include a list of recommended restaurants.

LEFT: strolling along the Malecón in Havana at sunset.

The new feature on Food was also contributed by Barrett who feels that Cuban cuisine is not as bad as it is often painted.

Journalist **Daniel Aeberhard**, who also wrote the *Insight Pocket Guide: Cuba*, updated the history features and the essay on Fidel Castro, and wrote a new chapter on the future of Cuba in the 21st century.

The music feature, *Cuba's Sizzling Sound*, was written by **Sue Steward**, an acknowledged expert on Latin American music and author of *Salsa: Musical Heartbeat of South America.*

The editor and her team of updaters built on the invaluable work of earlier editors and writers, including **Tony Perrottet**, **Joann Biondi** and **Jane McManus**.

Other contributors to earlier editions, whose work has provided a firm foundation, were **Liz Balmaseda**, **José Antonio Evora**, **Sergio Giral**, **Larry Luxner**, **David Lloyd Marcus**, **Naomi Peck**, **James Rodewald**, **Alfonso Silva**, **Ned Sublette**, and **Marjory Zimmerman**.

The quote from Colombian author **Gabriel García Márquez** from an article on his friendship with Fidel Castro (reprinted in full in previous editions) is the copyright of Gianni Mina and Ocean Press, and has been reprinted by kind permission of the Talman Company.

The main photographers were **Anna Mockford** and **Nick Bonetti**, **Glyn Genin**, and Joby Williams who captured the magic of Cuba. Thanks go to **Sylvia Suddes** for proofreading the guide and also to **Penny Phenix** for indexing.

◆ The **Travel Tips** listings section, with an orange bar, provides a point of reference for information on transportation, accommodations, sports, nightlife, the arts, festivals, outdoor activities, and more. An easy-to-find contents list for the Travel Tips is printed on the back flap, which also serves as a bookmark.

The contributors

This latest edition of *Insight Guide: Cuba* was reshaped by editor and regular Insight Guides contributor **Pam Barrett**, who along with Cuba-enthusiast **Joby Williams**, completely updated the Places section and Travel Tips listings.

Map Legend

▬ ▪ ▬	International Boundary
▬ ▬ ▬	Province Boundary
▬ ● ▬	National Park/Reserve
▬ ▬ ▬	Ferry Route
✈ ✈	Airport: International/ Regional
🚌	Bus Station
❶	Tourist Information
✝ ✝ ⚜	Church/Ruins
✝	Monastery
☾	Mosque
✡	Synagogue
◫ ◩	Castle/Ruins
∴	Archaeological Site
∩	Cave
⚑	Statue/Monument
★	Place of Interest
⚑	Beach

The main places of interest in the Places section are coordinated by number with a full-color map (e.g. ❶), and a symbol at the top of every right-hand page tells you where to find the map.

BELOW: coco-taxis are a fun way of getting around city streets.

Contents

LEFT: Santiago de Cuba: Cuba's early capital, and the cradle of the Revolution.

Maps

A map of Cuba is on the inside front cover; a map of Havana is on the inside back cover.

Travel Tips

THE BEST OF CUBA

From wonderful views and heroic sights to colonial architecture and great music venues, here at a glance are our recommendations, plus some handy money-saving tips

BEST HEROIC SITES

● **Monument to Che, Santa Clara** There's a dramatic statue, a small museum, and a mausoleum where the remains of Che Guevara and some of his fellow fighters are interred, and an eternal flame burns. *See page 240.*

● **Monument to Antonio Maceo, Santiago** The impressive monument to the great 19th-century independence fighter dominates the Plaza de la Revolución at the entrance to the town. *See page 295*

● **Playa Girón** The site of the disastrous Bay of Pigs invasion in 1961 is commemorated as "The First Imperialist Defeat in Latin America." *See page 232.*

● **Mausoleum of José Martí, Santiago** The Father of the Nation lies in a splendid marble mausoleum, where an armed guard is changed every half hour, accompanied by martial music. *See page 302.*

● **Moncada Barracks, Santiago** The unsuccessful attack on Moncada in 1953 launched the revolution. A museum gives details. *See page 295.*

● **Parque Nacional Desembarco de Granma, Niquero** On the edge of the Sierra Maestra, this is where the guerrilla war began, in 1956. There is a life-size model of the launch, *Granma*, and a museum. *See page 290.*

BEST THINGS TO BUY

● **Cigars** Cuba is justly renowned for the quality of its cigars – even though their most famous smoker has given them up. Always buy from a reputable outlet.

● **Rum** Called *ron* in Spanish, it is Cuba's second-most famous product and worth taking home.

● **Second-hand books** Magazines and books with a revolutionary theme can be found in book stores and in Havana's Plaza de Armas market, and are sometimes sold on the street.

● **Music** CDs of Cuban music are readily available. ARTex stores are a good source, or you can buy from musicians themselves if you specially like their sound.

ABOVE LEFT: the dramatic Che Guevara monument in Santa Clara.

LEFT: Cuban cigars and Havana Club rum are well worth buying to take home.

BEST VIEWS

● **Havana from Castillo del Morro** From the ramparts of El Morro fortress there is a splendid view across the bay. *See page 305.*

● **Santiago from Hotel Casa Granda** From the top-floor bar at sunset there are glorious views over the city. *See page 298.*

● **Valle de Viñales from the Hotel Los Jazmines** One of the most photographed views in Cuba is to be had across the valley from the hotel. *See page 206.*

● **Trinidad from the Convento de San Francisco** Climb 119 stairs in the bell tower to enjoy a view over Trinidad, and away to the Caribbean. *See page 260.*

BEST PLACES TO HEAR MUSIC

● **Casa de la Cultura de La Habana Vieja** Performances are held in the theater or in the churchyard. There is an enchanting atmosphere.

● **Casa de la Música, Havana** Late-night performances of salsa, songa and rock.

● **La Zorra y el Cuervo, Havana** Famous jazz club on La Rampa. Good acts every night.

● **Casa de la Trova, Santiago** One of the most famous *casas* in Cuba.

● **Casa de las Tradiciones, Santiago** A small, intimate, and very local venue where you will hear truly authentic music.

● **Casa de la Música, Trinidad** On the steps by the Plaza Mayor, there's music and dancing until the early hours.

● **Las Ruínas de Sagarte, Trinidad** Great Afro-Caribbean music and dance in a ruined building *For details of music venues, see page 356.*

BEST COLONIAL ARCHITECTURE

● **Palacio de los Capitanes Generales, Havana** Home to the Spanish governors during the colonial period, this fine building combines baroque with *Mudéjar* features. *See page 143.*

● **Casa de la Obra Pía** This lovely 17th-century building is one of Old Havana's finest colonial mansions. *See page 151.*

● **Palacio Cantero, Trinidad** The whole of Trinidad, a UNESCO World Heritage Site, is impressive, but the palace is one of the gems. *See page 257.*

● **Casa de Velázquez, Santiago** This 16th-century mansion on Santiago's main square has beautiful cedar-wood ceilings, and is believed to be the oldest house in Cuba. *See page 299.*

● **Museo de Artes Decoratives, Gibara** A magnificent 19th-century building with fine *mediopuntos* – the characteristic fan-shaped stained-glass windows. *See page 283.*

ABOVE: music in Cuba is infectious. **ABOVE RIGHT:** the view over Trinidad from San Francisco Convent.
RIGHT: the courtyard of the Palacio de los Capitanes in Havana is a fine example of colonial architecture.

BEST BEACHES

- **Cayo Levisa**
On the north coast of Pinar del Río province, Cayo Levisa is reached by a short boat trip. Thanks to the local fishing industry lobster is the lunch specialty in this attractive little beach resort. *See page 209.*
- **Cayo Largo**
Accessible by air from Havana or Varadero, Cayo Largo may not be "the true Cuba," but it has glorious white sands and clear, calm waters. *See page 328.*
- **María La Gorda**
Located in the far west of the island, this lovely beach flanks waters ideal for diving and sailing. *See page 210.*

- **Playa Esmeralda**
Esmeralda means emerald, which is the color of the water you swim in off this powdery white-sand beach in Holguín province. One of Cuba's most luxurious resort hotels is situated here. *See page 283.*
- **Playa Ancón** Some 12 km (8 miles) south of Trinidad, Playa Ancón has clean white sands backed by palm trees and is a popular place for snorkeling. *See page 262.*
- **Varadero** It was this long stretch of sugar-white sand, considered among the finest in the Caribbean, that made Varadero the island's major tourist resort. *See page 222.*

OUTDOOR ACTIVITIES

- **Walking in the Valle de Viñales**
Take walks with local guides through the breathtakingly beautiful valley. *See page 206.*
- **Birding on Cayo Coco** The protected home to 156 species of birds. *See page 269.*
- **Hiking in the Sierra Maestra**
Great hiking in the hills where Fidel's rebel army fought and hid out. *See page 288.*

- **Exploring the waterfalls of the Sierra de Escambray** Bracing walks and cooling dips amid pristine scenery. *See page 244.*
- **Scuba diving on the Isla de Juventud** One of the best of Cuba's scuba-diving sites. *See page 327.*
- **Discovering wildlife in the Zapata peninsula** Guides will take you to the best sites to see endemic birds, sea turtles and crocodiles. *See page 229.*

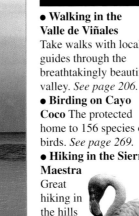

ABOVE RIGHT: the lovely Playa María la Gorda.
ABOVE: water sports are popular in Cuba.
RIGHT: Cuba has a wide variety of exotic bird life, such as the flamingo.

BEST HAVANA PLAZAS

● **Plaza de Armas** Havana's oldest square is lit at night by antique lamps, and is a center of action at all hours. *See page 143.*

● **Plaza de la Catedral** The baroque cathedral and handsome colonial buildings surround the square, where café tables invite you to sit and enjoy a *mojito*. *See page 144.*

● **Plaza Vieja** The square has been renovated with great care over recent years and is now one of the most gracious in the city. *See page 153.*

● **Plaza de la Revolución** The site of the stark memorial to José Martí and the illuminated mural of Che Guevara. The vast square is not beautiful, but it is impressive. *See page 177.*

● **Parque Central** This leafy square, home to the elegant Hotel Inglaterra, is always buzzing with life, especially in the *esquina caliente. See page 157.*

ABOVE: the leafy square known as Parque Central.
ABOVE RIGHT: painting in Museo Nacional Bellas Artes.

BEST MUSEUMS

● **Museo de la Revolución, Havana** Fascinating documentary material, photographs and more, plus, in a separate section, the *Granma*, the launch that brought the rebels to Cuba, and planes that were used to repulse the Bay of Pigs invasion. *See page 160.*

● **Museo Nacional de Bellas Arts, Havana** The museum is on two sites. Both are excellent, but for a real slice of Cuban culture, the Arte Cubano section is best. *See page 160.*

● **Museo Bacardí, Santiago** The museum created by the founder of the Bacardí rum empire is the oldest in Cuba. It contains some interesting Cuban artworks, plus an eclectic assortment of items, including an Egyptian mummy. *See page 296.*

● **Museo Romántico, Trinidad** Located in the mansion of a wealthy Spanish plantation owner, the museum has a wonderful collection of 18th- and 19th-century furniture, porcelain, and other priceless objects, culled from houses all over the city. *See page 259.*

MONEY-SAVING TIPS

● **Stay in *casas particulares*** Staying in rooms in private houses is considerably less expensive than hotels, and is an opportunity to get to know more about Cuba and the Cuban people. Some are housed in beautiful colonial mansions, but the accommodation and the hospitality can be just as good in more modest homes.

● **Eat in *paladares*** Privately run restaurants offer extremely good value.

Some of them are easy to find; others take a bit of seeking out. They usually have a good, local atmosphere, too (but you must pay in cash).

● **Travel on long-distance coaches** Although city buses tend to be overcrowded and uncomfortable, Cuba's long-distance coaches have comfortable seats, washrooms, and air conditioning, and offer a less-expensive alternative to renting a car. They will take you to most

of the places visitors want to go – although not to the more out-of-the-way destinations.

● **Bring cash or traveler's checks** While credit cards are useful for obtaining cash in an emergency, either through a bank or an ATM, they incur an 11 percent commission charge. And don't, of course, bring US dollars, or you will have to pay the high commission rate on cash transactions as well.

THE ISOLATED ISLAND

Cubans find it difficult to buy soap, yet have the
best health-care system in Latin America. It is such
contradictions that explode prejudices and make
the island such a fascinating place to visit

It is difficult to be unemotional about Cuba. This
Caribbean island thrills the senses, befuddles the mind,
and tugs at the heart. It is a magical place, full of romantic images: conga drums pounding late into the night; spicy
roast pork and sweet dark rum; baseball, ballet, and dazzling
nightclubs; quick conversations spiked with sexual innuendo
and wicked humor; people who are warm, expressive and
affectionate; music emanating from every window – all enveloped within
the aroma of hand-rolled cigars.

There are also more somber images of Cuba: frustrated youths willing to
risk their lives in search of a future elsewhere; an outmoded communist system, exacerbated by the privations engendered by a US trade
embargo, that is failing its citizens; political repression and a
stubborn, old dictator; crumbling buildings, empty stores, and
over-crowded buses. It is a place of great contrasts: immacu-
lately dressed schoolchildren emerge from tumble-down tenements. Political opponents portray it as a repressed dictatorship,
yet the people are infectiously exuberant.

Cuba's isolation, however, is becoming a thing of the past.
The Ministry of Tourism is eager to reinvent the island as a
sophisticated vacation destination, to bring in much-needed
income: pristine cays and sleepy fishing villages are being
transformed into modern beach resorts financed by foreign capital. Tourists,
however, are shielded from the harsh realities of life on the island. It is a rare
traveler who experiences the blackouts, the fuel and water shortages, the
inadequate food rations, the long lines, leaky roofs and heavy-handed bureau-
cracy that are daily hardships for the average Cuban.

For most visitors, Cuba is a taste of the good life, a tropical retreat and an
exotic escape. Even so, the average tourist will not leave Cuba unaffected.
Slowly but surely this Caribbean island gets under your sunburned skin and
touches your soul. Opinions – often contradictory ones – of the island and its
people form quickly. It's all quite an experience. ❏

PRECEDING PAGES: Cuba's new generation; a lazy day in Trinidad; boys at play
against a background of Havana's Vedado district at sunset.
LEFT: contemplating life through a haze of cigar smoke.
ABOVE: musical instruments are everywhere. **RIGHT:** a young Trinidadian.

THE CUBANS

Multiracial and multicultural, the vivacious Cuban people are universally hospitable and friendly. Most appear to support their government, but may not always feel free to express their opinions frankly in public

How do you describe the Cuban character? Words like fun-loving, spontaneous, and warm come to mind (not to mention long-suffering). Regardless of their status in society, Cubans tend to be a generous people. This generous nature, closely linked to the gregarious spirit that characterizes the country, is embedded in the Cuban psyche. For one Cuban to label another stingy is to tag him or her with one of the worst character flaws imaginable. The song written by popular songwriter Juan Formell and sung by his band Los Van Van captures the idea: "My hands are always empty, giving when there's nothing to give. Oh, but what can I do? These are the hands that I have!"

A mestizo people

Barely a trace remains in Cuban culture today of the peoples who were here when Christopher Columbus arrived in 1492. For the most part, Cuba's 11.4 million people are a mixture of European, African and indigenous ancestry. The government prefers to emphasize national rather than racial identity, so rarely releases statistics on

Cirilo Villaverde's famous 19th-century novel Cecilia Valdés o La Loma del Ángel *explores, brilliantly, the theme of the children of white "masters" and their black slaves, and the prejudice they faced.*

race, and for a while it deleted all questions about race from the official census. But some unofficial sources calculate that 70 percent of the population are of mixed race.

LEFT: a smile of welcome.
RIGHT: a sidewalk barber's shop.

With the onset of slavery in the 16th century, many Spanish colonizers satisfied their sexual appetites with their slaves – a practice that was common throughout the Americas. The criollo children born of these unions suffered as much social prejudice as did the black slaves.

From the late 1840s, Chinese immigrants began to form an important segment of the Cuban population. According to historian Juan Pérez de la Riva (author of *Slavery and Capitalism in Cuba*), about 35,000 Chinese were brought from Canton to the island to work as servants in conditions similar to that endured by African slaves. Eventually, more than 100,000 came to Cuba. Though only vestiges remain today, until the 1970s Havana's Chinese neighborhood was one of the city's most prosperous. The so-called *Barrio Chino* in central Havana has been revived over the past few years, and now has a popular market and foodstands attracting both local people and tourists – although it is but a shadow of its former self *(see page 171).*

Equality for all

Though once common, terms such as *El Chino* (the Chinese man), *El Negrito* (the black one), and *La Mulata* (the mixed-race woman) are rarely used today – even mentioning racial distinctions is a social taboo (although Chino, as a nickname, still exists). In the 1950s, skin color was a divisive issue. Black people had very little access to good jobs,

portionately from employment in the lucrative tourism industry during the recent boom. According to Carlos Moore, a black Cuban exile scholar, the color of power in Cuba has not changed at all.

The Catholic Church

The Catholic Church was officially separated from the Cuban Government with the birth of the

and were forbidden from joining certain clubs or attending private schools.

With its promise of "equality for all," the revolutionary government has gone a long way toward diminishing the effects of racial discrimination. Today, Cubans of all races and ethnic backgrounds are born in the same hospitals, attend the same schools and are buried in the same cemeteries. But some sociologists argue that, although opportunities for black people advanced dramatically after Fidel Castro took power, the country still suffers from institutional racism. There are only a handful of black people in the upper echelons of the government, and only about a quarter of Cuba's Communist Party are black or mulatto; and there's evidence that black people have not benefitted pro-

republic in 1902. Until the revolution, though, the government considered the Catholic Church its natural ideological ally. As in most Latin American cultures, it served as the foundation of an ordered society. But with the pronouncement of the socialist government in 1961, organized religion was condemned to disappear, and Catholic dogma was replaced by that of Marxism-Leninism. The church was not outlawed, but the revolutionary government viewed it as a dangerous rival and a focus for dissent.

For many years practicing Catholics were punished by limited access to schools and job opportunities. To attend Mass was to "lapse into the past," and the "past" was regarded by revolutionaries as a Bad Thing. Religious observation, however, continued in private, and following the break-up of the eastern bloc, reappeared in public again.

The papal visit

A landmark event occurred in January 1998, when Pope John Paul II visited the island – the last place in Latin America that he had not toured. The paradox was not lost on observers: that a Pope who had spent much of his papacy fighting communism should meet a Marxist like Fidel, who had completely relegated the role of the Catholic Church and institutional religion under his regime. The Pope was keen to advance the cause of reli-

lic holiday, as a one-off "goodwill gesture." The following year, after the Pope's visit, Christmas was reinstated as a permanent public holiday.

The state's position on religion has altered somewhat. Practicing Catholics are allowed to join the Communist Party, and the state is now described as "secular" rather than "atheist."

There seems to be far greater tolerance of religious observance in recent years, and while the number of people attending Catholic services is not high, neither is it negligible, especially among elderly people. Places of particular significance, such as the Basílica del Cobre, just outside Santiago, attract worshipers on a regular basis, while

gious freedom and human rights in Cuba; whereas Castro hoped to benefit from the international prestige of the event (demonstrating that his regime had nothing to hide), and on exploiting the fact that the Pope had publicly opposed the US embargo, so as to isolate the position of the US Government and the Miami exile community.

Vast crowds greeted the Pope at the open-air masses held all over the country, and hopes were high that his visit would herald a period of radical reform. For the first time since 1969, Fidel had declared that Christmas of 1997 would be a pub-

the festival here on September 8, venerating the Virgen de la Caridad, is a major event. A bust of the Pope, who visited the basilica when he was in Cuba, stands outside the church.

The Evangelical churches, too, have gained a foothold in Cuba, not on the same level that they have in some parts of Latin America, but they are a presence, nevertheless.

The power of Santería

Although all forms of religious devotion were proscribed for many years, Santería has survived. It is a mixture of Catholicism and traditional West African beliefs brought here by slaves in colonial times. The mixture of the rites and rituals of these two beliefs is classic religious syncretism (the

LEFT: onion sellers hawk their wares around the city streets.
ABOVE AND RIGHT: Catholicism is still strong in Cuba.

Virgen de la Caridad, for example, is also worshiped in Afro-Cuban religions as the goddess Ochún). Although it began as a religion of Cuba's black population, Santería followers now come from all walks of life. It is estimated that at least 90 percent of Cubans have participated in some form of Santería ritual, despite the fact that for many years it, too, was discouraged by the state.

The dominant influence behind Santería comes from the Yoruba religion and folklore of West Africa, which has had wider effects on Cuban popular culture: for example, many common Cuban proverbs are literal translations from the Yoruba language, and others are identical, except

wisdom differs. Instead of consulting one supreme being, *babalawos* use various instruments to interpret the wishes of the *orishas* or gods. These include the *tablero*, a circular board on which certain items are cast, and a *cadeneta*, a special necklace which is swung onto the floor to produce certain signs. Some *babalawos* use coconut shells or cards as their medium. Each sign carries many myths and stories which the priest will interpret for his client. A *babalawo* might advise a patient to sprinkle Catholic holy water around their home in order to chase away evil spirits. If the problem is caused by the spiritual presence of a dead loved one, they might instruct the patient to "steal a

that the cultural context has been altered – a Cuban animal swapped for a West African one, for example. Originally consisting of various tribes living near the African equator, the Yoruba had a common linguistic bond. In her study, *The Orishas of Cuba*, Natalia Bolívar wrote that two worshipers who lived in the Havana neighborhood of Regla unified all the Yoruba cults under the name of "Regla de Ocha." Then, the story goes, a Cuban slave who returned to Africa after the abolition of slavery was recognized there as a descendant of the kings *(obbas)*, and ordered to return to Cuba to found the sacred order of high priests, called the *babalawos*.

As in Catholicism, Santería priests offer guidance and counsel, but the source of their divine

mass." To do this, the patient would attend a Catholic Mass where the souls of the dead are being prayed for, and when the priest mentions the names of the dead who are being honored, they would whisper the name of their loved one. The annoying spirit then floats away and leaves the person in peace. *(See pages 104–5 for more on Afro-Cuban religions.)*

Machismo prevails

Born of two essentially patriarchal cultures, Cubans are largely *machista*, and traditionally homophobic. Only men are permitted to become Santería priests, for example, and women walking alone on the street are often bombarded with overt sexual comments from men. These *piropos* (flirtatious remarks) range from a courteous compliment to a blatant invitation for sex. Many Cuban women, however, accustomed to this from an early age, are capable of giving just as good as they get. *Cubanas* may be victims of *machismo* in some areas of life, but they appear remarkably self-confident.

Many years of official policy designed to achieve the "equality of women" have undoubtedly improved the lot of women in Cuba, but it has by no means dissolved the island's deep-rooted *machismo* spirit. Far from liberating them socially, the government's goal of incorporating women into the workforce has actually led to their

care. While this is obviously difficult to enforce, it was a move in the right direction.

A negative side effect of the revolution has been the increasing divorce rate. According to government statistics, about 5 percent of marriages ended in divorce in 1953. It is now estimated that, among Cubans aged from 25 to 40, a remarkable 60 percent of marriages fail. One reason for this is the lack of independent living space for newlyweds, who are forced to live in cramped apartments with their families. The decline of the influence of the Catholic Church has also been a factor, though another reason for the rise is the fact that the revolutionary government has made

having two jobs: one at the workplace and the other in the home, doing most of the cooking, shopping, cleaning and child-minding. However, this is not so different from what happens in the US and many European countries. Raúl Castro's wife, Vilma Espín, who died in June 2007, championed women's rights and lobbied for men to do more in the home and, especially, with raising children. She founded the Federación de Mujeres Cubanas (the Federation of Cuban Women), in 1960, and in 1975 drew up the Family Code, which obliged men to share housework and child-

LEFT: a Santería practitioner dressed all in white.
ABOVE: Vilma Espín, who championed women's rights.
RIGHT: carrying home the Mother's Day cakes.

MOTHER'S DAY

The role of mother is revered in Cuba, and Mother's Day, in mid-May, is a major event. Some say it is the only day in the year when the mail is bound to arrive on time, for the importance of Mother's Day cards getting to the recipient on the day is not taken lightly. Long-distance buses will be crammed with people carrying flowers and gifts en route to visit their mothers. Everywhere you go you will see people carrying large, square cakes, brightly iced in pink or blue, that are handed out of baker's stores by the dozen. And flower sellers, their trucks filled with blooms, do a roaring trade outside cemeteries as people come from far and near to visit the graves of their departed mothers.

it much easier to obtain a divorce: all it takes is a few hours and about half a month's salary. Again, this should be compared to the situation elsewhere: the US has the highest divorce rate in the Western world (44 percent) followed by the UK and Canada. Not as high as in Cuba, but indicative of a growing trend.

Homophobia and gay rights

Although official statistics estimate Cuba's homosexual population to be between 4 and 6 percent, the real figure is likely to be much higher since many gay people maintain public heterosexual relationships in order to avoid harassment. Since

suffered severe discrimination. However, there is more official tolerance of gay people these days. Homosexuality was legalized in 1979, and generally discrimination is less institutionalized today, although police harassment, for example, still exists. Groups of gay men and women have begun to form associations and meet formally to discuss gay rights – a move that even a few years ago would have raised quite a storm. Also, many say that much depends on where gay people work. Intellectuals and university students are far more tolerant of individual sexual preferences than blue-collar workers or farmers – but this is the same the world over.

the early 1960s, thousands of gay people have fled the island, including a large contingent that left during the Mariel boatlift of 1980 *(see page 75)*.

It is important to note that the most deprecating name used to refer to homosexual males in Cuba – *maricón* (queer) – is applied only to homosexuals who are "passive." Active homosexuals are generally referred to instead as *bujarrones*, or "butch." According to the *machismo* thinking that so esteems virility, these "active" gay people deserve less disrespect since they are "stronger." But because the political system does not consider them capable of performing "virile" tasks, and given that the cult of virility was so fundamental to the revolution, even so-called "butch" homosexuals have

Mariela Castro, Raúl's daughter, who now heads the National Center for Sex Education, has promoted homosexual-rights issues. It remains to be seen how much effect this will have.

Responses in cinema

The film *Fresa y Chocolate*, about a gay intellectual who falls in love with a straight Communist Party militant, brought the gay issue to the forefront in the early 1990s; it played to full houses in Havana and won several international awards. Julian Schnabel's 2000 film, *Before Night Falls*, starred Javier Bardem as the celebrated novelist Reinaldo Arenas (1943–90), who was imprisoned as a homosexual and political dissident before going into exile in 1981.

The film received international awards but has not, as yet, been shown in Cuba.

Changing attitudes

The appearance of Aids did nothing to help the status of gay people in Cuba. When the country's first Aids case appeared in 1985, the government quarantined patients in special sanitariums. The policy was condemned abroad as an abuse of human rights, but it helped contain the spread of the disease initially; many Aids-infected gay people voluntarily checked themselves into these sanitariums, where they had better access to food and medicines, and could live together openly.

of keeping a single patient in a sanatarium, some US$46,000 a year, was just too great to be sustainable. The places began to fall apart: broken furniture and equipment were not replaced, there were not enough lightbulbs and food quality deteriorated badly.

HIV-positive people are no longer confined in these places and, realizing that the government's original purpose of isolating the infected had failed, the system has been replaced with a "care in the community" policy. Emphasis is concentrated more on education, treatment, and assistance rather than isolation. Cuba's system today is acknowledged as being extremely effective and is frequently praised.

The picture has changed substantially since the growth of tourism in the 1990s and this, combined with rocketing levels of prostitution, a general hostility to the practice of safe sex, and the rampant promiscuity of Cuban society, has caused the number of heterosexual cases of HIV-infection to rise rapidly, and fears have been expressed that Cuba may be experiencing an Aids epidemic. But infection rates are still very low by comparison with other Caribbean countries.

The sanitarium system began to break down fairly quickly, partly due to lack of funds. The cost

LEFT: being gay in Cuba is less of a problem than it used to be. **ABOVE:** Reinaldo Arenas, who went into exile in 1981. **RIGHT:** waiting for changes.

Support or discretion?

It is difficult for an outsider to know exactly how Cubans feel about their government and society. If they are critical, they are unlikely to express it openly. On the one hand, people talk with apparent sincerity about the "triumph of the revolution," and appear supportive of Fidel, as he is invariably called. On the other hand, there are those who find the system insupportable, and who make their feelings known by leaving – or trying to. Most people would like some of the consumer goods and freedoms that tourists take for granted, but tend to blame shortages and hardships on the *bloqueo*, as they call the US embargo, while they wait, no doubt with mixed feelings, to see what changes are in store. ❏

DECISIVE DATES

PRE-COLUMBIAN PERIOD (6000BC–AD1492)

c. 6000–3000BC
First waves of native American settlers, pre-ceramic hunter-gatherer groups, sometimes known as the Guanahatabeys, the ancestors of the Ciboneyes.

c. AD600
Arawak-speaking Taínos reach Cuba, arriving in hollowed-out tree-trunk canoes. They come to dominate eastern and central Cuba, although Ciboney groups are never entirely displaced. The Taínos bring a more settled, agricultural way of life.

c. 1490
Native population estimated at over 100,000.

SPANISH SETTLEMENT (1492–1762)

1492
Christopher Columbus sights Cuba.

1508
Sebastián de Ocampo circumnavigates the island.

1509
Diego de Velázquez's first expedition.

1511–15
Velázquez returns to found Baracoa, followed by six other initial settlements (*villas*) around Cuba.

1512
Cacique Hatuey, the great Taíno chief, is burnt at the stake. Indigenous resistance crumbles. In the subsequent years most of the indigenous people are massacred, die of disease, or become forced laborers under the *encomienda* system.

1515
Santiago de Cuba becomes the capital.

1519
Havana is moved from the south coast to its present position on the north coast.

1523
The first African slaves are brought to the island to work in the mines and on plantations.

1537
First slave revolt crushed.

1546
French pirates plunder the eastern town of Baracoa.

1555
French forces sack Havana. On the orders of Felipe II (1527–98) fortresses are built to protect Havana and Santiago in the east.

c. 1560
Fewer than 3,000 indigenous people remain.

PRECEDING PAGES: flag waving in Havana's Plaza de la Revolución.

1607
Havana is named the official capital.

1668
English expedition under Henry Morgan sails upriver to Puerto Príncipe (modern Camagüey) and sacks the town.

1682
The Inquisition comes to Cuba, and strikes first in Remedios, which is torched after a Spanish priest discovers "devils."

1717
Tobacco trade declared a Crown monopoly.

THE BRITISH OCCUPATION (1762–3)

1762
Havana falls to a massive British invasion force. The port is opened up to international trade, breaking the monopoly of Spanish Crown.

1763
Havana is returned to Spanish rule as Britain swaps Havana for Florida (the Treaty of Paris).

SUGAR BOOM AND SLAVERY (1774–1840)

c. 1790s
Sugar replaces tobacco as Cuba's most valuable export. African slaves are imported in huge numbers to work on the plantations.

1795
French Haitian landowners flee the slave revolution and settle in Oriente (Cuba's eastern province).

Early 1800s
The price of sugar and land soars. Beginnings of independence movements in Cuba. Simón Bolívar leads anti-colonial revolts across Latin America.

1825
Cuba and Puerto Rico are Spain's only Latin colonies.

1837
Latin America's first railroad in operation between Bejucal and Havana.

TWO WARS OF INDEPENDENCE (1868–98)

1868
Carlos Manuel de Céspedes liberates his slaves near Manzanillo in Oriente and

issues call to arms against Spanish overlords, sparking the Ten Years' War.

1869
Rebels issue Constitution of Guáimaro.

1871
José Martí, independence fighter, poet and journalist, is exiled to Spain; he later settles in New York.

1873
Céspedes replaced as rebel leader.

1878
Peace treaty signed. Rebel factions split.

1879–1880
The "Little War" breaks out.

1886
Spain abolishes all slavery.

1892
José Martí founds the Cuban Revolutionary Party from exile in the US.

1895
The Second War of Independence, led by José Martí,

who dies in the first battle at Dos Ríos.

1896
Antonio Maceo, who took over the independence leadership role, is killed in western Cuba. Máximo Gómez returns from exile and continues the struggle. Spanish forces initiate a "scorched-earth" policy in the countryside.

1898
US battleship *Maine* sunk in Havana's harbor after an explosion, which prompts the US to enter the conflict. Spanish forces defeated at the Battle of San Juan Hill. Spain signs a peace treaty ceding control of Cuba to the US.

CORRUPTION AND COUPS (1901–59)

1901
The Platt Amendment adopted, under which the Guantánamo naval base is ceded to the US, and the US claims the right to intervene in Cuban affairs. Provokes widespread Cuban anger.

1902
Tomás Estrada Palma is inaugurated as president.

1906–9
Marines invade to protect US interests.

1912
Afro-Cuban Black Uprising is savagely repressed.

1924–33
General Machado's presidency prone to venality and violence. General strike forces him to flee.

1934
Fulgencio Batista stages a coup. Puppet president installed under army control. Abrogation of Platt Amendment, but Guantánamo left in US control.

1940–4
First Batista presidency after national vote.

1952
Batista seizes power and cancels elections.

1956
Fidel Castro's guerrilla force sails from Mexico in the *Granma*. Hideout established in Sierra Maestra.

1958
Guevara opens second front in Sierra del Escambray. Batista flees.

THE REVOLUTIONARY YEARS (1959–90)

1959
Castro enters Havana. First land reform introduced; literacy and public-health campaigns launched.

1960
Nationalization of major companies.

1961
US-backed invasion results in Bay of Pigs fiasco. Castro declares socialist nature of revolution.

1962
Cuban Missile Crisis brings world to brink of nuclear war. Cuba brought further into Soviet orbit. US economic blockade begins in earnest.

1964
Castro pays first visit to Soviet Union.

1965
Che Guevara resigns posts and leaves for Africa.

1967
Guevara killed in Bolivia.

1970
Failure of 10 million-ton sugar harvest target.

1976
Right-wing exile terrorist group bombs plane over Barbados, killing all 73 Cuban athletes on board.

1980
Mariel Boatlift: 120,000 leave Cuba – legally – for Miami.

1989
Execution of General Ochoa for alleged drug smuggling and corruption.

THE SPECIAL PERIOD AND RECOVERY (POST-1990)

1991
Russian economic aid axed completely after end of the Soviet Union. Chronic food

and fuel shortages begin. Industry crippled.

1993
Dollar is legalized, and limited forms of private enterprise allowed. Economic privations continue.

1994
Crisis of the boat people: 35,000 Cubans try to flee to Miami. US tightens immigration controls and limits number of asylum seekers.

1996
Draconian Helms-Burton legislation passed by US Congress tightens the embargo's stranglehold.

1997
Che Guevara's remains are returned from Bolivia.

1998
The Pope visits Cuba and criticizes the US embargo. Thousands attend masses across the country.

1999
Five-year-old Elián González survives a rafting accident on the way to the US. Despite fierce protests in Miami, Elián is returned home to his Cuban father.

2002
Nearly half Cuba's sugar mills close; 100,000 workers lose jobs and are sent for retraining. Two hurricanes strike the west of the island; 350,000 people are evacuated, and the tobacco harvest devastated.

2003
75 dissidents sentenced to jail terms of up to 28 years. Worldwide condemnation.

2004
The UN's Human Rights Commission votes to press for human-rights inspections. The USA tightens sanctions again, restricting visits by US Cubans and their remittances home. Castro retaliates by banning transactions in dollars.

2006
Castro hospitalized in July; temporarily hands over power to his brother, Raúl.

2007
Raúl continues in charge, and makes no policy changes. Fidel remains a strong presence.

CONQUISTADORS AND PIRATES

Long before Columbus arrived in Cuba the island had been populated by groups of indigenous people, who were to be subjugated to the European conquistadors. The island's early colonial history was a turbulent one as booms and busts in gold and sugar changed its fortunes

The first European to glimpse the coast of Cuba was Christopher Columbus, who on his initial voyage in 1492 pronounced it the most beautiful land "that eyes had ever set upon." This beautiful land had, of course, been discovered several thousand years beforehand by peoples Columbus assumed were Indians – a misnomer that has stuck.

The first groups of indigenous people to colonize Cuba were pre-agricultural hunter-gatherers. Quite how and when they first arrived is not known for certain, but it seems that they arrived in different waves of migration from about 6,000 years ago, from the Orinoco delta of modern-day Venezuela, from Central America, and possibly also from Florida and the Mississippi basin.

Historians have attempted to classify these peoples with different names at different times. Once known as Guanahatabey, they're more commonly referred to as Ciboney, but all shared a common pre-agricultural, pre-ceramic heritage. Their cultures were characterized by the use of shell implements, and they lived in caves or basic settlements across the island.

Some Taíno finds can be seen in the Museum of Anthropology in Vedado (Havana), and in the little Archeological Museum in Baracoa, close to the spot where a famous Taíno tobacco idol was found.

These hunter-gatherer groups were gradually displaced in parts of Cuba by waves of new immigrants – Arawak-speaking Taíno peoples – from about AD600 onward. These Taínos had followed

LEFT: a statue of the Taíno warrior Hatuey.
RIGHT: a depiction of Columbus's arrival in Cuba.

COLUMBUS: THE FIRST LANDING

Exactly where Columbus first weighed anchor in Cuba was once a matter of fierce debate. It was always agreed that it was in the east of the island, and the accepted spot is Bahía Bariay, near Gibara on the northeast coast, where a monument was erected in 1992 to celebrate the quincentenary of the event (*see page 283*). However, the people of Baracoa once claimed that the flat-topped mountain referred to by Columbus in his logbook was, in fact, their mountain, El Yunque (The Anvil) – rather than the Silla de Gibara. Baracoans have now come to accept, however, that Columbus arrived in their town only after making his first landfall at Bariay in 1492. His statue still stands proudly on the Malecón.

the arc of the Antilles islands in their hollowed-out tree-trunk canoes, arriving from the region of the Orinoco delta. The Taínos brought with them a more settled, agricultural way of life, and were the dominant group of peoples when Columbus arrived, although some earlier indigenous groups still survived.

The Taínos lived in communities of palm-thatched homes, described by Columbus as looking like large tents, scattered randomly around as if in a camp. For food, they combined fishing and hunting with agriculture – growing staple crops like cassava, peppers, beans, sweet potatoes, and fruits like guavas and pineapples. Society had a hierar-

traded everything they had, but they seemed to me a people short of everything." However, he admired their happiness and generosity. His sailors brought back to Europe tobacco, syphilis and news of a world ripe for conquest.

Spanish conquest

The Spanish first settled on the island of Hispaniola (present-day Dominican Republic and Haiti), where they enslaved and brutalized the indigenous population. Soon they started to look west, hoping to find gold in Cuba.

However, their reputation preceded them, and some indigenous *caciques* were determined to

chical structure, at the apex of which were hereditary chiefs *(caciques)* and shamans *(behiques)*. The shamans presided over curative rituals, linked to the worship of a pantheon of gods and ancestor spirits. Taínos believed in an afterlife, and revered idols, called *cemíes*, lovingly carved out of hardwoods, stone or coral, which they kept in special shrines.

Columbus's very first contacts with Cuba's native peoples were marked by mutual curiosity and, it seems, a certain respect, even if this wasn't to last for long. Columbus made sure his sailors took nothing from the first dwellings they entered, partly no doubt because he was more interested in gold and pearls than the fishing nets, spun cotton, silent dogs and tame wild birds that they found. Columbus noted, "They very willingly

SPEAKING WITH THE GODS

An early chronicler, the Jeronymite friar, Ramón Pané, recorded Taíno customs in his *Account of the Antiquities of the Indies* at the end of the 15th century. Of their ceremonies he writes: "To purge themselves, they take a certain powder, called *cohoba*, snorting it up the nose, which intoxicates them in a way that they don't know what they're doing; and in this way they say many incoherent things, in which they affirm that they are speaking with the idols." Once thought to be tobacco, *cohoba* is now believed to be the crushed seeds of an acacia-like tree – *Anadenanthera peregrina*. The seeds are still used today by some Venezuelan indigenous groups, where the snuff is known as *yopo*.

resist. The most famous of these was the great warrior Hatuey, who had witnessed Spanish massacres in Hispaniola and fled to eastern Cuba. When the conquistador Diego Velázquez landed in Baracoa in 1511 at the head of an expedition to settle the island, Hatuey fought back. But despite a long game of hide-and-seek in the caves and mountains of the east, Hatuey and his followers were captured and put to the stake in 1512. Offered baptism at his execution, the chieftain asked if there were any Christians in heaven; when told that there were, he proclaimed that he preferred to burn as a pagan. Statues of a defiant Hatuey can be seen in Baracoa.

WHY "CUBA"?

The name derives from a native term for the island, Cubanacán, and not, as some believe, the Spanish for barrel *(cuba)*, after the barrel-shaped hills seen by the first sailors.

skirmishes, or in massacres conducted by the more brutal of the early conquistadors – men like Pánfilo de Narváez. Some fled to the mountains, where they would be hunted down with muskets and dogs. Many more were forced to work as slaves, to grow food for the Spanish or to dig for copper and gold. But rather than be subjected to

Between 1512 and 1514, Velázquez and his men founded the seven original "villas" of Cuba – Baracoa, Santiago, Bayamo, Camagüey, Trinidad, Sancti Spíritus, and Havana. The Spanish then set about rounding up the indigenous population for forced labor. Indigenous resistance continued sporadically for the next couple of decades, but the outlook was bleak.

A Caribbean genocide

Thousands of Cuba's indigenous peoples were killed in the initial phase of conquest, either in

---

FAR LEFT: a Taíno figure in Baracoa's archeological museum. **LEFT:** a pre-Columbian idol from Banes Museum. **ABOVE:** the British assault on Havana.

such an existence, many indigenous families committed suicide by hanging themselves or by drinking poisonous untreated cassava juice. The Spanish perceived this as evidence of the indigenous people's inherent laziness.

Those who survived the initial brutality were in large part wiped out by European diseases against which they had no resistance – diseases like smallpox, measles, tuberculosis and even the common cold.

Champion of the people

Only a few brave Spaniards dared to speak out against what they were seeing. The most famous champion of the native peoples was Bartolomé de las Casas, so-called "Protector of the Indians." As one of the first settlers in Cuba in 1513, he had exploited indigenous slaves in the mines and on his estate, but turned against this system when a Dominican priest refused him absolution. On becoming a Dominican friar he passionately campaigned for the just treatment of native peoples at the court of Emperor Carlos V.

The writings of Las Casas laid the foundations for the "Black Legend," on whose record Spain's colonial history has often since been judged, yet he failed in his goal of abolishing the harsh *encomienda* system, which granted Spanish conquistadors land and the right to use the inhabitants of that land as forced labor.

had to be brought back safely to Spain via the Caribbean Sea, which was becoming infested with foreign pirates. A system of fortresses was established on the orders of Spanish king Felipe II, so that treasure could be conveyed in short hops from port to port. Havana was moved from the south to its current spot on the north coast, and acquired massive new walls and fortifications which took more than 40 years to build *(see page 187)*. It became the key point in Spain's whole transportation system: fleets from Cartagena in Colombia, San Juan in Puerto Rico and Panama City converged here for resupplying, while Latin America's first shipyard turned out merchant and

Although gold made some of the first settlers astonishingly rich, the supply quickly petered out. The conquistadors soon found other, more tantalizing rewards: Hernán Cortés set off to conquer Aztec Mexico, and soon afterward Francisco Pizarro toppled Inca Peru. Plundered gold and mined silver began streaming into the Spanish coffers, and Cuba was reduced to the status of supply post for the more lucrative plundering of South and Central America. While the ports of Panama overflowed with riches, and soldiers shod their horses with silver, the island's seven settlements remained little more than wretched provincial villages.

Cuba's strategic position, however, saved it from oblivion. Treasure from the New World still

warships. At the other end of the island, Santiago de Cuba was fortified as a secondary port.

First signs of wealth

These military accoutrements didn't make life in the towns any less squalid. On the contrary, the constant parade of seamen and desperate adventurers did the reverse, turning both Havana and Santiago into warrens of taverns, brothels and muddy, narrow streets. Even so, some of the wealth rubbed off; merchants could make modest fortunes loading up the galleons with provisions for the long journey to Spain.

While the average Spanish sailor was stuck with a scurvy diet of ship's biscuits, the officers could choose from a relatively gourmet menu that included live chickens, turkeys and piglets kept below decks for special meals, and jugs of Spanish wine. Wealthy passengers could bring along their own dried fruits, brandy, olives, and sweet almond cakes.

With the proceeds of these sales, Cuba attracted a rudimentary upper class and some magnificent stone buildings – a smattering of which still survive in Old Havana today. Like colonials everywhere, Spaniards trapped in this remote backwater tried desperately to hang on to their heritage: *caballeros* (gentlemen) would wear finery and frills despite the tropical heat, keep up with the latest in the arts in their homeland, and put on lav-

Pirates on the rampage

Despite Spain's best efforts, the uninhabited swamps of Florida and the island maze of the Bahamas became havens for freebooters and buccaneers of every nationality, ready to pounce on any ship passing along Cuba's coast. The more brazen found the cays and islands off Cuba's south coast to be perfect bases for their activities. The most famous (or infamous) names in the history of piracy all touched on the island's coast, and many became embroiled, over the years, in the shifting patterns of war between Spain and more recent interlopers in the Caribbean, the English, the French and the Dutch.

ish dinner dances in the midst of plagues of malaria and yellow fever.

As one traveler to Cuba remarked: "The palaces of the nobles in Havana, the residence of the governor, the convents, the cathedral, are a reproduction of Burgos or Valladolid, as if by some Aladdin's lamp a Castilian city had been taken up and set down again unaltered on the shore of the Caribbean Sea. And they carried with them their laws, their habits, their institutions and their creed, their religious orders, their bishops and their Inquisition."

LEFT: English pirates plunder the Cuban coast.
ABOVE: Havana's port was heavily fortified.
RIGHT: the infamous Henry Morgan.

Drake and Morgan

England's Francis Drake (1540–96), a favorite of Queen Elizabeth I, started the habit of calling in at Cabo de San Antonio, Cuba's westernmost point, for fresh water and turtle eggs on the way to and from raids on Cartagena and Panama. It was here that the dreaded buccaneer Bartholomew Portugués, whose small ship had just captured a vast, 20-gun man-o'-war, was surprised by the Spanish. Although he was flung in irons, the pirate knifed his jailers in Mexico and escaped, to be picked up by a band of passing cut-throats who helped him recapture the man-o'-war. They sailed it as far as the Isla de la Juventud on Cuba's south coast, where Bartholomew Portugués's luck finally turned: a hurricane smashed the ship to pieces.

The most ruthless and successful buccaneer of all arrived in the following century. This was Henry Morgan, son of a well-to-do Welsh farmer, who was hired by the English Government in 1668 to seek intelligence on Spanish activities in Cuba. Morgan took this as license to sail his 750 men the 80 km (50 miles) inland to Puerto Príncipe (modern Camagüey) and attack it. The Spanish governor got wind of his plan and had a force drawn up to meet Morgan, but, he reported, "the pirates were very dextrous." The Spaniards were defeated and the town surrendered. Morgan locked the inhabitants in the churches, and set about sacking the town.

torture of prisoners. This didn't stop the French governor of Tortugas signing L'Ollonois on for raids against the Spanish. On one occasion he attacked the village of De Los Cayos on the southwest coast of Cuba, capturing a frigate from Havana and beheading its surviving crew. Eventually L'Ollonois met his end at the hands of indigenous Nicaraguans, who slowly dissected him while still alive.

In 1715, the biggest Spanish treasure fleet ever gathered started off from Havana loaded with nearly 7 million "pieces of eight," and thousands of bars of silver. This time, it was nature rather than piracy that was to prove the venture's undo-

According to chronicles, Morgan's men "fell to banqueting ... and making great cheer after their customary way, without remembering the poor prisoners, whom they permitted to starve in the churches. In the meanwhile they did not cease to torment them daily after an inhuman manner, thereby to make them confess where they had hid their goods and money, though little or nothing was left them. They punished also the women and little children." Morgan went on to sack Panama City, and after retiring to London was appointed Governor of Jamaica.

Yet crueller than Morgan was the Frenchman L'Ollonois, who came to the Caribbean as an indentured manservant, joined a buccaneer crew and soon won a reputation as a psychopath for his

THE INQUISITION STRIKES

The Inquisition descended most famously on the town of Remedios in 1682, when the parish priest declared that the village had been invaded by 800,000 devils (making more than 1,000 devils per inhabitant – which is quite a lot). After burning the odd, unfortunate possessed victim, 40 soldiers torched the settlement, ordering the villagers to relocate to relatively useless land, where the new town of Santa Clara was being established. This could be regarded as Cuba's first real-estate scam: the property was owned by the parish priest who had "discovered" the devils, and who hoped to rent it out at a tidy profit. The villagers, however, defied pressure and decided to rebuild their town.

ing. Though the fleet waited until after the hurricane season, it ran straight into a storm in the Gulf of Florida. Nearly 1,000 of the 2,500 passengers lost their lives, and wreckage littered the entire Florida coast, where it was picked off by passing buccaneers.

The tyranny of "white gold"

Dramatic as these events were, Cuba's real future was being shaped in its first sugar fields. When Columbus first landed in the Americas, sugar was one of the most valuable commodities in Europe, imported for a fortune from the Orient and weighed out by the tablespoon. He realized the

Africa to work them. The first African slaves were brought to Cuba as domestic servants, but soon they were being forced to work in the mines and sugar or tobacco plantations. With the indigenous population wiped out, the Spanish needed an alternative source of labor and Africans were deemed more robust and resilient. Even Fray Bartolomé de Las Casas *(see pages 35–6)* had spoken out in favor of the African slave trade, as a way of protecting his beloved "Indians" from rapacious exploitation. And before long, a second phase of brutalization had begun.

Until the late 18th century, the slave trade was run under license from the Spanish Crown,

Caribbean's potential, and on his second voyage he brought the first sugar-cane roots from the Canary Islands and planted them in the modern-day Dominican Republic. Within a century, sugar cane had spread across the Caribbean islands and to the coast of Brazil.

Cuba started off as a comparatively minor sugar producer – cattle ranching and then tobacco were more important initially – but gradually more and more lush forests of mahogany and ceiba were uprooted to make way for sugar-cane plantations, while boatloads of slaves were transported from

LEFT: a 19th-century woodcut depicting a contemporary tobacco plantation.
ABOVE: African slaves in the sugar fields.

although a sizable illegal slave-smuggling trade existed too. And although the trade was initially on a far smaller scale than it was to become in the 19th century, nevertheless thousands of peoples from across Africa – from countries like Senegal, Mali and Sierra Leone; Yoruba-speaking peoples from present-day Nigeria; Bantú peoples from the Congo and Angola; and even from as far away as Mozambique – were hauled across the ocean, all bringing different cultural traditions and languages. With the slaves came African gods, myths and rituals, which the Christian priests could not eradicate despite their zeal.

Life on the plantations was terribly harsh – thousands died from overwork, disease and poor nutrition; beatings were common; there was a dearth of women, as slavers preferred importing young men who were stronger and therefore represented better value; women were raped by their overseers; and slave families could be broken up by selling their children.

Desperate measures

There were uprisings throughout the colonial period, one of the first ones taking place as early as 1537, when slaves rose up and joined in an assault by French pirates on the city of Havana. And the Spanish lived in constant fear of slave rebellion. Some slaves, termed *cimarrones*, chose to escape, fleeing to the mountains where they sometimes

THE CORNISH IN EL COBRE

El Cobre copper mine has a link with the southwest English county of Cornwall. The Spanish abandoned the mine in the early 19th century, and a visiting English businessman, finding that there were still rich copper deposits, founded the Cobre Mining Company. He imported steam engines and labor from Cornwall, a prominent tin-mining area. Thousands of Cornishmen came to the area in the 1830s but harsh conditions, and mosquito-borne yellow fever, resulted in a high death rate, and the number of workers dwindled. By 1870 the enterprise was over: the seam was becoming exhausted, and the destruction caused by the uprising against the Spanish *(see page 49)* was the final straw.

developed small communities *(palenques)*, possibly joining too with remnant indigenous communities, but they always lived under the fear of recapture by slave-hunters and their savage dogs. Just outside Santiago stands a monument to slaves who fled from the harsh conditions of forced labor in the copper mine, El Cobre, in the 18th century. Other slaves, in desperation, even chose mass suicides – many believing that after death they would be resurrected in Africa.

Magical, medicinal powers were attributed to women slaves – although it seems they were ones that it suited their white masters to believe. "There was one type of sickness the whites picked up, a sickness of the veins and male organs," one former slave recorded. "It could only be got rid of with black women: if the man who had it slept with a Negress, he was cured immediately."

The Last Supper

Just how bizarre Cuban rural society had become by the end of the 18th century can be seen by the events that took place near Santa María del Rosario, a village southeast of Havana. The account comes from historian Manuel Moreno Fraginals (1920–2001), a leading authority on plantation slavery in Cuba, and was captured in the classic Cuban film *La Última Cena – The Last Supper* – made in 1976 by leading Cuban director Tomás Gutiérrez Alea.

In a fit of religious fervor, the Count de Casa Bayona (whose former home now houses the Colonial Art Museum in Havana) invited a dozen of his slaves to a feast on Maundy Thursday (the day before Good Friday). Acting out the role of Jesus Christ, he washed the feet of each slave personally. When the overseer refused to give the slaves a holiday on Easter Sunday, as had been promised by the count, because the Bible teaches that Sunday should be a day of rest, they rose up in rebellion, burning the plantation to the ground.

Hearing the news, the count arrived with armed horsemen to repress the uprising. Horrified at what he perceived to be their ingratitude, he ordered the 12 slaves to be hunted down and executed. Their heads were placed on pikes in the cane fields as a warning to their fellow-workers that, whatever the Bible might say, all men were not created equal in Cuba. ❏

LEFT: the film *La Última Cena* was based on a real, and horrific, event.
RIGHT: an idealized depiction of slave life.

THE STRUGGLE AGAINST COLONIALISM

Cuba was one step behind the liberal changes that spread
through other Latin American colonies in the 19th century.
But Spain's "Ever Faithful Isle" did eventually fight to
gain independence from Spain. Inevitably that meant
it came within the sphere of influence of the USA

I n the early 1800s, every Spanish possession in the New World rose up against colonial rule – except Cuba and Puerto Rico. In Havana, barely a voice was raised in support of the romantic liberation movements being led by heroes such as Simón Bolívar and José de San Martín, much to the embarrassment of modern Cuban historians. On the contrary, Cuba became Spain's military springboard for the many attempts to reconquer her tattered empire, which dragged on for decades and left much of South and Central America in ruins. But by 1825, the Spanish gave up on the New World and retreated to its two loyal Caribbean possessions – the more valued of which, for the next 40 years, remained Cuba – referred to in Madrid as "the Ever Faithful Isle."

Predictions of ruin

Cuban Creoles, masters of a slave society, were in fact desperate to avoid independence. They had been kept in a state of constant terror since the bloody slave rebellion in neighboring Haiti in the 1790s: French refugees had landed on the beaches around Santiago, starving, desperate and telling

The Cafetal La Isabelica near Santiago, now under UNESCO *protection, was the plantation house of a coffee estate belonging to a family of French descent, fleeing from Haiti's slave rebellion*

wild tales of race slaughter, laced with lurid images of voodoo and throbbing African drums. Napoleon's army of 20,000 men was defeated on the shores of the new black republic, and white

LEFT: 1901 cartoon satirizing US involvement in Cuba.
RIGHT: Carlos Manuel de Céspedes.

Cubans were worried that their island might follow suit. "There is no country on earth where a revolutionary movement is more dangerous than Cuba," declared one planter, predicting "the complete ruin of the Cuban race."

Even so, greed was stronger than fear. The expansion of the slave population during the later 18th and early 19th centuries was unparalleled, for two main reasons. First, in 1762, the British had captured the heavily fortified city of Havana, after storming the main forts guarding the harbor. This was simply a consequence of a wider war Britain was waging against France and her ally, Spain. They then trained the very guns that were meant to protect the city against its own walls, forcing its capitulation in just two weeks. The

Governor of Havana was sent back to Spain in disgrace, but the heroic resistance of the captain commanding El Morro fortress, Don Luís de Velasco, earned him a posthumous ennoblement from his king.

The British divided up the tremendous spoils of the city's public monies and warehouses, and then endured sickness and disease, until Havana was returned to Spain a mere seven months later. Spain regained possession of her beloved colonial city by handing Florida over to the British, but an important legacy of the occupation was that the British had allowed Havana to trade freely with other nations, thus breaking the monopoly

that Spain had enjoyed since the 16th century, and this liberalization vastly increased the trade in slaves. Once broken, this monopoly could not realistically be reimposed by the returning Spanish. Freed from this economic straightjacket, the Cuban economy boomed, and there were real incentives to increase production of its chief commodity: sugar.

Secondly, the Haitian rebellion destroyed the sugar plantations there, pushing sugar prices sky-high, and many of the refugees who resettled in Cuba brought with them expertise and improved production techniques. Cuba soon became the world's biggest producer of "white gold." It was a

HUMAN LIFE DEVALUED

German naturalist Alexander von Humboldt, on his first visit to Cuba in 1800, witnessed at first hand life on the island's sugar plantations. He was appalled by the attitude of Cuban slave owners: "I have heard discussed with the greatest coolness whether it was better for the proprietor not to overwork his slaves, and consequently have to replace them with less frequency, or whether he should get all he could out of them in a few years, and then have to purchase newly imported Africans."

new era of fabulous wealth and sudden fortunes.

Nothing could stop sugar cane consuming the countryside – citrus fields were replanted, the last forests uprooted, even tobacco plantations were plowed over (growth of the crop being restricted to the narrower fields of the province of Pinar del Río). A steadily increasing supply of slaves was needed for the plantations, especially as workers survived for an average of only seven years. The number of slaves in Cuba leapt from 40,000 in 1774 to 470,000 in 1840, when they made up half the population.

Africans were bought and sold in newspaper classifieds, next to advertisements for horses and farm implements. In a rare gesture of leniency, some planters allowed their slaves to dance at night to drums, praying that they were not communicating news of rebellion.

A new "sugarocracy" arose in Cuba: the sugar center of Trinidad sprouted resplendent palaces with names like Hope, Gamble and Confidence. Their owners could afford to take shopping trips to Europe, bringing back Persian carpets, Italian paintings and French chandeliers. Sumptuous mansions transformed Havana from a "large village," in foreigners' eyes, to Spain's "jewel of the Caribbean," a city of elegant iron grilles *(rejas)*, gracious curlicues and beautiful stained glass. The streets were paved with granite imported from New England, and trade with the United States boomed – the beginning of a relationship that would dominate much of Cuba's modern history.

Meanwhile, in 1837, Latin America's first railroad was built from the Güines sugar fields to Havana, using the labor of African slaves, Chinese workers and indentured Irishmen. Conditions were so miserable that 13 workers perished for every kilometer of track laid.

However, the economic euphoria couldn't last: in 1857, the bottom fell out of the sugar market, and Cuba went into a downward spiral. The names of mansions in Trinidad went from "Good Results" to "Wit's End," "Woe" and "Disenchantment."

The push for independence

By 1868, many Cubans were at last ready to end Spanish colonial rule. In that year, a small-plantation owner, Carlos Manuel de Céspedes, freed the slaves at one of his plantations near Manzanillo, and declared Cuba independent, sparking off the Ten Years' War with Spain. Free and runaway slaves swelled the Liberation Army's ranks: known as *mambises* – a word that meant "rebel" in the African Congo. They often fought with machetes for lack of guns and went barefoot and near-naked for want of boots and uniforms.

Antonio Maceo, the "Bronze Titan," was a black soldier who rose from the ranks to become major-general and one of the most popular leaders in the struggle. Like a character in a García Márquez novel, he is said to have survived innumerable assassination attempts, fought in 900 battles, been wounded 25 times, and lost his father and nine of his 13 brothers in the war. Many pro-Spanish whites were afraid that he would attempt

LEFT: slaves' lives were hard and short, and owners began to fear rebellions.
RIGHT: a monument to two independence leaders.

to become president, and gathered under the slogan: "Cuba, better Spanish than African!"

Adventurers came from around the world to join the struggle against Spain. One was former American Union army officer Henry Reeve, who signed up, only to be captured and shot by a Spanish firing squad. Left for dead, he survived and became a leading general and anti-slavery voice,

remembered as *El Inglesito*, the "little Englishman." But the war ground on for a decade, took 200,000 lives and ended in stalemate. It also left a crippled economy, and, with land prices at a level lower than they had been in years, US companies began to invest heavily in Cuban real estate, developing a significant financial interest in the country's future.

The fighting starts again

In 1895, the carnage began again with the Second War of Independence, this time led by the great Cuban theorist José Martí *(see page 48)*. Martí had infused the independence movement with earlier, nascent ideas of social justice: the goal was not just a free Cuba, but a Cuba without its vast inequalities of wealth and racial divisions. Unfortunately, he was shot dead in his first battle in 1895. However, the seemingly indestructible Antonio Maceo was still around to keep the flame of revolution burning, until he too was killed in a skirmish with Spanish troops on the border of Havana and Pinar del Río provinces, at the end of 1896. The tragedy left the Cuban cause in the hands of another stalwart veteran of the earlier war, General Máximo Gómez, who had been persuaded by Martí to return from exile to help lead the independence struggle.

Unable to engage the elusive rebels directly, Spanish forces started a scorched-earth policy in the Cuban countryside, executing *guajiros* (farmers), burning farms and putting the survivors into labor camps. The strategy failed; by 1898, the Spaniards were exhausted and at the point of withdrawing entirely. But another colonial power had been watching the conflict with increasing interest: the United States of America.

Enter the United States

As long as a century before, North American thinkers had decided that Cuba was crucial to their country's strategic interests. Throughout the 1800s, there were calls for outright annexation, and several filibustering expeditions set out from Florida to the Cuban shores, hoping to provoke a popular revolt that would cause Cuba to fall "like a ripening plum into the lap of the Union" (in the happy phrase of John Quincy Adams). Four US presidents even offered to buy Cuba from the Spanish during the first half of the 19th century, seeing the island as part of the natural orbit of their increasingly powerful and expansionist country. With more than US$100 million invested in Cuba by 1898, there were many in Washington who worried that radicals would take over an independent Cuba.

American emotions had already been whipped up by the press. Newspaper barons William Randolph Hearst (Orson Welles's model for *Citizen Kane*) and Joseph Pulitzer (who would give his name to America's greatest journalism prize) competed to offer the most lurid and heart-rending tales of the Spanish troops' cruelty: images of Cuban streets awash with blood, bayoneted babies and deflowered virgins became daily fare for millions from Kansas to New York.

"Remember the Maine!"

The pretext for intervention came on February 15, when the USS *Maine* – a battleship sent to protect US interests – mysteriously blew up in Havana harbor, killing 260 people. Hearst and Pulitzer both claimed that the explosion on the USS *Maine* was caused by a Spanish mine (it was Hearst who coined the immortal, and very catchy, slogan, "Remember the Maine, to hell with Spain!"), and though some Cubans today subscribe to the belief that it might have been a deliberate explosion caused by the US itself to precipitate their involvement in the war, the evidence points to an accidental munitions explosion in the hold. Today there is a monument to the *Maine* in Havana on the Malecón.

Within a month, President McKinley had declared war; three months after that, the US Navy had blockaded the Spanish Navy in the harbor of Santiago de Cuba, at the eastern end of the island. A huge American expeditionary force landed north of the city. It was led by an obese veteran of the Indian wars, General William Shafter (1835–1906), and accompanied by a boatload of eager, albeit diarrhea-ridden, journalists.

Although the US Congress passed an amendment stating that they were not claiming sovereignty in Cuba, nationalists quickly had cause to doubt the benefits of US assistance.

Juan Hill, on the outskirts of Santiago. The American Rough Riders were led in a famous charge by Edward Roosevelt, a short-sighted weakling as a child who had taken up *machista* pursuits from tiger hunting to soldiering in compensation. The Spanish were defeated, although the Americans took heavy casualties. Roosevelt's first missive to the US President was sheepish, but the national press hailed it as an extraordinary military achievement. Roosevelt rode the wave of popularity on to the governorship of New York and, in 1901, the US presidency. Two days after San Juan, the Spanish Navy made a quixotic sally from Santiago only to suffer a rapid defeat.

Shafter and his men took one look at the ragged Cuban Army and refused to allow them into battle – publicly blaming their lack of shoes and poor weapons, in private appalled that so many of them were black and mulatto (mixed race) – the reporter Stephen Crane called them "real tropic savages."

Shafter suggested that the Cubans keep up the rear, digging trenches and latrines. Unsurprisingly, the commanding general, Calixto García, refused to cooperate.

The Spanish Army had very little fight left in it, but a showdown of sorts came at the Battle of San

It had been a "splendid little war," as one US official noted, giving the Americans an instant empire (Puerto Rico, Guam and the Philippines were snapped up at the same time). General Shafter arranged a victory march through the streets of Santiago, but the Cuban forces were barred from participating.

The highjacked revolution

The US set up a military government to administer the country. After 30 years of fighting, Cubans had, in fact, traded one set of colonial masters for another. But not all Americans were caught up in the jingoism of the moment: the vitriolic Mark Twain wrote that the Stars and Stripes should be replaced with a Skull and Crossbones.

LEFT: a United States version of the Battle of San Juan Hill.
ABOVE: a Spanish depiction of the same battle.

In 1901, US Congress agreed to withdraw its troops in exchange for guarantees that the country would remain an American protectorate. The so-called Platt Amendment – composed in Washington to be included verbatim in the Cuban Constitution – allowed the United States to intervene in Cuban internal affairs: it forced Cuba to lease them a naval base at Guantánamo Bay, and gave the US the right to veto Cuba's trade or loan pacts with third countries. Understandably, news of the legislation caused rioting around Cuba, but the US military governor made it clear to the constitutional convention in Havana that the *yanquis* would not be leaving on any other terms. Tomás

for American immigrants in places such as Isla de la Juventud.

The final tragedy of Cuba's false freedom was the so-called Black Uprising of 1912. Afro-Cubans – many of whom had fought courageously in the wars of independence – were disgusted to find that the new republic was happy to leave them in effective serfdom. They formed their own political party, the Partido Independiente de Color, only to have it banned.

Finally, open rebellion spread throughout the country. Cuban forces led by General Monteagudo crushed the uprising with the help of US Marines and, more viciously, local Creoles, who took

Estrada Palma, Cuba's first president, reluctantly signed the amendment.

The independence that wasn't

The Stars and Stripes came down in May, 1902, and Cuba began its stunted, compromised freedom. In the coming years, US Congress sent in the marines on a regular basis to protect American interests, and even reinstated US military rule entirely from 1906 to 1909. None of the social reforms envisaged by José Martí would be enacted; elections were held, but were usually fraudulent, and corruption was rife. At the same time, American investment in Cuba rocketed. United States companies snapped up land at bargain prices, and even set up mini "colonies"

revenge on the Afro-Cubans in retaliation for a century and a half of fear.

"It is impossible to tell the number of dead," the general soon reported, "because it has degenerated into widespread butchery in the hills," while one contemporary writer stated that "entire families were machine-gunned in their *bohíos* [huts]." Some 3,000 Afro-Cubans are estimated to have been massacred in a period covering a little over two months. The "black fear" had been wiped out with blood, and Cuban racism was more brutally ingrained than ever. ❏

ABOVE: African-American soldiers fought in the US army in the War of Independence, but black Afro-Cubans found that peace did not bring prosperity.

José Martí

Even the tiniest Cuban village has a bust of José Martí in its main square. Indeed, images of this incandescent romantic visionary can be found in cities across Latin America and wherever Cubans have settled: he remains Cuba's only historical figure whose greatness is undisputed, both as a man of action and of letters.

Born in 1853, Martí began his career as an independence fighter at 15, when he helped start an anti-colonial newspaper, *The Free Fatherland*, in Havana and denounced a fellow student for marching in a Spanish procession. He was charged with treason and sentenced to hard labor in a stone quarry. A frail youth, the experience ruined his eyesight, gave him a hernia and permanent scars on his ankles from the shackles he wore (in later life, he would always wear a ring made from these shackles). After six months, Martí was pardoned but sent into exile in Spain – the beginning of a journey that took him to France, England, Mexico, Guatemala, back secretly to Cuba, to exile again in Spain, escape to France, then to the US and south to Venezuela.

In 1881 Martí, with his wife and son, finally settled in New York City, a center for Cuban exiles, and was initially intoxicated with the United States ("One can breathe freely," he wrote. "For here, freedom is the foundation, the shield, the essence of life.") The enthusiasm was short-lived, and Martí soon saw the United States as the greatest threat to Latin American independence. He viewed as crucial the prevention of "the annexation of the peoples of our America by the turbulent and brutal North which despises them... I have lived within the monster and I know its entrails – and my sling is the sling of David."

For 15 years in the US, the wire-thin Martí kept up a punishing routine of political organizing, lecturing, purchasing weapons, and writing firebrand speeches, newspaper columns and exquisite, avant-garde poetry (his *Versos Sencillos* were married to the music of *Guajira Guantanamera* in the 1960s, in what has become the unofficial Cuban national anthem). He ate little, slept only in snatches, but glowed with nervous energy. Traveling to Florida – always in a heavy black suit and bow tie, his pointed moustache neatly clipped – Martí visited cigar factories to recruit Cuban exiles

RIGHT: José Martí, an undisputed hero.

to his cause. Cuba would not be truly free, he argued, without economic, racial and sexual equality – thus adding an inspiring social element to the provenly potent rhetoric of nationalism.

Martí, though, was not content to remain an intellectual. In 1892, he founded the Cuban Revolutionary Party. Three years later, plans had been laid to rekindle the independence struggle: a message, hidden in a Havana cigar, was sent to the black general Antonio Maceo in Cuba. Martí and Máximo Gómez landed secretly on the southeast coast, in a tiny boat that was nearly dashed to pieces in the middle of a storm. Escaping to the sierra of the Oriente, they were joined by hundreds

of supporters. But life as a guerrilla was harsh: Martí's emaciated frame, still covered by a heavy coat, was weighed down by pack and rifle, and he often fell on the mountain trails.

On May 19, 1895, near Bayamo, Martí went into his first day of battle with a picture of his daughter over his heart. He was shot dead almost immediately as he charged toward the enemy, without ever having drawn his gun. A martyr to the cause, he has been worshiped by Cubans ever since. Today, his words have been appropriated by both sides of the political divide: Fidel Castro views Martí as the home-grown ideologue of the revolution, while right-wing Miami Cubans named their anti-Castro broadcast stations Radio Martí and TV Martí. ❑

THE AGE OF DECADENCE

From the 1930s to the 1950s, the decades spanning US Prohibition and Depression, Havana was a playground for wealthy Americans seeking guilt-free sex, cheap alcohol and the chance to win – or lose – everything on the gaming tables. The Mafia and corrupt Cuban politicians joined forces to preside over this hedonistic era

A t the height of Prohibition in the United States, which lasted from 1920 to 1933, "personal liberty" became the euphemistic reason for thousands of US tourists to take the short boat ride to Cuba from Florida, to drink and have the sort of fun they wouldn't have at home.

Basil Woon, author of the classic 1928 travel guide *When It's Cocktail Time in Cuba*, remarked "*Have one in Havana* seems to have become the winter slogan of the wealthy." Like a P.G. Wodehouse character, Woon sums up the reasons for visiting Cuba:

● *You may drink as much as you want to.*
● *You may buy as many drinks for your friends as you want to.*
● *You may chance your luck at the lottery.*
● *You may lose as much money as you desire at the casino.*
● *You need not carry your marriage certificate with you.*
● *You may stare at the pretty señoritas, because staring in Cuba is considered a compliment – not a crime.*

From these innocent beginnings, Cuba in general and Havana in particular were well on the way to becoming international symbols of decadent pleasure. The flow of Americans visiting for sun, sex and alcohol that began in the Prohibition years would turn into a flood after World War II. In Havana, refined nightclubs raged all night and the casinos rivaled those of Las Vegas.

Lovely, long-legged mulattas trod the boards of the Tropicana for the entertainment of audiences drunk on daiquirís, while the more adventurous visitors headed for live sex acts in seedier surroundings; a regular show-time favorite was Superman, who measured his spectacular erection by lining up 12 silver dollars side by side.

The seamy side

Havana quickly became the prostitution capital of the Western hemisphere. Businessmen could choose their mulatta for the weekend from photographs at the airport; the notorious Casa Marina specialized in 13-year-old girls and boys from the provinces (with only a minor surcharge for virgins). In its prurient, watered-down way, Hollywood helped export Cuba's image as the world's sex capital: in *Guys and Dolls*, Sky Masterson would bring his virgin Salvation Army love down to Havana to be seduced. In real life, stars like Errol Flynn and Gary Cooper visited every winter in their luxury yachts. George Raft, who specialized as a film-star gangster, was full-time host of the Red Room at the Hotel Capri.

And the whole, rum-soaked party went on to the fabulous rhythms of mamba, rumba and *son* (folk music). Cuba's 12-piece bands, musicians all decked out in white tuxedos, were in demand from Manhattan to the Parisian Left Bank, though the big money in Havana went to American jazz bands and front-liners like Nat King Cole and Maurice Chevalier. Nevertheless, the city became invaded with penniless hopefuls from the provinces. And all this was going on against a sordid background of Cuban domestic politics: the spiraling decadence of Havana was aided and abetted by a series of increasingly corrupt, brutal, and authoritarian regimes.

hopped on a plane to Miami, supposedly carrying five revolvers and as many bags of gold bullion.

In the ensuing chaos, the figure who took control was a young army sergeant called Fulgencio Batista, who organized a revolt of lower officers. A mulatto of humble social origins, Batista had mostly only been noticed for a winning smile, but in quick succession he took the rank of colonel, then gained full control of the army. Before long, he emerged as the major player in Cuban politics, managing the government through a string of puppet presidents. The "Batista Era" had begun.

In 1934, the US Government, perhaps confident that its interests were secure, repealed the

The "Batista Era"

The Great Depression, which began after the US stock-market crash in 1929, sparked off a string of riots against President Gerardo Machado, who had been elected more or less fairly in the mid-1920s but made so much money that he refused to leave office. Troops were regularly called out to break strikes; demonstrators were gunned down; hired thugs, called *porros*, abducted and tortured enemies of the regime, who then "disappeared." The country was teetering on the brink of civil war in 1933 when a general strike was called. Machado

Platt Amendment that guaranteed its power of intervention – although the Americans retained their lease on the naval base at Guantánamo. By 1940, Batista had wearied of running Cuba through others and ran for president himself, winning an apparently fair election. He enacted various social reforms during his first term and stayed in power until 1944.

Havana and the Mob

In a city where fabulous sums could be made from booze, drugs, gambling and prostitution, it is not surprising that the American Mafia was not far behind. In December, 1946, the most important Mafia conference since the Depression was held in Havana. Organizing the meeting was the power-

LEFT: grand hotels, like the Sevilla-Biltmore (now the Mercure Sevilla) sprang up during Havana's heyday.
ABOVE: Sloppy Joe's, a famous Havana bar.

ful Meyer Lansky. Known as "the Jewish god-father," Lansky was a diminutive, bookish man who was the brains behind the USA's national crime syndicate, formed by uniting the various warring families in the 1930s. Guest of honor was "Lucky" Luciano, Lansky's more high-profile Sicilian partner, who had recently been deported from the United States for his notorious activities, and was now entering Cuba under a false passport. Every Mafia boss from New York, New Jersey, Tampa, Chicago and New Orleans made the pilgrimage to Havana for the event.

The Cuban capital was a logical meeting place. The Mob had gained a foothold here during the Prohibition years, using Cuba as a base for running rum to the Florida Keys. But a much more lucrative opening had come in 1938, when Batista had invited Meyer Lansky to take over the operation of two casinos and a racetrack at Havana's Oriental Park, all of which had gained a reputation for being crooked.

Lansky brought in his own pit crews to replace the Cubans and soon had the places "reformed." The establishments flourished, and more casinos soon followed – with regular kickbacks to Batista, brokered by Lansky. What was better, as far as the Mafia was concerned, was that the whole thing was perfectly legal.

PLAYING FOR THE PLAYERS

The writer Oscar Hijuelos captures the unequal and divisive atmosphere of those heady days when American high-rollers flooded toward the glitzy Havana scene. In *The Mambo Kings Play Songs of Love*, he describes how: "A musician's life in Havana was poor, sociable. Pretty-boy singers, trumpet players, and *congueros* (conga drummers) gathered everywhere – in the arcades, plazas and bars. Cuban musicians were paid shit. Ten dollars a night, with cleaning charges for uniforms; black skins and mulatos in one door, white musicians in another, no drinks on the house, no overtime, and Christmas bonuses of watered down, resealed bottles of whiskey."

Business was slow in 1946, but the Cuban capital was still the most comfortable and safe place to discuss Mob business. Frank Sinatra was even flown down to sing for them: the New Jersey crooner came in with two of Al Capone's cousins, and bringing a gold cigarette case for Luciano. Top of the Havana agenda at that time was what to do with Benny "Bugsy" Siegel, a sociopath, but a charming one, who had blown a fortune of the Mob's money on the Flamingo Hotel, the first casino in Las Vegas (there is a memorial to him there today).

Meyer Lansky had the last word on his longtime partner and bosom buddy: "There's only one thing to do with a thief who steals from his friends. Benny's got to be hit."

The Las Vegas of the Caribbean

Although Siegel was duly gunned down the next year, his formula of "high-stakes, high-class gambling joints for high-rollers" soon took off in Las Vegas – convincing Meyer Lansky that the slowly degenerating operations in Havana were chicken feed. The ever-greedy Batista, who had retaken power after a brief hiatus with a bloodless coup in 1952, agreed. Scandals were again rocking the Cuban casinos, with allegations of rigged games: their rooms were full of US-born dice hustlers, who would fleece tourists of their spending money in games like cubola and razzle-dazzle, even as they dined at their restaurant tables.

When he was asked why American gangsters were so welcome in Cuba, the US Ambassador replied: "It's strange, but it seems to be the only way to get honest casinos."

The second Batista presidency (1952–8) became the climax of Cuba's age of decadence, a time when corruption reached mythic proportions. The revitalized casino industry was part of a massive push to promote tourism: a new airline was started, visas were waived for visiting Americans, and all new hotels were granted tax-free status. The number of hotel rooms in Havana nearly doubled in six years. Almost any hotel could and did have a gaming room, so educated Cubans gave

Worse, a friend of Californian Senator Richard Nixon lost a considerable sum in Havana, creating a great deal of poor publicity when he refused to pay up.

In 1953, Batista appointed Meyer Lansky his personal adviser on gambling reform, to clean up Havana as he had done in the 1930s. From his base in the Montmartre Club, Lansky soon proceeded to turn Havana into a tropical Monte Carlo. Games were regularized, and the secret police were employed to arrest and deport card sharps. The irony was not lost on many people.

up their jobs as doctors and teachers for much more lucrative work as croupiers. Oiling the gears was a Byzantine system of bribes – Meyer Lansky is said to have deposited more than US$3 million in Batista's personal bank account in Switzerland, and this was just a tiny fraction of his own share. The Mafia boss and Cuban president continued to get on famously; according to one observer, they were "like brothers."

Meanwhile, Batista's secret police became less secret and more savage in hunting down opposition figures. The corpses of tortured dissidents were strung from the lampposts as a warning for anyone who dared to speak out against the relentless turning of the roulette wheels and poker machines in Havana.

Far Left: casinos were the playground of the rich.
Left: "Bugsy" Siegel, who came to a sticky end.
Above: Batista and Meyer Lansky: "like brothers."

The lure of the tropic

Cuba's combination of unlimited sensual pleasures, lawlessness and corruption – along with the
frisson of danger – exerted an almost irresistible
fascination for the many writers and artists who
passed through Havana.

In 1923, the 19-year-old Anaïs Nin paid a visit
to her high-society family, indulging in a rigor-
ous routine of horseback riding, garden parties,
and flirtation. Initially attracted to the sensuality
of Havana, the future feminist icon was soon
repelled by the city's superficiality and "unsub-
dued coarseness." "Mental idleness, vacuity, are
what I read in most passing faces," she wrote in her

country: it was in Cuba that he wrote his play
The Public, the first published Spanish work to
center on male lovers.

Two years later, the US poet Hart Crane, who
had always had problems with his sexuality, had
much less success with Cuba's fabled freedoms:
arriving depressed from a failed trip to Mexico,
he made advances to the wrong sailors in Havana
harbor and was beaten senseless. Leaving Cuba
the next night, he jumped off the boat and
drowned himself.

Of all the foreign visitors, Ernest Hemingway
was the most notorious, visiting throughout the
1930s for marlin fishing, and then moving to Cuba

Early Diaries. "Eyes seeming to wander forever,
alighting on everything but carrying no thoughts to
the mind, eyes devoid of vision, gleaming only
when the senses are pleased."

More impressed with Cuba was the Spanish
poet Federico García Lorca, who came here in
1930 and stayed for three months. "This island is
a paradise," he rhapsodized in a letter to his parents. "If I ever get lost, they should look for me
either in Andalucía or Cuba." Already a recognized poet, Lorca was befriended by a string of
habanero bohemians and took full advantage of
Cuba's pleasures.

The atmosphere of sexual liberation apparently
made García Lorca more overt about his own
homosexuality than he had been in his own

permanently. Although he regularly drank himself into a stupor, and could become aggressive,
Hemingway's streak of midwestern puritanism
was strong enough for him to remain largely innocent of the seedier side of Havana life.

No such qualms restrained the English writer
Graham Greene. During a brief visit in 1957,
Greene explored romantic, decadent Cuba and
immortalized it in his novel *Our Man in Havana,*
the story of a vacuum-cleaner salesman supplying
the British secret service with bogus information.
Greene found the Cuban capital a place "where
every vice was permissible and every trade possible," and lapped up "the brothel life, the roulette
in every hotel, the fruit machines spilling out jack-
pots of silver dollars, the Shanghai Theater where

for one dollar twenty-five cents one could see a nude cabaret of extreme obscenity with the bluest of blue films in the intervals."

Greene even became caught up in his own minor intrigue when he flew to Santiago in the hopes of interviewing guerrillas in the Sierra Maestra, carrying a suitcase of clothes for them. On the plane was a *Time* reporter whom Greene decided was a CIA spy. There were surreptitious meetings with revolutionary contacts in Santiago (where he stayed in the Casa Granda Hotel), and Greene became convinced that he was being followed. The interview fell through and Greene left Cuba soon after.

and young faces ripped apart by tortures so savage – vividly described by the *revolucionario* driver – that the daiquirís, the sweet roast pork, the yummy yams, the fine Havanas, the hot sex, nothing tasted good any more."

But not everyone noticed the changing of the winds – including Mob boss Meyer Lansky. In 1957, he opened his own hotel, the Riviera, right on the Malecón – it is still there today. It was the largest, and perhaps the most tasteless, place in Havana. Ginger Rogers performed in the hotel's Copa Room on opening night; Abbott and Costello, the hugely popular American comedy duo, flew down to entertain soon afterward.

Last days of the frenzy

For many, the disparity between Cuba's fun-loving image and brutal reality was becoming too great. Many Cubans were disgusted with the levels of corruption into which their country had sunk and the spectacle of the opulent, Mafia-run casinos alongside Cubans sleeping on the sidewalks and in burned-out cars. Even some foreigners felt moral qualms. As the Cuban-American writer Enrique Fernández-Más put it: "On the road to pleasure, your driver could turn around at a stop light and show you photos of bodies bloodied with bullets

LEFT: Federico García Lorca came to Havana in 1930; and Graham Greene immortalized the city in fiction.
ABOVE: high times in a Havana nightclub in 1946.

There seemed to be no limits to the money Havana could produce: gamblers' checks were flown to Miami every morning to make sure that they cleared. In April 1958, the Nevada Gaming Board, enraged that Havana's success was hurting Las Vegas, banned holders of Nevada gambling licenses from operating in Havana. Several Vegas operators withdrew their money. Regardless of this, and seemingly oblivious to what was going on in Cuban politics, Meyer Lansky stayed put. The consummate gambler this time got it wrong. He gambled everything on Havana – and, as he would later have cause to put it, "I crapped out." After the revolution, the casinos were closed, the Mob's properties nationalized. Havana's age of decadence was at an end. ❏

THE REVOLUTION

The 1959 Revolution was one of the 20th century's most distinctive political triumphs for the underdog. It ended the blatant corruption and inequality of the Batista years, but conflict with the USA, and support from the USSR, brought the world to the brink of nuclear war

As the age of decadence flourished in Havana, the roots of a revolution were beginning to take hold in the countryside. Under Batista's rule, a small elite enjoyed a grand lifestyle, while the majority of the rural population endured appalling poverty. Few had running water, electricity, or access to health care and education. A quarter of all Cubans were unable to read or write, and a quarter of adult males were unemployed. The country was rife with corruption, oppression, and inequality.

One year after Batista began his second term in office, a brazen young lawyer named Fidel Castro concluded that an armed uprising was the only way to end the dictator's reign. This was not Castro's first attempt at power. A year earlier he had tried to run for a seat in congress but, in a Machiavellian move by Batista, the elections were surreptitiously canceled.

The Moncada attack

Hoping to spark a mass uprising of the Cuban people, on July 26, 1953, Castro and 128 of his fellow anti-Batistas mounted an attack on the

You may still see slogans – especially in and around Santiago – declaring "Es Siempre el 26" (It is always the 26th), a reference to the 26th July Movement and the attack on the Moncada barracks.

army barracks at the Moncada Garrison in Santiago. But as the music of Carnival blared in the background, the young revolutionaries were brutally defeated. Despite being a total failure,

LEFT: Fidel and his brother Raúl (to his right) in 1957.
RIGHT: time runs out for Fulgencio Batista.

the hapless coup marked the beginning of the Cuban Revolution.

Six rebels died in the attack, and 55 more were later killed by the police. Those who escaped, including Castro, took refuge in the nearby Sierra Maestra mountains. But soon afterward they were rounded up and sent to jail. Fortunately for Castro, the arresting officer was sympathetic to the rebel cause, and took him to a local jail rather than the government prison where he would surely have been killed.

That officer, Sergeant Pedro Sarría Tartabull, was later court martialed and jailed by the Batista regime, but years down the track, he would be rewarded for his good deed: a grateful Castro appointed him as personal private secretary to the first president to take office after the revolution – Oswaldo Dordicos.

History will absolve me

For Batista, having Castro executed in secret would have solved many problems, but Castro's capture had become public knowledge, so any such attempt would have fomented even more anti-government sentiment. Instead, he had to put the rebel on trial. Acting as his own lawyer, Castro delivered a five-hour speech that would sink deeply into the minds of the Cuban underclass when it was eventually smuggled out of prison. He called Batista the worst dictator in Cuban his-

years, he was released on Mother's Day in May 1955 (El Día de La Madre is a major event in Cuba) under a government amnesty. This was a decision that Batista would later regret.

Soon after his release, Fidel Castro and his comrades went into exile in Mexico. There, he met a young Argentinian called Ernesto "Che" Guevara and together they created the 26th of July Movement (M-26), named for the attack at Moncada in 1953. M-26, which had roots in Cuba's 19th-century struggles, was the philosophical foundation that became synonymous with Castro's revolution. Castro traveled to New York and Miami to raise money for the impending revolt,

tory, and described in detail the sorry living conditions of the majority of the Cuban people.

He also called for universal education, agrarian reform, and a total restructuring of the government. He then delivered his famous words: "Condemn me if you will. History will absolve me." Significantly, he did not mention a single word about the principles of Marxism-Leninism.

Time to reflect

Sentenced to 15 years, Castro was imprisoned on the Isle of Pines (now the Isle of Youth). While in jail, he read the works of Marx and studied successful peasant uprisings. He also lectured to fellow inmates and plotted the revolution that would bring him to power. After serving less than two

gathered guns and ammunition, and campaigned for support from abroad.

In November 1956, Castro, Che, and 80 other revolutionaries left Mexico aboard a leaky 18-meter (60-ft) yacht. The boat, *Granma*, is said to have been named by its first (presumably English-speaking) owner for his grandmother. Later, *Granma* would become the unlikely name of Cuba's Communist Party newspaper, as well as the name of a whole province.

After several days floundering in stormy seas, the rebels landed on December 2 in the Gulf of Guacanayabo, about 160 km (100 miles) west of Santiago. The plan had been to arrive in Santiago at the end of November, to assist a potential uprising led by M-26 member Frank País, but the delayed arrival of Castro and his men meant that this uprising was crushed in just a few hours. A few days after the seasick revolutionaries finally disembarked from their boat they were ambushed by Batista's troops who captured and killed about three-quarters of the crew.

Among the dozen or so survivors were Castro, his younger brother Raúl, and Che. Joined by a group of peasants and a few fellow revolutionaries, the ragged band quickly slipped away into the Sierra Maestra where they founded the Rebel Army. One of those who joined them was a wealthy and spirited revolutionary named Vilma Espín, who became Raúl Castro's wife, founded

the airwaves for a democratic Cuba. Needing the support of the underground movements in Havana, they aligned themselves with the Students' Revolutionary Directorate and the Civic Resistance Movement.

In a clever public-relations coup, the rebels smuggled Herbert Matthews, a reporter for the *New York Times*, into their mountain camp for a clandestine interview with Castro. Swayed by the boisterous bravado of Fidel and his men, Matthews' account praised the Rebel Army and gave the world a romantic first impression of the dashing young revolutionary. Batista insisted that Matthews' story was fabricated, and Castro was

the Federation of Cuban Women, and remained active in politics until her death in June 2007.

Guerrillas in the mountains

Entrenched in the mountains, the Rebel Army saw themselves as warriors of the common people, and set out to infiltrate the country with their revolutionary ideas. During the next few years, they set up an informal government, drew up a manifesto, and organized schools and hospitals in rural areas. They also established their own radio station, Radio Rebelde, and campaigned on

LEFT: Raúl Castro and Che Guevara in the mountains.
ABOVE: Fidel Castro with his long-time companion, Celia Sánchez.

actually dead. Days later, the *New York Times* responded with irrefutable evidence: a photograph of Matthews and Castro smoking cigars together in the mountains.

With his name and face now known the world over, public support for Castro in Cuba multiplied. In March 1957, students stormed the Presidential Palace in an attempt to kill Batista, while another group took over a radio station and falsely announced his death. The following year a general strike was called in support of the Rebel Army, and disgruntled naval officers tried to stage a rebellion in the port of Cienfuegos.

The turning point of the revolution came in July 1958, when a battalion of Batista's forces surrendered to Castro's troops after a 10-day siege. The

Che Guevara

To this day, decades after his death, Ernesto "Che" Guevara is a glorified Marxist hero and model for Cuba's ideal socialist man. An icon by government decree, he is known throughout the island simply as Che, an affectionate Argentinian expression equivalent to the cockney/Australian "mate" or the American "pal" or "buddy."

Each morning, Cuban schoolchildren begin their day by reciting the patriotic slogan: "Pioneers of communism, we shall be like Che." Throughout the country, posters of his handsome face hang on

thousands of living-room walls. Government officials try to emulate his ideals, and women swoon for him as if he were a movie star.

Born in Argentina in 1928, Guevara came from a left-leaning, middle-class family. As a child he developed a severe asthma condition that later brought about his decision to become a doctor. He graduated from medical school in 1953, and then took off to travel through Latin America, seeking political adventure.

After witnessing the CIA-inspired overthrow of the socialist Árbenz government in Guatemala in 1954, Guevara moved to Mexico, where he met the then exiled Fidel Castro. Soon afterwards, he joined Castro's 26th of July Movement and was later to command the guerrilla attacks that led Batista to flee Cuba. He also became Castro's principal ideological counselor and closest friend.

Once the government was established, he supervised agrarian reform, served as the president of the National Bank of Cuba, and negotiated trade agreements with eastern-bloc countries. In 1960 he wrote a book called *Guerrilla Warfare* that became a manual for revolutionary strategies in the Developing World. In it, he advocated the use of guerrilla tactics to defeat imperialism; moral rather than material incentives for work; and working-class solidarity.

During the 1960s, an entire generation of radical youths idolized his purist Marxist beliefs, selfless devotion and relentless work ethic, and his dramatic image blessed protest movements in Paris, London, Washington, Montreal, Tokyo, Bombay and Baghdad.

A member of the macho world of brave guerrilla fighters, Guevara was impetuous, daring and reckless. He was also a brilliant intellectual who spoke French, wrote poetry, and represented Cuba in international chess competitions. Thrilled by the staccato beat of machine guns, he flaunted his Achilles heel: a total disregard for danger. In 1965 he resigned from his posts (some historians say he'd fallen out with Castro over the growing influence of the Soviet Union in Cuban affairs), and, after a brief spell fighting in the Congo, he settled in the highlands of Bolivia where he attempted to foster revolution among the local peasants. The campaign proved a disaster and Guevara was captured and killed by the Bolivian Army in 1967.

After his death, Castro declared a three-day period of national mourning, and then spent years creating a Guevara cult that surpassed his own. When the country began to feel the strain of the collapse of the Soviet Union, Castro tried to rekindle some revolutionary passion by implementing a nationwide "Let's Be Like Che" campaign. Then, in 1997, Che's mortal remains were discovered in Bolivia and returned to Cuba *(see page 234)*.

Che Guevara remains Latin America's most celebrated modern revolutionary. Hindsight reveals him as a martyr glorified by circumstance whose dream of spreading socialism around the world never really had a chance, yet he achieved enough in his brief life for French philosopher Jean-Paul Sartre to describe him as "the most complete human being of our age." ❑

LEFT: Che Guevara, iconic revolutionary.

Rebel Army, which by this time was about 50,000 strong, charged ahead.

Followed by troops, Castro advanced into Santiago, Raúl into northern Oriente and, in the most decisive move of all, Che Guevara into Santa Clara. By December 1958, the rebels had shattered Batista's army, which retreated in defeat. A terrified Batista fled the country to the Dominican Republic.

The following morning, people all over the island rejoiced. Ebullient revelers danced in the streets, applauding Batista's downfall. In Havana, throngs of Cuban peasants stormed into the fancy casinos, which had been off-limits to them for years. Some vandalized the slot machines, while others brought their pigs in to have a look.

The victory drive

After announcing the triumph of the revolution from the balcony of Santiago's town hall on January 2, 1959, the handsome 32-year-old Castro took off with his guerrillas for a victory drive to Havana. Euphoric crowds cheered as they passed through the countryside. When they arrived in the capital a week later, tens of thousands of supporters welcomed them. As Castro delivered a victory speech in Havana, a flock of white doves was released into the air; one of the birds landed on his shoulder, and this was taken by followers of Santería *(see pages 104–5)* to be an omen that he had been chosen by the gods to deliver them from oppression.

The world approves

Cubans in New York and Miami celebrated the fall of Batista and made plans to return to the island. The revolution was praised worldwide as a true victory for the Cuban people, and even the US Government was initially optimistic about the changes taking place.

Meanwhile, back at the Riviera Hotel, workers walked out of their jobs. Meyer Lansky , the boss, found himself in the kitchen cooking dinner for befuddled guests as his wife waited tables and mopped the floors. For Lansky and his cronies, the good life was over. Words from Castro's speech echoed in his head: "We are ready not only to deport the gangsters, but to shoot them." Lansky knew he meant it. He moved his gambling business to the nearby Bahamas, and offered a large bounty for Fidel Castro's head.

RIGHT: a revolutionary poster (now in Havana's Museum of the Revolution) invites Batista to flee the country.

NOTHING TO DECLARE

Shortly after midnight on New Year's Eve (1958–9), Batista fled Cuba for the Dominican Republic and then Florida, supposedly with US\$300 million in his suitcase.

A new Cuba

In the spring of 1959, a victorious Castro declared himself the prime minister of Cuba, and Che Guevara was appointed president of the National Bank. Hundreds of Batista supporters were jailed, many of them executed, and by the following year sweeping political changes were taking place across the country.

The new government passed an agrarian reform act which limited private land ownership; under Batista, 70 percent of the land had been owned by a mere 8 percent of the population. Fidel's regime also confiscated foreign-owned industries in an effort to end US control of the island (North Americans owned more than 165 major companies including 90 percent of the public services and 40 percent of the sugar industry).

Farms, plantations, oil refineries, and communications systems were nationalized. The government also outlawed racial discrimination, created a low-income housing program, made free health care and education available to all, and implemented new policies for farming, sports, music, the arts, and defense.

The redistribution of wealth meant instant rewards for the peasant class, but just as quickly, the middle and upper classes were stripped of the privileges they had once enjoyed. Already having had their homes confiscated, many feared what might come next, and fled the country for exile in Miami. Forbidden to take any possessions with them, most left with nothing more than the clothes on their backs. Women sewed their wedding rings into the hems of their dressses to smuggle them out. Once in Miami they established a vocal anti-Castro community of exiles that freely criticized the new government, and looked forward to the day they could return to their homes.

In 1960, Fidel Castro delivered his first speech to the United Nations and was introduced to Soviet Premier Nikita Khrushchev. While in New York, he also met the radical American Black Power leader Malcolm X.

At about that time, the US Government began to see Castro as a threat to its national security, and mysterious things started happening. A French ship, *La Coubre*, delivering Belgian armaments, inexplicably exploded in Havana harbor as unidentified low-flying planes flew over the city. The US was the prime suspect.

In response, Castro took an aggressive stance. In January 1961, he expelled 11 US diplomats. Soon afterward, the two countries severed diplomatic relations, and the US began an economic embargo that brought the import of American goods to a halt. It further isolated the island by persuading all but two Western-hemisphere nations (Canada and Mexico) to cut trade and diplomatic ties with Cuba.

The Bay of Pigs

In April 1961, a CIA-trained brigade of 1,500 mercenaries, mostly Cuban exiles from Miami, landed at Playa Girón in the Bahía de Cochinos (Bay of Pigs) on the south coast, hoping to instigate an anti-Castro coup. The invasion was a complete fiasco. The element of surprise was lost because US bombers attacked Cuban airfields days beforehand; the raids failed to destroy the Cuban airforce, thus leaving the attackers open to assault from the air. The counter-revolutionaries were no match for Cuba's military, led by Castro himself; and the local populace, whom it was hoped would be sympathetic to the exiles' cause, were strongly pro-Castro.

Within 72 hours the US brigade was defeated. A few men were killed and the rest taken prisoner. For their release, the US traded $50-million worth of medicines that Cuba had been unable to buy due to the embargo.

Castro emerged as the clear victor, while Kennedy was humiliated. The invasion was seen by the Cubans as a blatant imperialist stunt, and relations between the two countries worsened still further. The incident also garnered support for Castro throughout Latin America, and rendered him forever fearful of a US military invasion.

The United States did little to alleviate those fears, instigating covert activities including plots to assassinate Castro *(see panel, left)*. The Cuban leader estimates that there have been 20 CIA-

FIDEL THE SURVIVOR

The CIA's ingenious (if ineffective) ways of attempting to assassinate Castro (apart from simply shooting him). included:

• contaminating his cigars with botulism.
• giving him a toxic dose of LSD.
• lacing a chocolate milk-shake with cyanide.
• smearing his wet-suit with tuberculosis spores.

Cuban exiles in Miami and the Mafia were the agency's two natural partners in crime, but their plots never worked.

inspired attempts on his life; one CIA director, William Colby, expressed surprise, saying he was aware of only five.

Socialism or pragmatism?

By the end of 1961, Castro's platform for a freely elected democratic government had changed. Following the Bay of Pigs invasion he had shocked the world by pronouncing Cuba's revolution to be a "socialist revolution." Some believe that Castro's conversion to Marxism was merely a pragmatic move to gain favor with the Russians, without whom the island did not stand a chance of surviving the US embargo.

The US demanded that the Soviets remove the missiles, and threatened to bomb Cuba if they refused. The world watched in horror as the possibility of war came closer. The Soviets eventually relented and an uneasy peace was restored.

Despite the fact that an agreement was reached, the US was not happy with the outcome. In 1963, President Kennedy relegated relations with Cuba

On the brink of war

In order to support of the new socialist Cuba, the USSR supplied Castro with economic aid, as Castro had anticipated, and shipped nuclear missiles to Cuba to defend the island. The threat of nuclear weapons stationed just 140 km (90 miles) away was too much for the US Government, and in October 1962, the Soviet Union and the United States came face to face with the reality of nuclear war, over what has gone down in history as the Cuban Missile Crisis, and Cubans refer to as the Caribbean Crisis.

LEFT: a memorial to those who died at the Bay of Pigs in 1962.
ABOVE: Krushchev welcomes Fidel to Moscow.

to fall under the US Trading with the Enemy Act, which tightened the embargo and prohibited all commercial and personal contact between the two nations. The US became the only country in the world to forbid its citizens to travel to Cuba; the political impasse became even more intractable.

Castro was incensed that he had not been consulted during the talks between the two superpowers, but the reality was that he had thrown in his lot with the Soviets and was powerless to prevent them from dictating terms. He had to content himself with an unwritten assurance that the US would not sponsor a further invasion of Cuba, and with the fact that, for the briefest of periods, he'd managed to turn the tables on his enemy in the insecurity stakes. ❑

SOCIALISM OR DEATH

During the 1960s and 1970s, Cuba played a role in world affairs out of all proportion to its size. Since then, progress has been curtailed by crippling domestic problems, taxing even Fidel Castro's ingenuity

Although resolved diplomatically, the Cuban Missile Crisis *(see page 63)* provoked even more Cold War hostility from the United States, and pushed Castro firmly into the Soviet camp. In addition, it helped to turn the country into an audacious socialist experiment and a feisty Third World power.

Cuba's Communist Party was established in 1965, and the following year, despite Soviet disapproval, Castro was determined to export his revolutionary ideals. In 1966 he claimed that the Andes would become the next Sierra Maestra. But the Soviet Union (which provided money and arms) pressed Castro to pursue a less independent foreign policy. It seems that Che Guevara was determined to carry out a policy of directly fomenting revolution, with or without Soviet support, and left Cuba to fight first in Africa and then Bolivia.

Friends and foes

With the death of Guevara in Bolivia in 1967, Castro realized he had to take a different path to global influence. In 1968 he personally endorsed the Soviet invasion of Czechoslovakia, and cemented the bond with his powerful ally.

Castro then directed his energy inward. Trying to lessen the country's dependence on the sugar industry, he tried to diversify the economy through industrialization. But, by this time, thousands of educated Cubans had fled and the country lacked skilled labor. The US embargo limiting the import of industrial equipment was another hindrance, and eventually the industrialization plan failed. So sugar, once again, became the main force of the economy.

LEFT: a 1970s May Day parade in Havana.
RIGHT: a supportive T-shirt.

NEIGHBORHOOD WATCH

To help dissuade counter-revolutionary activities, Castro created neighborhood-watch groups known as Committees for the Defense of the Revolution (CDRS). Although CDRS did organize labor and implement health and education programs, they also served as vigilantes and as the Big Brother of the revolution. Members monitored their neighbors and reported all non-conformist behavior to the government. Still in operation today, there are more than 100,000 CDRS on the island, comprising about 75 percent of the total population. Membership is voluntary, but belonging to a CDR brings a guarantee of social benefits, while not belonging may possibly bring trouble.

Big Brother is watching

In the name of the revolution, the 1960s marked the beginning of decades of political repression. Anyone seen as non-supportive of the government was deemed "socially unacceptable," and thousands of these "dissidents" were jailed.

Government police sealed off the bohemian neighborhoods of Havana and interrogated artists, writers and intellectuals. Non-supportive poets were silenced. Education and cultural policies became more severe, trade unions were disbanded, and the media fell under absolute control of the government. By the late 1960s, an ideological straitjacket seemed to have smothered the country.

increased and was measured in billions of dollars. At the time, Cuba was receiving generous shipments of oil priced far below standard OPEC rates, and about one-half of all Soviet aid to the Third World. Its sugar crop was bought at inflated prices. Boosted by Soviet weapons and fighter planes, Cuba's defense system developed into the most powerful military force in Latin America, much larger than those of Brazil or Mexico.

The heady 1970s

For most Cubans, the 1970s are remembered fondly as the heady days of the revolution. With the utmost confidence, Castro became the inter-

Practicing Catholics, Protestants, Jews, and Santeros were persecuted – religious affiliation was deemed anti-revolutionary. Prostitutes were sent to vocational schools for rehabilitation, homosexuals were imprisoned in labor camps, and all remnants of bourgeois society were eliminated.

Throughout the 1960s, the "better-dead-than-red" communist-obsessed US continued covert activities against Cuba, including more CIA-backed assassination attempts on Castro. In addition, several of Cuba's trade missions in Europe were bombed by anti-Castro terrorists. As a result, the Soviet Union beefed up its military and economic support to Cuba. Eastern-bloc technicians were sent to the island while Cuban students were invited to study in Moscow. Financial aid steadily

national spokesman for Developing World causes, traveling to South America, China, Vietnam, and Africa. In 1974 the Soviet premier Leonid Brezhnev visited Cuba and publicly endorsed his Caribbean comrade. In front of enraptured crowds, the two men predicted that communism would some day triumph throughout the world. The next year, the Organization of American States lifted its sanctions against Cuba and many Latin American nations resumed ties with the country.

Economically, Cuba advanced, and the gains of the revolution were indisputable. Unheard of in most Third World countries, Cuba's health-care system eliminated infectious diseases, drastically lowered the infant mortality rate, and curtailed population growth. The number of doctors grew from 6,000 to over 25,000. The government also paved roads throughout the countryside, built low-rent apartment buildings, and eradicated illiteracy. Cubans felt proud.

Although Cuba's political system was re-designed to mimic the Soviet model, Castro remained very much his own man. This was especially so when it came to foreign policy. He saw Cuba as part of the non-aligned movement, but nevertheless got heavily involved in Africa where, capitalizing on Cuba's Afro-Cuban heritage, he aligned himself with left-wing revolutionary movements. In 1975 he flexed his military mus-

Back on his own side of the world, Castro befriended left-leaning leaders in nearby Jamaica and Grenada and, in 1979, hosted the annual conference of the non-aligned nations. That same year Cuba supported the Soviet invasion of Afghanistan, and the socialist revolution in Nicaragua which brought the Sandinistas to power. An elated Castro strutted the world stage like a proud peacock.

In 1976, Cuba finally approved its new constitution which canonized Marxism-Leninism, and Fidel Castro's position as head of state became constitutional. The new constitution redrew provincial boundaries, adding eight more

cles by sending 200,000 soldiers to Angola. Cuban troops fought on the side of the Marxist SWAPO government, following South Africa's decision to assist Angolan UNITA rebels. This conflict continued a tradition of Cuban assistance with what Castro saw as anti-imperialist movements in Africa, which went back to the days of Che. In 1978 he did the same for Ethiopia. But Angola was Cuba's greatest triumph – as attested to by Nelson Mandela, who says the defeat of South African troops there helped precipitate the downfall of the apartheid state in his own country.

LEFT: Cuba's literacy campaign created the most literate population in Latin America.
ABOVE: the island's military on parade.

provinces to the original seven inherited from the Spanish. It also created the assemblies of People's Power *(Poder Popular)*, governing bodies of elected officials who delegate power at municipal, provincial and national levels.

Socialismo o Muerte

At the beginning of the 1980s, Cuba was still a Latin American symbol of independence from US imperialism, but the quality of life in the country was beginning to decline. Productivity dropped off, and health care, education and social services deteriorated. Castro blamed the country's problems on the "workers who do not work and the students who do not study," and then fired many government economists.

Many of Cuba's economic problems, however, were caused by blatant mismanagement. The government had appointed Communist Party members to professional positions for which they were not qualified, destroyed the plantation system, and refused to develop the tourism industry. And a political system designed for the Soviet Union did not translate well to Cuba.

In 1980 public protests escalated to the point that the government permitted anyone who wanted to leave to do so – including, it is said, many criminals who were freed from prison in order for them to leave. That year, 125,000 Cubans fled to the US in the so-called Mariel

SUGAR FOR OIL

A sugar-for-oil deal with the USSR meant that Moscow guaranteed a price for Cuba's harvest, and payment was made in oil at a price well below the going rate.

boatlift *(see page 75)*, adding to the several hundred thousand who had left in the early years of the revolution. In 1985, the Cubans in Miami set up Radio Martí, an anti-Castro propaganda station aimed directly at Cuba. The station's reports of how great life was in the US stirred up even more discontent, although Castro limited this by jamming its frequency.

REJUVENTATING SLOGANS

By the late 1980s, Cuba was billions of dollars in debt to the Soviet Union, and the government was forced to cut food rations. In an attempt to rejuvenate the revolutionary spirit, Castro revised his *¡Patria o Muerte!* (Fatherland or Death) slogan used to punctuate his dreadfully long speeches during the 1960s, and *¡Socialismo o Muerte!* became the slogan of choice. In an appeal to Cuban nationalism, "100 percent Cubano" became another motivational motto. Both were plastered on billboards throughout Cuba.

Criticisms and scandals

On the international level, Cuba received harsh criticisms for its human-rights violations. A report filed by Amnesty International condemned the country for its abuse of political prisoners, and the beatings, psychological torture and solitary confinement taking place in Cuba's prisons became a thorny issue.

In 1989, more disgrace fell on the country. General Arnaldo Ochoa, a much-decorated military figure, and six other military officials, were charged with corruption and drug trafficking. Found guilty of pocketing millions of dollars and allowing Colombian cocaine smugglers to use Cuba as a way-station en route to the US, the officers were put before a firing squad.

The scandal made a mockery of Castro's insistence that Cuba had an impeccable record when it came to involvement with illegal drugs, and cynics saw the public execution as overly dramatic. Some accused Castro of ordering the punishment in order to mask his own involvement with drugs. Others suggested that Ochoa had been conspiring to oust Castro.

The eastern bloc crumbles

As the Ochoa scandal shook the country, communist dominoes in eastern Europe were beginning to tumble. When Mikhail Gorbachev assumed power in Moscow and put forth his *perestroika*

were a privileged class in Cuba. With access to food, cars, gas, travel abroad, and imported goods, they bitterly resisted change.

When the USSR finally fell apart in 1991, the impact on Cuba was devastating. At a stroke, the country lost annual subsidies of US$6 billion in economic aid, $1 billion in military assistance, 10 million tons of oil, and $6 billion worth of imported goods. It also lost its major trading partner, and now had to sell its sugar at market value. The scarcity of available oil paralyzed Cuban industry and transportation systems. Adding to the turmoil, Cuba's sugar harvest was the lowest in 30 years.

economic reforms, many predicted that Soviet money would flow less freely, causing chaos for the Cuban Government. But Castro made it clear that he had no interest in multiparty governments or a free-market system. "For us to adopt *perestroika* would be like living in our home with another man's wife," he said.

Members of Cuba's Communist Party agreed with their leader. For them, *perestroika* and Gorbachev's other main goal – *glasnost* (transparency and freedom from censorship) – were dirty words. Untouched by the looming crisis, party members

LEFT: standing in line outside stores has become a monotonous feature of Cuban life.
ABOVE: most commodities are in short supply.

The "Special Period"

Beset by economic crises, but unwilling to adopt either *perestroika* or *glasnost*-style reforms, the Cuban Government implemented a belt-tightening survival strategy known as the "Special Period in Time of Peace." In order to compensate for the loss of Soviet subsidies, Castro told the Cuban people to work harder and be patient. He then set about stripping them of the basic necessities of daily life, and demanding sacrifices like none they had ever known before.

Energy consumption was drastically reduced, oxen replaced tractors in the fields, and food rations were slashed to a minimum survival level. Government-produced television programs instructed citizens on how to grow their own vegetables, make their own candles and soap, and turn dried banana skins into sandals. Horse-drawn buggies were put back in service, and cheap, low-grade oil was substituted to fire electric plants, causing a pall of dirty smoke over Havana.

In addition, the government imported a million Chinese bicycles and ordered the people to start pedaling. Encouraging Cubans to adopt cycling, Fidel Castro told them: "Expanding the use of the bicycle is an indicator of cultural advancement." But for the millions of secretaries, teachers, and factory workers who had to spend hours a day riding to work, it was more like pedaling back in time.

The "Special Period" – which only officially ended in 2005 – meant that life for the average Cuban citizen was bleak. People watched as the crowded apartments in which they lived slipped further into disrepair. Electric wires dangled in the streets, telephones rarely worked, elevators were often out of order, and clocks no longer told the time.

Hungry, frustrated Cubans soon tired of waiting in long lines for pitiful goods. Sugar, coffee and rum – the backbone of the Cuban economy – became a luxury for most people. And while Cubans had lived with the *libreta* or ration book since the early 1960s, less and less seemed to be actually avail-

LIVING ON THE *LIBRETA*

A Cuban's typical monthly ration amounts to 3 kg (6 lb) of rice, 3 kg (6 lb) of sugar, 10 eggs, seven bread rolls, 125 g (4 oz) of coffee, some cooking oil, 250 g (8 oz) of dried beans, plus 250 g (8 oz) of minced soya-based "meat" product or a quarter of a chicken if available. Real meat is available only for those with children under 12, and under-7s and pregnant women are entitled to a daily supply of milk. Many of these items, which are sold at heavily subsidized rates, are often out of stock at local shops, and the quality is poor.

However, farmers' markets *(agropecuarios)* wherein farmers are allowed to sell their surplus products, do offer access to a wider variety of foodstuffs, especially

fruit and vegetables when in season, and these can be purchased with Cuban pesos but they are expensive. Meat, which is often sold at street stands called *puntas de carne,* is even more expensive. The rural population fares better: those who grow fruit and vegetables and keep chickens for eggs usually have a reasonable supply, with some to share with urban relations, after they have delivered their quota to the state, but they are not allowed to eat the meat from their own oxen – this is a state monopoly.

The days of rationing may be coming to an end: in a speech in November 2005, Castro said Cuba was "creating conditions for the *libreta* to disappear."

able. Even today the *libreta* entitles its owner to precious little *(see panel, previous page).*

Patients had to get used to bringing their own sheets to hospitals, and surgeons were allotted only one bar of soap a month with which to wash their hands. Herbal remedies replaced drugs and hemp was used for sutures. In schools, textbooks were shared and work in exercise books erased so they could be passed on to the next class. Factories sat idle, there were no fertilizers for crops, and harvests rotted in the fields for want of distribution. Newspapers and magazines shut down for want of paper. Toilet tissue, toothpaste, shampoo and aspirin became luxuries Cubans had to buy

It was a sign of just how serious the crisis had become when, in 1993, Fidel Castro swallowed his pride and legalized the use of the American dollar, to which previously only a few privileged citizens (including high-ranking members of the Communist Party) had had access.

In the same year Castro permitted people to go into business for themselves by offering licenses in over 100 categories, including mechanics, fishermen, farmers, taxi drivers, hairdressers and restaurateurs. The government ensures the self-employed have to pay a small fortune for a trading license and in income tax to prevent them from benefitting too much from their efforts, thus

in what were then dollar shops – but first they had to get access to dollars.

Capitalist tinkerings

Faced with rousing discontent, Castro has made some compromises that in the past were non-negotiable. In 1991, he eased travel restrictions abroad, released some political prisoners, permitted more free speech than ever before, and granted autonomy to farmers, who were now permitted to sell a proportion of their surplus produce on the open market, often at cripplingly high prices.

LEFT: refilling cigarette lighters; buying produce at a farmers' market. **ABOVE:** revolutionary literature for sale. **RIGHT:** foreign stores appeared in the 1990s.

putting a sharp brake on both private enterprise and dollar investments from Miami Cubans.

Meanwhile, to make up for lost Soviet subsidies and to combat the United States embargo, Cuba began to woo new investors – notably Canada, Mexico and members of the European Union – in what are commonly known as "joint ventures". These countries are pumping hundreds of millions of dollars into the economy, above all into tourism but also in the fields of nickel mining, oil exploration, and the pharmaceutical industry.

Tightening the noose

During the 1990s, Castro alluded to a reconciliation with the US – something that proved a phantom hope, even in the post-Cold-War era. In 1992, the powerful Cuban-American lobby helped ensure the passing of the so-called Torricelli Act in the US, which sought to tighten sanctions in an effort to bring down the struggling Cuban regime. It prohibited subsidiaries of US companies from trading with Cuba, and linked any repeal of sanctions to Cuba hosting free and fair elections.

Sanctions were ratcheted up again in 1996, when the then US President, Bill Clinton, gave way to pressure from Cuban Americans and approved the Helms-Burton legislation *(see panel below)*, named after its sponsors in the US Congress. Among other provisions, the Helms-Burton legislation raised the threat of suing any company worldwide that did business with Cuba involving assets on the island that had been confiscated by the Castro regime in the 1960s. Consequently, relations between the US and countries that were investing in Cuba – especially Canada and some members of the EU – came under strain.

It also helped polarize the debate on sanctions within the US – some powerful business and humanitarian interests spoke up against sanctions, which they believed had failed in their primary objective of bringing down the Castro regime, and which were denying US companies investment opportunities. Some, too, believed the Cuban-American lobby had overreached itself.

THE CESSNAS INCIDENT

In February 1996, Cuban MiGs (Russian-built fighter planes) shot down two unarmed Cessnas piloted by members of the Brothers to the Rescue organization *(see page 77)*, on the look out for rafters crossing to Miami. The Cessnas had crossed into Cuban airspace in defiance of a warning issued by the Cuban authorities, who viewed these flights as violations of an agreement with the US to clamp down on those encouraging emigration from Cuba. The Cessnas' four Miami Cuban crewmen were killed, and the subsequent outcry in the US helped smooth the passage of the Helms-Burton legislation, which President Clinton had previously opposed.

The *bloqueo*

The US embargo (called the *bloqueo* in Cuba) also attracted international disapproval. In 1997, 143 countries in the UN General Assembly voted against the embargo, with just three in favor (the US, Uzbekistan and Israel). The figures for the same resolution in 1992 were 59 in favor, 3 against and 71 abstentions.

Cuba's regime was also given a shot in the arm by the much-publicized visit of Pope John Paul II in January 1998. Castro agreed to release some 300 political prisoners ahead of the papal visit; the Pope, for his part, criticized Cuba on human-rights issues, but he also spoke out indirectly against US sanctions, calling any such embargo "deplorable." This saw the US Government relax the embargo slightly: direct flights between Miami and Havana resumed in July 1998, and more US politicians and businessmen began visiting Cuba, though under tight restrictions.

Dollars or death

However, Cuban society was showing the strain. Decriminalizing the dollar had a devastating effect on a society brought up at least to pay lip service to egalitarianism. The island was essentially divided into two classes – those with dollars, and those without. Dollars could be acquired through fair means or foul: on the one hand through relatives living abroad or through a thriving business;

den closures, and laws passed and repealed without notice. Police would appear at the door at 6am to close "illegal" businesses – the dispossessed businessman discovering in that morning's edition of *Granma* that some new law had been enacted, making his business illegal. Such tactics, together with high taxation, fines and overwhelming bureaucratic control, created tremendous insecurity and unease in a population that felt it must earn dollars to survive.

From 1999–2003 there were 1,400 house confiscations, 548 expulsions of illegal occupants, and more than US$1.5 million levied in fines for "property crimes" (which were mostly unlicensed

on the other from black-market dealing or prostitution. Since there is little of worth that pesos can buy, many Cubans also converted their hard-earned pesos into dollars at exchange bureaux known as *cadecas*. They got a miserable return – with an average monthly salary worth less than US$10.

For those with dollars, life improved beyond measure, hence the booming, clandestine economy and rocketing crime rate. Fear that the dollar sector was getting out of control – that some people were becoming "too rich" – led to a seesaw economic policy: shop openings followed by sud-

lets and illegal sales). This crackdown came in 2000 after a decree gave the authorities sole right to authorize constructions and to seize property if they felt the law was being broken. In 2001, there was also a crackdown on *casas particulares* (rooms rented out to tourists). This was later reversed, but is strictly controlled, and taxes are high, as they are on *paladares* (privately run restaurants).

One effect of the property crimes legislation was that prosperous householders would never paint the exteriors of their homes for fear of attracting unwanted attention. So the shabbiness of some buildings in Havana is misleading: the peeling, crumbling facades may sometimes hide freshly painted, air-conditioned interiors full of the latest electrical goods.   ❑

LEFT: Pope John Paul II visits Cuba in 1998.
ABOVE: there's time to dance, between socialism and death.

DREAMING OF MIAMI

Over the decades thousands of Cubans have fled to Miami as political or economic refugees. Ironically, the remittances they sent back to their families helped keep the Cuban economy afloat during its most difficult period

On Havana's Malecón, a small crowd gathered to watch as fishermen battled to rescue the little raft – a black inner tube lined with fishing net – that had drifted in and out of the bay all morning, held by a current that no one could breach. Finally, three men, fishing for snapper in similar crafts, managed to get hold of the raft and bring it to shore. Too late for the two young men inside: one had already died of dehydration, the other died soon after the rescue.

A weeping sore

In the weeks following the start of the "rafters crisis" during the summer of 1994, people in Havana began to get used to the sight of bodies washing up in the bay – many of them chewed up by sharks. Although about 40,000 Cubans made it to the United States that year, it is estimated that between five and nine thousand died in the attempt. This exodus was just the most recent in a series of migrations.

A generational change

In 1959–60, hundreds of thousands of the rich left, with many more following in 1961 and 1962, after Castro's declaration that the revolution was "Marxist-Leninist," and the increasingly evident socialist slant of policies.

Landless peasants and poor farmers then came from the countryside and took over the vacated mansions. Their children grew up in cities living lives very different from their own, becoming doctors, professors and engineers. Yet many Cubans still wished to emigrate to Miami.

LEFT: inner tubes, once a means of floating to Miami, are now used for fishing. **RIGHT:** youngsters play by the bay but can't cross the water.

In 1980, after a week-long crisis in which more than 10,000 Cubans sought asylum in Havana's foreign embassies, Castro announced that anyone who wanted to leave could do so. Around 125,000 promptly did, aided by small craft from Miami, in what became known as the Mariel Boatlift.

For the Castro regime, these people were traitors or "worms" *(gusanos)*, and were denounced by the state media as *escoria* (scum). Castro ensured that thousands of criminals were disgorged from Cuban prisons to join the exodus. But the refugees turned out to be mostly respectable, hard-working people: doctors, teachers, academics and members of Castro's new middle class. In other words, people who owed their education and status to the revolution they had rejected.

What had gone wrong? Why, after 20 years of a revolution marked by great social changes, of a revolution that was still popular in some sectors and that was marked by a vehement anti-Americanism, did so many Cubans still yearn for a life in the United States?

Opportunity stifled

Most of the people who still seek to leave Cuba say the revolution has failed because it denies two freedoms. Political freedom, and also, especially for young people, economic freedom. They complain bitterly about the lack of opportunity to "get on" in the world. Those who have trained to be

Miami their home – near enough to Cuba to keep alive their dreams of a successful return or of counter-revolution.

José Martí was there in the 19th century, plotting the overthrow of Spanish colonial rule. Cubans fled there in the 1930s during the brutal dictatorship of Machado. Castro visited exiled Cubans there in 1955 when seeking funds for the overthrow of Batista. After more than a hundred years, Miami has taken on a strong Cuban flavor – the city is essentially Spanish-speaking, largely because of its dominant Cuban community; restaurants and stores sell American-made replicas of Cuban brands, and strong, sweet "Cuban" cof-

professionals often can't afford a house – many married couples live with their children in a single room at their parents' house. Doctors earn less in a month than a waiter or taxi driver can make in convertible peso (CUC) tips in a day.

As one young émigré – an agricultural engineer – said, "In the United States I will have the chance to live my life. I may fail – there's always a risk. But at least I will have had the chance. Here, if you do not conform, if you are not a revolutionary man, you have no chance to succeed. None at all."

Home away from home

These emigrants have settled in different Cuban-American communities across the United States, but most Cubans make the tropical city of

fee scents the air of Little Havana (the coffee is not the real thing, of course – federal politics ensures that no goods from the island ever reach the United States).

Escaping the "Special Period"

The obsession with Miami reached a peak in the early 1990s, when Cuba faced crippling hardships after the fall of the Soviet Union, and people were so desperate to leave that they were willing to risk their lives on a fragile raft.

Many had no idea of the difficulties they faced. A distance that seemed small on a map took many days, even weeks, to reach. All too often, empty rafts would wash up on the Florida Keys. The horror stories did not deter those determined to leave, usually sailing with a large painted banner to catch the attention of the Brothers to the Rescue, an exile organization that launched planes from Miami to search for rafters.

Between 1989 and 1994, more than 10,000 rafters made it to Miami. The Cuban coastguard stopped a further 37,800. Castro claimed that the US precipitated the crisis – by refusing to grant entry visas to people who were then welcomed as heroes after risking their lives on rafts, as any Cuban arriving in US waters was eligible for US citizenship. Castro retaliated by saying he would no longer prevent Cubans from leaving, sparking a mass exodus – between August and September

WILL THEY EVER STOP?

In 1998, three Cuban-Americans in their seventies were captured in the mountains of Pinar del Río, trying to incite guerrilla war against Castro.

for US visas doubled until 1999 when the US State Department claimed it had received as many applications as there were families living in Cuba.

The agreement didn't stop rafting completely though, and the Cuban authorities were still angered by the US policy of granting citizenship to rafters who made it to dry land. But the measures put in place after the crisis helped to alter

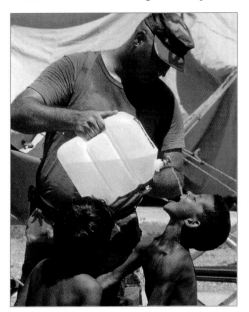

1994, around 2,000 rafters a week set sail. The US authorities feared the consequences of a mass migration like that of the Mariel Boatlift, and started to ship those picked up at sea to internment camps at its Guantánamo military base.

The crisis led to talks between the US and Cuba, whereby the Cuban authorities agreed to clamp down on would-be refugees, rafters picked up at sea would be returned home, and the US would grant 20,000 visas a year by lottery to Cubans seeking to leave the island. This lottery proved popular – each year the numbers applying

LEFT: makeshift raft crossing the Florida Straits. **ABOVE:** young refugees at Guantánamo. **RIGHT:** baseball is equally popular in Cuba and the US.

the perspective of some would-be refugees. Some began to look to emigration to other Latin countries – Costa Rica and Mexico were favorites. Marriages to tourists – sometimes pre-arranged and paid-for – also became an increasingly popular means of leaving Cuba.

An ongoing exodus

To this day, Cubans still try to make the sea crossing, although not in the numbers seen during previous crises. An upturn in Cuba's economy has meant some islanders have begun to see more of a future in their homeland and are no longer prepared to countenance the risk of an illegal crossing. Others are put off by reports – true or not – of Cubans going to Miami but ending up disillusioned by the rampant consumerism, the widespread waste of resources, the hours of work needed to maintain the coveted lifestyle, the threat of unemployment, and the difficulties of being confronted with large medical bills and tussles with insurance companies.

These days, a significant proportion of illegal Cuban emigrants who still risk the crossing travel with professional immigrant smugglers. It's a multimillion dollar industry. Cubans, usually funded by their relatives in Miami, pay up to US$10,000 per person. Nevertheless, in 2006, US coastguards intercepted more than 2,800 Cubans who were trying to cross to Florida illegally. And in Cuba there are – despite massive security measures – still attempts to hijack boats and planes. You will see a heavy police presence at places like the ferry that crosses Havana bay to Regla; and in April 2003, three alleged ferry hijackers were put to death by Castro's courts. The security checks for domestic flights are often more stringent than for international ones; and in May 2007, a gun battle in Havana's airport thwarted another unsuccessful attempted hijacking.

The grass is always greener

While those in Cuba dream of life in Miami, the old guard there still dreams of returning to

INTERNATIONAL BATTLE

One of the most dramatic immigration cases took place in 1999. Five-year-old Elián González was one of a handful of people who survived when the small craft he had been traveling in overturned. His mother and nine others drowned. His father (divorced from his mother) called for Elián's return to Cuba, and the boy became the subject of a fierce international custody battle between relatives in Miami (backed by Cuban-American organizations) and the US Government, which backed Elián's father's demands, in rare agreement with the Cuban regime. Elián did return home, to the jubilation of hundreds of thousands of Cubans who had demanded his return at daily rallies organized by the authorities.

Havana. Veterans of Batista's time and the Bay of Pigs still gather in Miami's Little Havana to plot and scheme over cups of coffee at the Café Versailles. Old men now, they still cling to their dream that Castro will be overthrown and they will return home. Miami-based terrorist organizations such as Alpha 66 and Omega 7 have carried out several unsuccessful incursions into Cuban territory. Exile leaders admit that the bombs that exploded in Havana's hotels in the summer of 1997, killing an Italian tourist, were organized and paid for in Miami.

These desperate acts, though, are the work of the older generation. Those Cuban-Americans born in the USA, or who arrived since the Mariel Boatlift, have a different way of taking on the regime, using their prosperity to fund businesses in Cuba. Most of Cuba's *paladares* (family-run restaurants) started up using Miami money, either as a loan or by direct investment, with the investor taking a cut of the profits. Many Cubans who left on rafts returned as tourists or entrepreneurs, helping friends and family set up new businesses that have changed the once moribund face of Havana.

Cubans without Miami connections resent this: they see the families of exiles able to live well while they suffer on a monthly ration that barely lasts two weeks. Havana's shopping malls have been fueled by the spending power of those who

And not all Miami Cubans feel the same about remittances – some people complain that their families back home are too demanding, seeing them as cash cows to be milked at every opportunity. Many are working-class people with mortgages and heavy financial commitments who can find the burden of helping families in Cuba too much for them.

Room for dialogue

These days, too, there's more contact between the two communities than there was in the aftermath of the Revolution, when political refugees vowed never to return until Castro was ousted. Subsequent refugee groups like the *marielitos* and the rafters,

receive money from abroad. Ironically, some argue that remittances sent by the exile community helped prevent economic collapse during the "Special Period". And even with restrictions on remittances, tightened up by President Bush in 2004, perhaps as much as US$1 billion still gets sent on an annual basis.

In November 2004 Castro responded to tighter sanctions by banning commercial transactions in dollars in Cuba, and urging people to tell their relatives in the US to send money home in currencies other than the dollar.

LEFT: demonstration in Miami in favor of keeping Elián González in the US.
ABOVE: Miami Cubans wait for Castro's demise.

having left Cuba for economic rather than political reasons, are not troubled by the idea of vacations in Cuba. Journeys "home" increased after the resumption of direct flights from Miami to Havana in 1998. Policy swung back again in 2004, when President Bush tightened travel restrictions, in a move that got a mixed reception from within America's Cuban community. Now US-based Cubans are only allowed to visit "close family," and only once every three years, for a maximum of two weeks. Nevertheless, contacts like this have helped ensure that the Miami Cuban community no longer has a monolithic approach to the Cuban state. The majority remains anti-regime, but at the same time, most now back calls for dialogue rather than confrontation with the Cuban Government. ❑

CUBA IN THE 21ST CENTURY

It is difficult to predict what direction Cuba will take after the demise of Fidel Castro, but most believe that change will be peaceful, and controlled from within the state rather than imposed from outside

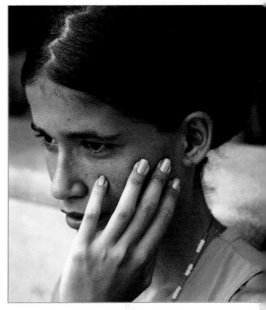

A s Cuba moved into the 21st century, the Revolution was already four decades old, and in many ways the island seemed to be stuck in a time warp.

The demise of Cuba's great *caudillo*, Fidel Castro, has been predicted for decades, but even the man who outlasted the nine US presidents before George W. Bush can't fight Father Time. In July 2006, Castro handed over supreme power "temporarily," to undergo operations on an unspecified condition that some foreign observers guessed to be diverticulitis – a debilitating bowel disease. Whether or not he recovers sufficiently to resume his duties, this marked the effective beginning of the post-Fidel phase of Cuba's history. Not yet post-Castro, of course, as he handed power to his brother Raúl, five years his junior, and the long-standing head of the Revolutionary Armed Forces.

This early, "temporary" post-Fidel phase has so far been peaceful, and the Cuban state is apparently continuing pretty much unaltered. The state still has great control over its population through its network of organizations like the neighborhood

Castro's illness meant that celebrations for his 80th birthday in 2006 had to be postponed from August to late November, but even then he was not well enough to attend them.

CDRs *(see box, page 65)*; and the army seems to be firmly wedded to the state, benefitting as it does from running parts of the lucrative tourism business through its subsidiary arm, Gaviota.

LEFT: optimistic boys in Santiago.
RIGHT: a thoughtful look at life.

A rosier future

Cuba's economic future is much rosier than it was at the end of the 20th century – so much so that in 2005, the authorities declared the end of the "Special Period" *(see pages 69–71)* that had been in place since the fall of the Soviet Union. But the benefits of this have been slow to trickle down, and life for normal people continues in much the same way as during the "Special Period."

The economy has been helped by Cuba's continued tourism growth, along with the shift away from older mainstays. In 2002, Cuba finally recognized that its sugar industry was no longer sustainable as it existed. In a significant decision, it closed almost half of the sugar-processing plants, and in 2007, the harvest was the smallest in a century. Nowadays, exports like nickel are worth four times those of sugar.

International agreements

New agreements with China and, above all, with Venezuela, have helped Cuba thwart US attempts to isolate it diplomatically and economically. President Hugo Chávez of Venezuela, a firm admirer and ideological ally of Fidel Castro, agreed massive oil deals on favorable fixed terms, which have alleviated Cuba's energy crisis. In return, Cuba exports services – in the case of Venezuela, some 30,000 doctors and health-care workers. This is the most obvious example of a long-term strategy

Rico. But the reality seems different, and Cuba appears unlikely to undergo either this type of radical transformation or the one that occurred in Europe's former eastern-bloc countries when the Soviet Union imploded.

Other options include a move to a more capitalist model, as seen in China, where there is still a totalitarian type of control. This was an economic model that Fidel refused to adopt in the 1990s, but in July 2007, Raúl said that Cuba might have to turn to foreign investment. Whether this will happen is uncertain, as Fidel remains a strong presence, but Raúl has acknowledged that "structural and conceptual changes" are needed.

of "health diplomacy," which sees Cuban doctors working in other Latin American countries like Bolivia, but also in regions like West Africa. However, many Cubans complain that their own health service has suffered as a consequence.

Options for change

Quite what form Cuba's post-Fidel era will take is far from certain. For decades, many observers outside Cuba presumed that the regime would collapse after its charismatic leader was removed from power, died or was incapacitated. This scenario envisaged a flood of dollar-rich Cuban exiles from Miami and New Jersey sweeping into the island on a tide of capitalist counter-revolution, with Cuba turning perhaps into a type of Puerto

A challenging time

In the meantime, the challenges facing any immediate post-Fidel administration are legion. Wages have been increased slightly, but are still minimal by Western standards. The administration has the difficult task of trying to keep the generation of young Cubans – a generation born well after the Revolution – from wanting to leave the island, while at the same time maintaining social provisions in health and education.

One of these battlegrounds is likely to be in the form of access to information technology – for the time being, the authorities are maintaining strict controls on Cubans accessing the full World Wide Web, allowing access only to a country-wide intranet. Then there are continuing challenges, such as reinvesting in outdated infrastructure and industries, and fighting corruption. And there are new ones, too, like preventing power struggles in an age when there is no clear, charismatic leader who carries with him the legitimacy of the original Revolution.

However, the chances of violent upheaval in Cuba – feared by many observers – seem to be receding, although they are still possible after Fidel's death. Even though the years ahead will bring change and transition, it seems that this is likely to be largely peaceful, and will probably be controlled by the internal authorities rather than from abroad. In 2007 it was announced that a new National Assembly would be formed the following year. This, in turn, would elect the president for the next five-year term; whether or not Fidel would stand for re-election was not specified.

Cuba's internal political opposition is weak – and although the US seeks to fund opposition groups, many Cuban dissidents choose to retain their independence, preferring to express themselves in the context of Cuban nationalism. In 2002, the so-called Varela Project was organized by one prominent dissident, Oswaldo Payá, calling for a number of political and economic reforms. The petition gained 11,000 signatures, but came to nought, and the following year, a crackdown on many of the people involved saw 75 opposition figures arrested and imprisoned. This reaction led to widespread international condemnation (Amnesty International declared the activists prisoners of conscience), and precipitated a split with the European Union.

The role of the United States

Of course, the position of the United States has a significant role to play in future developments in Cuba. Relations between the two are still stuck in a time warp of their own. These days, there is an ongoing debate in the US about the merits of sanctions – some groups believe US policy has been hijacked by the influential Cuban-American lobby. But the United States' official foreign policy is still resolutely anti-Castro, firmed up by the rigid Helms-Burton legislation *(see page 72)*.

The US Government refuses to deal with anything that it considers a "succession" government rather than a properly "transitional" one, and will

only end sanctions once this projected transitional government is committed to free and fair multiparty elections. It also insists that the government contains none of the old guard – people such as Raúl Castro; and that all political prisoners – believed to number between the scores and the low hundreds – are released. What is more, the United States Government backs the claims of the highly influential Cuban-American lobby, which is pushing for compensation for property confiscated after the Revolution. Meanwhile, the US Government continues to enforce strict financial sanctions and diplomatic efforts to isolate Cuba. Only time will tell what the outcome will be. ❑

NEW LEADERS

A generation of new Cuban leaders has been emerging – officials who have been working within the system for a number of years, but who are increasingly in the spotlight: Ricardo Alarcón, the head of the National Assembly; Vice-President Carlos Lage (pronounced "La-hey"); Francisco Soberón, the head of the Cuban Central Bank; and Felipe Pérez Roque, the Foreign Minister. People such as these could form part of a collective leadership with Raúl Castro after Fidel's death. The generation that fought in the Sierra Maestra is moving into its twilight years, as marked in June 2007 by the death of Vilma Espín, Raúl Castro's wife, who was known colloquially in recent decades as Cuba's "first lady."

LEFT: socialist posters adorn walls and billboards throughout Cuba.
RIGHT: Raúl Castro, his brother's heir.

FIDEL CASTRO

Fidel Castro's illness of 2006 made a man who had seemed immortal to some look very mortal for the first time.
He was never conventional, but will he go down in history as a megalomaniac dictator or a unique statesman?

Fidel Alejandro Castro Ruz was born in Birán in Oriente in 1926. His father, Ángel Castro, was a brash Spanish businessman who carried a whip and a gun at all times. His mother, Lina Ruz González, a servant in his father's home, bore Fidel out of wedlock. The couple married some years after Ángel's first wife died. With a farm employing 300 people, the Castros were wealthy, but not of the cultured class.

Prone to temper tantrums, the young Castro was a troublesome child. Sent to a Jesuit boarding school in Santiago de Cuba, he was teased about his crude manners. Later, he attended Belén College in the capital, before going on to obtain a law degree from the University of Havana, where he frequently instigated student protests. During this period he honed his skills in oratory.

After graduation Castro briefly practiced law, but since he refused to accept money from his impoverished clients, he survived on the largesse of his family. In 1948 he traveled to Colombia where he was arrested for inciting anti-imperialist demonstrations. That same year he married Mirta Díaz-Balart, a wealthy philosophy student with family ties to Batista. The couple honeymooned in Miami and New York, and received US$1,000 from Batista as a wedding gift. In 1949 their son, Fidelito, was born, but five years later they divorced. Mirta remarried and left Cuba, and has never spoken publicly about her ex-husband.

In 1959 Castro swept into the limelight with his Christ-like demeanor and outlaw charisma, and seized control of Cuba. As an international statesman and icon of the radical left, he mesmerized cheering crowds in cities all over the world, from Baghdad to Hanoi and Prague. For years, he was the self-proclaimed leader of the developing world.

A determined grip

Castro set about ruling his island with absolute power, surrounding himself with an entourage of yes-men who would cater to his ego and bathe him in adulation. His national-security apparatus, embedded in every crevice of the island, helped maintain total authority. Anyone opposing him was labeled subversive and harassed or jailed.

Many loathe him or have deserted him – his children, Alina and Fidelito, now live abroad, and Alina attacked him in a book published after she fled to the US in the 1990s. Others, the *fidelistas*, revere him as the man who brought them cradle-to-grave health care, free education and social-security benefits. Castro has many names, including El Comandante or El Jefe Máximo

(The Maximum Leader). He is sometimes affectionately referred to as El Caballo (The Horse).

Castro's personal life

If Castro the politician is hard to understand, Castro the man is even more elusive. Although a public figure, he gained a reputation as a very private person and a master of self-concealment. When working, he rarely got a good night's sleep, for to sleep is to be off-guard. Instead, he would take short naps at his office. Though fluent in English, he does not speak it in public. In his spare time he reads voraciously, but he stopped puffing on his trademark cigars in the 1980s, as part

Cuban people, and also held substantial power in the government. Celia's death from cancer in 1980 reputedly hit the Cuban leader hard.

Castro is still an icon for some, especially on the Latin American left – above all, Venezuelan President Hugo Chávez, who is in many ways his natural political heir on the international stage. At home, Castro named his younger brother Raúl as his successor in 1997, acknowledging that he wouldn't be around forever, "I am not eternal," he said. "Suddenly, one discovers that almost everything is behind and that life has its limits." However, he has also said, "I am a revolutionary and revolutionaries do not retire." ❑

of a public no-smoking campaign. His recent illness and operations have no doubt curtailed many of his other hobbies – gardening, swimming, fishing, playing chess and driving his jeep.

Rumors say that Castro had hundreds of romantic encounters and fathered dozens of children. But following his divorce, he was linked publicly to only one woman, Celia Sánchez. A vivacious upper-middle-class *cubana* and devoted companion during the rebel campaign, Sánchez was the love of his life. A champion of social causes, she was always popular with the

LEFT: a youthful Castro released from jail in 1955.
ABOVE: Castro with his friend and supporter, Hugo Chávez, president of Venezuela, in 2006.

THE GREAT IDEALIST

Gabriel García Márquez, the Nobel Prize-winning Colombian author and long-standing friend of Fidel's, recalls: "He has the nearly mystical conviction that the greatest achievement of the human being is the proper formation of conscience, and that moral incentives, rather than material ones, are capable of changing the world and moving history forward. I think he has been one of the greatest idealists of our time and this, perhaps, may be his greatest virtue, although it has also been his greatest danger."

CUBA'S ARCANE TRANSPORT SYSTEM

Fascinating, exotic, frustrating and divisive, depending on your standpoint, the beleaguered transportation system is a visible microcosm of Cuba's economic woes

In the late 1980s, oil supplies from the eastern bloc that had provided the island with 90 percent of its fuel began to dry up as the Cuban-sugar-for-Soviet-oil deal came to an end. Scarcity of fuel meant that outside the main cities motorized transportation virtually vanished, a situation that has changed little today. Roads are all but deserted, oxen pull plows that till the fields, and horses and traps ply the streets of provincial towns.

But, most noticeably, bicycles are everywhere – more than 1 million were imported from China in the early 1990s, and in this make-do-and-mend society many of them are still going strong. It's as if the clock has been turned back to a pre-industrial age. Cycling has become part of the fabric of everyday life, with special parking lots for bicycles and tire-repair shops everywhere.

The island's current tribulations and its decades of isolation from the Western world have resulted in other memorable forms of transport. Wonderful old Cadillacs get top billing, but also look for veteran motorcycles with sidecars, rickshaws created from two bicycles welded to armchairs, and on the railroads anything from magnificent steam trains to wheel-less buses that can run along the tracks. And if you think horses and traps are charming, how about goats and traps? They take children on circuits round the main squares of provincial towns on weekends.

ABOVE: hitching a ride: while tourists have the choice to whizz around in air-conditioned buses and rental cars, for most Cubans getting around is not much fun. Hitching is often the only option.

ABOVE: horse and trap: *coches*, or horses and traps, serve as buses and taxis all over the island. An average ride will cost just a few pesos.

LEFT: coco-taxis: these are a fun way to get around Havana and some other cities – as long as you don't have any luggage. They use less fuel than conventional taxis and are therefore cheaper. Drivers wear helmets – passengers don't.

RIGHT: kit cars: many Cadillacs and Chevvies may look ready for the scrapyard, but their owners somehow keep them on the road. The cars are often ingeniously customized with spare parts (sometimes even from Ladas) acquired illegally on the black market.

THE STRUGGLE TO GET AROUND

The recent purchase of many new buses (called *guaguas*) means fewer lines and less overcrowding than in the "Special Period," but things still get bad at peak times and cancellations are common. Cubans still need to book in advance for a seat on a crowded long-distance bus – a form of transportation tourists are steered away from – they are expected to use the dedicated convertible peso services *(see Transportation in the Travel Tips section, page 338).*

Hitchhiking *(la botella)* is a way of life for Cubans of all ages, but definitely not for tourists, as anyone who was kind enough to pick you up would risk a fine. This is not any old hitchhiking: state officials, called *amarillos*, because they wear yellow jackets, supervise crowds of hitchers at designated places, usually on the edge of towns and cities. State vehicles are obliged to stop, and *los amarillos* will allocate people to each vehicle on a first-come, first-served basis. Pregnant women and children get priority.

BELOW: "camels": Cubans say these two-humped giant buses are like the Saturday movie on TV: they always contain sex, violence and swearing.

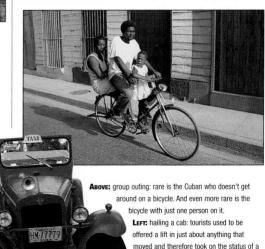

ABOVE: empty tank: the chronic fuel shortage in Cuba means that even main highways can be virtually bereft of traffic, including the six-lane highway from Havana to Pinar del Río. Cars abandoned by the roadside while drivers go in search of fuel, are a common sight.

ABOVE: group outing: rare is the Cuban who doesn't get around on a bicycle. And even more rare is the bicycle with just one person on it.

LEFT: hailing a cab: tourists used to be offered a lift in just about anything that moved and therefore took on the status of a "taxi." This can be a great Havana experience but the imposition of heavy fines on illegal drivers means that the practice is not as common as it used to be.

TOURISM: SALVATION OR SELLOUT?

Post-Revolutionary Cuba viewed the tourist industry with disdain, but nowadays it has no option but to embrace it. That is good news for those who want to visit this alluring island, but dramatically underlines the differences between local people and visitors

Revolutionary Cuba, a land of socialist ideals and egalitarian values, once said "never again" to tourism. Back in the decadent 1950s, the island was the king of Caribbean tourism. Havana, with its sophisticated hotels, clubs and casinos, was an exotic getaway that catered to the whims of wealthy Americans, and had a worldwide reputation for gambling, drugs, prostitution, pornographic films and live sex shows. But although the industry was lucrative, much of the infrastructure was foreign-controlled, leaving few in Cuba who actually benefitted from the profits.

Rejecting excess

Part of Fidel Castro's struggle against Batista stemmed from his revulsion at the excesses of tourism, and the neo-colonialism he believed it represented. Castro denounced tourism as a vulgar example of the dichotomy between the haves and the have-nots. After he took power, one of his goals was to change forever the sinful image of the island. Cuba would never again be a playground for the rich and beautiful, he promised.

There is a rather cynical joke circulating around the island: an adult asks a child the classic question: "What do you want to be when you grow up?" The child answers: "A tourist."

Instead it would rely on sugar and other natural resources to fuel its economy.

The new government set about closing casinos and nightclubs, the prostitutes were rounded up

LEFT AND RIGHT: Cuba's waters and beaches are idyllic playgrounds for foreign visitors.

and sent to learn trades, and the hotels were put to use as vacation retreats for local workers. In the 1960s and 1970s, many of the foreign visitors to Cuba were either journalists or people wanting to express solidarity with the revolution. Others were eastern-bloc communists on a government-paid Cuban vacation. The island promoted "social tourism," whereby sympathetic visitors from around the world were invited to visit model communities, hospitals, schools and other places where the achievements of socialism were put on display. Between 1963 and 1975, the island received only about 3,000 foreign visitors a year.

When the economy began to show signs of strain in the early 1980s, the government reconsidered its policy toward tourism, and "health tourism" became the new trend. Foreigners were invited to Cuba for a first-rate face-lift or coronary bypass at low cost. But by the mid-1980s, the government realized that "health tourism" was not going to provide the economic boost the island needed, and it launched an international campaign to promote pleasure tourism. After the collapse of the Soviet Union, this campaign became much more aggressive.

Tourism is gold

"In the past we feared that tourism would defile us," Castro told his compatriots, "but tourism is gold." So began the push to make tourism the new

A pact with the devil

Having come full circle, the tourism industry has created embarrassing ideological problems for the Castro government. Most pro-Castro Cubans see tourism as a way of preserving their independence, but it comes at a social cost.

Tourism employs more than 80,000 people, but this represents only about 2 percent of the overall workforce. Tourism jobs are highly sought after because they offer access to tips in foreign currencies or convertible pesos (CUCs). Many teachers, doctors and engineers leave their professions to work in more lucrative jobs as waiters or bellhops. Tourism has also bred corruption. Cubans

business frontier of the island – one that saw investors from places like Europe, Mexico and Canada being offered extremely non-socialist incentives that would allow them to operate in Cuba for at least 10 years without paying taxes on their income.

Progress came quickly. In 1995, as the sugar industry weakened still further, tourism became, for the first time, the island's biggest source of hard currency. In 1984, fewer than 200,000 foreign tourists visited Cuba; by 1998 there were more than a million – which was triple the number that came during the booming 1950s. Nowadays, well over 2 million visitors come to Cuba each year, bringing more than US$2 billion into the Cuban economy.

DANGEROUS LIAISONS

More often than not, the sex scene these days revolves around bars and clubs, either through none-too-subtle flirtation that in some places can border on harassment or through young pimps. These days, few *jineteras* are prepared to offer their services for the sake of a dress or a meal – many make more money in a week than a government minister earns in a year. Western men should also know that during crackdowns, even entirely innocent talk with Cuban women can lead to those women being arrested and jailed by the authorities on suspicion that they're plying a trade. There's also a parallel, though much smaller, type of sex tourism where Western women hook up with young Cuban men.

wishing to work in a foreign currency/CUC enterprise often have to bribe managers for the privilege of doing so.

The superb colonial architecture, impressive scuba diving, open-sea fishing and fine flora and fauna attract a certain number of high-spending tourists, but many more are deterred by the dilapidated infrastructure and relatively poor service.

Sex tourism flourishes undercover, despite crackdowns. One such crackdown, in the summer of 1999, targeted the hoards of scantily clad girls (called *jineteras* after the Cuban word for jockey) who used to hang around tourist hotels. The authorities had probably been embarrassed into

with hard currencies and those without. This enclave system, often referred to as "tourism apartheid," is as divisive as the former Berlin Wall was in Germany.

Hotels are like private country clubs that no Cubans can join. Local people are usually not

action by the scale of this sex trade, and the all-too-evident parallels that could be drawn with the sordid side of tourism in pre-Revolutionary Cuba. Many *jineteras* were arrested and sent to "re-education" camps in the countryside.

Tourism apartheid

The most distasteful aspect of Cuba's tourism industry is the division it has created between local people and tourists. Isolated from the public, most modern resorts have a "Club Med" mentality that accentuates the differences between those

LEFT: most Cubans can only hope that the benefits of tourism will trickle down to them.
ABOVE: selling souvenirs brings some income.

allowed in even if they are accompanied by a foreigner. At plush restaurants, the wine flows freely and the steaks are tender, but in most Cuban homes, the walls are crumbling and the cupboards are bare.

Although the electricity grid is now being improved after years of neglect, the authorities will still prioritize fuel supplies for the hotels while private homes suffer regular blackouts *(apagones)*. Tourists can easily buy gas for their rental cars, while local people must ride bicycles or squeeze into overcrowded buses. And beautiful beaches, which were once the domain of the islanders themselves, are being gobbled up by developers. In theory, there are no private beaches in Cuba, but in many resorts they might as well be. ❏

CUBA'S SIZZLING SOUND

**There's nowhere else like it: for "Cuba," read "Rhythm."
Here you will find a depth of musical talent that is,
perhaps, unequaled anywhere in the world**

Music and Cuba have been synonymous for well over a century; in no other communist country have music and revolution marched so closely, hand in hand. Even during the final build-up to the 1959 Revolution, at the dramatic closure of that legendary era when Havana was a fantasy island playground for American tourists, the bands played on and visitors rushed to the city's casinos, bars, hotels, glitzy nightclubs and beaches.

Revolution never quashed the music: film footage of Castro's guerrillas moving toward Havana show Che Guevara with a guitar on his back. All through the "Special Period," the state still supported musicians, and the music began to launch a new flush of tourism.

The beat goes on

Today, music is the state tourist board's golden egg; millions of visitors flock to Cuba for the same reasons the Americans once did: the rum, sun, sex, music and dancing (no gambling, however, which is strictly counter-revolutionary). Ironically, they often travel in the same, now

Many people were introduced to Cuban music by the Buena Vista Social Club, liked what they heard, and went on to discover much more about the island's rhythms, its musical history and changing styles.

patched-up Oldsmobile taxis to the same still glitzy nightclubs, bars and hotels built by the Americans and abandoned in 1959. The Hotel

PRECEDING PAGES: a *quinceañera* celebration for 15-year-old girls. **LEFT:** sweet sounds on the Malecón. **RIGHT:** a dancer in Havana's Callejón de Hamel.

Nacional, where Sinatra sang and American high society (and gangsters) partied, is still hugely impressive; the breathtaking Tropicana nightclub still sees dancers in towering headdresses parade across galleries between the palm trees, and singers today perform on the same stage that shook to the voice of the future Queen of Salsa, Celia Cruz, and the delights of Nat King Cole. Hotel Rivera's elegant nightclub is now the Palacio de Salsa (Salsa Palace).

The ruffle-sleeved shirts survive yet the decadence is gone. But most hotels and restaurants provide some kind of live music, and salsa venues in the capital include the prestigious Casa de la Música, and small rooftop bars like the Pico Blanco in the Hotel St John's, a must for smoochy boleros. Compay Segundo's old haunt, the beer garden, El Tropical, is today a landmark venue for the raunchy Cuban salsa called timba *(see box, page 100)*, and the narrow alley, the Callejón de Hamel, in the Vedado district hosts rumba drumming, dancing and singing on Sundays.

Music wherever you go

Visitors today are never far from music, with timba trombones ricocheting around the narrow streets, scorching jazz drumming rising from basement bars, and sweet guitar melodies in Buena Vista style, drifting from pavement cafés in Old Havana. The 70-year-old song *Guantanamera* is

Breaking it down

Many tourists visit Cuba for the salsa dancing, often on special packages, and the chances are that leading salsa bands like Los Van Van *(see pages 100 and 101)*, will provide music for their classes back home, and the live soundtrack to their vacation. To navigate the overwhelming range of music, the local radio stations Taíno (bilingual and for tourists) and Rebelde (mixing news, interviews and music, in Spanish) are more useful than the solitary newspaper, *Granma*, and Cuban TV presents home-grown bands live and on video.

While Havana is the epicentre of Cuban music, it doesn't hold the monopoly on variety or excite-

as ubiquitous as images of Che Guevara, and the evocative *Chan Chan* is a reminder of the impact the Buena Vista Social Club film and album has had on the surge of tourism since the late 1990s.

While tourist hotels worldwide traditionally offer cheesy clichéd and stereotyped shows, Cuba's conservatoire-trained musicians treat tourists to music that is often of a spectacularly high standard (although they trot out plenty of *Guantanamera*s, as well) and they are often internationally acclaimed, even Grammy-winning artists, such as the Afro-Cuban jazz pianist, Chucho Valdés (founder of the trailblazing band, Irakere), who is a regular at the rooftop Jazz Café, playing with his scat-singing sister, Mayra or his own small group.

ment. Santiago, in the eastern state of Oriente, is equally rich in traditional and modern music, and its Carnival (held in late July) beats Havana's hands down.

Santiago is a heavily African city with its own musical identity. The latest dance music sensation, Sur Caribe, is an upbeat salsa-rap big band, influenced by the winning combination of violins and trombones pioneeered by Los Van Van but also involving traditional Santiago carnival instruments – the raucous *corneta china* (Chinese cornet) and portable drums made world famous in the 1930s by Desi Arnaz, and still alive and kicking in conga bands today. In contrast, Septeto Tipico de Tivoli is a neo-traditional *son* band, the *corneta* replacing the conventional trumpet.

Trova

Santiago is a focus for the trova song style, which is supported around Cuba in *casas de la trova*. Santiago's is a celebrated meeting place, where singers, composers, guitarists, and friends met to drink rum, smoke cigars and be transported by the guitar melodies, vocal harmonies, sensual rhythms, and lyrics inspired by the country life and work, patriotic or revolutionary themes.

Some guitarists once lived a troubadour's life, playing *trova* songs alongside soldiers during the 19th-century Independence War with Spain, and during Castro's guerrilla war. The latter spawned a *nueva* (new) *trova* movement linked to Latin

Today, tourists crowd the bar, and crane their necks to read their autographs, most famously that of Hemingway, with whom the bar is most closely associated. *Trova* musicians' repertoires roam through guitar-based styles, and include the ubiquitous *son*, which is at the root of most popular Cuban music, including salsa.

Son

Son became universally familiar through the Buena Vista Social Club phenomenon. Its origins lie in Oriente state, against a backdrop of late 19th-century tobacco fields and sugar-cane plantations. By the 1920s, it had reached Havana, and

America's 1960s revolutions, and key figures, Pablo Milanes and Silvio Rodríguez, are now superstar elder statesmen who perform internationally. Their songs are almost as familiar as those of their international contemporaries such as Bob Dylan, and their successors, including Carlos Varela and Amaury Pérez, have moved closer to rock's singer-songwriter tradition.

One of Havana's celebrated *trova* hang-outs is the Bodeguita del Medio, a small bar in Old Havana where writers, poets and musicians rehearsed new works and debated revolution.

LEFT: dancing is part of the Cuban way of life.
ABOVE: Ibrahim Ferrer, vocalist with the Buena Vista Social Club, who died in 2005.

THE BUENA VISTA SOCIAL CLUB

The mid-1990s brought a great upsurge of interest in traditional Cuban music, especially with the release of the Buena Vista Social Club film and album. Pride of place among the elderly stars who were "re-discovered" by American guitarist, composer and singer Ry Cooder went to Compay Segundo, one half of the superb 1950s duo, Los Compadres, who came out of retirement and recorded a Grammy-winning CD in 1998. He was still touring the world in his nineties, but died in 2003. Sadly, most of the other greats from the 1950s have since died, too: the pianist Rubén González in 2003, and vocalists Ibrahim Ferrer in 2005, and Pío Leyva in 2006. Only Omara Portuondo is still going strong.

rapidly adapted to an urban style. *Son* is both truly African and truly Cuban, built around call-and-response singing, rough, often high-pitched lead voices, repetitive guitar riffs working in percussive harmonies with the hand percussion. Most crucial are the two hard-wood blocks *(claves)* clacking out the *clave* rhythm, which underlies Cuban popular music. *Clave*'s syncopated beat forces dancers into action, and musicians into the basic rhythm around which they can improvise.

In 1920s Havana, the country migrants initially busked on the streets and in cafés, but their infectious sweetness and catchy rhythms seduced wider audiences, and trios expanded to more sophisti-

the docks, but are now polished, finely tuned instruments, often played in multiple, differently tuned "nests." The word "nest"describes both the music and the parties at which it is played. Master conga drummers have played key roles in the development of original new styles, including the imaginative percussionist Chanquito's role in Los Van Van, and that of the late Angá Diaz, who developed a symphonic sound.

Matanzas still has some of the most brilliant *rumberos* in Cuba: Los Munequitos de Matanzas (The Little Dolls) and Clave y Guaguanco both perform at international festivals and the city's squares. Of the scores of varieties of rumba, three

cated sextets and septets, boosted with bongos, double bass and eventually trumpets. In salons and dancehalls the guitars would be replaced by pianos. Don Azpiazu's Cuban big band recording of *El Manicero (The Peanut Vendor)* in 1931, ignited an international rumba craze. Although known as rumba, his popularized *son* differs from the Afro-Cuban rumba that originated in the slave communities and involves drumming, dancing and chant-singing.

Rumba

Rumba is thought to have emerged among the Congolese dock workers in the late 1800s in the port of Matanzas, following the abolition of slavery. The original drums were boxes taken from

main types are preserved: *guaguanco*, *yambu* and Columbia, each with specific drums, rhythms and dance styles. One of Cuba's most famous singers, the late Lázaro Ros, who died in 2005, could sing in around 800 different African languages, and his rumba group, Olorun, worked with rock groups that blended Afro-Cuban religious music with modern styles. A true rumba is a profound experience which can be shared in street sessions in Matanzas, near the Teatro Sauto, and at Rumba Saturdays in Havana's Vedado district.

Country music: *guajira*

Cuba's country music, *música guajira*, is rooted in Andalusia in southern Spain, descended from the Spanish peasants who came to the island two centuries ago, but blends influences from the African cultures of fellow workers. It was originally a form of after-work escapism for exhausted Spanish peasant farmers and cattle herders, and for African workers in the sugar-cane plantations, tobacco fields, and factories. Like country workers elsewhere, they would pull out a guitar and sing, with family and friends joining in, adding touches of their own.

Its gorgeous melodies are carried on lilting acoustic guitars or *laoud* (a version of the Arabic oud) with verses in the poetic song tradition, praising landscapes, detailing everyday lives and loves, and adding improvised gossip.

Many *guajira* singers, including Compay Segundo, were known for harmonizing duets. Compay's Buena Vista companion, Eliades Ochoa is a quintessential *guajiro* with his cowboy hat, nimble-fingered guitar playing and high-pitched, soaring voice, but it was the late Polo Montañez's raw countryman's voice that re-ignited the traditional sound in two great albums, *Guitara Mia* and *Guajiro Natural* ("Discovered" relatively late in life, Montañez died, far too young, in a car accident in 2002).

Taking country music to town

Musicians who rose beyond the family porch left the land to busk or play in town bars and cafés, and, if lucky, to perform on the radio. Most significant composers and performers ended up in the cities; the early 20th-century composer Guillermo Portabales recorded songs whose sensual lilting melodies accompanying images of ox-cart drivers and untouched landscapes, have resonated with economic migrants everywhere.

In 1950s Havana, the country duo, Celina y Reutilio performed romantic, upbeat songs heavily African-influenced and delivered in harmonies led by Celina's powerfully expressive voice. Celina González became an ardent defender of the New Cuba through her long-running country-music radio show.

It was the 1930s radio singer, Joseito Fernández, who launched the classic *La Guajira Guantanamera* onto the world. The song, about a girl from Guantánamo, became popular through a 1935 radio soap opera, but had lyrics based on a poem by independence hero and poet José Martí.

LEFT: you will find musicians playing in the streets, as well as in bars and clubs, all over the island.
RIGHT: Polo Montañez, much-loved *guajiro* singer.

It is now heard in every tourist niche in Cuba. *Guajira* music still inspires national pride today, and was central to the Buena Vista Social Club's repertoire, and its success.

Danzón to cha-cha-cha

A small but significant French element in the Cuban mix is traceable to the late 18th-century arrival in Oriente (eastern Cuba) of French colonizers' families and slaves escaping the Haitian revolution. They brought the *contredanse*, a variation of the English country dance, played by trios on piano, violin and flute, and this laid the foundations for the elegant dances called *danzóns*.

Expanded into orchestras called *charangas*, they gradually incorporated a mild African syncopation, which extended its popularity. The most significant Havana *charanga* was run by flautist Antonio Arcano, and featured the double-bass player Israel "Cachao" Lopez and his brother, the pianist Orestes. In the late 1930s, they invented a mutant version with a syncopated ending they called mambo, which was declared devil's music for some years. But the 1940s hit records by the brilliantly eccentric Cuban pianist Perez Prado, spread mambo's popularity to the US, and from there, around the world in a sanitized, softened guise by the band leader Xavier Cugat. Mambo was the dance craze in 1950s Manhattan, and laid the trail to salsa.

Another offshoot of the *danzón*, the cha-cha-chá, possessed fewer African qualities than mambo, and was deliberately tailored by its creator Enrique Jorrín (director of Orquesta América) for American tourists and dancers. The first cha-cha-chá, *La Engañadora*, in 1953, ignited a fever that overwhelmed mambo's popularity around the world. The greatest *charangas* remained in Cuba – Orquesta Riverside, and the sensational Orquesta Aragón, still playing today.

Son montuno to timba salsa

As the *danzón* was being modified into the cha-cha-chá, a blind Cuban musician of Congolese descent, Arsenio Rodríguez, updated the *son* by extending the repetitive instrumental section to create *son montuno*. The master *tres* guitarist manipulated the slackly strung, resonating strings to create a searing, unmistakably Cuban sound, which has been extensively imitated by modern groups, including Sierra Maestra.

Throughout the 1940s and 1950s, La Sonora Matancera also occupied an important place in the story. Formed in Matanzas in the 1920s, it moved to Havana in the late 1940s, and introduced a fireball singer named Celia Cruz who became everybody's favorite (they all relocated to the United States after Castro's arrival). Cruz's male coun-

TIMBA SALSA

Salsa comes in scores of varieties all over Latin America, but in Cuba, the dancers' soundtrack is a sizzling mutation called *timba*. The trail to *timba* was laid by young musicians creating music for the post-revolutionary era. Chucho Valdés' Afro-Cuban big band Irakere transformed jazz, and Juan Formell's Los Van Van reinvented dance music through the brassy, swinging *songo* rhythms. *Songo* is a feast of conversations between violins and trombones, and the jagged rhythms that backed hit songs packed with gossip and catch phrases. Irakere's ex-flautist, José Luís Cortés, founded N.G. (New Generation) La Banda in the 1980s and crystallized the *timba* sound with brass choruses, funk-bass lines and risqué slang. NG was a university for *timba* stars including the brilliant Issac Delgado, who took it into America's salsa charts, and the heart-throb, Paulito F.G. The 1990s opened to David Calzado's outrageous Charanga Habanera, whose compellingly edgy songs caused fan hysteria, official panic and a ban. The acrobatic break-dancing female singers left to found the stunning Azucar Negra. Manolin "El Medico" de la Salsa and Manolito y su Trabuco continue a more conventional line but Los Van Van's dreadlocked vocalist, Mayito, remains frontman for the still-dynamic band. Today's leaders include the electronic-acoustic orchestra, Chispa y los Complices, which are infecting the new *timba* dancers around the world.

terpart was Beny Moré, a sensational dancer and intuitive singer and arranger who spent the 1940s in Mexico City, performing mambos and boleros (made for his searingly expressive high voice) and appearing in Mexican films – as himself. Back in Havana, "El Bárbaro del Ritmo" (the Barbarian of Rhythm) launched his horn-driven Orchestra Gigante, noted for its up-tempo arrangements of brass, percussion and interlocking piano, whose influence continued into salsa.

The Cuban variety of salsa is called *timba (see panel, previous page)*, and was a product of experimentation by the dazzling Los Van Van, and its founder and bass player, Juan Formell, with the singer, Adalberto Alvarez, has shifted toward a more pan-Caribbean beat, but remains 100 percent Cuban, while the trombone band Dan Den, founded by the pianist Juan Carlos Alfonso, became popular for its modern, electronic sound.

Other key salsa bands include Yumurí y Sus Hermanos (Yumurí and His Brothers) and the Vocal Sampling. This six-piece a-capella group reproduce perfectly the sound of an entire salsa band, using only their mouths, cupped hands and slapped bodies, and are an international phenomenon. The radical Bamboleo introduced shaven heads, break dancing and wildly sexual routines to the musical scene, but the wildest

original *songo* rhythm created for the band by conga player Changuito Formell's revolutionary exchanges between violins and trombones, which were the sensation of the 1980s and 1990s.

Timba is the soundtrack to 21st-century Cuba, through its propulsive, edgy rhythms, braying trombone choruses, and driving funk bass lines. Contemporaries of Cortés, including the popular idol Issac Delgado, followed a more traditional singer/band route, but he broke the rules by recording a hit in New York with leading 1980s salsa producer, Ralph Mercado. The popular

LEFT: Los Van Van reinvented dance music with swinging *songo* rhythms.
ABOVE: Chucho Valdés and his band, Irakere.

1990s bunch, David Calzado's Charanga Habanera, who were once banned from performing live because of their so-called "lewdness," inspired the new wave of rap-based performers that are poular today.

The electronic invasion

The 1990s international explosion of hip-hop slowly but inevitably penetrated the Cuban scene, via illicit American radio and TV, which, of course, captivated the imagination of Cuban youth. The pioneering Orishas emerged in Cuba as a popular rap duo but transferred to Paris and sprang a future Grammy-winning album, *A lo Cubano* (In the Cuban style) on the market. Its fusion of electronic and "live" Cuban rhythms, rapped and sung vocals, influenced today's thriving Cuban hip-hop scene.

This scene is officially endorsed by the government, and showcased annually at the Havana Hip-hop Festival, held every August, and for which the state provides the sound system. Early on, Fidel Castro apparently performed alongside rappers Doble Filo at a baseball game, and today, the state supports more than 500 hip-hop artists, many with international reputations.

The jazz thing

From the 19th century onward, the sea links between Havana and New Orleans enabled impor-

tant musical interchanges: Afro-Cuban rumba became a basic part of New Orleans' jazz musical vocabulary, and African-American jazz came to Havana almost at birth.

Modern Cuban musicians understand both European-style musical theory and Afro-Cuban traditions and those skills have been exploited particularly in the new jazz. Pioneering the move, Cachao López made a series of legendary recordings of *descargas* (jam sessions) in the 1950s with leading soloists from the dance bands, expanding the ad-lib solo slots in popular music to become the entire piece. *Descargas* is still an inspirational best-selling CD, as fresh today as in 1959.

Jazz is central to Cuban music, though many exponents are often easier to catch live during foreign tours. Irakere, the 15-piece group founded in 1970 by pianist Chucho Valdés, fused North American jazz idioms, and has operated as a university for young soloists, including the *timba* pioneer, José Luís Cortés. Two original members, Paquito D'Rivera and Arturo Sandoval, are now international stars based in the US, and Valdés is an elder in Cuban music, professor at the University of Havana, and a multi-Grammy-winning solo artist who occasionally still rejoins Irakere. His recent reunion concerts and recordings with his father, Bebo Valdés, who has lived outside Cuba since 1960, produced some marvelous, moving musical conversations.

New generation

Groups like AfroCuba, Cuarto Espacio and Perspectiva continue the explorations. But a new generation emerged from the Buena Vista Social Club project. Pianist Roberto Fonseca, who made his name with the singer Ibrahim Ferrer, is the latest to mesmerize, with sparkling, inventive performances that betray his early experience as a drummer. In 2007, his album *Zamazu* was released to international acclaim. Composer and pianist Omar Sosa is another explorer who blends Cuban, African and European music with jazz, to great effect. This restless search for new music has characterized the story of Cuban music for centuries, and shows no sign of diminishing. So, whatever your musical taste, you will find much to please you in Cuba, in clubs and bars, at high-profile festivals, or simply in the city streets. ❏

CUBAN HIP-HOP

Cuba's 500-plus approved hip-hoppers don't run with the gangstas; their lyrics concentrate on social issues, criticisms and humor, and their electronic beats vie with "live" brass, guitars, and percussion. Following the first Havana Hip-hop Festival (1995), Castro legitimized the underground, and encouraged newcomers like Obsesión and Amenaza (Threat) – who re-formed in Paris as the Grammy-winning Orishas and put Cuba on the rap map. Subsequent compilation albums including *Hora de Abrir los Ojos* (Time to Open Your Eyes) and *Cuban HipHop All-Stars* exposed the scene, and the international DM Ahora! label showcases the rap big band Interactivo, and rap-poet sensation, Telmary.

LEFT: Yotuel Romero, lead singer with the platinum-selling rap group, Orishas.
RIGHT: Telmary, the latest rap sensation.

SANTERÍA AND AFRO-CUBAN RELIGIONS

Three main religions developed in Cuba out of the rich heritage of West Africans brought to the island as slaves. Of these, Santería is the most important

Santería (the "Way of the Saints"), also known as Regla Ocha or Regla Lucumí, stems from the beliefs of the Yoruba people of West Africa – the dominant ethnic group of slaves in Cuba. Forbidden by their Spanish Catholic masters to practice their native religion, believers hid their worship by syncretizing traits and characteristics of individual African *orishas* (gods) with those of particular Catholic saints. For this reason, the religion became known as Santería, and for this reason, too, the term "Santería" is considered to be derogatory by many believers.

In the Regla Ocha, Olofí is the highest god – the source of *ashé* or spiritual energy that makes up the universe and everything in it. He interacts with humankind through his emissaries or lesser gods called *orishas,* who rule over every aspect of life and every force of nature. There are hundreds of gods in the Yoruba pantheon, but around 15 feature regularly: Oshun, the goddess of sweet waters, love and fertility, is represented by Our Lady of Charity – Cuba's patron saint.

Santería is not just a faith but a way of life. Walk down a street in any Cuban town and you are likely to find someone dressed all in white who has recently been initiated into Santería – an *Iyawó* – and is undergoing a year of communion with their *orishas*. In the religion, communication between *orishas* and humankind is by means of ritual, *ebó* or offerings – including sacrifice and divination. The latter can be performed only by a *babalawo* or priest of Orula – the *orisha* of Knowledge and Wisdom – who will use pieces of coconut or shells. Music, dance, and trance possession are also ways through which believers interact with the *orishas*, and are integral to the spiritual experience.

ABOVE: A BOVEDA, OR SPIRIT ALTAR
Glasses of water, candles, a rosary, and photographs of the dead are placed at this altar, as they are believed to aid communion with the spirits of the deceased known as *eggún.*

RIGHT: BATÁ
The sacred *batá* is a kind of drum that represents the tones of Yoruba. They are used to call the *orishas.* Each rhythmic pattern varies and is a prayer to a particular deity.

LEFT: IYAWO
Santería initiates dress all in white and adhere to a strict code of conduct.
The necklaces worn are sacred; each represents one of the *orishas*.

BELOW: ELEGUÁ
The guardian of roads and doors, Eleguá stands at the crossroads of the
human and the divine. Nothing should be done without his permission.

ABAKUÁ AND PALO MONTE

Abakuá is the name given to the esoteric religion practiced by all-male secret societies
that still exist in Cuba, especially in places like Guanabacoa near Havana, and Matanzas.
Visitors, however, are only likely to see it as part of a
tourist show, characterized by the hooded figure of the
diablito (little devil), who dances among the *ñáñigo*
(initiates), ritually cleansing them. Real initiates join
by invitation, and then only after their good character
has been verified.

The way of the religion is laid down in the sacred
book called the *Estatuto*.

Another all-male religion is Palo Monte, also known as
Regla de Palo ("Rule of the Stick"). It is similar to Santería,
but has its roots in Congolese religion, rather than
Yoruba. Importantly, its practitioners *(paleros)* work
with the forces of the underworld, and cannot be
consulted by anyone except a *babalawo*.

RIGHT: CHANGÓ
The fiery god of lightning, passion,
and dance, Changó is represented by
Santa Bárbara, by a double-headed
ax, and the colors red and white. For
many believers, he embodies virility.

LEFT: TRANCE
During a *bembé* (drumming party), a
santero or *santera* may be "mounted" by an
orisha who is thereby able to offer counsel
through the body of its human host.

THE ARTS

Elitist and derivative art of colonial times was replaced in the 20th century by a creative, inclusive, home-grown tradition in painting and architecture. Literature, dance and cinema have all flourished, too, although censorship has inevitably taken its toll

Cuba has one of the most vibrant artistic histories in the Caribbean, largely due to its location and cross-cultural history. Forming a maritime crossroads between Europe, Africa and the Americas, it has long fed off cultural exchange across the Atlantic Ocean.

Although the island was originally inhabited by various indigenous groups *(see page 33)*, relatively few pre-Columbian artifacts have been discovered in Cuba, especially when compared with the marvels that have been unearthed in Peru or Mexico, for example. However, a few beautiful Taíno pieces have survived – stone and wooden idols, and wooden ceremonial seats. The first Western chroniclers were, for the most part, unimpressed with the material culture of the people they encountered on the island.

With the rapid extermination of the indigenous population, whatever else there may have been of the non-material side of native culture died out too, leaving the Spaniards with an almost blank cultural slate on which to write their own forms of music, dance and decorative arts – a situation unlike that in most of their other colonial possessions, such as Peru, for example, where Spanish and indigenous art were blended.

However, the one-sided nature of this cultural imposition was tempered in the late 18th century by African slaves, brought to the island by the French plantation owners escaping from the Haitian revolution in 1790. To a less significant extent, the Chinese brought in as contract laborers in the second half of the 19th century also made a cultural impact. America's intercession in Cuba's war against Spain in 1898 added yet another cultural

outlook – best exemplified in the grandiose Capitol in Havana, which closely resembles the Capitol in Washington, DC – but this aspect waned after Castro came to power.

Architecture

The sugar industry and concomitant slave trade brought great wealth to the Spaniards, who imported from Europe gold and silverware, precious stones and fine furniture, and the skills of glass-blowers to adorn the nouveau-riche palaces they constructed around cool, shady courtyards. They also built fortresses and churches, mixing baroque with the distinctive *Mudéjar* style – a blend of Christian and Islamic traditions born from centuries of contact between the Spanish

---

LEFT: Alicia Alonso with the late Marcel Marceau.
RIGHT: frescoed ceiling in the Teatro de la Caridad.

and the Arabs, mainly in Andalusia in southern Spain *(for more on colonial architecture, see pages 166–7)*.

In the early 20th century, Art Nouveau and Art Deco became popular in Havana and other Cuban towns, as it did in many European and North American cities. A notable example of Art Deco is the Bacardí building in Old Havana, built in the early 1920s.

Art in the 20th century

But while Cuba was endowed with so much fine colonial architecture, the pictorial arts were dull and staid – stiff portraits of wealthy ladies and

his life in Madrid and Paris, and was greatly influenced by Picasso's cubist legacy. Other major artists were Leopoldo Romanach (1862–1951), with his robust country people and gloomy interiors; Fidelio Ponce (1895–1949), who painted young women, children, and saints in faint monochromes; Mariano Rodríguez (1912–90), who famously incorporated roosters into all his vivid, powerful paintings; Amelia Peláez (1897–1968), who evoked the Cuban spirit in her tropical still-lifes; Servando Cabrera (1923–81), who painted robust countrymen and some impressive nudes; and Antonia Eiriz (1929–95), who fascinated the art world with her Goya-esque monsters and

tepid landscapes tended to decorate aristocratic homes and offices, mimicking the high-society tastes of Europe.

In the 20th century, however, things began to change. From 1900 to the end of the 1950s, Cuban art gained international acclaim and, thanks to the many foreign artists visiting the island, Havana became one of the most celebrated cultural centers in Latin America.

Cuba's most prominent artists from this era include René Portocarrero (1912–85), who created fantastic versions of Havana and beautiful Creole women; and Wifredo (usually called Wilfredo) Lam (1902–82), who incorporated the mystical dimensions of his Afro-Cuban heritage with erotic and magical symbolism. Lam spent much of

ghostly nightmares. The work of all these artists has been displayed in galleries in Europe and the United States, but the best place to see a wide selection of their works is in the Arte Cubano section of the Museo Nacional de Bellas Artes in Havana *(see page 157)*.

Art and revolution

When Castro seized control, a new class of artists rose to power. Along with social and economic reforms, Castro brought an aggressive program of cultural reforms that tried to enhance artistic expression. In 1959, one of the first acts of the new government was the creation of the Instituto Cubano del Arte e Industria Cinematográficos (Cuban Film Institute; ICAIC) and the Consejo

Nacional de Cultura (National Cultural Council; CNC). The Escuela Nacional de Arte (National School for Art; ENA), founded in 1962, served as the cradle for new artists in the fields of painting, music, dance and drama, and teachers of art were sent out to schools all over the island. The ENA building was also a fine example of contemporary architecture.

State sponsorship opened the door to many artists. However, having the state as patron could have its drawbacks, particularly in terms of freedom of expression. In 1962 Castro defined his political policy toward artists and intellectuals: "Within the revolution, everything; outside the rev-

After this, the strength of the arts was greatly diminished. Directors and writers became more cautious as they were forced to fulfil the government's artistic and cultural requirements. Socialist ideology began to dominate. In 1973 another Education and Cultural Congress introduced further reforms designed to increase censorship. Hundreds of actors, writers and directors lost their jobs, and the totalitarian ring tightened around the art world.

Post-Revolutionary painting

Painting is a field in which Cuban artists have managed to retain a fairly healthy degree of free-

olution, nothing," and during the mid-1960s the position of the government hardened. This forcibly removed all those who had differing opinions about the cultural program, as well as those who were noncommittal. Many liberal artists were condemned to silence, while others were forced to seek asylum, and some were persecuted as "antisocial elitists," or exposed as homosexual. The most unfortunate were despatched to prison or to one of Cuba's new labor camps, known as UMAPs – "Military Units for Aid to Production," which were set up in 1965.

LEFT: René Portocarrero's *The Evening Meal*.
ABOVE AND RIGHT: paintings by Mariano Rodríguez and Eduardo Abela, both from 1938.

ARTISTIC HIGHLIGHTS

A handful of works that will help you familiarize yourself with the arts in Cuba, and get a broad-brush picture of the country, include:
● *Soy Cuba*: an extraordinary film made in 1964 by a team of Russian film makers, and still occasionally shown at independent cinemas and festivals.
● *Before Night Falls*, a hard-hitting and moving memoir by Reinaldo Arenas.
● The dynamic and quintessentially Cuban paintings of René Portocarrero.
● The Ballet Nacional de Cuba: go if you can while the legendary Alicia Alonso is still in charge.
● The often whacky productions of Teatro Buendía.

dom of expression, in spite of the difficulties involved. Surviving the sclerosis of socialist realism, the contemporary generation of Cuban artists has developed diverse styles, many with strongly anti-establishment undertones, through their often abstract art.

Afro-Cuban mythology and folklore are more apparent in Cuban art than ever before, as seen in the works of Manuel Mendive (b. 1944), one of Cuba's most famous contemporary artists. He has cultivated an intricate, primitivist style laden with Afro-Cuban symbolism, and his work is appreciated worldwide. The Cuban booth at the Venice International Biennial Exhibition of Modern Art in

1988 was dedicated to his work. You can see his paintings in the Arte Cubano section of Havana's Museo Nacional de Bellas Artes. Look out, also, for the work of Flora Fong, (b. 1941), of Cuban-Chinese descent, who combines Caribbean colors with a light touch that hints at her ethnicity.

A movement known simply as Street Art developed, whereby young artists displayed their highly expressive work outdoors, away from the official galleries where their paintings could be censored. The streets of Havana became a living exhibition where painters not only displayed their canvases, but also turned the streets into studios in which they created their work. Because of its dissident style, this rejection of official art was finally suppressed. Some exponents were harassed by the police and most of their work was confiscated.

Many young artists left Cuba for other countries, although some established themselves abroad without breaking their ties with the government.

Painters such as Humberto Castro and Moises Finale, both born in 1957, established themselves in Paris. Many others moved to Miami, where a Cuban artistic network was already in place. Respected artists José Bedia, Luís Marín, José Iraola, Tomás Esson, Nereida García, Frank León, Juan-Si and the outstanding Tomás Sánchez (whose symbolist landscapes won him the Joan Miró prize at an international exhibition in Barcelona) have all defected, and are now leaders of a new generation of Cuban artists residing in the United States.

It became much easier to buy Cuban art during and after the "Special Period." Old Havana is now chock-a-block with state-run art galleries, and artists selling their works on the street.

Theater

Following the 1959 Revolution, Cuban theater experienced its best, and its worst, years. At the outset of the Revolution, there was tremendous development in different theatrical currents; everything from Sartre to Ionesco was performed, and an annual International Theater Festival, attracting playwrights and directors from across Latin America was established.

The Teatro Escambray, a mobile drama group that took theater to the masses, is still trumpeted as a great revolutionary achievement, but it did more to spread the message of the Revolution than entertain the Cuban people. While theater remains the least favored of Cuba's art forms, there are a few companies worth looking out for, most notably Teatro Buendía, an internationally respected company, formed in 1986, who are based in Havana but are often away on tour.

Dance

Ballet is held in high esteem in Cuba. The Ballet Nacional de Cuba, founded by Alicia Alonso in 1948, has won international acclaim for its repertoire, which includes classical and modern ballets, many choreographed by Cuban masters. When not touring abroad, the company performs mainly in Havana's Gran Teatro or Teatro Nacional. Now well into her eighties, and nearly blind, Alonso, who was made a UNESCO Goodwill Ambassador in 2002, still directs the company. The Camagüey Ballet, a newer company founded shortly after the Revolution, once had an impressive reputation, but has lost some of its best dancers to the bright lights of the capital. A number of younger Cuban dancers, most famously Carlos Acosta, who was born in Havana in 1973, have become international stars.

Contemporary dance is also flourishing. Danza Contemporánea de Cuba, under Miguel Iglesias, grew out of Conjunto Nacional de Danza Modernas, begun by Ramiro Guerra in the early post-revolutionary years. And Ballet Rakatan fuses contemporary and traditional dance styles with flamenco and Afro-Cubans rhythms.

The Ballet Folklórico Cutumba, based in Santiago de Cuba, has been performing vibrant ritual

poet, playwright and critic Severo Sarduy (1937–93), and poet and novelist José Lezama Lima (1910–76), are leading lights of Latin American literature. Backtracking to the 19th century, Cuba's brightest star was, of course, poet and revolutionary, José Martí *(see page 48)*.

Before the Revolution, many Cuban writers had gone abroad, and several returned during a period of literary renaissance in the early 1960s, when they received preferential access to housing and a guaranteed income. Writers like the poet Nicolás Guillén were given official patronage by the revolutionary government, and some were even sent overseas as cultural attachés.

dances and chants from the Afro-Cuban cultures for more than three decades; and there are many amateur dance groups across the country who dedicate their efforts to maintaining elements of African culture.

Literature

Cuba has produced some outstanding writers, some of whom have won an international reputation. Guillermo Cabrera Infante *(see below)*; Alejo Carpentier (1904–80), who moved to Paris in 1966 where he served as Cuban Ambassador;

LEFT: naïve art inspired by Santería.
ABOVE: a striking performance by Danza Contemporánea de Cuba.

However, the international literary scandal known as the Padilla Affair changed all that. In 1968, Herberto Padilla (who died in Alabama in 2000) won an award for his book *Fuero del Juego (Out of the Game)*, a collection of poems that discredited the myths of revolutionary society. Though the award was given by a prestigious international jury, the book was banned in Cuba, and Padilla was arrested. This caused an outcry among intellectuals abroad, including writers like Gabriel García Márquez and Jean-Paul Sartre, who had until then been supportive of Castro's regime.

After this, a large number of writers were marginalized and their books taken out of circulation. The era of limited toleration of literary dissent had ended. Many writers left, including Guillermo

NICOLÁS GUILLÉN

Nicolás Guillén (1902–89) was a lifelong communist and after the Revolution enjoyed the prestige of being Cuba's National Poet.

Cabrera Infante, winner of the 1997 Cervantes Prize, the most prestigious Spanish-language literature award, and often described as Cuba's greatest 20th-century author. He lived in London from 1965 until his death 40 years later, and remained highly critical of Castro and his regime.

In 1987, the Cuban leadership re-evaluated the issue of artistic censorship, and in the 1990s,

York in 1990. His autobiography, *Before Night Falls*, was made into a highly acclaimed film in 2000 *(see page 24)*. His major work was *Pentagonia*, a series of five novels published over a number of years.

Cinema

Film is the most favored of the arts. Cuban cinema kicked off with the arrival of Castro and the Cuban Institute of Cinematography (ICAIC). A militant cinema industry set about promoting the advantages of the socialist system. Cuban documentaries were shown in the most remote corners of the island. Inspired by this movement, other

because of the massive exodus of writers and artists, the government took a more lenient attitude toward literary taboos.

In addition to the writers mentioned above, other Cuban writers well worth reading – both those who stayed and those who left – are anthropologist Miguel Barnet (b. 1940), whose best-known work is *Biografía de un Cimarrón (The Autobiography of a Runaway Slave)*, published in 1967; Lydia Cabrera – famous for her studies into Afro-Cuban religions – who died in 1991; Lisandro Otero González (b. 1932), whose most recent work, *Charada*, was published in Havana in 2004; and Reinaldo Arenas, whose openly gay lifestyle led to his imprisonment, and who left for Miami in the Mariel Boatlift. He committed suicide in New

Latin American film makers created political documentaries that became a vehicle for left-wing liberation movements around the world.

At the suggestion of Gabriel García Márquez, Castro founded an international film school in San Antonio de los Baños *(see page 188)* in the suburbs of Havana in 1986. Sponsored by a group of Latin American film makers and by García Márquez himself, the school caters to students from Asia, Africa and Latin America, and is relatively free from following the constraints of the official party line.

The leading light among Cuba's film directors was Tomás Gutiérrez Alea (1928–96). His 1969 movie *Memorias del Subdesarrollo (Memories of Underdevelopment)*, about a middle-class

Cuban who refuses to leave for Miami in the early 1960s but is unable to fit into revolutionary society, is a modern classic. His 1966 comedy *La Muerte de un Burócrata (Death of a Bureaucrat)* is also well worth seeing; and *Fresa y Chocolate (*1994), co-directed by Juan Carlos Tabío, created a stir inside and outside Cuba.

Although Cuba is full of creative energy, most cultural institutions felt the crunch of economic crisis during the "Special Period" in the 1990s. The film industry was all but shut down and most new movies were made with foreign money. Book publishing was badly hit, too. Writers, artists, actors, and film makers struggled to survive. For-

THE LATIN OSCARS

The New Latin American Film Festival, founded in 1979 and held in Havana every December, attracts film makers and actors from all over the world. Its Coral prizes are the Latin American equivalent of the Oscars.

The head of ICAIC, Alfredo Guevara (a lifelong communist and friend of Castro) gave an emotional press conference defending the films. But after a flurry of resignations and a meeting between Castro and leading artists, the official position prevailed, and Guevara stated that artistic "mistakes" had been made, and that the artistic

tunately, things are picking up again now.

Economic woes also saw a return to a harsher government attitude, and it seemed that the period of relative tolerance had been a false dawn. Movies such as the well-received 1995 comedy *Guantanamera* and the Oscar-nominated *Fresa y Chocolate* (both directed by Gutiérrez Alea and Juan Carlos Tabío) were severely criticized by Castro in a speech in 1997, arousing fears among the artistic community – and those who simply enjoyed cinema – of a return to the dark days of total censorship.

FAR LEFT: Guillermo Cabrera Infante. **LEFT:** poster for the groundbreaking film, *Fresa y Chocolate*. **ABOVE:** a still from the 2005 film *Habana Blues*.

community must be careful not to damage public morale or values.

More recent films depicting contemporary Cuba include *Suite Habana* (2003), directed by respected Cuban film maker Fernando Pérez Valdés. A documentary without dialogue, chronicling a day in the life of several real people in the city, it has been widely praised. His latest work, *Madrigal* (2007) produced by ICAIC, was screened at the 2007 Berlin Film Festival, and opened in Havana a few weeks later. Meanwhile, *Habana Blues* (2005) is a Spanish-Cuban co-operative effort, directed by Benito Zambrano, a Spaniard who studied at the San Antonio de Baños film school and who has described the film as his homage to Havana. ❑

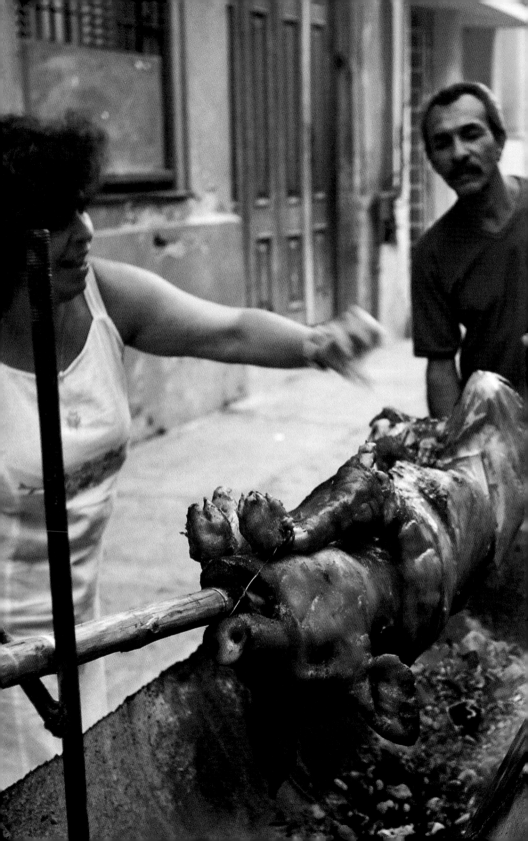

THE ESSENCE OF CUBAN FOOD

The items on Cuban menus may all seem pretty similar,
but there is good-quality food to be found, although
not always in the obvious places, along with some
delicious fresh fruit – not to mention the cocktails

Most Cuban food is simple. It is the fare of
el campo (the countryside), which reflects
local harvests and earthy suggestions of
its Spanish and African roots. It allows, for
instance, a dish of Galician inspiration to be
served with African-style accompaniments. Cuban
cooking isn't fancy, but Cubans love food.

The Cuban staples

If Cuban creole *(criollo)* cuisine had a national
dish, it would be roast pork *(puerco* or *cerdo)*
served with black beans *(frijoles)*, white rice
(arroz) and plantains *(plátanos)*. Rice and beans
are traditionally prepared in two forms: black
beans with rice known as *moros y cristianos*
(Moors and Christians) or red kidney beans with
rice *(congri)*. A delicious soupy stew of black
beans *(potaje)* is sometimes served alongside
plain white rice. Root vegetables are also popular
accompaniments, particularly *yuca* (also called
cassava, a starchy tuber), *malanga* and *boniato*.
Malanga is not unlike yucca, and *boniato* is a
tasty kind of sweet potato.

*Food gets into the music. The island's most famous
singer, Beny Moré, teased the* marranito, *the little
pig: "We're going to make you* jamón *(ham) and*
chicharrón *(pork scratchings)".*

Chicken *(pollo)* appears on many menus –
invariably fried, and invariably free range. Goat
(cabrito) doesn't – although herds of goats can be
seen grazing in the countryside. Fish *(pescado)*
makes relatively rare appearances, and when it

does it is usually *pargo* (snapper) or a plain steak
of white fish simply called *pescado*.

The ingredients, herbs and spices most used in
traditional Cuban cooking are cumin, oregano,
parsley, sour oranges and *ajos* – garlic. The *sofrito*,
a paste of chopped onion, garlic and green pepper
sizzled in good olive oil, is the basis of many
dishes. In these days of scarce ingredients, a popular seasoning for vegetables and meat is a tasty mixture of sour orange, garlic and oil, called *mojo*
(see recipe on page 119). You won't often find meat
stews on the menu, but look out for the *ajiaco*, a
classic infusion of meat and vegetables.

Although you sometimes see piles of vegetables
in markets, you don't often find them in restaurants. Salad often means a heap of grated white

---

LEFT: spit-roast pig to celebrate New Year.
RIGHT: waiting for customers at an *agropecuario*.

SWEET THINGS

Sugar is the basis for Cuba's fine rum, but also for one of its favorite non-alcoholic drinks, *guarapo*, which is the cloudy, sweet juice of raw, pressed sugar cane. You will see it being sold from carts in the street.

cabbage. However, when you do get the real thing – tomatoes, for example – they can be delicious, full of flavor, and invariably organic.

During the "Special Period," the tough years after the collapse of the Soviet Union when there were shortages of absolutely everything, Cuba became the land of "no hay" – which means,

ever was available, planning vegetarian meals in a culinary culture obsessed with meat. On the other hand, it wouldn't be unusual to find a Cuban bartering a chicken for a bar of soap, or any other items considered a luxury, because they were so hard to obtain.

The opening of farmers' markets *(agropecuarios)* in 1994 made a wider choice of ingredients available. These are markets where farmers sell their surplus produce, after the state has bought its quota, and you will find a wide range of goods on sale, from fresh vegetables to meat, eggs and honey. The food you eat in *paladares* will have come from an *agropecuario*.

"there isn't any," and people had to learn to cook with whatever was available. Culinary expert Nitza Villapol, well-known before the revolution as the author of a book called *Cocina al Minuto* (Cooking to Order), appeared on television offering tips on how to cope with ration books and food shortages, rather in the way that food experts in Britain during World War II gave similar advice on the wireless. She advised people to substitute lemon peel, dried avocado and celery leaves for hard-to-find spices. Villapol, who died in 1998, believed that people were infinitely adaptable – and she certainly helped them become so.

Lean times forced a new kind of cuisine upon the Cuban people, who became masters of improvisation, stretching and enhancing rice with what-

THE VERSATILE PLANTAIN

Cuban cooking exalts lowly ingredients. Take, for instance, the plantain, *el plátano*. You can fry it ripe *(maduro)* in slices cut diagonally, or green *(verde)* in paper-thin chips *(chicharitas)*. You can fry thicker wedges of green plantain, squash them, and fry them again for *tostones*. You can boil plantain chunks, ripe or green, mash them with a fork, drizzle with olive oil and sprinkle with crunchy fried pork rinds for *fu fú* – a dish of western African origin and something of an acquired taste. You can fill mashed plantains with *picadillo*, minced meat, and melted white cheese to make a *pastel de plátano*. In fact, you can do just about anything except eat them uncooked

Some things, such as beef and lobster, can only be sold by the state, but there is, of course, a black market in these things. If you stay in a *casa particular (see page 340)* and order dinnner, your host may ask you, with a knowing wink, if you would like *pollo de mar* (sea chicken), as if the word lobster should not even be mentioned. But if you want it, it will be available.

Fruit

Fruit in Cuba is a delight, and so are the juices made from it. It's due to the tropical climate, of course, and the fact that everything is harvested in season, when it is at its peak. Sweet, juicy pineap-

Sweet treats

Unless you buy it yourself in markets you are most likely to come across fruit on the breakfast table of a *casa particular* or the breakfast buffet in a hotel. Despite being plentiful and cheap it is rarely offered as a dessert. That role is played by ice cream (and that is usually good, too) or the ubiquitous *flan*, a caramel custard. Cubans do, on the whole, have a sweet tooth – you just need to look in a bakery window at the fluffy pink and baby-blue iced confections to realize that. If you are in Cuba for Mother's Day (the second Sunday in May) you will see special versions of these cakes being handed out of bakers' storefronts to

ples, grapefruits that need no sugar, mangos like you've never tasted, and bananas – the small, chunky ones are the best – will all introduce you to flavors completely lacking in fruit that has been picked before it is ready, packaged, refrigerated and flown to its faraway destinations. Avocados, too, whether you categorize them as a fruit or a vegetable, are at their perfect, creamy best when picked straight from the tree. Freshly squeezed fruit juices can be found in many bars, in whatever variety is most available at the time – ask for *jugo natural* to get the real thing.

LEFT: *comida criolla* for sale on a street stall.
ABOVE: a baker in Santiago de Cuba prepares bread rolls and delicious iced cakes.

waiting crowds and, everywhere you go, notice people carrying them home, often one in each hand, or balancing them on bicycle handlebars.

If you are in the east of the island, you should try the *cucuruchu* for the ultimate in sweetness. This is grated coconut, sometimes flavored with fruit juice and (mostly) sugar and sold in ingeniously fashioned banana-leaf wrappings.

Drinking in Cuba

The first thing that comes to mind is rum. Along with cigars, this is Cuba's best-known product. Rum, of course, is a sugar-based alcohol, and Cuba has always had plenty of sugar. The best known and biggest brand is Havana Club. There are various types, but you will most often find

Añejo 3 Años, Añejo Reserva, and Añejo 7 Años, of which the latter is the best. There is also a white rum, Añejo Blanco. Although Bacardi rum originated in Cuba (in Santiago) it is no longer made or sold here. The Bacardi family, fiercely opposed to Castro, had their business appropriated and left the island after the Revolution. Bacardi is now made in Puerto Rico.

A good, aged rum (*ron* in Spanish) can be drunk neat, like a brandy or whisky (ask for *ron de siete años*), but white rum is used as the basis of Cuba's famous cocktails: the *mojito* (rum, lime, mint and soda water), the *daiquirí* (rum, lime juice, sugar and crushed ice), the *piña colada* (rum with pineapple juice and coconut) and the Cuba Libre. The latter – which means Free Cuba – originated at the end of the 1898 War of Independence and was made with rum and Coca-Cola. Now, of course, it cannot be made in Cuba with Coca-Cola, so local versions – TuCola and Tropicola are used instead. swaped

As well as rum, Cubans are also fond of beer. Hardly surprising in this hot climate. Bucanero is a popular brand, as is the ubiquitous (and lighter) Cristal. The once-popular Hatuey beer, named after a Taíno chief whose picture appeared on its label, was made by the Bacardi company. It is now produced in the US and unavailable in Cuba.

MOJO CRIOLLO

The classic sauce for pork, but it is also used to add flavor to vegetables, such as *malanga*.
For four people:
8 garlic cloves, chopped, 1 tsp salt
1 tsp ground oregano (optional)
½ tsp ground cumin (optional)
½ cup sour orange juice
½ cup olive oil
Mash the garlic with the salt to form a paste. Blend in the spices. Add the sour orange juice and leave for 30 minutes; stir in the olive oil. Sour orange juice appears in many Cuban recipes but you can substitute a mixture of sweet orange juice and lime or lemon juice.

You can buy wine in some places, certainly in better hotels and restaurants, but don't expect to find it everywhere. There is small-scale wine production in Pinar del Río province *(see page 199)*, but most of the available wine comes from Chile or Argentina.

Cuba produces and consumes some excellent coffee. Ask for a *café con leche* if you want coffee with hot milk. A *café cubano* or *cafecito* is small and strong like an espresso, except that it comes ready sweetened unless you ask for it "*sin azúcar*," although many Cubans think this is a bit odd. ❏

ABOVE: Havana Club white rum is usually used for cocktails such as the mojito; the dark version can be drunk neat.

Paladares

For many years after the 1959 Revolution, family-run restaurants were illegal, like virtually every kind of private enterprise. They operated clandestinely, yet everyone knew where they were; even policemen and party members could be seen dining there. Then, in 1994, the law

was changed and these establishments, called *paladares* could start doing business more openly. Cuba was suddenly full of *paladares* offering cheap home cooking. The golden year of the *paladar* was 1995, when every other house in Havana seemed to be a restaurant – usually serving the traditional menu of pork, beans and rice.

But in 1996, the government realized that it had created a highly successful, profitable sector of the economy that was not making money for the state – indeed, that was competing, perhaps a little too successfully, with the lackluster state restaurants. So the *paladares* were obliged to register with the state, pay a license fee, meet strict public-health standards and pay devastatingly high taxes – as much as US$1,000 a month in Havana, regardless of how many meals were served. Consequently, many *paladares* were driven out of business. A series of crackdowns closed many more. There were commando raids (often shown on television evening news) to root out supplies of illicit lobster, shrimp, turtle and beef (all state monopolies that *paladares* cannot sell). Tax evasion, dirty kitchens, black-market cheese used on pizzas – all were used as an excuse to close more *paladares* which – bitter owners believed – had become too successful for the anti-capitalist government to bear.

ABOVE: a more down-to-earth *paladar*.
RIGHT: enjoy a hearty, home-cooked Cuban meal.

Government policy drastically reduced the numbers of *paladares*, and also pushed up prices but, from the customer's point of view, there were advantages, as the survivors had to compete, and draw in more customers. They began to make more of an effort, erecting neon signs, placing tables in gardens, making sure there were clean tablecloths, and providing flowers and candles – even printing menus. Standards of cooking rose and menus became more imaginative – some places began to specialize in foreign cooking – Chinese, Arabic, Spanish or Italian. These have moved beyond being traditional *paladares* – they now operate like professional restaurants. You have to book to get a table at some of the more popular establishments. In the case of the most famous one in Havana, La Guarida, reservations must usually be made far in advance, and confirmed on the day.

The days of the cheap meal eaten in the family sitting room are not entirely over, however. These *paladares* have simply moved back underground.

Refusing to register and paying no taxes, they come and go, but, as in the old days, everyone in the neighborhood knows where they are. Just ask around: any local person will be able to tell you the addresses of two or three that are open.

Menus are often limited to fried or grilled pork, chicken or sometimes fish, accompanied by rice and beans *(moros y cristianos)*, salad and a starchy vegetable *(vianda)* such as *yuca*, plantain, *malanga* or *boniato (see page 115)*. This is what Cubans eat at home: the majority do not seem to want anything else, and scorn even the slightest attempts to alter traditional dishes. They reject spices in favor of oil and garlic and all vegetables in favor of large quantities of meat. ❑

SPORT

One irrefutable triumph of the Revolution has been in the domain of athletics. Cuban sportsmen and women regularly dominate world-class opposition, and sporting opportunities for all are regarded as a right

I n 1944, the young Fidel Castro was voted athlete of the year at Belén College in Havana, where baseball was his specialty. "If I hadn't been an athlete, I wouldn't have been a guerrilla," Castro has said. He was once offered a professional contract to pitch for a US team but, by his own admission, he was not major-league material. Had Castro's arm been better, he might never have taken up arms against Batista, Cuba might still be a playground for wealthy Americans, and it is extremely unlikely that there would now be a large sign displayed outside the Cuban national sports training center, proclaiming *"Fidel: Atleta Número Uno."*

The right of the people

Less than a month after taking power, Castro addressed Cuba's assembled sports organizations and declared: "It is a shame that sport has been so undervalued. Less than 10 percent of our youth participate in sports. We must promote them at all costs. We must inundate every corner of the island with sports equipment. We should strive to improve our athletes rapidly."

Another Castro quotation is plastered around sports arenas: "Sport is the right of the people." With the creation of the National Institute of Sports, Physical Education and Recreation (INDER) in 1961, Cuba began to fulfil this pledge. Today, nearly half the population has participated in organized sports.

The base of Cuba's sporting pyramid is its 80,000 elementary school children. Every year students compete in the School Sports Games. Those that excel are invited to be tested for admis-

CLASH OF THE TITANS

It would have been the clash of the century – Muhammad Ali, US Olympic gold-medal winner in 1963, the dominant professional heavyweight of his age, against Teófilo Stevenson, amateur's subsequent king of the ring as a three-times Olympic heavyweight champion. But despite multimillion-dollar offers, these two champions never fought – loyal to Castro's revolution, Stevenson refused to defect. These two pugilists later cemented a friendship, and visited each other in the US and Cuba.

LEFT: Yargelis Savigne, world champion triple jumper.
RIGHT: baseball is a national obsession.

sion to the Schools for Sports Initiation (EIDE), whose students range in age from 11 to 16. EIDE students attend regular classes, but they are also given advanced coaching and face high-level competition. Those who perform best graduate to one of the Schools of Higher Athletic Performance (ESPA) where students hope to be noticed by a coach from the national ESPA in Havana.

Incentives

It took more than a decade for this system to make an impact on the sports world, but when it did, it did so with a bang. Teófilo Stevenson, a heavy-weight boxer from eastern Cuba, won a gold medal at the 1972 Olympics in Munich. Stevenson won another gold at the 1976 games in Montreal, where another great Cuban athlete, Alberto Juantorena, won gold medals in the 400- and 800-meter races – the first man ever to win both events in one Olympic Games. Stevenson won a third gold medal in Moscow in 1980 *(see also panel on previous page)*. Both Stevenson and Juantorena now hold posts in INDER. They are two illustra-

tions of another Cuban sports philosophy: "The greatest incentive that can be given to an athlete," Castro said in 1959, "is security in their retirement and a proper reward for champions."

International events

Overall, Cuba has performed well at international sporting events for a nation of its size. In the Pan-American Games, Cuba stands second behind the US in the overall medals table. Its greatest success in these games came in 1991, when it played host to the event. Cuba had staked significant prestige on the outcome, managing to stage the games despite the financial strictures caused by

2000 they came ninth in the overall table (one above the UK); and in Athens in 2004 they came 11th, winning 27 medals, including nine golds. And the wins continue, in 2007 Yargelis Savigne *(see page 120)* won gold in the Triple Jump at the World Championships in Osaka.

Although it has a good record in athletics and some martial arts like judo and taekwondo, the real mainstay in terms of medal-winning is in boxing – one of the island's sporting passions. "To beat an American is the most important thing," said one Cuban boxer. "Knocking out an American is better than knocking out a better boxer. It's transcendent."

the collapse of the Soviet Union and the subsequent loss of Soviet subsidies. The risk paid off, with Cuba becoming only the second nation ever to displace the US at the top of the tree – an obvious reason for national pride.

The nation has likewise punched above its weight at the Olympics, although it seems to be slipping slightly in the table of nations. At the 1992 Olympics in Barcelona, Cuba was the fifth-highest medal winner with 31, surpassing larger countries such as France and Britain. In Atlanta in 1996, they came eighth with 25 medals; in Sydney in

LEFT: youngsters are encouraged to take up sports.
ABOVE: the Cuban national baseball team wait for play in the dug-out.

Baseball

Another Cuban passion is baseball, which came to the island at the end of the 19th century, when the North American influence was starting to outweigh that of Spain. The first games were played in around 1865 between Cuban dock workers and US sailors. Spanish authorities associated the game with the cause of Cuban independence – and revenues from baseball games did, indeed, support José Martí's independence movement. As a result, the game was banned in parts of the country in 1895.

Repeated visits from US marines after independence heightened baseball's popularity, as did the increasing numbers of North American players seeking Caribbean warmth and winter paychecks. Though the sport was originally the realm of Cuba's economic elite, it quickly caught on among all classes of society.

All over Cuba you will see evidence of the game's popularity. Even the smallest community has a baseball pitch, and in city streets you will see small boys practicing shots – even when they only have a stick, and perhaps a tin can for a ball.

Major-league riches

The island has totally dominated baseball since it was made a full Olympics sport in Barcelona in 1992, winning three of the four golds awarded since then. The only blemish came in 2000 in Sydney, when they were beaten into silver-medal

ing for a small local team, Morales and his companions were sent home to Havana. Six weeks later, the baseball star was back in the US, having paid an undisclosed sum to one of the many illegal immigrant smugglers. Dozens of Cuban baseball players have defected over the past 15 years, but not all of them elect to stay in the United States – many go on to a third country to negotiate a lucrative contract which is free of US baseball's rules on exclusive rights.

The legal way

Cuba does export some of its athletic talent through official channels, and INDER takes half the earnings

position by the USA. Cuban players assert that they play for the love of the game and their country, and are not interested in the millions of dollars they could earn in major leagues.

Defections, however, have become increasingly common, and some of the island's finest players have abandoned Cuba for multimillion-dollar contracts and the chance to play in prestigious United States major leagues. Two of the biggest stars to do so were half-brothers Liván and Orlando "El Duque" Hernández, who left in 1995 and 1997 respectively.

The Cuban authorities hoped they had put a stop to baseball defections when Andy Morales was repatriated after being intercepted at sea by the US coastguard. After a year in disgrace, play-

of coaches and athletes who go abroad legally to work and compete. Cuban sports personnel work in some 40 different countries and, in 2002, the authorities came to an agreement with Japan's professional baseball leagues for Olympic stars like slugger Orestes Kindelán and third-baseman Omar "El Niño" Linares to play there. But when it comes to the United States, that avenue is firmly closed. INDER refuses to sanction players leaving for the US, and the US does not permit the wages of professional players to go back to Cuba.

Despite defections, Cuba's baseball still seems to be in rude good health; 2006 saw the inaugural World Baseball Classic – the only international competition in which top stars from the US major leagues tend to compete. Initially, it seemed that

Cuba was going to be prevented from competing in the US by the American authorities, as prize money would fall foul of the same anti-Cuban financial sanctions. But the Cuban team received the all-clear (and goodwill, in some quarters) when they offered to donate any prize money to victims of Hurricane Katrina, and went on to surpass their hosts in the tournament, eventually only losing in the final to Japan.

In the footsteps of the greats

Two of Cuba's outstanding athletes of the 1990s were the runner, Ana Fidelia Quirot, who triumphed in the 800-meter race at the World Cham-

However, Sotomayor was stripped of the gold medal he won at the 1999 Pan American Games in Winnipeg, Canada, when he allegedly tested positive for cocaine. The Cubans reacted angrily, accusing the United States of doctoring the tests in order to tarnish Cuba's sporting reputation. Castro launched a campaign to try and clear Sotomayor's name and Cuba refused to suspend him. After his ban was reduced from two years to one, Sotomayor came back to win a silver medal in high jump in Sydney in 2000. After more than 20 years in the limelight he retired in October 2001, just before his 34th birthday, which is a grand old age for a high jumper. ❑

pionships in 1997 – having made a remarkable comeback from a severe burns accident – and the phenomenal high jumper, Javier Sotomayor (who enjoys the additional prestige of being a deputy in Cuba's National Assembly). Sotomayor can rightfully lay claim to the title of greatest high jumper of all time: he frequently broke the world record (pushing the mark up to 2.45 meters in 1993 – a record that still stands); claimed Olympic gold in 1992 (Cuban boycotts meant he missed the 1984 and 1988 games); and won World Championship golds in 1995 and 1997.

***

FAR LEFT: baseball pitcher Yadel Marti's family watch him on TV. **LEFT:** Ana Quirot, 800-meter champion. **ABOVE:** world champion Javier Sotomayer.

OPEN TO ALL – BIG AND SMALL

In Havana, top budding gymnasts train at the Provincial School for Gymnastics, housed in an ornate colonial building on the Prado. While they practice their world-class routines, on the other side of the building a group of five-year-olds might be working on cartwheels. Despite the disparity between these extremes of talent and experience, there is an air of accessibility to the elite athletes that meshes nicely with the pleasing irony of this formerly exclusive club being put to popular use. It is difficult to imagine a top-level national athlete in any other country training alongside primary-school kids, but, like so many of Cuba's apparent contradictions, it seems to work.

PLACES

A detailed guide to the entire archipelago
of Cuba, with principal sites clearly
cross-referenced by number to the maps

Most visitors to Cuba arrive at either Havana or Varadero – two places that, while only 140 km (85 miles) apart, mark the opposite extremes of the Cuban experience. Varadero is a vacation resort built purely to attract tourists, with glitzy, high-rise hotels, restaurants and nightclubs, and golden beaches that are largely free of local people. Havana, on the other hand, is where five centuries of Cuban history coalesce, a city saturated by romance, nostalgia and intrigue. Although sadly dilapidated in parts it should not be missed, as there is nowhere else like it in Latin America.

Whichever city you choose as a jumping-off point, the "real Cuba" lies out in the provinces. A shortage of parts and fuel has made public transportation a serious problem, but things are gradually improving and tourist transportation services are now widely available. With a judicious combination of short domestic flights, organized tours, comfortable long-distance buses, taxi rides and rental cars, you will be able to penetrate the less-frequently visited hinterland.

For a pure taste of rural life, to the west of Havana lies the province of Pinar del Río, the tobacco-growing region that is one of the lushest and most spectacular parts of the island. A journey to the central south coast should include visits to Playa Girón on the Bay of Pigs, the wildlife-filled Zapata peninsula, the port of Cienfuegos, and Cuba's colonial jewel, Trinidad. Offshore, Cayo Largo is the favored beach resort, while the Isle of Youth is a major diving center.

The vast sugar-cane fields of the rural heartland make up the slowest and least-visited part of Cuba, where cities such as Santa Clara, Camagüey and Holguín are interesting stopover points. The east has its own thriving identity and traditions. Santiago, Cuba's second city, is often a few steps ahead of Havana in culture and music. The little colonial town of Baracoa is a delight, and exploring the highways, remote beaches and craggy mountains of the Oriente remains one of Cuba's great adventures. ❏

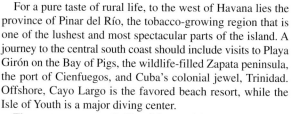

PRECEDING PAGES: children in Santiago; visitors on one of the Eastern Beaches (Playas del Este); Old Havana, with the Capitolio in the background.
LEFT: a trusty old car in Trinidad. **ABOVE:** a proud fisherman and a watchful youth.

Cuba

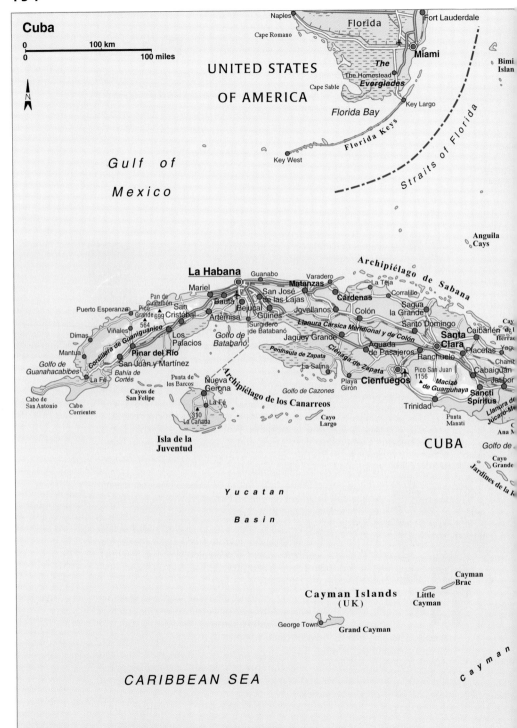

0   100 km
0   100 miles

N

Naples

Cape Romano

Florida

Fort Lauderdale

Miami

Bimi
Islan

UNITED STATES

OF AMERICA

The Homestead

Cape Sable

The
Everglades

Key Largo

Florida Bay

Florida Keys

Straits of Florida

Gulf of

Key West

Mexico

Anguila
Cays

La Habana   Guanabo

Archipiélago de Sabana

Varadero

La Teja

Mariel

Pan de
Guajaibón

San José
de las Lajas

Matanzas

Corralillo

San
Cristóbal

Bauta

Bejucal

Cárdenas

Sagua
la Grande

Puerto Esperanza

Pico
Grande 699

564

Artemisa

Güines

Jovellanos

Colón

Santo Domingo

Caibarién

Cay

Dimas

Viñales

Guaniguanico

Surgidero
de Batabanó

Llanura Cársica Meridional y de Colón

Santa

Placetas

Yegr

Mantua

Cordillera de Guaniguanico

Los
Palacios

Golfo de
Batabanó

Jagüey Grande

Aguada
de Pasajeros

Clara

Ranchuelo

Chamb

Golfo de
Guanahacabibes

Pinar del Río

San Juan y Martínez

Bahía de
Cortés

Península de Zapata

Ciénaga de Zapata

Pico San Juan
1156

Macizo
de Guamuhaya

Cabaiguán

Jatibor

La Fé

Punta de
los Barcos

Nueva
Gerona

La Salina

Playa
Girón

Cienfuegos

Sancti
Spíritus

Llanura de

Cabo de
San Antonio

Cabo
Corrientes

Cayos de
San Felipe

Archipiélago de los Canarreos

Golfo de Cazones

Trinidad

Punta
Manati

Júcaro-Mo

La Fé

310
La Cañada

Cayo
Largo

Ana M

Isla de la
Juventud

CUBA

Golfo de

Cayo
Grande

Jardines de la R

Yucatan

Basin

Cayman
Brac

Cayman Islands
(U K)

Little
Cayman

George Town

Grand Cayman

Cayman

CARIBBEAN SEA

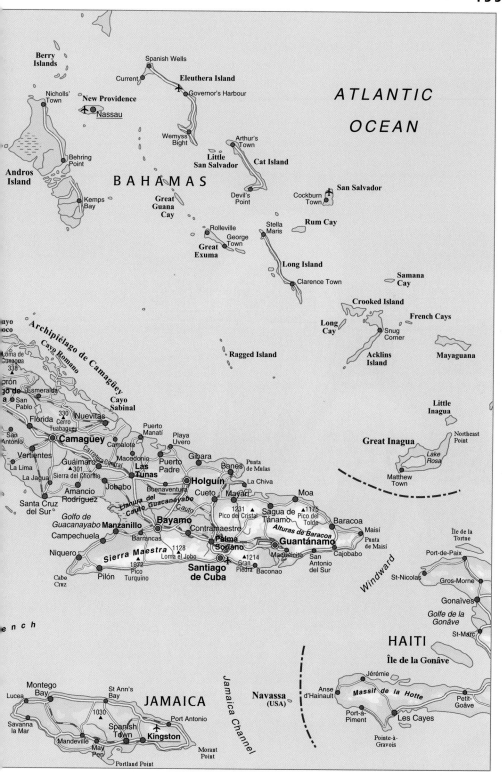

Berry
Islands

Spanish Wells

Current

Eleuthera Island

Nicholls'
Town

New Providence

Governor's Harbour

Nassau

ATLANTIC

OCEAN

Wemyss
Bight

Arthur's
Town

Behring
Point

Little
San Salvador

Cat Island

Andros
Island

BAHAMAS

Devil's
Point

San Salvador

Cockburn
Town

Kemps
Bay

Great
Guana
Cay

Rolleville

Stella
Maris

Rum Cay

George
Town

Great
Exuma

Samana
Cay

Long Island

Clarence Town

Crooked Island

French Cays

ayo
oco

Archipiélago de Camagüey

Long
Cay

Snug
Corner

Acklins
Island

Mayaguana

Cayo Romano

oma de
uaga
338

rón
jo de
a

Esmeralda

San
Pablo

Cayo
Sabinal

Little
Inagua

Florida

330
Cerro

Nuevitas

Great Inagua

Northeast
Point

Tuabaguey

San
Antonio

Camagüey

Puerto
Manatí

Playa
Uvero

Lake
Rosa

Matthew
Town

Vertientes

Camalote

Macedonio

Gibara

Punta
de Mulas

La Lima

Guáimaro

301

Puerto
Padre

Banes

La Jagua

Sierra del Chorrillo

Las
Tunas

La Chiva

Amancio
Rodríguez

Jobabo

Buenaventura

Holguín

Llanura del

Cueto

Mayarí

Moa

Santa Cruz
del Sur

Cauto Guacanayabo

Cauto

1231

Pico del Cristal

Sagua de
Tánamo

1175
Pico del
Toldo

Baracoa

Golfo de
Guacanayabo

Manzanillo

Bayamo

Contramaestre

Alturas de Baracoa

Maisí

Campechuela

Barrancas

Palma
Soriano

Guantánamo

Punta
de Maisí

Île de la
Tortue

Niquero

Sierra Maestra

1128

1972

Loma el Jobo

Maqueicito

1214
Gran
Piedra

San
Antonio
del Sur

Cajobabo

Port-de-Paix

Gros-Morne

Cabo
Cruz

Pilón

Pico
Turquino

Santiago
de Cuba

Baconao

St-Nicolas

Windward

Gonaïves

Golfe de la
Gonâve

ench

HAITI

St-Marc

Île de la Gonâve

Montego
Bay

St Ann's
Bay

Jérémie

Anse
d'Hainault

Massif de la Hotte

Lucea

JAMAICA

Jamaica Channel

Navassa
(USA)

Petit-
Goâve

Savanna
la Mar

1030

Port Antonio

Port-à-
Piment

Les Cayes

Mandeville

Spanish
Town

Kingston

Pointe-à-
Gravois

May
Pen

Morant
Point

Portland Point

INTRODUCING HAVANA

A city of more than 2 million inhabitants, Cuba's capital offers far more than just its astonishing colonial core

Seen from a distance, Havana looks spectacular. Waves crash over the city's famous promenade, the **Malecón**, where lovers stroll past pastel-colored buildings. Stone fortresses turn golden in the Caribbean light, recalling the days when Havana was the jewel in the Spanish Crown, its harbor full of galleons loaded with South American silver.

For many years after the Revolution turned its attentions to the impoverished countryside, the city didn't see a lick of paint, but serious attempts have now been made to stem the tropical decay. The partly UNESCO-funded renovation of 17th-century Old Havana started the ball rolling in the mid-1990s, and now numerous colonial buildings have been restored to their former splendor – many of them housing museums and galleries. In 1998, work began on the salt-pitted Malecón, where individual Spanish provinces sponsor major works. In the early 21st century many parts of the badly decaying Central Havana (which borders Old Havana to the west) and Vedado districts are receiving long-overdue attention.

There are two areas, linked on the sea side by the Malecón, on which most visitors will concentrate. First, **La Habana Vieja** (Old Havana), a mixture of beautifully renovated squares and buildings, and narrow, noisy streets where Cubans live in cramped conditions. Second, **Vedado**, which was modeled on Miami; most of its tallest buildings are the hotels originally financed by the US Mafia in the 1940s and 1950s. Here and in the other main western suburb, Miramar, farther afield, the pre-revolutionary mansions of the rich are today occupied either by Cuban families – whose homes lie rotting splendidly amid lush foliage – or by a growing number of embassy officials, foreign investors and Cuban bureaucrats.

Havana is exhilarating, but it can also be exhausting. There is a neurotic, anxious edge to life here, unlike anything you'll find in the rest of Cuba. It is one of the most fascinating places on earth – a city of great paradox and tremendous presence. As Cuba's political and economic center, it has become a monument to a broken communist dream. Yet it is also the focus of Cuba's artistic life, its youth culture and its aspirations for the future. ❑

LEFT: a colorful couple in Havana. **ABOVE LEFT:** drums can be heard on any street corner. **ABOVE RIGHT:** models of Cuba's famous old cars make popular souvenirs.

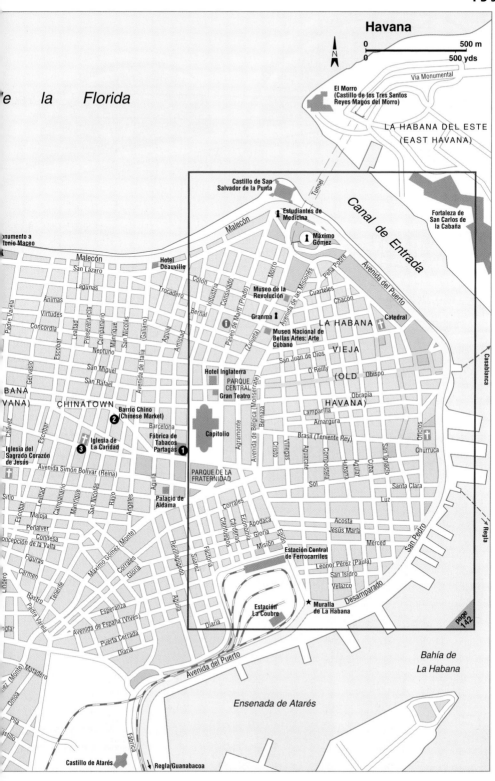

e la Florida

Havana

Via Monumental

El Morro
(Castillo de los Tres Santos
Reyes Magos del Morro)

LA HABANA DEL ESTE
(EAST HAVANA)

Castillo de San
Salvador de la Punta

Tunel

Canal de Entrada

Fortaleza de
San Carlos de
la Cabaña

Malecón

Estudiantes de
Medicina

Máximo
Gómez

Avenida del Puerto

Monumento a
tonio Maceo

Malecón

San Lázaro

Hotel
Deauville

Lagunas

Colón

Industria

Morro

Peña Pobre

Casablanca

Trocadero

Consulado

Museo de la
Revolución

Avenida de las Misiones

Cuarteles

Chacón

Ánimas

Bernal

Virtudes

Concordia

Granma

LA HABANA

Catedral

Padre Varela

Gervasio

Escobar

Lealtad

Perseverancia

Campanario

Manrique

San Nicolás

Galiano

Aguila

Amistad

Paseo de Martí (Prado)

Zulueta

Museo Nacional de
Bellas Artes: Arte
Cubano

VIEJA

Neptuno

Avenida de Italia

San Juan de Dios

O'Reilly

Obispo

(OLD

San Miguel

San Rafael

Hotel Inglaterra

BANA
VANA)

CHINATOWN

PARQUE
CENTRAL

Gran Teatro

Bernaza

HAVANA)

Obrapía

Oficios

Chávez

Escobar

Barrio Chino
(Chinese Market)

Barcelona

Lamparilla

Amargura

Iglesia de
La Caridad

Fábrica de
Tabacos
Partagás

Capitolio

Agramonte

Avenida de Bélgica (Monserrate)

Cristo

Villegas

Aguacate

Brasil (Teniente Rey)

Compostela

Habana

Aguiar

Cuba

San Ignacio

Churruca

Iglesia del
Sagrado Corazón
de Jesús

Avenida Simón Bolívar (Reina)

Aguila

PARQUE DE LA
FRATERNIDAD

Sol

Santa Clara

Luz

Sitio

Lealtad

Campanario

Manrique

San Nicolás

Rayo

Angeles

Palacio de
Aldama

Maloja

Peñalver

Condesa

Concepción de la Valla

Máximo Gómez (Monte)

Corrales

Gloria

Revillagigedo

Corrales

Economía

Cárdenas

Cienfuegos

Apodaca

Gloria

Misión

Egido

Acosta

Jesús María

Merced

San Pedro

Figuras

Carmen

Suárez

Factoría

Estación Central
de Ferrocarriles

Leonor Pérez (Paula)

San Isidro

Lindero

Castro

Paula Varela

Tenerife

Esperanza

Avenida de España (Vives)

Puerta Cerrada

Diaria

Diaria

Estación
La Coubre

Muralla
de La Habana

Velazco

Desamparado

Regla

Bahía de
La Habana

nglar

ez (Monte) Matadero

Omoa

Pila

stillo

Avenida del Puerto

Ensenada de Atarés

Fábrica

Castillo de Atarés

Regla/Guanabacoa

page 142

OLD HAVANA

Restored grandeur reveals the might of Spain's most precious colonial city, but Old Havana is more than a living museum. Life on the streets is vibrant and noisy, and just as interesting as the fine architecture

Havana

CUBA

La Habana Vieja, Old Havana, is the city's vibrant heart, and this is where most visitors to Cuba spend the first day or two of their trip – a tremendous place to begin any vacation.

The compact grid of narrow colonial streets, graceful squares and aristocratic mansions that make up Old Havana was, for some 350 years, the entire city. It was only in the 1860s that the massive city walls were knocked down and *habaneros* began distinguishing the district as "old." For many years, the area was allowed to languish – a blessing in disguise, since it meant Havana escaped the Disneyland-style restoration of some other colonial Caribbean cities. Castro's government prioritized putting money into developing the impoverished countryside, and left the capital untouched. In spite of the decay, evident everywhere after such chronic neglect, the 1959 Revolution saved Old Havana. The Batista regime had had the area scheduled for demolition: cars could not easily pass down the narrow streets, and more land was needed to satisfy the fever for high-rise hotels, casinos and nightclubs.

Since the old city was placed on the UNESCO World Heritage List in 1982, and with the added incentive of turning it into a major tourist attraction, the authorities, under the directorship of the indefatigable Dr Eusebio Leal Spengler, the city historian, have embarked on an ambitious process of restoration. This has rescued sections of the city from decay, and restored many buildings to their for-

mer glory, but in other areas, buildings continue to collapse after bad weather – more than 600 have been lost in this way over the past two decades. Still, some 150 of Havana's remaining buildings date back to the 16th and 17th centuries, 200 from the 18th, and 460 from the 19th, making it the best-preserved colonial city in the Americas.

The restoration of the island's most historical site has resulted in demographic changes in what was once one of the liveliest *barrios* (neighborhoods) in the city. People were moved out of

Main attractions

PLAZA DE ARMAS
PLAZA DE LA CATEDRAL
MUSEO DE ARTE COLONIAL
CASA DE LA OBRA PÍA
PLAZA VIEJA
CAPITOLIO
MUSEO NACIONAL DE ARTE CUBANO
MUSEO DE LA REVOLUCIÓN

LEFT: a beautifully renovated building in Plaza Vieja.
BELOW: greenery festoons many balconies.

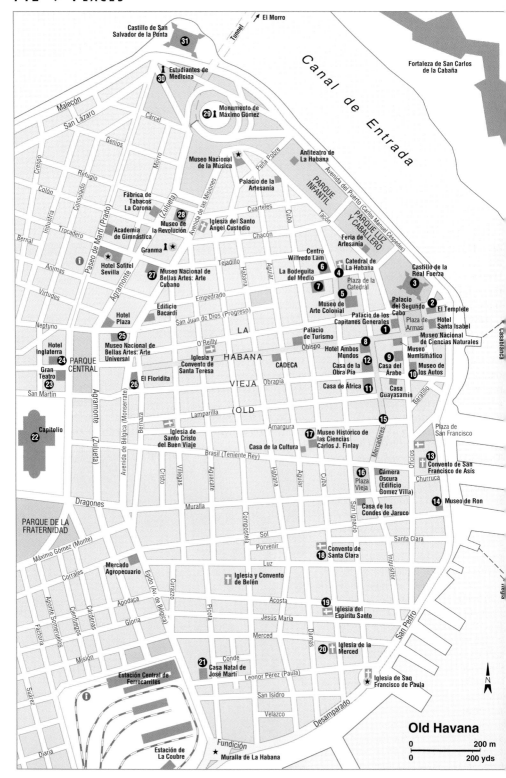

El Morro

Castillo de San Salvador de la Punta
31

Fortaleza de San Carlos de la Cabaña

Estudiantes de Medicina
30

Monumento de Máximo Gómez
29

Malecón
San Lázaro
Cárcel
Genios
Morro
Crespo
Refugio
Colón
Consulado
Industria
Trocadero
Bernal
Ánimas
Virtudes
Neptuno

Canal de Entrada

Museo Nacional de la Música
Palacio de la Artesanía

Anfiteatro de La Habana

Fábrica de Tabacos La Corona
Museo de la Revolución
28
Academia de Gimnástica
Granma
Iglesia del Santo Ángel Custodio

Cuarteles
Chacón

PARQUE INFANTIL

PARQUE LUZ Y CABALLERO

Feria de Artesanía

Museo Nacional de Bellas Artes: Arte Cubano
27
Hotel Sofitel Sevilla

Centro Wilfredo Lam
6
La Bodeguita del Medio
7
5

Catedral de La Habana
4
Plaza de la Catedral
Museo de Arte Colonial

Castillo de la Real Fuerza
3

Palacio del Segundo Cabo
2
El Templete

Hotel Plaza
Edificio Bacardí
San Juan de Dios (Progreso)
Empedrado

LA
HABANA
VIEJA
(OLD

Palacio de los Capitanes Generales
1
Plaza de Armas
Hotel Santa Isabel

Museo Nacional de Ciencias Naturales

Hotel Inglaterra
24
Gran Teatro
23
Parque Central
26
El Floridita

25
Museo Nacional de Bellas Artes: Arte Universal
Iglesia y Convento de Santa Teresa

CADECA
Obispo
Palacio de Turismo
Hotel Ambos Mundos
12
Casa de la Obra Pía
Casa de África
11

8
9
10

Casa del Árabe
Museo Numismático
Museo de los Autos

San Martín

Capitolio
22

Lamparilla
Amargura
Iglesia de Santo Cristo del Buen Viaje
Casa de la Cultura
Brasil (Teniente Rey)
Muralla

17
Museo Histórico de las Ciencias Carlos J. Finlay

Casa Guayasamín
15

Plaza de San Francisco
13
Convento de San Francisco de Asís

PARQUE DE LA FRATERNIDAD

Máximo Gómez (Monte)
Corrales
Mercado Agropecuario
Apodaca
Gloria
Misión

Sol
Porvenir
Luz
Iglesia y Convento de Belén
Acosta
Jesús María
Merced
Conde

16
Plaza Vieja
Cámara Oscura (Edificio Gómez Villa)

Casa de los Condes de Jaruco
Santa Clara
18
Convento de Santa Clara

19
Iglesia del Espíritu Santo

20
Iglesia de la Merced

14
Museo de Ron

21
Casa Natal de José Martí
Leonor Pérez (Paula)
San Isidro
Velazco

Iglesia de San Francisco de Paula

Estación Central de Ferrocarriles

Estación de La Coubre
Muralla de La Habana
Fundición

N

Old Havana

0 _____ 200 m
0 _____ 200 yds

Old Havana in their thousands, their homes becoming cafés, restaurants, hotels, and museums. Most were re-housed in the less picturesque (but far more comfortable) projects of Lamar that disfigure the city vista east of El Morro. As a result, the well-kept and well-policed streets and squares have lost much of their appeal, becoming unnaturally quiet, especially at night. However, current thinking has become more sensitive to social change, and there is now an attempt to allow people to remain in or return to the renovated buildings.

Vestiges of the life that filled this once-bustling *barrio* can still be seen in the grid of largely unrestored streets between Calle Brasíl (Teniente Rey) and the train station, where hundreds of families inhabit waterless, crumbling mansions. Music blares from every window, washing hangs from balconies, boys practice baseball shots, scraggy dogs scavenge for food, and life is lived outdoors to escape the heat of crowded rooms in which air conditioning is not an option. Catch it while you can – it may soon be gone.

The heart of the Old City

The **Plaza de Armas** is Havana's oldest square, and the best place to begin any walking tour of the city. In the evening, it is lit by antique filigree lamps, and on many nights an orchestra plays in the open air. It is the focus for much of the street life of the restored city, and is surrounded by cafés, bars and restaurants, such as the Café Mina. In the center of the leafy square is a statue of Carlos Manuel de Céspedes, rebel president and leader of the first War of Independence in the 1860s. A secondhand book market, which sells revolutionary literature in various languages, is held here (Wed–Sat 9am–6pm); and you will often see costumed troupes of entertainers – stilt-walkers, dancers and drummers – performing here.

The majestic building on the west side of the plaza is the **Palacio de los Capitanes Generales ❶** (Palace of the Captain-Generals), perhaps the finest

example of baroque architecture in Havana. Completed in 1780, this was home to the Spanish Governor until independence, and of the US Military Governor for the few years thereafter. Cuban presidents lived here until 1917, when they moved to the Capitolio and this became the mayor's office.

Today the palace houses the **Museo de la Ciudad** (City Museum; open daily 9am–6pm; entrance charge), which has by far the most lavish of Havana's many collections of colonial artifacts. You can visit independently but you get to see more if you take the guided tour. Keep an eye out for the machete of independence fighter General Antonio Maceo, and the dining room with 400 plates hanging on the walls. The King of Spain's Hall was kept constantly ready in case His Majesty ever decided to inspect Havana, though no monarch ever did so. The courtyard garden is delightful, hung with vines and bougainvillaea, with a statue of Christopher Columbus at its center.

Nearby (still on the Plaza de Armas, although the actual address is Calle Obispo 61), is the **Museo de Ciencias**

La Giraldilla on the Castillo de la Real Fuerza is a symbol of Havana.

BELOW: entertainers take a break in the Plaza de Armas.

TIP

On one side of La Mina restaurant is a tiny store, the Casa del Agua, which dispenses glasses of pure water from a natural source, kept cool in old ceramic urns. On the other side (actually in Calle Obispo) is an atmospheric store in the oldest surviving house in Havana, where antiquarian books are displayed in glass-fronted cabinets.

BELOW:
bookstalls and ornate lamps in the Plaza de Armas.

Naturales (Museum of Natural History; open Wed–Sun 11am–6.30pm; entrance charge). Working with the American Museum of Natural History in New York, it has become far more user-friendly of late. Among its wide collection of flora and fauna is a beautiful exhibition of Cuban snails.

At the plaza's northeast corner is **El Templete ②**, a Doric-style temple with three large paintings by French artist Jean-Baptiste Vermay inside. One canvas is said to be the first in Cuba to portray black and white people in close company. A column marks the spot where the city was refounded in 1519 as "La Villa de San Cristóbal de la Habana," with a mass being said under the sacred ceiba tree. The original tree was uprooted by a hurricane in 1828 and replacements have been planted several times. The current descendant is still credited with magical powers, partly because ceibas are considered sacred to the Yoruba religion (on which Santería is based). During an annual festival on November 16, *habaneros* celebrate that first mass: thousands of people fill the square, and wait many hours to fulfil a

ritual – circling the tree three times and placing coins at its roots to bring good luck in the coming year. Visitors to the temple are encouraged to do the same.

Nearby stands the beautiful **Hotel Santa Isabel**, which was originally built in the 18th century as the Palacio del Conde de Santovenia; a ruin for many years, it has now been restored to five-star status *(see page 341)*, and is one of the nicest in the city.

Across the street from El Templete is the **Castillo de la Real Fuerza ③** (currently closed for renovation), the oldest building in Havana. This powerful fortress, complete with drawbridges, iron cannon and murky green moat, was built on the orders of Felipe II after the city was sacked by pirates, and was completed in 1577.

Topping its tower is the city's symbol, the bronze figure of **La Giraldilla de la Habana** (a replica, in fact – the original is in the Museo de la Ciudad). Called Iñez de Bobadilla, she was the wife of conquistador Hernando de Soto, who left Cuba to search Florida for the fountain of youth. Instead, he found only miserable death. La Giraldilla spent every afternoon for four years in the tower, watching for his return. From the roof there are good views of the harbor, and there is a small ceramic art museum and gallery inside. When renovation is completed more facilities may be available.

The impressive baroque building on the northwest side of the square is the **Palacio del Segundo Cabo**, the headquarters of the Spanish vice-governor in colonial times. It has a beautiful courtyard, and houses the Instituto del Cubano del Libro, and a small book store.

Plaza de la Catedral

Two blocks north is the **Plaza de la Catedral**. This beautiful square was once a rather seedy place, known as Plazuela de la Ciénaga (Little Swamp Square). It was the place where the city's rainwater drained, and was once dominated by the 16th-century Zanja Real or "Royal Ditch" *(see page 152)*. The site of a fish market before construction began in the

18th century, it was the last square to be built in Old Havana.

It is named for the baroque **Catedral de La Habana ❹** (opening times vary, but usually open 8am–noon or 12.30pm; free, but small charge to go up the tower), which dominates the square and forms part of the most harmonious collection of buildings in the city.

Officially termed the Catedral de la Virgen María de la Concepción Inmaculada, the building was finally finished in 1777, after several setbacks. It was begun as a church by the Jesuits in 1748, but was halted when King Carlos III ordered them out of Cuba in 1767, and gained cathedral status only in 1793. There are bells in both of the towers: the shorter tower has a bell from the Cuban city of Matanzas; the taller one, a bell from Spain. At midnight on New Year's Eve, the cathedral bells ring and crowds gather to rap at the great timber doors for luck in the new year. The interior holds an altar of Carrara marble inlaid with gold, silver and onyx.

For many years the cathedral held the supposed ashes of Columbus, though most people now believe they were those of his son, Diego. Brought from Santo Domingo in 1796, they were returned to Spain after Cuba won independence in 1899. Pope John Paul II held the final mass of his Central American mission here, in January 1998. The square was packed with the faithful (and the merely curious), and surrounding buildings were decked with flowing silk banners in the Vatican colors: yellow and white. A small store to the right of the cathedral sells postcards, T-shirts and other memorabilia of the historic papal visit.

Colonial homes

On the east side of the square is the **Casa de Lombillo**, built in 1741. The former mansion of a Cuban slave trader, it housed Cuba's first post office, and is now the headquarters of Dr Eusebio Leal Spengler, the city historian. Beside the Casa de Lombillo is the **Casa del Marqués de Arcos**, built in 1742 for Cuba's royal treasurer and now an art gallery.

Directly opposite the cathedral is another beautifully restored colonial building, the **Casa del Conde de Casa Bayona**. Constructed in 1720 for Governor General Chacón, it now contains

Ornate knocker on the door of Havana's cathedral

BELOW:
Havana's 18th-century cathedral.

Tuning up in the Plaza de Armas, ready to entertain customers in El Patio restaurant.

the **Museo de Arte Colonial** ❺ (open Wed–Sun 9.30am–7pm; entrance charge), which is packed with a variety of artifacts from four centuries of colonial rule. Most of the rooms, centered on a blue-and-yellow colonial courtyard shaded by a huge palm tree, are open to the public, and are furnished to give an idea of the lifestyle of a wealthy Havana family in the 19th century.

There is one room dedicated to the city's famous *vitrales*, the stained-glass windows and panels that are a Cuban specialty, including the distinctive swing doors known as *mamparas*. Note also the superb wooden *Mudéjar* (Arab-inspired) ceilings upstairs, known as *alfarjes (see pages 166–7)*.

Just off the southwest corner of the square is the **Callejón de Chorro**, a tiny cul-de-sac where a wonderfully restored Art Nouveau building houses the **Taller Experimental de Gráfica** (Experimental Workshop of Graphic Arts). Here you will find good-quality silk screening and printing for sale, and you can often watch local artists at work in the studios.

Next around the square is the **Casa de Baños** (Bathhouse), rebuilt in 1909 over

a 19th-century original; the water was fed directly into the baths from the Zanja Real water ditch. A plaque marks the spot. Today, the building houses the Galería Manuel which sells excellent art, clothes and Tiffany-style lamps. Next door, taking up most of the west of the square, is **El Patio** restaurant. This beautiful colonial building was formerly the **Casa de los Marqueses de Aguas Claras**, the 16th-century former home of Governor General Gonzalo Pérez de Ángulo. Outside, a talented house salsa band plays sets for those sipping cool *mojitos* on the terrace or at tables and chairs set in the floodlit square. Inside, the palm-filled courtyard is the setting for a formal and somewhat overpriced restaurant, where you may be serenaded with music from the grand piano if there's no competition from the salsa band. Though the surroundings are elegant, the food is mediocre.

Art and artesanía

Farther along, next to the cathedral, in a pretty, pinkish building, is the **Centro Wilfredo Lam** ❻ (open Tues–Sat 10am–5pm; entrance charge), a cultural center

BELOW: restoration in Old Havana is an ongoing process.

Restoration

Visitors to Old Havana should bear in mind that the huge amount of restoration work going on in the city may mean that some of the sights they wish to see are closed for renovation – a process that may be short-lived or may take several years to complete. Similarly, some of the places under restoration at the time of writing may once again be open. The process is a fascinating one, as buildings that were under wraps and encased in scaffolding, billowing building dust, emerge in a pristine state. A splendid book about the restoration program, highly illustrated with photographs showing buildings before and after they were rescued from collapse, can be found in the book store in the Palacio del Segundo Cabo in the Plaza de Armas and the one in Calle Obispo, just off the same plaza.

dedicated to one of Cuba's most famous 20th-century artists (1902–82). It exhibits the works of artists from Latin America, Africa and Asia, and is one of the venues for the Havana Arts Biennial, which has been running since 1984.

To the east of the cathedral is **Calle Tacón**, a good place to park if you are driving, as official "minders" keep parked cars under watch – theft from vehicles is rife in this part of town. Car minders should be given a tip for their pains. This is also a place for the foot-sore to find a taxi. At Tacón 4, a lovely blue-and-white colonial building with a cool tiled patio is home to the D'Giovani Italian restaurant, with a small cake and pastry store tucked into the corner.

A bustling artisans' market, **La Feria de Artesanía** (open Wed–Sat 9am–6pm), is permanently located on Tacón, one block northeast from the Plaza de la Cat-edral, toward the bay. It *is* touristy, but there are many lovely things to be bought here at bargain prices. Check out the cro-chet work, Tiffany-style lamps and other objects made from stained glass, painted papier-mâché toys and wonderfully carved wooden statuettes. There is also

plenty of jewelry – everything from the bead *collares* of the Santería saints to beautiful pieces featuring small native pearls, coral, shells and hematite – but refrain from buying red and black coral and tortoiseshell since these are seriously endangered species. Contemporary artists sell their works here too.

Behind the cathedral

Between calles Empedrado and Chacón is the **Seminario de San Carlos y San Ambrosio**, a solid building of coral lime-stone that runs along the harbor front. Built by the Jesuits in 1721, it is still used as a seminary and the doors are rarely opened to the public; when they are, step into the deliciously peaceful green court-yard, perfect for quiet contemplation amid the noise and heat of the Old Town. Behind this building is a sturdy castle that looks very much like the Castillo de la Real Fuerza. Attempting to sightsee here would be a mistake, however, as it is a police station.

Just around the corner, at Calle Cuba 64, is the **Palacio de Artesanía**, another delightful colonial building, with bright blue shutters, which has an artisans' mar-

TIP

Even if the subject mat-ter of some of Havana's museums does not par-ticularly appeal to you, they are usually worth visiting for the buildings alone, mostly set around shady, flower-filled courtyards, some cooled by gently splash-ing fountains.

BELOW:
Restaurant El Patio in the Plaza de la Catedral.

*Many of Havana's
buses are school
vehicles, obtained
from other countries
when they went out of
service. You will
notice that many still
have the words
"Escoliers" or
"Schulbus" on the
front.*

ket on three floors set around a beautiful plant-filled courtyard. It's an obligatory stop on the bus party trail. Most of the stores sell postcards and – surprise, surprise – Che Guevara T-shirts.

Calle Empedrado

Leading off the Plaza de la Catedral, Calle Empedrado's first main site is the famous bar and restaurant, best-known for its Hemingway connections, **La Bodeguita del Medio** , which started life in 1942 as a grocery store. The story is that poets and writers from a nearby print shop used to drop by to check their galleys here, so the owner first offered a few drinks, then lunch. Gradually, more and more tables were set up, until the place became the epicentre of Havana's bohemian life, frequented by talented writers such as Alejo Carpentier and Nicolás Guillén. Cuba's national drink, the *mojito,* was perfected here.

Today, La Bodeguita is still informal and atmospheric, although the only Cuban bohemians here are likely to be working as waiters. Photos and memorabilia from famous diners clutter the

walls, which have been tattooed with so many signatures that they are almost black. A sign over the bottles in the front bar was supposedly written and signed by regular customer Ernest Hemingway: *"My Mojito in La Bodeguita, My Daiquirí in El Floridita."* Not perhaps, his most profound statement, but typically pithy, and a whole lot less banal than some other people's contributions to the great graffiti debate that plasters the bar's walls. According to Tom Miller in *Trading With the Enemy (see page 376)*, it was a hoax anyway, made up by Papa's drinking pal Fernando Campoamor to attract customers. If so, it has certainly worked: from morning to closing, the barman can't pour out *mojitos* fast enough. Errol Flynn was another frequent visitor, but nowadays the mix is mainly camera-toting tourists and *jineteros* (hustlers). The food is not great value but if you decide to eat here as well, pork is the specialty, served with *moros y cristianos* (rice and black beans), and plantains.

At Empedrado 215 is the beautiful **Museo Alejo Carpentier** (open daily 8.30am–4.30pm; free) dedicated to the Cuban writer (1904–80). The house, also called the Casa del Conde de la Reunión, is centered around a lovely courtyard and contains many interesting artifacts. All the objects and the house itself, built in 1820, were given to the state on Carpentier's death by his widow, along with the rights to his royalties, to be used for maintaining the museum.

One block south along Calle Cuba is **Calle O'Reilly**, named after a Spaniard with Irish ancestry, Alejandro O'Reilly, who was the first Spanish Governor after the island was handed back by the British in 1763. A plaque on the corner of Tacón reads "Cuba and Ireland: Two island peoples in the same seas of struggle and hope." This street is still awaiting restoration – it is fairly run-down and dirty for the most part, but there's the enjoyable Café O'Reilly (No. 205), with some fine little upstairs balconies. On the corner opposite, the café has an open-air barbecue area.

BELOW: lots of artists have studios in Calle Obispo and the surrounding streets.

Opulent Calle Obispo

Calle Obispo is one of the best-known and most pleasant streets in Old Havana: it was the first street in the old city to be pedestrianized and restored. It is also one of the busiest, and contains a number of places visitors will find useful *(see margin tip)*. One classic 1920 guidebook to Havana likens Obispo's open-air stores to caves, with windows full of "diamonds and Panama hats, tortoise shells, Canary Island embroidery and perfumery." Café windows were stacked with chocolate and almond cakes, wine stores offered Russian liqueurs in miniature glass bears.

Things have changed a lot since the 1920s, but though Havana is still far from being a consumer paradise, many expensive-looking stores have opened, all selling goods for *pesos convertibles* (known as CUCs), at prices well out of the reach of all but a handful of Cubans – even those who have access to convertible currency. They sell everything from designer clothes to bed linen and smart sunglasses, although there are still a few, but dwindling, Cuban peso stores with almost nothing for sale. You can also see, and buy, the work of local artists displayed in small upstairs rooms or the spaces they rent at the front of private houses.

The famous pharmacy, **Drogería Johnson** (on the corner of Aguiar), suffered a serious fire, and is now being refurbished, a process that looks set to take some time. No doubt it will eventually look as good as before, with polished mahogany benches and ceramic medicine jars. Another wonderful old pharmacy, **Sarrá**, on the corner of Compostela and Brasil (also called Teniente Rey), has been refurbished and returned to its original state, as part of the city restoration program.

Walking west up Obispo from the classical, columned **Banco Nacional de Cuba** on the corner of Calle Cuba, you find the beautifully refurbished Hotel Florida – an 18th-century mansion with 25 plush rooms *(see page 341)*. At the far (Capitolio) end is the Art Deco book store La Moderna Poesía.

Another Hemingway haunt

Heading back down Obispo toward Plaza de Armas, you pass the **Hotel Ambos Mundos ❽** (No. 153). For

TIP

On Obispo you will find an Infotur office (between Bernaza and Villegas) and an Infotur kiosk (corner of San Ignacio), as well as the Etecsa office (corner of Habana) with phone kiosks and Internet access; and a branch of Cadeca (between Aguiar and Habana) for exchange facilities and ATMS. For more details on all of these, see the A–Z section.

BELOW: there are lots of public phones, but making a call isn't always easy.

Stained-glass mediopuntos are one of the loveliest features of Havana architecture.

BELOW: musical instruments and old cars: a familiar image of Old Havana.

CUC$2 you can visit room 511 where Ernest Hemingway wrote *For Whom the Bell Tolls*: the room is tidily kept, with an antique typewriter (though not Ernesto's) and several copies of 1930s US magazines. The rooftop bar is a regular stop on the tour-group trail. The hotel has been extensively refurbished and has a wonderful piano bar in the lobby. Opposite the hotel hangs a bell marking the original site of the University of Havana, founded here in January 1728. This bell originally tolled to signal the beginning of students' classes.

South along Calle Oficios

The next, cobbled section of Obispo leads back to the Plaza de Armas. Turning south out of the plaza onto Calle Oficios, you reach almost immediately the **Museo Numismático** (open Tues–Sat 9.15am–4.45pm, Sun 9am–1pm; entrance charge) – one of Old Havana's least-visited museums, dedicated to coins. At Oficios 12 is the **Casa del Árabe** ➒ (open Tues–Sat 10am–3pm, Sun 10.30am–3pm; free). A surprising number of Cubans are of Middle Eastern origin and this beautiful colonial mansion celebrates

Arab culture. On the first floor is a small museum of costumes, tiles and carpets. Upstairs is a beautiful, tiled fountain, where worshipers wash before attending prayers in the adjoining one-room mosque. A knowledgeable and friendly curator will unlock the upstairs rooms and take you in. His little tour is given free, but a donation is much appreciated. Next door is a restaurant, Al Medina, in which you can eat *tabbouleh* and *houmous* and other eastern dishes in a pretty courtyard (*see page 163*).

Across the street is the **Museo de los Autos** ➓ (Car Museum; open daily 9am–7pm; entrance charge) – although just about any street in Havana could claim this title. Here resides a fabulous collection of venerable roadsters and limos, including vehicles in which revolutionary young bloods like Camilo Cienfuegos and Celia Sánchez would tour around Havana on affairs of state.

Down the little Calle Justiz alongside is a place for dance enthusiasts: the **Caserón del Tango**, dedicated to the promotion of this Argentinian art form, which is a world apart from some of the more spontaneous, lively Cuban dances.

On the corner of Oficios and Obrapía is the **Hostal Valencia**, the first colonial home in Old Havana to be converted into a hotel. Its rooms are grouped around a vine-draped courtyard with a pleasant bar and a restaurant. While a lovely place to stay, the hotel is regularly invaded by sightseers during the day.

Around Obrapía

Turn right into Calle Obrapía and you pass the **Casa de Oswaldo Guayasamín** (open Tues–Sat 9am–2.30pm, Sun 9am– 1pm; free), the house of one of Latin America's foremost 20th-century artists. Though Ecuadorean by nationality, Guayasamín (1919–99) always had a close affinity with Cuba, and belonged to the left-leaning artistic community that found inspiration here. There are a few original paintings in the house, which mainly stages temporary exhibitions. A portrait of Guayasamín's friend, Fidel Castro, can be seen in the Fundación La Naturaleza y el Hombre in Miramar *(see page 185).*

Farther along Obrapía is the **Casa de Africa** ⓫ (open Tues–Sat 2.30–6.30pm, Sun 9am–1pm; entrance charge) with an impressive display of African artifacts, many of them donated by the city's African embassies. The third floor is dedicated to the Afro-Cuban religions of Santería, Abakuá and Palo Monte *(see pages 104–5).*

Opposite, at No.158, is the delightful lemon-yellow **Casa de la Obra Pía** ⓬ (open Tues–Sat 10.30am–4.30pm, Sun 9am–1pm; donation), once the home of the Calvo de la Puerta family. The *obra pía* (pious act) commemorates Martín Calvo de la Puerta's action in providing dowries for five orphan girls every year. The imposing doorway leads into a creeper-strewn courtyard and one of Old Havana's finest colonial mansions. Built in 1665 and enlarged in the 1700s, the building's best rooms are upstairs. Highlights include the rare *cenefas* – painted floral borders – on the staircase, and the elegant, open-sided dining room. On the roof are the small rooms where the family's slaves were housed. A room on the first floor is dedicated to Alejo Carpentier, housing some of his photographs and personal effects, and his car, a Volkswagen Beetle.

A waterfront square

Walking in the rest of the Old City can be pleasant in any direction. Returning to the Hostal Valencia and walking south along Oficios brings you to another historic square, the **Plaza de San Francisco**. At its center is the Fuente de los Leones (Lion Fountain), built in 1836, and on one side the immense and refurbished business center in a former commodities market, the **Lonja del Comercio**. The main landmark here, however, is the **Convento de San Francisco de Asís** ⓭ (open daily 8.30am– 6pm; entrance charge).

First built in 1608 and rebuilt in 1737, San Francisco has a 40-meter (130-ft) bell tower that is one of the tallest on the continent and was once Havana's best lookout for pirates. The building was taken over by the British in 1762–63 and, as it had been used for Protestant services, Catholic *habaneros* would never again worship in it. Since the 1840s, it

TIP

The old kitchen of the Casa de la Obra Pía is temporarily being used as a classroom, while a local school is being refurbished. Museums throughout the city are encouraged to offer rooms for teaching purposes, to help compensate for a shortage of classrooms.

BELOW: the beautiful Casa de la Obra Pía.

TIP

Running from the north-ern end of Plaza de San Francisco is Calle Baratillo where there is a sculpture garden founded in memory of Diana, Princess of Wales.

has been a customs office, a post office and a warehouse. Its two cloisters house a **Museo de Arte Religioso** (Museum of Religious Art). One of the strangest exhibits is the pickled remains of Teodoro, a Franciscan monk, in jars set into the left side of the church. The beautiful cloisters are perhaps more interesting than the items on display. The convent is now a venue for classical recitals, often held in the early evening.

If you continue a short way south along the waterfront you will reach the **Museo de Ron ⓮** (open Mon–Fri 10am–5pm, Sat 10am–4pm, Sun 10am–1pm; guided tours; entrance charge), on the corner of San Pedro and Sol. The tour takes you through the whole process of rum production and ends with sampling and an opportunity to buy. The adjoining Havana Club bar is wood paneled and appealing, and sometimes has live music.

Calle Mercaderes

BELOW RIGHT: El Caballero de Paris – a statue with a strange history.

Stretching away from Plaza de San Francisco on all sides are newly restored cobbled roads and freshly painted mansions, many of them now cafés, stores or art galleries. Walking west along Calle

Brasil (Teniente Rey) where you can see excavated parts of the old watercourse, the Zanja Real, you reach the Plaza Vieja, and off to the right runs the traffic-free **Calle Mercaderes ⓯**, one of the prettiest and best-restored streets in the old city. Among its pleasures are two extremely popular restaurants – the Café Taberna, which has great *son* music, and El Mesón de la Flota, which hosts flamenco shows *(see page 164)*.

Mercaderes also houses an eclectic clutch of small museums and atmospheric stores. There's the **Museo de Chocolate** – really a café with displays related to chocolate making and consumption, which serves cups of delicious, thick, pure chocolate. Lining up in temperatures of 35°C (95°F) to drink cups of hot chocolate in an air-conditioned interior may seem odd, but it's worth it.

The Cuban-Mexican Society for Cultural Relations is housed in the **Casa de Benito Juárez**, which has a display of artifacts and costumes from different parts of Mexico.

At No. 117, you'll find one of the many elegant stores springing up in Old

El Caballero de Paris

O utside the Convento de San Francisco is a statue of a man nick-named El Caballero de Paris (The Gentleman of Paris). There are many stories attached to this figure, but the most commonly accepted is that he was a man who became insane while in prison in the 1920s, falsely accused of theft. (In other versions he was incarcerated simply because he *was* insane – something that used to happen under General Machado's regime.) On his release he wandered the streets of Havana, wearing a flowing cloak even in the hottest weather, never begging even when destitute, and distributing flowers and feathers to passers-by. He became a much-loved figure in the city, which erected this monument in his memory. You will often see people stroking the statue's prominent beard, which is said to bring good luck. The beard has been rubbed to a shiny gold, as has one of the elegant fingers on his left hand.

There are also a number of explanations given for his unusual name: while it is agreed that he did not come from Paris, theories range from one that his French wife-to-be died in a shipwreck while on her way from France to Cuba, to the more mundane explanation that he had worked in a Havana restaurant called the Paris.

El Caballero died in a psychiatric hospital in 1985, at the age of 86, and is buried within the church.

Havana – the **Tienda de Los Naveg-antes**, beautifully fitted out in polished wood, which sells maps and navigation charts, both old and new. The **Casa del Tabaco** (open Tues–Sat 10am–5pm) is a fascinating little museum, well worth a quick visit. Many of the exhibits were donated by the world's most famous ex-smoker, Fidel Castro himself. Notice the cigar box in the shape of the house where Castro was born. You can also buy cigars fresh from a large humidor. Then there is the **Maqueta de la Habana Vieja** – a scale model of the old city; a little garden with a statue of Simón Bolívar, and the **Casa de Simón Bolívar**, funded by the Venezuelan Government, where music is played in a blue-and-white courtyard.

Plaza Vieja

Back now to **Plaza Vieja** ⑯ (Old Plaza), built in the 1500s to create a space for bullfights and fiestas, and once one of Old Havana's principal squares. A famous fountain with four dolphins once stood here, but it fell victim to 1930s "modernization." For decades an underground parking lot ruined any chance the

square had of being picturesque, while the surrounding buildings crumbled. But this has all changed and, except for one building, renovations are now complete. The plaza is again one of the most beautiful in Havana, and a place where children are brought to play ball games.

On the northeastern corner, on the roof of a yellow-and-white wedding cake of a building, is the **Cámera Obscura** (open Tues–Sat 9am–5.30pm, Sun 9am–1pm; entrance charge). A lift takes you to the eighth floor, where the flat roof offers amazing views over the city, and the camera obscura hones in on details of surrounding buildings as well as the general vista.

To the south of the square is the **Casa de los Condes de Jaruco**, home to the Fondo Cubano de Bienes Culturales (Cuban Fund for Cultural Products). This fine 18th-century colonial house has various galleries of contemporary art and glass work, and some rare murals upstairs. Its trio of *mediopuntos* are among the best examples of stained-glass windows in Havana. The building also houses the **Galería Plaza Vieja**, which specializes in Afro-Cuban works.

The broad expanse of the Plaza Vieja has become a playground for children.

BELOW:
the Plaza Vieja has been returned to its former glory.

A smart new store in the Plaza Vieja, catering to the tourist market.

On the southwestern corner of the square is a restaurant-bar, the **Cervecería Taberna de la Muralla**, with its own organic microbrewery. On the western side, at San Ignacio 352, in the colonial Casa de las Hermanas Cárdenas, is the **Centro de Desarrollo de las Artes Visuales** (open Tues–Sat 10am–5pm; entrance charge), which focuses on contemporary works by Cuban and other Latin American artists. On the southeastern corner of the plaza, the amazing Art Nouveau **Hotel Palacio Viena**, built in 1906, was for a long time a *solar* – a residential hotel where many families live cheek by jowl – but is currently undergoing much-needed restoration.

Just to the northeast of the plaza (at Calle Cuba 460) is the **Museo Histórico de las Ciencias Carlos J. Finlay** ⓱ (open Mon–Fri 9–11.30am, 1.30–5pm, Sat 9am–3pm; entrance charge), a museum dedicated to the history of science in Cuba, named after the doctor who discovered the vector for yellow fever, once a massive killer, but something that has now been eradicated. The museum includes an elegant neoclassical lecture theater (where Einstein once

gave a lecture) and an atmospheric 19th-century pharmacy.

Heading south down San Ignacio and turning right on Santa Clara you come to the **Convento de Santa Clara** ⓲ (open Mon–Fri 9am–5pm; entrance charge), an enormous 18th-century former convent that was renowned as a refuge for dowerless girls. You can visit the vast, tree-filled main courtyard, the Clarisa nuns' cells, and the lovely cloisters. The convent now houses a conservation institute where you can see all the restoration techniques being utilized in the renovation of Old Havana – including carpentry, the restoration of old tiles, and the making of new ones. All the works in the old town have been undertaken using, wherever possible, the same materials and techniques as the original craftsmen. There are also inexpensive accommodations here, mainly designed for visiting students.

A duet of churches

South of here, on Calle Acosta, is the delightful **Iglesia Parroquial del Espíritu Santo** ⓳ (open daily 8am–noon, 3–5pm), one of Havana's oldest churches. Built in the 1670s as a religious retreat for "free negroes," this fully renovated gem displays Moorish influence in its facade and the cedar ceiling, and features catacombs whose roofs are supported by tree trunks. The chapel vault has a mural (sadly almost erased by the passage of time) depicting the Dance of Death.

A little farther down Calle Cuba you will reach the lavish **Iglesia de la Merced** ⓴ (open daily 8am–noon, 3–5pm), dating from 1746. This is one of Havana's most famous churches as it is dedicated to Santa Mercedes, who becomes Obatalá in the Santería faith. On September 24, hundreds of worshipers – often wearing white or carrying white flowers (white is Obatalá's color) – congregate here to pay tribute. And at any time of the year, you may see white-clad Santería devotees worshiping here. Note the flower sellers all around, for flowers are a common gift of thanks for

requests granted by the saints. The church itself is dark and ornate with wonderful trompe l'oeil frescos and a peaceful, leafy cloister.

Along the waterside

The atmosphere changes as you hit the busier streets on the fringes of Old Havana. This is not an area that attracts many visitors, but there are a few sights worth seeing if you have time to spare.

By the harbor, where Calle San Ignacio meets the dock road (here called Desamparado), is a pretty little former church, now beautifully renovated, the **Antigua Iglesia de San Francisco de Paula** (open Mon–Sat 9am–5pm, Sun 9am–1pm; entrance charge). It has an interesting collection of modern art with a Christian theme and some fine stained glass. A variety of classical concerts are held here in the evening.

Farther along the waterfront you come to some interesting remnants of the old city walls, the **Cortina de La Habana**. Slaves worked for 23 years to build these walls, which were 1.5 meters (5 ft) thick and more than 10 meters (30 ft) tall. The first walls were begun in 1674, but were altered and expanded up until the late 18th century. They ringed the old city until 1863, when they were torn down to allow for expansion.

Nearby stands a stark, dramatic monument to the Belgian ship *La Coubre*. Carrying armaments for the Cuban Army, it blew up on March 4, 1960, killing 72 sailors and dock workers: was it an accident or – as the Castro government has always maintained – the work of the CIA?

Three blocks north up Avenida de Bélgica (Egido) at No. 314 Leonor Pérez (confusingly also called Leonor Paula), is the house where Cuba's most revered figure was born. The **Casa Natal de José Martí** ㉑ (open Tues–Sat 9am–5pm; entrance charge) is a small, simple house, painted yellow and blue in typical Havana style. Martí was born here in 1853 and lived here until he was five years old. The house contains letters, first editions, manuscripts, photos, even locks of his hair. There is sometimes a line to get in as the house is a popular place for school visits. It is worth seeing simply because Martí is such an iconic figure *(see page 48)*.

Serving coffee in the Café de Paris.

BELOW: Havana girls on their way home from school.

The Capitolio, modeled on the Capitol building in Washington DC.

BELOW: shiny old cars wait to take tourists on trips round the town.

Around the corner is the Moorish-Victorian **Estación Central de Ferro-carril** (central train station) – unmissable with its soaring twin towers.

Capital projects

Officially, the sights that follow belong in Central Havana, but they are so closely integrated with Habana Vieja that we have included them in this chapter.

From the station, follow Avenida de Bélgica northward. This is a broad, busy street with a number of CUC stores that sell soap, shampoo and the like to local people who have access to *convertibles*. It follows the line of the old city walls, and leads you north (past a small farmers' market – an *agropecuario*) to the enormous, grandiose **Capitolio ㉒** (open daily 8.30am–8pm; entrance charge), which dominates the skyline all around.

Built in the 1920s as the new presidential and governmental palace, it closely resembles the design of the Capitol in Washington DC, continuing the process of Americanization begun in 1902 when the United States effectively took over from Spain as Cuba's colonial master. Before the revolution it was the home of the National Congress, but it now houses the Cuban Academy of Sciences. Guided tours run through its proud interior into the former presidential offices and halls of congress, but you can also go round on your own.

The huge bronze doors and marble floor of the domed entrance hall are impressive, as are the broad staircases, but it's a rather soulless place. There are some interesting photographs on the walls of the phases of its construction. At the entrance and exit are small galleries and stores tempting you to buy carved wooden figures, and paintings done with differently colored sawdust. There is also a bar/café, a lovely place to sit and watch the world, but at the time of writing it was closed for renovation.

Next door to the Capitolio is the flamboyant **Gran Teatro ㉓**, completed in 1837, and sometimes called El Teatro García Lorca. It contains several auditoria – the gold auditorium is grand, if surprisingly small inside, with plush red seats and a bewitching painted ceiling. The theater building also houses cultural institutions, including the Centro Gallego for descendants of Galician immigrants,

Sightseeing in Style

Outside the Capitolio there are always a number of 1950s limousines – Buicks, Chevrolets, Packards, Chryslers. But unlike the many beat-up models you see traveling slowly and noisily around town or stopped with their hoods open while the driver works wonders with a screwdriver, these have shiny bodywork and gleaming hubcaps. They belong to Grancar, a state-owned company that specializes in taking visitors for tours around the city – or as far afield as they want to go.

Driving through Havana in one of these limos is a great experience, and not as expensive as you might think, as all rates are strictly controlled. You do, however, usually get a better deal if you ring the company office (tel: 07-577-338) rather than making an arrangement with a driver on the street.

one of several Spanish social clubs in the city (the Andalusian one in the Prado is currently under renovation). Ballet dancers and theater companies rehearse here, and tours are sometimes offered. There are still regular performances by the national ballet and opera companies (tel: 07-861-3096), usually at weekends. It is well worth getting a ticket if you can.

Parque Central

The Gran Teatro occupies one corner of the **Parque Central**, which, with its stately royal palms (many bearing tourist graffiti from the 1940s and 1950s), always seems to be buzzing with activity from early morning until midnight. In the center is a white marble statue of José Martí. The corner of the park nearest the Capitolio is called the Esquina Caliente or "Hot Corner" where men gather and debate (hotly), mainly about baseball.

Next door to the Gran Teatro is the splendid, neo-baroque facade of the **Hotel Inglaterra** ㉔, so named because it was popular with early travelers from England. The sidewalk outside its doorways, nicknamed "the Louvre Sidewalk," has been one of the busiest spots in Havana for generations. The covered café here is a great place for people-watching, but you will get plenty of hassle from the street.

This was a popular place for pro-independence conspirators to speak, and one such occasion in 1869 prompted Spanish soldiers to open fire. Not all Spaniards were so ruthless: an officer protesting the execution of eight Cuban students in 1871 broke his sword against the hotel door, and a plaque commemorates his bold, humanitarian gesture.

The Inglaterra was once one of the most opulent hotels in Havana, and the Arab-influenced dining room off the lobby is still impressive – unlike the food – although some say that the café serves the best ham and cheese sandwich in Havana. The rooftop bar holds a salsa cabaret (Wed–Mon; entrance charge), and there is Internet access to the left of the hotel lobby.

Artistic corner

Close to the park is the *Arte Universal* section of the **Museo Nacional de Bellas Artes** ㉕ (open Mon–Sat 10am–6pm, Sun 10am–2pm; entrance charge; com-

TIP

A statistic that your Capitolio tour guide will tell you is that the bronze statue symbolizing the republic in the entrance hall is 17 meters (56 ft) high, weighs nearly 50 tonnes, and is said to be the third largest indoor statue in the world.

BELOW: the elegant Hotel Inglaterra and the Parque Central.

Watching the world go by in one of the many streets that have not been renovated.

BELOW: white weddings are still as popular as ever.

bined ticket available for this and the Arte Cubano section, *see page 160*). Housed in the old Asturian cultural center on Calle San Rafael (en route to El Floridita), it contains Latin America's largest collection of antiquities, as well as works by Goya, Rubens, Velázquez, Turner, Gainsborough, and Canaletto.

On the east side of the park are the Cuban Supreme Court and a rather seedy shopping mall – in the process of restoration that never seems to end – and on the northeast corner the **Hotel Plaza**, with its grand, columned lobby. The café-bar on the first floor behind the lobby, with stained-glass skylights, parrots and plants, is a popular meeting place for foreign business people.

Behind the hotel is the Art Deco **Edificio Bacardí**, an extravagant confection topped with the statue of a giant bat. Formerly the headquarters of the Bacardí Rum Company, which was based in Cuba until the family fled the island in the early 1960s, the building, dating from 1929, is a strange mixture of Swedish granite, Cuban limestone, tiles and terracotta, resembling a giant three-dimensional mosaic.

Hemingway's bar

Two blocks south of the Edificio Bacardí is **El Floridita** ㉖, made famous as Ernest Hemingway's favorite haunt (it features in his novel *Islands in the Stream*). It was frequented by the Hollywood set who came to Havana in the 1950s – Errol Flynn, Frank Sinatra, Ava Gardner, Gary Cooper and Marlene Dietrich were all regulars. *Esquire* magazine in 1953 ranked it with the 21 Club in New York, the Ritz in Paris and Raffles in Singapore as one of the best bars in the world. It is claimed that the daiquirí cocktail was perfected here, though it was probably originally invented in Santiago province as an antimalarial potion for miners. Certainly it was at El Floridita that the drink became famous, and Hemingway even invented his own version, the "daiquirí special," which is still served.

Not much else is the same as in Hemingway's day, when it was an informal, old-fashioned place, with ceiling fans and a three-piece band. Like an ordinary *bodega* (wine cellar), it opened out onto the street (which made it convenient for Hemingway to throw people he'd beaten

Sealing Deals and Tying Knots

The Prado is important territory. The area between Colón and Refugio has become widely known as an unofficial property market. Cubans are not permitted to sell property – only to exchange it. "*Se permuta*" signs pinned to doors and balconies around the city mean the residents want to exchange their house either with another in a different area, or, more commonly, because family pressure means they want two small houses for one large one. These are more difficult to fix since almost everyone has one large house and wants two smaller ones. This means money as well as property changes hands, illegally, so people gather on the Prado to make deals. Sometimes the equivalent of thousands of dollars change hands, in a country where the average wage translates at around US$12 a month.

At Prado No. 306, on the corner of Calle Animas, is the **Palacio de Matrimonios** (Wedding Palace), where on Monday, Wednesday, Friday and Saturday you can see wedding parties in hired tuxedos and frothy white dresses make their grand entrances and exits. Take a look inside, too, at the gilded, chandeliered luxury of this former aristocrat's palace. The non-religious ceremony has a strong socialist feel – the man promises to help his wife with housework and childcare (though few Cuban men ever do).

up directly onto the sidewalk). Today it has been renovated and polished up into one of the most expensive restaurants in Cuba, with a life-size bronze statue of Hemingway near his favorite seat, on the far left of the original wooden bar. It still serves the best, if overpriced, daiquirís in town but, although friendly, the bar lacks the atmosphere of the Bodeguita del Medio *(see page 148)*, and it is, of course, a blatant tourist trap.

The faded glory of the Prado

Running north of the Parque Central is the **Prado** (officially known as the **Paseo de Martí**), the historic, popular promenade lined with trees and lion statues, that stretches all the way to the Malecón. Like the previous few sights, the Prado is officially part of Central Havana, but is generally considered to be part of Old Havana, and forms an easy landmark in the transition between the touristy Old Town and the real city of working *habaneros*. This boulevard, with its raised walkway set with colored marble and stone, has seen better days. Construction began in the late 1700s and continued until 1852, and its buildings were once home to Havana's richest, most aristocratic families. Some of them are extraordinarily beautiful – and extraordinarily dilapidated. Renovation work is proceeding, but slowly, and there is a great deal to do. Some of the renovated buildings house stores and restaurants, and there is one excellent *paladar*, Doña Blanquita, oozing with atmosphere.

The area began to decline in the early 20th century when the mansions of the rich were mostly turned into casinos and nightclubs. The upper levels became notorious brothels, adorned with skimpily dressed girls who would stand on the balconies to lure in custom. The practice did not entirely die with the Revolution, since nowadays the Prado attracts some of the worst pimps and *jineteras* (prostitutes) in Havana, along with the odd bag-snatcher.

However, they are outnumbered by ordinary people going about their daily business or simply taking a stroll. Fur-

thermore, some of the old buildings nearby have been turned into schools, and as they have no playgrounds, you will often see the children in their red and white uniforms having sports lessons or just playing on the Prado's raised walkway. On Saturday there is small art market where paintings and photographs by local artists can be bought.

Slightly farther along the boulevard stands the **Academia de Gimnástica**, where Cuba's budding young gymnasts and current stars train together. Strictly speaking, the building is not open to the public, but with a little gentle persuasion, you can sometimes get the caretaker to let you inside for a look at the stunning galleries upstairs.

Take a short detour off the Prado to the ornate **Hotel Mercure Sevilla**, which was a notorious Mafia hangout, and featured prominently in Graham Greene's *Our Man in Havana*: secret agent Hawthorne stayed in Room 501. Beautifully restored since the mid-1990s, the Sevilla has a wonderfully Spanish ambiance, with a cool lobby and a delightful blue-tiled patio café, complete with fountain. The best view in the area

A weekend walk down the shady center of the Prado.

BELOW:
the Prado is lined with pastel-colored buildings, some in need of attention.

The patio of the Museo de Bellas Artes.

BELOW: a Mariano Rodriguez painting in the *Arte Cubano* section of the Museo de Bellas Artes.

is to be had from the lavish ninth-floor restaurant: it is closed during the day, but the person on the door may be happy to let you in for a look.

The hotel has a pool, on the side backing onto the Prado, and will allow non-guests to use it, but charges CUC$20 per person for the privilege.

The national art collection

Between Agramonte (Zulueta) and Avenida de las Misiones are two of Havana's most important museums, presenting two very different aspects of Cuba. The first of them, in a modernist building is the excellent *Arte Cubano* section of the **Museo Nacional de Bellas Artes** ❷ (National Museum of Fine Arts; open Tues–Sat 10am–6pm, Sun 10am–2pm; entrance charge; combined ticket available for this and the Arte Universal section, *see pages 157–8*). The museum re-opened in 2001 after five years of extensive renovation. It contains the largest collection of works by Cuban artists in the country, and the excellent 20th-century section includes pieces by Wilfredo Lam, Carlos Enríquez, René Portocarrero, and Eduard Abela, well dis-

played in a series of interlinked air-conditioned galleries. It is generally considered the best museum in the city.

Museum of the Revolution

Directly opposite the Fine Arts Museum is the **Monumento Granma**, which is part of the **Museo de la Revolución** ❷ (open daily 10am–5pm; entrance charge), housed in deposed dictator Fulgencio Batista's former palace. The 18-meter (56-ft) yacht *Granma* was used by Fidel, Che and 80 other guerrillas to cross from Mexico to Cuba in 1956. The boat is painted brilliant white with green trim and set in a huge glass case as one of the Revolution's great icons. Around the yacht, in a fenced off and closely guarded area are other relics of the Revolution: a tractor converted into a tank by rural guerrillas; an old Pontiac with a double floor for smuggling arms and documents; and the bullet-riddled delivery van used for an attack on the Presidential Palace in 1957 in an unsuccessful attempt to assassinate Batista. March 13, the anniversary of the attack, in which 35 rebels and five palace guards were killed, is commemorated each year.

There are also airplanes that were used to repulse the CIA-backed Bay of Pigs invasion (the invading boats are decorated with a skull and crossbones), and a fragment of the U2 spy plane shot down over Cuba shortly before the Missile Crisis of 1962. The star-shaped monument to the Heroes of the New Fatherland, with an eternal flame, is just like the Kremlin's master model in Moscow. Every day at 3pm there is a changing of the guard ceremony here. You can see quite a lot from the street, but if you want a close-up look at any of the above, you must enter the Museum of the Revolution first.

War memorabilia

Permanently parked outside the front of the museum is an SAU 100 Stalin Tank, which Fidel Castro used during the battle at the Bay of Pigs. The Presidential Palace was worked in and lived in by all Cuba's presidents from its completion in 1913 until 1957, when Batista built the present Palacio in what is now the Plaza de la Revolución. The delicious white-and-gold interior was created by Tiffany's of New York. The memorabilia laid out

with quasi-religious reverence in these splendid rooms offer a vivid picture of the Revolution, and the earlier struggle for independence. Information panels about the exhibits all have English translations, and quite good ones, at that.

There are bloodstained uniforms from the failed attack on the Moncada Barracks in 1953, as well as the heavy black coat that Fidel wore during his trial, when he made his famous "History will absolve me..." speech. Photographs of a young, beardless Castro come as quite a surprise. Also here are a guitar that revolutionaries played in prison, a doll that was used to smuggle messages, and, strangely, old poker machines from the casinos of the 1950s.

Graphic black and white photographs show victims tortured by Batista's secret police alongside little-seen images of Fidel and his band in the Sierra Maestra. Giant, complicated, three-dimensional maps show the various guerrilla campaigns, while two somewhat disturbing life-sized dummies of Che and Camilo Cienfuegos bound through a model forest. There is a separate Che Guevara section that tells his own story, complete

TIP

You have to check your bags in when you go into the Museo de la Revolución but you are allowed to take a camera in with you and, unusually, you don't have to pay an extra charge for using it.

BELOW:
a model of Che Guevara in the Museo de la Revolución, and an improvised tank outside.

CONSTRUIDO POR LOS OBREROS DEL C. ANDREITA

George Bush Snr in the Rincón de los Cretinos.

BELOW: the imposing monument to Máximo Gómez, independence campaigner.

with exhibits including cuttings from his beard, his Bolivian body bag and his (over-) stuffed horse.

A small gift store on the way out sells Che T-shirts, posters, and postcards and a few books about the Revolution. Just before you get to the shop you pass **El Rincón de los Cretinos** (Cretins' Corner), devoted to three figures: Ronald Reagan (shown in life-sized caricature with a cowboy hat and six-shooters), George Bush Snr, and the deposed Fulgencio Batista. Inscriptions on the wall beside each figure thank them because their "cretinous" behavior has contributed to the continuing success of Cuba's Revolution.

The end of the road

Not far from the Presidential Palace, at the bottom of the Avenida de las Misiones, where it meets the Malecón, the **Museo Nacional de la Música** has an extensive collection of Cuban instruments and a store selling recordings, but is currently closed for renovation.

Set proudly and unmissably on an island in the middle of a swirl of traffic and parkland is the **Monumento de Máximo Gómez** ⓩ, an equestrian statue of Gómez who was one of the great campaigners for Cuban independence, although he actually came from the Dominican Republic. Nearby, people line up for the *ciclobus*, which takes cyclists through the tunnel under the bay to Habana del Este.

To the left of the Gómez statue, in the Parque de los Martires, is the **Memorial a los Estudiantes de Medicina** ⓚ, commemorating those shot by the Spanish in 1871 for allegedly desecrating the tomb of a Spanish journalist who had attacked the independence movement. Behind it, in a gorgeous, ornate *palacio*, is the Spanish Embassy.

On the waterfront opposite stands a small 16th-century fortress, the **Castillo de San Salvador de la Punta** ⓛ housing a museum of maritime archeology (closed for renovation at the time of writing). Like El Morro across the water, the fortress was designed by Italian engineer Juan Bautista Antonelli during the reign of Felipe II. In the 17th century, to further protect the harbor against pirate incursions, a heavy chain linked the two fortifications. ❏

RESTAURANTS, PALADARES, BARS & CAFÉS

Restaurants

Café del Oriente
Calle Oficios, 112,
Plaza de San Francisco
Tel: (07) 860-6686. Open
daily noon–midnight. **$$$**
This is an extremely formal restaurant, with a
resident pianist and a
full international menu.
The food is very good,
but there's not much
atmosphere. Tea, coffee
or cocktails at tables in
the square may be a
better bet.

El Floridita
Calle Obispo,
corner Monserrate
Tel: (07) 867-1300/1301.
Open daily noon–1am. **$$$**
Havana's most fabled
dining spot, and Hemingway's favorite for his
daiquirís (the best in
town, but not cheap),
is elegant but dark and
overpriced. You pay
for the name (and the
waiters' red jackets) as
well as for the food.
Main courses include
grilled lobster, shrimp
flambéed in rum, turtle
steaks and other exotica. If you just want to
check it out, you could
simply opt for a daiquirí
at the bar.

El Patio
Plaza de la Catedral
Tel: (07) 867-1034. Open
daily noon–11pm. **$$$**
Go for the fabulous location, in an old colonial
palace, rather than the

food. You can eat either
on the ground floor, surrounded by palms and
serenaded from the
grand piano, or upstairs
in the Parillada del Marqués. Reserve a table
overlooking the plaza.
International menu.

La Bodeguita del Medio
Calle Empedrado, 207,
off Plaza de la Catedral
Tel: (07) 867-1374. Open
daily noon–midnight. **$$$**
Bohemian atmosphere
with creole cooking in
this old Hemingway
haunt, but the quality of
the food and service
suffers due to the constant flow of tourists.
Walls downstairs are
decorated with the autographs of celebrities
who have eaten here
over the years, but the
roof terrace is a more
congenial place to sit.
Reservations advised.

La Mina
Plaza de Armas
Tel: (07) 862-0216. Open
daily noon–midnight. **$$$**
Cuban *criolla* cooking in
a restaurant with a
beautiful courtyard and
a broad terrace right on
the Plaza de Armas.
Very popular with
tourists.

The Roof Garden
Hotel Sevilla, Calle
Trocadero, 55
Tel: (07) 860-8560. Open
daily 7–10.30pm. **$$$**
The food is good – much

better since the recent
takeover and renovation
of the hotel – but the
views are the reason
many people come here
for dinner. Panoramic
vistas of Old Havana on
three sides. Wonderful,
elegant, candlelit
ambiance.

Vuelta Abajo
Hotel Conde de Villanueva,
Calle Mercaderes, 202,
between Lamparilla and
Amargura.
Tel: (07) 862-9293. Open
daily L & D. **$$$**
Named after a tobacco
plantation in Pinar del
Río, this cool, stonearched restaurant specializes in old *criolla*
favorites, such as
pescado trapiche – fish
with ginger, and *fonguito*

– streamed, seasoned
plantain.

Al Medina
Casa de Los Arabes,
Calle Oficios, 12.
Tel: (07) 867-1041. Open
daily noon–11pm. **$$**
Tasty Arabic dishes,
based on lamb and
couscous in the courtyard of a lovely old colonial mansion attached
to the Casa del Arabe.
The menu is padded out
by Cuban dishes.

PRICE CATEGORIES

Price categories are for a
three-course meal for one
with a beer, or *mojito*.
Wine puts the price up:
$ = under $25
$$ = $25–35
$$$ = over $35

Bar Cabaña

Calle Cuba, 12, corner of Peña Pobre (by the seafront) Tel: (07) 860-5670. Open daily 10am–midnight. **$$** Good *criolla* and international food served in an unpretentious setting.

Café el Mercurio

Calle Oficios, corner of Plaza de San Francisco. Tel: (07) 860-6118. Open daily 9am–midnight. **$$** Good for breakfasts and for light meals throughout the day – salads, omelets, etc. Particularly recommended are the ice creams and cocktails, especially the excellent *mojitos*.

Café Taberna

Calle Mercaderes, 531, corner of Brasil (Teniente Rey). Tel: (07) 861-1637. Open daily 11am–midnight. **$$** Reasonably good Cuban food in cheerful, atmospheric surroundings, done out in 1950s style. There's a tremendous band of elderly *son* and mambo specialists to serenade you while you eat. And there's dancing later on.

Don Giovanni

Calle Tacón, 4, between Empedrado and O'Reilly. Tel: (07) 867-1036. Open daily 10am–midnight. **$$** Don Giovanni has pulled up its socks after a low period and the food has returned to the standards of its early years. They serve pizzas, including one with lobster, mushrooms and olives.

Jardín del Eden

Hotel Raquel, Calle Amargura, corner of San Ignacio

Tel: (07) 860-8280. Open daily L & D. **$$** Havana's only kosher restaurant. Delicious food (no pork or seafood, of course) in the Hotel Raquel's elegant restaurant, with a chandelier and attractive stained-glass screens. Surprisingly reasonable prices.

La Dominica

Calle O'Reilly, corner of Mercaderes. Tel: (07) 860-2918. Open daily noon–midnight. **$$** You can sit inside or out at this lovely courtyard restaurant. Excellent pizzas and pasta and other Italian-influenced dishes. Good band.

La Paella

Hostal Valencia, Calle Oficios, 53. Tel: (07) 867-1037. Open daily noon–11pm. **$$** Authentic, filling and tasty Spanish food in a breezy, delightfully old-fashioned room. Spanish wines. Paella is, of course, a specialty, but there are lots of other choices.

La Zaragozana

Avenida de Bélgica and Obispo. Tel: (07) 867-1040. Open daily 10am–midnight. **$$** Filling *criolla* and Spanish dishes, including thick bean soups, fish and paella, but the quality is rather inconsistent. The restaurant tends to be livelier at lunch time than in the evening.

El Castillo de Farnés

Avenida de Bélgica (Monserrate), 361, corner of Obrapía.

tel: (07) 867-1030. Restaurant open daily noon–midnight; bar daily 24 hours. **$–$$** Pictures of Fidel and Raúl adorn the bar – this is supposed to have been a favorite haunt. There are authentic Spanish dishes on the menu. The chickpeas *(garbanzos)* with ham are a specialty and are worth trying.

El Mesón de la Flota

Calle Mercaderes, between Amargura and Brasil (Teniente Rey). Tel: (07) 863-3838. Restaurant open daily 11am–11pm; bar daily 24 hours. **$–$$** A restaurant-bar in Old Havana serving authentic and delicious tapas and full Spanish-influenced meals. There are good Spanish wines, beer on tap, and excellent service. Flamenco performances daily. All very refreshing. There are a few rooms to rent above the restaurant.

Hanoi

Calle Brasil (Teniente Rey) corner of Bernaza. Tel: (07) 867-1029. Open daily noon–midnight. **$** Despite the name, the food is more *criolla* than Vietnamese. Lots of pork, shrimp and rice. Cheap cocktails and relaxed atmosphere.

La Lluvia de Oro

Calle Obispo 316, corner of Habana. Tel: (07) 862-9870. Open daily 8am–early hours. **$** The name means Golden Rain. This is a good place for a snack and a drink in a very local Cuban atmosphere

with live (and loud) music.

La Torre de Marfil

Mercaderes 121, between Obispo and Obrapía. Tel: (07) 867-1038. Open daily noon–midnight. **$** Tasty Chinese food in pleasant surroundings.

Los Nardos

Paseo de Martí (Prado), 565, between Teniente Rey and Dragones Tel: (07) 863-2985. Open daily noon–midnight. **$** This is a quirky and popular place, with a busy, buzzing atmosphere. No reservations taken, so you have to wait in a well-regulated line outside till a table is free. Decorated with soccer memorabilia and hunting trophies. Good wine list. Huge portions, of pork, lamb, chicken, fish, shrimp, and lobster with all the trimmings. Service is efficient and friendly.

Paladares

Doña Blanquita

Paseo de Martí (Prado), 158, first floor, between Colón and Refugio Tel: (07) 867-4958. Open daily noon–midnight. **$** One of Havana's best-known *paladares*. Well-cooked food – the usual Cuban dishes of pork, chicken, rice and beans, and excellent *malanga con mojo* (a *yuca*-like vegetable with garlic sauce). It's pink, kitsch and great fun, with plastic flowers and candles on the tables. Try for a table on the sweet little balcony overlooking the Prado.

La Julia

Calle O'Reilly, 506, between Bernaza and Villegas. Tel: (07) 862-7438. Open daily noon–11pm. **$**

One of the real old-style *paladares* where you feel as if you are eating in someone's home – although the dining room opens out onto the street. Excellent *comida criolla* – some of the best *frijoles* (fried beans) you will find – together with good prices and good service from members of a friendly family make this a recommended choice.

La Moneda Cubana

Calle San Ignacio, 77, between O'Reilly and Empedrado. Tel: (07) 867-3852. Open daily noon–late. **$**

This very small *paladar* has four set-price menus on offer. The usual *criolla* dishes, but well-cooked. Fish and omelets make an appearance. Lots of pesos and bank notes from all over the world are glued to the walls. Despite the restaurant's name, you pay in CUCS, not *moneda nacional*.

Bars and Cafés

Bar Monserrate, (Avenida de Bélgica (Monserrate), 401, corner of Obrapía). Good, reasonably priced cocktails in a bar with a laid-back, local atmosphere, next door to the far more swish and expensive El Floridita.

Casa de las Infusiones (Calle Mercaderes, between Obispo and Obrapía). An attractive courtyard bar where you can get a variety of infusions (herbal teas), along with soft drink and cocktails – but no beer. Also serves snacks and light meals.

Bosque Bologna (Calle Obispo, 424). A cheerful place on this busy street, with green-painted trellises, and live music day and night.

Café O'Reilly (Calle O'Reilly, 203). An atmospheric little bar with a spiral staircase leading to a small upper room where you can sit on the tiny balcony and drink one of the best cups of coffee in Havana. Good fruit juices, too. Tapas and other snacks are available, and on the adjacent corner the bar has an open-air barbecue area with a few tables and chairs.

Café de Paris (Calle San Ignacio, 202, corner of Obispo). Live music and reasonable street-style pizza, but fried chicken and fries always seems to be the most popular dish.

Café la Logia (Capitolio, Paseo de Martí). The café is currently closed for renovation, but when it re-opens, pop in to enjoy excellent fresh fruit juices, or a beer and a sandwich along with wonderful views from a seat on the broad terrace.

Dos Hermanos (Alameda de Paula, south of Plaza de San Francisco). For many years, the Two Brothers was a rough sailors' and dockworkers' bar serving cheap shots of *aguardiente* and coffee. Now refurbished to appeal to tourists, it retains some of its atmosphere. Serves tapas-style snacks with the drinks.

Hotel Inglaterra (Parque Central). The terrace bar is a great place for people-watching. Among other things there are good fresh fruit juices and home-made lemonade, and what some say are the best ham and cheese sandwiches in Havana (and there's Internet access in the lobby).There is always a group of musicians playing, and as often as not it's *Guantanamera*.

Hotel Ambos Mundos (Calle Obispo, 153). It's fun to take the ornate old elevator to the rooftop bar for a drink with a wonderful view over the old city. The piano bar on the ground floor is pleasant, too, in a hushed and intimate kind of way.

RIGHT: the courtyard of Don Giovanni.

CUBA'S COLONIAL ARCHITECTURE

Colonial architecture in Havana may not be as decorative as that found in other Spanish colonies such as Peru, but it has a simple, solid elegance

ABOVE: Cuban baroque: Havana's Palacio de los Capitanes Generales is an example of the use of baroque in secular buildings. It marks the peak of baroque refinement, but still uses *Mudéjar* features, as in the courtyard.

Old Havana is, without doubt, the finest showcase of colonial architecture in Cuba. Its features are seen all over the island, however. Other cities particularly worth visiting for their architecture are Camagüey, Gibara, Remedios, Santiago, and, especially, Trinidad.

The strongest influence on Cuban colonial architecture came, of course, from Spain. In particular from Andalusia, where the so-called *Mudéjar* style – a fusion of Christian and Arabic architectural traditions that developed in medieval Spain – predominated at the time of the colonization of Cuba. Many of the early buildings in Havana were built by *Mudéjar* craftsmen, who came by ship from Seville and Cádiz and adapted the styles they knew to suit the conditions in the Caribbean: primarily the hot climate and the relative paucity of materials. The talent of these craftsmen lay above all in carpentry. Woods such as mahogany and cedar were abundant in Cuba at that time, and were used to construct ceilings, doors, columns and railings, as well as furniture.

The other predominant style is baroque, which reached Havana in the late 18th century, and was primarily used in the building and decoration of churches. This more flamboyant, sophisticated architecture proved to be a perfect medium for expressing the new-found confidence of a nation enjoying its first real economic boom – though the wealth was concentrated in the hands of a few. While undoubtedly grander than anything that had gone before, fusion with the existing *Mudéjar* styles kept Cuban baroque relatively simple.

LEFT: grilled windows: grilles *(rejas)* are a common architectural feature. Originally made of wood, it became popular in the 1800s to fashion them from wrought iron.

BELOW RIGHT: the square: this image of Havana's Plaza Vieja shows a typical square in the colonial period. The arcades at ground level were a practical feature that enabled people to walk in the shade.

ABOVE: *Mudéjar* ceilings: the Museo de Arte Colonial in Old Havana has some of Cuba's finest *alfarjes* – the wooden ceilings built by Spanish carpenters, who would often adorn them with Islamic, geometric designs.

HOW TO BE COOL IN CUBA

The most striking features of Cuban colonial design are solutions to the problem of how to keep cool – namely, by creating the maximum amount of shade and ventilation.

● Courtyards: many houses were laid out around a courtyard, with arcades enabling residents to move from room to room in the shade.

● Doors: these were very tall and had small windows or *postigos* that could be opened to provide light and ventilation without having to disturb the residents' privacy by opening the whole door.

● Ceilings: vaulted ceilings *(alfarjes)* were not easy to build but were higher than flat ones and kept rooms cooler.

● *Mamparas*: these swing doors, with decorative glass panels and fancy woodwork *(above right)*, were popular in the 1800s and allowed air to circulate between rooms.

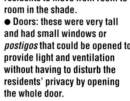

BELOW: floral frescos: murals, called *cenefas*, usually with floral motifs, were frequently used to decorate the lower half of interior walls. The delicate examples in the lovely Casa de la Obra Pía *(see page 151)*, and shown below, are among the few to survive.

ABOVE: restrained baroque: the swirls on the facade of Havana's cathedral are typical of Cuban baroque. Because the local limestone was hard to work with, the style was less elaborate than that found in Europe, and some believe that to be a good thing, more in keeping with the Caribbean surroundings.

LEFT: glass as art: panels of brightly colored glass (known as *lucetas*, *vitrales* or *medio puntos*) over doors or windows were decorative features, but were also functional, as they filtered the harsh sunlight. Numerous examples survive in Havana and other Cuban cities.

CENTRO HABANA AND VEDADO

Centro Havana is a run-down but colorful place with crumbling tenements and bustling markets, while Vedado's broad streets are quieter, more elegant, and the centerpiece is the stark, impressive Plaza de la Revolución

Havana
CUBA

Bounded by the giant avenues of the Malecón to the north, Prado to the east, and Calzada de Infanta to the west, **Centro Habana** is a bustling, overcrowded district seething with life and noise. The area dates mostly from the 19th century, when Havana, having burst out from its city walls, began to spread across the swampy lands and rocky pastures to its west. The restoration program has spread to Centro, most notably to the Malecón, Monte, Cayo Huseo and parts of Chinatown. But most of this district is as it has been for decades: salt-pitted and tumbledown, narrow streets lined with tall crumbling mansions divided between a dozen families into *ciudadelas* (little cities).

But look beyond the crumbling facades and you will see that many of these houses are true palaces, even if their glory has faded: pizzerias lit by priceless chandeliers; a narrow passage-way lined with lofty marble columns; a pink marble bathroom with gold fittings, but nevertheless waterless and sometimes shared by 30 families. The city may slowly be falling into ruin, but the inhabitants certainly don't let that interfere unduly with their lives.

Centro Habana is full of life. The street theater of everyday normality (Cuban-style) lights up each corner and offers visitors a different kind of experience – of life as it really is lived in the city. However, although there are points of genuine interest, Centro is not really a tourist destination.

Behind the Capitolio

Tucked just behind the Capitolio at Industria No. 502, on the corner of Dragones, is the **Fábrica de Tabacos Partagás ❶** (Partagás Cigar Factory; open Mon–Fri 9–11am, noon–2.30pm; regular 45-minute tours; entrance charge; no photos; store open Mon–Sat all day). The famously strong Partagás cigars have been rolled here since 1845 *(see pages 212–13)*. The factory has a cigar store attached, but prices are often higher than they are in hotel stores. Real cigar smokers should resist the temptation to

Main attractions

FÁBRICA DE TABACOS PARTAGÁS
MALECÓN
HOTEL NACIONAL
CALLEJÓN HAMEL
COPPELIA ICE CREAM PARK
PLAZA DE LA REVOLUCIÓN
CEMENTERIO DE COLÓN

LEFT: a golden glow on the Malecón.
BELOW: the Partagás Cigar Factory.

REAL FABRICA DE TABACOS
Partagás
FUNDADA EN 1845

There are still a number of old-style mail boxes to be found.

BELOW:
colorful washing on
a Malecón balcony.

buy from the *jineteros* (hustlers) gathered outside. Despite the stories they tell, most of their cigars are fakes and definitely not worth the high asking price. Immediately behind the factory at Amistad No. 407, the equally famous **H. Upmann** cigar factory also offers guided tours. Some of the best Montecristos are rolled here.

Flanking the southern side of the Capitolio is the **Parque de la Fraternidad**, a busy, pleasant park with the Friendship Tree at its heart. This ceiba tree was planted in the soil of 17 nations by the delegates of the 1928 Pan-American conference to cement friendship between the countries of the Americas. Also here are rows of old American cars in varying states of repair whose owners tout for business from passers-by. They're not supposed to pick up tourists, though some may do so at night, when they stand less chance of being seen and fined by the police. (For trips in " official" vintage American cars, *see box, page 156*.) On the west side is this area's main bus terminal, and you will see long lines for the buses and the clumsy-looking *camello* buses or "road-trains" that roar

out to all parts of the city – although these are gradually being phased out.

On the southwest corner of the park is the beautiful, 19th-century **Palacio de Aldama**, which houses an institute detailing the serious matter of the history of communism and socialism. The building has some unique painted ceilings, now somewhat spoiled by striplighting, but it is not open to the public on a routine basis.

The Queen's Avenue

The hectic **Avenida de la Reina** effectively forms the southern boundary to Centro Habana for most tourists. Somewhat confusingly, this street is also known as Avenida Simón Bolívar, and becomes Avenida Salvador Allende as it heads out toward Vedado. Two sites are worth noting among the multitude of stores and apartment blocks along its length. First, a magnificent Gothic church with lovely stained-glass windows, the **Iglesia del Sagrado Corazón de Jesús**; and a little farther on, the splendid **Casa de Cultura de Centro Habana**, which is always alive with musicians, dancers and other aspiring

artistes, who rent magnificent, decaying practice rooms for a pittance.

Running southwest from the end of Reina is Calle Máximo Gómez, better known as **Monte** (Hill). This area has been crumbling away for decades but is now in the process of renovation. The imposing 19th-century mansions were once the summer homes of the city's colonial aristocracy, as it was cooler here than in the rest of the city during Havana's steamy summers.

The street begins to the south of the Parque de la Fraternidad, at the bustling farmers' market of **Cuatro Caminos** – the largest market in the city, with separate sections for fruit and vegetables, meat, flowers and prepared foods. There is a *guarapera* selling freshly pressed sugar-cane juice for around a Cuban peso a glass. This entire area is good for peso street food, such as peanut *turrón* (nougat) candy bars, reasonably cheesy pizza, *refrescos*, and *granizados* – shaved ices flavored with syrup, for those with stronger stomachs. The area has some good *paladar* restaurants, too. There is an interesting herbalist, with strong links to Santería, opposite the market, selling medicinal herbs alongside votive jars, candles and the bead necklaces dedicated to the *orishas* or gods of the religion.

Chinatown

Easily reached by heading west along Dragones from the Partagás cigar factory is the **Barrio Chino** ❷ – Havana's once huge but now tiny Chinatown, centered around calles Cuchillo and San Nicolás. The first Chinese arrived in Cuba in the mid-19th century to build the country's railroads, but the community lost much of its homogeneity after the Revolution, and has to a large extent been integrated into wider Cuban society. Still, many people in the area have distinctly Asiatic features and, confusingly, almost everyone is known by the nickname "Chino."

This area used to be notorious as the center of Havana's red-light district. Times have changed, and the infamous **Shanghai Theater** – described in Graham Greene's *Our Man in Havana*, and

which once specialized in live sex acts and pornographic movies – has now re-opened as a nightclub specializing in karaoke. Castro and Hemingway were both regulars of the once-renowned Restaurante Pacífico, at the end of Calle Cuchillo on San Nicolás, but these days the food is not distinctively Chinese. Hemingway's son Gregory described a 1950s visit to the Pacífico with a five-piece Chinese orchestra on the second floor, a whorehouse on the third floor and, on the fourth floor, an opium den. On Calle Cuchillo, a small, not especially Chinese market is a hive of activity and does sell a few unusual things – fresh lychees and goose eggs for example – but watch out for pickpockets. There are also several places specializing in Chinese medicine.

The neo-Romanesque Santería church, **Iglesia de la Caridad** ❸ is to be found at the edge of Chinatown on calles Manrique and Salud. This glorious frescoed and golden church – its dark interior lighted by candles and full of incense, flowers and choral music – is undergoing lengthy restoration, so you won't yet be able to appreciate its beauty. Just inside

Chinatown has lost much of its atmosphere, but you can still find street stands selling Chinese snacks.

BELOW:
fresh produce at a farmers' market.

TIP

Take Calle Italia down from Chinatown to the Malecón. This noisy commercial street, lined with crumbling tenements, has lots of *agropecuarios* (produce markets) and CUC stores. It is also home to the Casa de la Música. Set on the first floor of a huge apartment block, it looks unprepossessing but is known for its great music.

BELOW:
waves batter
the Malecón.

the door is a shrine to the eight saints who are the most powerful *orishas* of the Santería faith.

The Malecón

The area of Centro Havana that most tourists visit is to the north. Emerging from the Castillo de la Punta at the end of the Prado, the 5-km (3-mile) **Malecón** seafront stretch is Havana's main artery, running straight through to Vedado. Hitchhikers, runners, young couples, families out for a stroll, wheeler-dealers, prostitutes, elderly women walking the dog – such is the cross section of city life you will see here. Salsa bands rehearse in the buildings above, while children splash in the crashing (and heavily polluted) surf, or play makeshift games of baseball, fearless of the traffic as they run out to collect their balls, and musicians sit on the sea wall and play, hoping for a few pesos from tourists who show an interest. On weekend nights the Malecón turns into one huge party, when hundreds gather to dance and drink rum.

The first ornate building you see is the **Centro de Cultura Hispano-Americano**, with its second-floor balcony supported by caryatids (classical, draped female figures). Known as the Casa de las Cariátides, it re-opened after renovation in May 2004, and stages temporary art and photographic exhibitions.

Many houses along the seafront here, having suffered from decades of neglect, are now undergoing desperately needed renovation, with many individual buildings having been sponsored by different Spanish provinces. Consequently, you find severely dilapidated, overcrowded buildings standing next to smartly painted new ones.

There are plans to completely rebuild the dangerously pitted seafront walkway; the plans also include barriers to prevent waves crashing over the sea wall. The spectacle of the sea roaring up against the Malecón is a part of the Havana scene, but the "big seas" (during storms, giant breakers can reach up to 10 meters/30 ft) do tremendous damage to roads, paths and buildings. In winter, the road is often closed to traffic, and on some occasions the sea wall is severely breached, flooding Centro Havana.

For the time being, at least, you can still enjoy the dramatic spectacle from

September to April – the biggest and best waves are to be seen in Vedado, by the Hotel Riviera and the statue of Calixto García, where the Malecón meets Presidentes. In contrast, when the tide is low and the sea calmer, you can see the remains of 19th-century stone baths carved from the limestone at the Old Havana end of the Malecón. The area, known as the **Elysian Fields**, was a fashionable place to see and be seen. There were once separate bathing areas for men and women, and for blacks.

The Hotel Deauville at Malecón and Avenida de Italia (Galiano) is one of Centro Habana's only tourist hotels – a pretty grim-looking building, although the interior has recently been refurbished. Halfway along the promenade is the **Monumento a Antonio Maceo ❹**, a huge bronze statue of the 19th-century revolutionary hero. There is a code to the city's equestrian statues of heroes: when the horse is rearing up, with both hoofs in the air, the subject died in battle; if only one hoof is raised, the man died of wounds sustained in battle; if the horse has all four hoofs firmly on the ground, the hero in question died peacefully in his bed. Maceo's horse is rearing since he died fighting the Spanish in 1896. Close by is the 18th-century watchtower, the Torreón de San Lázaro.

The large tower block behind the statue, reached by sinuous drive, was built before the Revolution as a bank, but it is now Cuba's flagship hospital, the Hospital Nacional Hermanos Ameijeiras.

A couple of blocks inland is **Callejón de Hamel ❺** – take San Lazaro behind the hospital, then turn left on Calle Hospital *(see panel below)*.

Vedado

West of Centro Habana, the Malecón courses through to the green and leafy suburbs of Vedado. The district was loosely modeled on Miami: the streets are identified by numbers (running east to west) or letters (running north to south); and some Art Deco buildings vaguely recall the shabbier corners of South Beach in the 1970s, before its restoration. With palm trees lining many streets, it is a pleasant place to stroll or stay, even if it has less character than Old Havana. There are far fewer tourists, and more of a local feel.

Callejón de Hamel is a fascinating spot, quite unlike anywhere else in the city.

BELOW LEFT: musician in the Callejón de Hamel.

Callejón de Hamel

Anyone who takes an interest in Afro-Cuban religions and the powerful, percussion-driven music and dance that accompanies their ceremonies, should check out the Callejón Hamel in the district of Cayo Hueso – a tiny backstreet off San Lázaro and Lucena in northwestern Centro Habana. The area has been dedicated to Palo Monte and Santería, with shrines to the various *orishas* and tiny stores selling art and artifacts. The walls and houses of the alley have all been plastered with enormous, boldly colored murals, pieces of sculpture, old typewriters, and bath tubs turned into seats. The project was initiated in 1990 by artist Salvador González. A nattily dressed man with the air of a showman, he is fired by his religious heritage, and there is considerable local pride in his achievement, especially considering the scarcity of available resources.

It's interesting to see at any time, but Sunday is the best day to go (noon–3pm), when an Afro-Cuban band strikes up with *batá* drums and fierce dancing for the mixed crowd of tourists and local people. The atmosphere is good, but it gets very crowded, so take care of your valuables, or better still, leave them behind in your hotel. You are welcome to take photos, but expect to make a contribution. Women sit at the gated entrance offering good-luck charms and fortune telling for an "offering," and the bands' CDs are for sale.

TIP

There is a television station in Vedado's hotel zone, from which Castro traditionally made his speeches. When he was due to arrive the streets were blocked off and residents were not allowed out on their balconies.

BELOW: the Black Flag monument outside the US Interests' Section.

The suburb is heralded by the twin towers of the **Hotel Nacional ❻**, Havana's most splendid hotel, perched on a rocky outcrop overlooking the Malecón. Modeled in the 1920s on the Breakers Hotel in Palm Beach in Florida, it has serene gardens with conveniently placed chairs and tables, good views of the sea and a long, shaded verandah with comfy wicker chairs where you can escape for a while the hubbub of the city. The café bar has walls lined with pictures of those who stayed here in its glory days – movie stars such as Errol Flynn, Frank Sinatra, Ava Gardner, and Clark Gable, plus more recent celebrity visitors, such as Naomi Campbell.

The Malecón rolls on past the **Monumento al Maine ❼**, dedicated to the 260 US sailors who were killed when their ship blew up in Havana in 1898 *(see page 46)*. A plaque on the monument declares, "Victims Sacrificed by Imperialist Voracity in its Eagerness to Seize the Island of Cuba." The US eagle that once topped the two graceful columns was felled by an angry mob with a crane in 1960.

The **US Interests' Section** – a faceless mass of concrete and tinted glass – lies a little father west. Throngs of overdressed Cubans hoping to join the "*Señores Imperialistas*" with an entry visa gather in a little park on Calzada and K as they wait to be interviewed by the consulate. Many come from out of town and sleep in their cars for days waiting to be interviewed.

In February 2006, Castro unveiled a large monument in front of the Interests' Section, blocking the view of an electronic billboard that scrolled out illuminated propaganda messages. It consists of 138 black flags, each with a white star, symbolising those who have died as the result of violent acts against Cuba since 1959. Professor Carlos Alberto Cremata, who stood beside Castro when the monument was unveiled, is the son of the co-pilot of a Cuban airliner that was bombed in 1976, killing all 73 people aboard. CIA documents released in 2005 indicated that the agency had known the bombing, instigated by a Cuban exile, Luis Posada Carriles, was going to take place. At the inauguration, members of the crowd held posters showing pictures of the dead.

The Posada Debâcle

I n 1976 former CIA agent Luís Posada Carriles, was jailed in Venezuela for his part in bombing the Cuban airliner *(see above)*, but he escaped from prison nine years later. In 2005 he arrived in the United States, where he was originally charged with illegal entry. To the anger of both Cuban and Venezuelan authorities, the charges were dropped two years later, even though the US Justice Department described him as a danger to the community, and "an admitted mastermind of terrorist bombs and attacks." Both governments are pressing for his extradition, which to date the United States has refused to grant. Posada is also under investigation for an alleged role in the bombing of the Copacabana Hotel in Havana in 1997, in which an Italian tourist was killed.

A couple of blocks south, on calles 13 and L, is a building right out of Gotham City, designed by the firm of architects (Shreve, Lamb and Harmon) who built the Empire State Building in New York. The families of many famous revolutionaries lived here. Next door, by the park, is the Hospital Camilo Cienfuegos (convertible pesos only), specializing in eye diseases. Another Vedado landmark is the blunt, curved **Edificio Focsa 8**: although reminiscent of Stalinist architecture, it was actually built in the capitalist 1950s, and the Russians liked it so much that they copied the design for 10 buildings in Moscow.

Vedado's hotel zone

The Monseigneur, the basement bar opposite the Hotel Nacional, once the scene of many Mafia meetings, is still functioning. Inland from the Nacional are numerous hotels, including the elegant Hotel Victoria, on calles 19 and M, with a pleasant coffee bar. The Hotel Capri on Calle 21 was co-owned in the 1950s by actor George Raft and, like the Sevilla, was a Mafia haunt. Today it stands empty, awaiting refurbishment. Calle O contin-

ues across the famous commercial artery of Calle 23 – known as **La Rampa**. Here there are three budget hotels, many of the city's airline offices, a few nightclubs, an excellent jazz club, and a whole host of fairly cheap but good snack bars.

One block away, on Calzada de Infanta, is the **Museo Casa de Abel Santamaría 9** (open Mon–Fri 10am–4pm; free), home of the joint leader (with Castro) of the 26th of July Movement in the 1950s. He was tortured to death after the failed Moncada attack of 1953. Castro attended many meetings here. Today, it contains Santamaría memorabilia.

To the west is the **Hotel Habana Libre 10**, a tall building emblazoned with a bold blue-and-white ceramic mural. For three months before the Revolution it was open as the Havana Hilton, but afterward Fidel and his embryonic government took over an entire floor for several months. The first-floor café that was the scene of a famous poison attempt on Castro – who used to spend late nights here chatting to kitchen staff (the cyanide capsule intended for his chocolate milkshake broke in the freezer) – has disappeared in a refurbishment that replaced

A blue-and-white ceramic mural is emblazoned across the Hotel Habana Libre.

BELOW LEFT: a monument commemorates the sinking of the USS *Maine*. **RIGHT:** the Hotel Nacional.

Savoring the very special ice cream at Coppelia Ice Cream Park.

---

the atmospheric 1950s interior with a more bland, modern design. The view from the 25th-floor bar is one of the best in the city, but the hotel charges non-guests several CUCs to visit. There is a shopping mall on the first floor, with a pharmacy and clothes stores.

Opposite the Habana Libre is the famous **Coppelia Ice Cream Park** ⓫, built by the revolutionary government to replace the notoriously elitist Vedado ice-cream parlors (where poorer and darker-skinned clients need not even have bothered lining up). This institution has re-opened after undergoing repairs and the old dollar section, where the lucky few could jump the line, went before the dollar did. There have been reports of foreigners turned away by over-zealous police who insist they go to convertible peso (CUC) establishments. There is no legal reason for them to do so: tourists are entitled to wait for two hours or more with everyone else if they wish. The ice cream is still the best in Cuba, but is less rich and creamy and more icy than it used to be – employees say that less butter is used now because of the cost. You can always get the seriously rich Cop-

pelia brand from the stands on the fringes of the park, as long as you pay in CUCs. It was in the park that the opening scenes of the 1994 film *Fresa y Chocolate* were filmed – the title refers to the two most common flavors, sometimes the only ones – strawberry and chocolate.

Around the university

The **Universidad de La Habana** ⓬, two blocks southeast of here, is a lovely group of classical buildings in golden stone placed around a cool and leafy garden, reached by climbing an impressive flight of steps at the head of San Lázaro. Anyone can stroll around the campus, and it is a good place to meet young Cubans, who love to practice their English. On the campus lies the **Museo Antropológico Montané** (open Mon–Fri 9am–noon, 1–4pm; entrance charge), with an excellent collection of pre-Columbian artifacts including the famous wooden Taíno Tobacco Idol, dating from around AD 900, found in Maisí, at the far eastern tip of Cuba.

Opposite the university is a stark **monument to Julio Antonio Mella**, containing the ashes of the student who

CENTRO HABANA AND VEDADO | Map on pages 138–9 | **177**

founded the Cuban Communist Party and was assassinated in Mexico in 1929. On January 28 – José Martí's birthday – a tremendous torchlit march starts from the monument.

Around the corner, the **Museo Napoleónico** ⓭ (open Tues–Sat 8.30am–4.30pm, Sun 9am–1.30pm; entrance charge) is housed in a delightful mansion with a small garden at San Miguel, 1159. Much of this unexpected collection of Napoleonic memorabilia was brought by Julio Lobo, a 19th-century politician, from his travels in Europe. It includes Napoleon's death mask, pistols from the Battle of Borodino and a fine library.

Where Calzada de Infanta meets Avenida Salvador Allende (also called Carlos III) you'll find the **Quinta de los Molinos** ⓮, reached via a tree-shaded drive. This was the site of 18th-century snuff mills built alongside the Zanja Real watercourse to Old Havana *(see page 152)*, and parts of the 16th-century aqueduct have been incorporated into the water garden and grotto. Now quiet and neglected, the gardens were popular in colonial times, when the rich owners of summer palaces nearby could inspect slaves before they went to market. They are now home to La Madriguera, a center for young artists, and a music venue where musicians are often found practicing beneath the trees. The lovely house here, once the colonial governor's summer palace, is now a rundown museum dedicated to General Máximo Gómez.

Revolution Square

South of here is the **Plaza de la Revolución** ⓯, the governmental heart of modern Havana. It is an extraordinary place – a vast, bleak square, big enough to hold the masses who came to hear Fidel's famous eight-hour May Day speeches, but normally empty of anyone except camera-toting tourists and the taxis that brought them. The exception to this is October 9, the anniversary of Che's death, when schoolchildren come here to lay flowers.

The whole region has been given over to eastern European-style monolithic architecture, where bureaucrats labor behind concrete walls. Yet the Revolution is not entirely to blame: many of the buildings, including the Martí monument, went up during Batista's time, when the dictator expressed his taste for intimidating, uninspired design, as seen in the gray former Justice Ministry, finished in 1958, that now houses the Central Committee of the Communist Party.

At the center is the mighty **Monumento José Martí** ⓰ (open Mon–Sat 9am–5pm; entrance charge), which houses an informative museum, including the original design plans for the plaza and Martí monument. Ascend the monument (extra charge) for an impressive 360-degree view of the city: Habana Vieja looks a very long way away. Behind the monument is the monolithic Palacio de la Revolución, where senior ministers, including Fidel Castro, have their offices. Visitors are not permitted to photograph the palace, or even loiter behind the monument.

The Ministerio del Interior is Cuba's most sinister and secretive organization

TIP

The Martí statue at the foot of the monument is made of marble from the Isla de la Juventud. The monument itself is the highest point in Havana, as the site is on a slight hill.

BELOW: the dramatic José Martí monument.

There is a philatelic museum – the Museo Postal Guerra Aguiar – to the northeast of the square, with exhibitions of stamps from all over the world.

(although vast, it has just one number listed in the phone book, which no one ever answers), yet it is housed in Cuba's most photographed building. The outside wall has a giant mural of Che Guevara executed in black metal, and best viewed at night when clever lighting gives the face an eerily three-dimensional look. The plaza is also the location of the Television and Radio Information and Communications Building, the Biblioteca Nacional, and the Teatro Nacional de Cuba (tel: 07-879-6011) – a stark building containing three theaters, the lively Café Cantante, a piano bar, a discotheque in the basement, and a large sculpture garden where works by Cuban artists are displayed.

Nuevo Vedado

Lying just south of the Plaza de la Revolución, in the area known as Nuevo Vedado, on Calle 26 is the somewhat inconspicuous office of the Víazul bus company, from where you can get buses to major destinations throughout Cuba (*see page 338*). Behind it, on Avenida Zoológico, is a small zoo, where bears can be seen pacing.

City of the dead

You could get a taxi from the Plaza de la Revolución – there are usually several lingering there – or from the nearby bus terminal to the **Cementerio de Colón**  (Columbus Cemetery; open 9am–5pm; entrance charge includes a guided tour), with its arched entrance gate. This is one of the largest necropolises in the world. Work began in the 1860s, when *habaneros* ran out of catacombs. A competition for its design was won by a Spaniard, Calixto de Loira y Cardosa. Although the Latin motto reads "Pale Death enters both hovels and the palaces of kings," Calixto used a pattern to ensure that the dead could be separated by social standing. He died before it was completed and became one of the first to be buried here. Wealthy *habaneros* competed to create the most impressive tombs, and the result is a decadent, morbid atmosphere that would have appealed to Edgar Allan Poe: a stone forest of Grecian temples and columns, crucified Christs and angels of mercy. The mausoleums are an eclectic mix of Gothic and neoclassical styles, and faithful stone dogs lie at their masters' feet.

BELOW: the mural of Che Guevara in the square.
BELOW RIGHT: the tomb of Amelia Goyre de la Hoz.

Cubans make pilgrimages to the tomb of Amelia Goyre de la Hoz, known as La Milagrosa (The Miraculous One), who died in childbirth. She was buried in 1901 with her child at her feet, but when she was exhumed the child was supposedly found in her arms. Nobody seems clear about *why* she was exhumed, but La Milagrosa is an object of devotion.

Southwest of the cemetery is the **Parque Almendares**, bordering the river of the same name. It's an attractive green, woody space, but local people will advise you not to go there alone.

Western Vedado

Three very different places of interest are scattered around western Vedado. Closest to the cemetery, on Calle 8 between 15 and 17, is the **Parque Lennon** ⓲, centered on a realistic bronze statue of John Lennon, lounging nonchalantly on a park bench and inscribed with the line "Dirás que soy un soñador, pero no soy el único" (You may say that I'm a dreamer, but I'm not the only one). The statue was unveiled by Castro himself in December 2000. It's a favorite hang-out spot for young people and there are occasional concerts.

At Calle 17, between Avenidas D and E, is the **Museo de Artes Decorativas** ⓳ (open Tues–Sat 11am–6pm, Sun 9am–1pm; entrance fee). It has a wonderful collection of European and Oriental decorative arts, especially porcelain, which is displayed in a series of furnished rooms ranging from a rococo salon and Regency dining room to a gorgeous Art Deco bathroom.

If you missed out on these two attractions and are coming directly from the Plaza de la Revolución, you will have come (on foot or by taxi, depending on stamina) along the broad **Avenida de Los Presidentes**, which crosses La Rampa, and is lined with lush, formal gardens and the former homes of the rich, most now government buildings.

En route, you pass a gigantic marble tribute to past Cuban presidents. Once a favored hang-out for disaffected youths, it has now been cleaned up. Next door to Hotel Presidente, the elegant cultural center, the **Casa de Las Américas** ⓴ (open Mon–Fri 8am–5pm; entrance charge) was founded by Che Guevara. Housed in a landmark Art Deco building, it contains archives and a fine collection of Latin American art, and hosts workshops, lectures and other cultural events.

Toward Miramar

From here, the Malecón heads west. There is a dusty artisans' market, the Feria del Malecón, on the corner of Calle D, and just beyond rises the Hotel Riviera, built by mob boss Meyer Lansky as a last attempt to recreate Las Vegas in the Caribbean. Lansky had a suite on the 20th floor, which can be booked by hotel guests. The interior of the Riviera is still pleasantly evocative of the 1950s, but the hotel has been both dwarfed and outclassed by the Hotel Meliá Cohiba next door, which was Cuba's first five-star hotel *(see page 342)*.

A couple of blocks west is the expensive Club 1830, in the **Torreón de la Chorrera** castle by the sea. Alongside, the Malecón disappears into the tunnel under the Almendares River, re-emerging as Quinta Avenida in Miramar. ❑

When Meyer Lansky owned the Hotel Riviera he was listed, for tax reasons, as the hotel's kitchen manager.

BELOW: John Lennon's statue in the little park named after him.

RESTAURANTS, PALADARES, BARS & CAFÉS

Restaurants

1830

Malecón, 1252 and 22, Vedado.
Tel: (07) 55-3090–2.
Open daily L & D. **$$$**
Located just before you go under the tunnel to Miramar, this romantic restaurant is known for a well-respected chef. There is a bar attached, and a pleasant garden.

La Torre

Focsa Building, calles 17 and M, Vedado.
Tel: (07) 55-3088–9.
Open noon–midnight. **$$$**
At the top of Havana's highest building, La Torre offers a fantastic panoramic view. The menu, which is domi-

nated by steaks and fish, has a decidedly French influence.

Casona de 17

Calle 17, between M and N, Vedado.
Tel: (07) 838-3136. Open noon–midnight. **$$–$$$**
Serves reasonably priced Cuban dishes, and more international food in the elegant sur-roundings of an old villa, opposite the Focsa Building. Two air-conditioned indoor restaurants and a patio barbecue-grill.

El Conejito

Calle M, 206 and 17, Vedado.
Tel: (07) 832-4671. Open daily noon–11pm. **$$**
A supposedly "English" restaurant, though the

architecture and decor is more of a strange mix of English and Swiss styles. It special-izes in rabbit (conejo), but serves a wide range of international dishes.

La Roca

Calle 21, 102, between L and M, Vedado.
Tel: (07) 334-501. Open daily noon–midnight. **$–$$**
A classic 1950s club – with an atmospheric cocktail bar – that has been well-renovated. Well cooked, if rather bland, international menu, with a choice of meat, fish and shell-fish. One of the few restaurants in Cuba to offer a cigar after din-ner. A word of warning: the air conditioning is fearsome.

Restaurante Monseigneur

Corner of O and 21, Vedado.
Tel: (07) 832-9884. Open noon–1am. **$$**
Opposite the Hotel Nacional, the Mon-seigneur cellar restau-rant is famous as a former meeting spot for 1950s Mafia bosses. The Cuban singer, the late Bola de Nieve, made it his home, too, and his piano is still there. The restaurant now has a long seafood menu and a moody ambiance.

Restaurante Pacífico

Calle Cuchillo and San Nicolás, Centro.

Tel: (07) 863-3243. Open daily 11am–11pm. **$$**
Fairly authentic Cantonese cooking (but there's a lot of Cuban influence) in Havana's most famous Chinese restaurant, in the heart of Chinatown.

Restaurant Tien Tan

Calle Cuchillo, 17, between Rayo and San Nicolás.
Open daily 10am–11pm. **$$**
Extensive menu of gen-uinely Chinese food. Good stir-fries, and duck as well as pork and chicken.

Trattoria Maraka

Hotel St John, Calle O, between 23 and 25, Vedado.
Open daily L & D. **$$**
Authentic Italian food, including pizzas cooked in a wood-fired oven. Pasta, steaks and interesting salads on offer, as well.

Paladares

In Centro and, espe-cially, Vedado, there is a wide variety of paladares and they are by far the best places to eat. They do come and go, but the following are well-established.

De Cameron

Línea, between Paseo and Calle 2, a block from Hotel Riviera.
No phone. Open Wed–Sun, noon–late. **$**
Specializes in pizzas, with a good range of toppings and generous amounts of cheese.

Also pasta, and meat and fish dishes. Meals are served in an airy room full of plants and a talkative parrot. Be warned that service is terribly slow. Also does takeouts.

El Aladino
Calle 21, between K and L. No phone. Open daily L & D. $
Serves mostly Cuban dishes, but occasionally couscous, lovely salads of mint and cucumber, and great houmous.

El Amor
Calle 23 between calles B and C.
Tel: (07) 38-150. Open daily L & D. $
Grand surroundings in a crumbling mansion full of dusty antiques. Wonderful air of faded grandeur. Specializes in fish dishes.

El Gringo Viejo
Calle 21, 454, between calles E and F.
Tel: (07) 831-1946. Open daily L & D. $
"The Old Gringo" is popular for its efficient service as well as the menu, which features seafood as well as the usual offerings.

La Guarida
Calle Concordia, 418, between Gervasio and Escobar, Centro.
Tel: (07) 866-9047. $$–$$$
You must book well in advance, as this *paladar* featured in the famous Cuban film *Fresa y Chocolate* – or, rather, the film featured

the crumbling tenement building, and the *paladar* followed two years later. It is always full. The decor is kitsch and eclectic, the food is varied and excellent, and portions are "nouveau" without being small. Prices are high, as the restaurant trades on its movie connections, but it is well worth a visit.

Jardín de los Siete Esferas
Calle 19, corner of Calle B. No phone. Open daily noon–10pm. $
Here, you eat in a vine-draped garden. Mostly Cuban dishes with good pastries and an excellent chocolate and coconut pie.

Marpoly
Calle K, 154, between calles 11 and 13, Vedado.
Tel: (07) 322-471. Open daily lunchtime–midnight. $
A mixture of *comida criolla* and international food. Marpoly makes an effort to serve somewhat unusual dishes – a platter of pineapple and toasted cheese may sound odd, but is particularly delicious.

Nerei
Calle 19, 110, between calles L and M, Vedado.
Tel: (07) 832-7860. Open daily noon–midnight. $
Good Cuban dishes and fast, friendly service. *Lechon asado* (roast suckling pig) is a specialty, and it does taste very different from the

usual slices of pork. *Malanga con mojo* (starchy tuber with garlic sauce) is another favorite. Eat in a dining room furnished with antiques, or outside on a plant-filled terrace.

Paladar El Hurón Azul
Calle Humboldt, 153, corner of Calle P
Tel: (07) 832-4551.
Open Tues–Sun L & D. $
A well-recommended *paladar*, which specializes in interesting fish dishes. Because it's popular, and you can't book, there is sometimes a line, but it's worth the wait.

Bars and Cafés

Opus Bar (Calzada, corner of Calle D, Vedado). Above the Teatro Roldán, this is a tranquil, comfortable bar.

Bar-Café Centro de Prensa (Calle 23, corner of Calle O, Vedado). A pleasant place for a drink, where you can feel you are joining the intellectual café society. It closes at 7pm.

Hotel Nacional (Calle O and 21, Vedado). An excellent *mojito* or daquirí on the broad, landscaped terrace overlooking the sea is one of the delights of Havana, especially when the sun is going down.

PRICE CATEGORIES
Price categories are for a three-course meal for one with a beer, or *mojito*. Wine puts the price up:
$ = under $25
$$ = $25–35
$$$ = over $35

LEFT: enjoy a *mojito* before your meal.
RIGHT: kitsch decor in La Guarida.

AROUND HAVANA

The area around Havana contains an eclectic mix of things to see – from classy Miramar in the west to the Parque Lenin, a delightful botanical garden, two majestic forts, a couple of Hemingway sites and an eastern beach

Visitors to Havana generally concentrate on La Habana Vieja, Centro and Vedado, but there are other areas not far away that are well worth visiting if you have time.

Continuing westward from Vedado, where the previous chapter left off, you will soon come to the suburb of Miramar, which is divided from Vedado by the Río Almendares. You can cross into Miramar by tunnel, close to the bay, or farther inland by the road bridge, an extension of La Rampa (Calle 23).

Miramar

Miramar ❶ is a suburb of broad, tree-lined avenues, once the home of Havana's wealthiest residents, and still pretty smart compared with much of the city, although many of the buildings have seen better days. It is also an area that seems to have no center, perhaps because it was modeled on Las Vegas, rather than on colonial Spanish cities, as was the case with Habana Vieja. High-rise hotels and business centers are springing up all over the area, and the building work seemingly forever in progress between Quinta Avenida and the sea is designed to produce luxury apartments to rent to foreigners, and yet more hotels.

Quinta Avenida (Fifth Avenue) is a broad promenade, planted with vividly flowering trees and bushes, where most of the foreign companies who have chosen to defy the US ban and invest in Cuba have their offices. Signs are everywhere: Benetton, Castrol, Bayer, Philips.

It is also the home of the city's foreign embassies, housed in beautiful buildings, set in lush gardens.

Quinta Avenida (at Calle 14) is home to one of the city's quirkiest museums – the **Museo del Ministerio del Interior** (open Tues–Fri 9am–5pm, Sat 9am–4pm; entrance charge), which catalogs the CIA's numerous attempts to destabilize the Cuban state and to assassinate Castro.

A little farther along, between calles 24 and 26, there is a pretty little park, shaded by enormous, ancient banyan trees. Heading from here toward the sea

Main attractions
MIRAMAR
MARINA HEMINGWAY
TROPICANA
PARQUE LENIN
EL RINCÓN
EL MORRO
CASTILLO DE SAN CARLOS
SANTA MARÍA DEL MAR

LEFT: Castillo de San Carlos de la Cabaña. **BELOW:** the stark Russian Embassy building.

A Night at the Tropicana

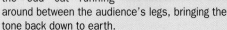

The roulette tables may be gone, but not a great deal else has changed in the Tropicana nightclub – which has been Havana's most famous cabaret spot ever since it first opened in 1931, and the only place of its kind that has operated more or less continuously throughout the austere years of the Revolution. Kitschy, crass and unashamedly sexist, the Tropicana (located between Avenida 43 and Línea T in the Marianao district in western Havana; tel: 7267-1717) is everything that Cubans love in live entertainment.

Shows start at 10pm every evening except Monday, weather permitting, and last 1 hour and 45 minutes. Billed as an open-air paradise *"bajo las estrellas"* (under the stars) it is forced to cancel shows regularly in the rainy season. Doors open from 8.30pm, when guests start arriving for drinks or dinner. The place is lit up like a Christmas tree: blue neon signs announce the entrance, and a huge fountain with statues of frolicking naked women is bathed in blue and red. A small band warms up the crowd at the entrance, to add to the carnival atmosphere.

Whatever you think of the actual show, the Tropicana's setting is breathtaking. Tables fan out like sunbeams around the semicircular stage, with enough room to seat 1,400 and stand many more; tropical trees enclose the amphitheater in a sheltering cocoon; among the foliage, large neon lights spell out the names of legends who performed here in pre-revolutionary times, such as Carmen Miranda and Nat King Cole. On a good night, the warm tropical air is seductive and the stars are visible through the treetops. This being Cuba, there may also be the odd cat running around between the audience's legs, bringing the tone back down to earth.

With the triumphant blare of a 20-piece band, the show begins. Women in silver lamé coats and top hats float across the stage on trapezes. Dancers leap past in a blur of feathers, glitter and long legs. A bizarre pageant may be thrown in. Then, as if to mock the power shortages elsewhere, dancers appear with giant, blazing candelabras sprouting bizarrely from their heads.

It's the sort of extravaganza preserved in the rest of the world only in old black-and-white movies. In fact, to enjoy the Tropicana, it's best to turn your mental clock back about 50 years. Despite the Revolution's progressive social legislation, flirting is still alive and well in Cuba, and Cubans love their vast, hectic, titillating shows; lesser versions can be seen around the island – the best, also called the Tropicana, in Santiago de Cuba.

Another reason that Havana's Tropicana has survived is that it brings in tourist revenue: entrance fees (85 CUCs for the "preferential" seats, 65 CUCs for less good ones) include a quarter-bottle of rum and a mixer, but not the use of a camera. Meanwhile, the Tropicana is a prime haunt for Cuba's most gorgeous and voracious *jineteras* (prostitutes) who hunt out single men, and introduce themselves as "dancing students" who just happen to be catching the show. The discotheque attached to the club goes on, very loudly, till 2am. ❑

LEFT AND ABOVE: Tropicana's extravaganza has changed little over the decades.

you will come to the **Maqueta de La Habana** (open Tues–Sat 9.30am–5pm; entrance charge), at Calle 28 between 1st and 3rd avenues. This vast scale model of the city took 10 years to construct, and is the largest of its kind after a model of New York. Every street, every house, every vacant lot, every tree is faithfully represented, constructed out of cigar boxes; different colors show which districts date from which period.

Back on Quinta, farther west at No. 6502, between 62 and 66, the giant **Russian Embassy** towers over Miramar. This huge, ugly complex of offices and apartments once housed the various delegations of the Soviet Union. Now the independent former Soviet states have moved out and have their own embassies, leaving the greatly reduced Russian mission somewhat lost and lonely, but hard to overlook.

Close by, on **Tercera Avenida** (Third Avenue) between 60 and 62 is the **Acuario Nacional** (National Aquarium; open Mon–Sat 10am–9.30pm, Sun 10am–6pm; entrance charge), which has an endangered-species breeding program, and treats injured animals before returning them to the wild. It also stages dolphin and sea-lion shows regularly throughout the day (small extra charge) and is a great favorite with local families, especially on weekends, when it gets quite crowded. Opposite is a little complex of bars and restaurants.

Just inland from the Russian Embassy, on Avenida 5B, between calles 66 and 70 (the western end of Avenida 7), is the **Fundación La Naturaleza y el Hombre** (open Mon–Fri 10am–4pm; advance booking essential; entrance charge). This fascinating place displays the canoe in which naturalist Antonio Nuñez Jimenez and his team traveled from the source of the Amazon to the sea in 1987. There is a wealth of objects gathered from the indigenous people they met, including lots of erotic ceramic figures. The foundation also has an excellent photographic collection, and Oswaldo Guayasamin's portrait of Fidel Castro.

Retracing your steps eastward, one further attraction in Miramar is the Teatro Karl Marx (tel: 07-209-1991), on Primera Avenida (corner of Calle 10), which is good for concerts and movie premieres.

Nightlife and sea life

South of Miramar, in Marianao, is the famous **Tropicana** nightclub *(see page 184)*, while to the west extend endless green suburbs, such as **Cubanacán** and **Siboney**, where many government offices are located, and a lot of party functionaries also live. Cubanacán is also the location of the Institito Superior de Arte, and a large conference center.

At the farthest outskirts of Havana is the marine resort called **Marina Hemingway** ❷. There are hotels and villas for rent and several expensive restaurants and duty-free stores here, but apart from the name, there is not the slightest connection to the writer. It has also borrowed his name for the Ernest Hemingway International Marlin Fishing Tournament in late May, and is a popular center for sport fishing, sailing and scuba diving *(see Activities, page 363)*. From the marina, the coastal road carries on west

Marina Hemingway is a center for all kinds of water sports.

BELOW: a visit to the National Aquarium makes a popular family outing.

*Heliconia – one of
the vivid blooms in
the Jardín Botánico.*

toward the province of Pinar del Río. It passes a few small resorts, such as **Santa Fé**, **Playa Baracoa**, and **El Salado**, pleasant, sleepy places with wooden houses along the seafront and small rocky beaches, before it reaches Mariel *(see page 201)*.

Lenin lingers on

Directly south of Havana on the airport road (officially called Rancho Boyeros, but Avenida Independencia on most street signs) is **Parque Lenin ③** (park open daily; attractions Tues–Sun 9am–5pm; free entry, but charges for some amenities and attractions), a vast

stretch of gently rolling parkland with tall trees and bamboo stands. After years of stagnation in the "Special Period", the park is slowly gaining a new lease of life. Some rides and shows, and the 19th-century miniature steam railway have reopened and there are new cafés serving Cubans in pesos and foreigners in convertible pesos (CUCs). Among the attractions is an artificial lake with rowing boats, an aquarium, a monument and museum dedicated to the park's creator, Celia Sánchez; and, most famously, a giant, well-tended stone head of Lenin – one of the last such monuments left in the world. There is also an equestrian center,

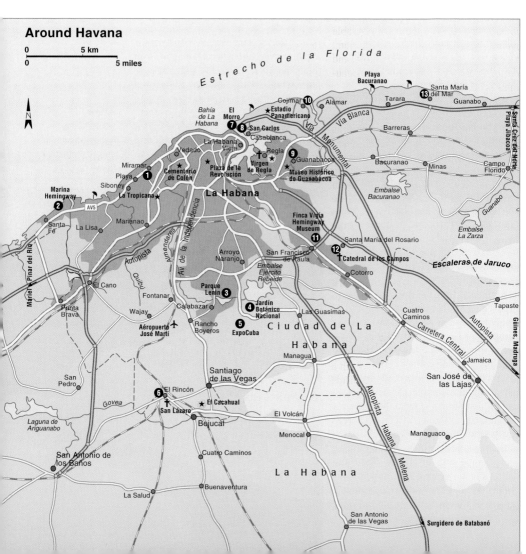

Club Hípico (open Wed–Sun 9am–4.30pm), where you can hire horses.

South of the park is the largest botanical garden in Latin America, the **Jardín Botánico Nacional** ❹ (open Wed–Sun 9am–4pm; Mon–Tues by arrangement; entrance charge). Looking after the vast areas of pasture and woodland is quite a struggle, and some areas are sorely neglected. The beautiful Japanese Garden is well maintained, however, and there are attractive greenhouses with large collections of tropical, desert, and temperate flora (there are poinsettias the size of Christmas trees), as well as an extensive herb garden, which supplies medicinal plants to many of Havana's *yerberos* (herbalists). Your entrance fee includes the services of a knowledgeable guide. The garden has a herbal tearoom, a botanical book store, a plant store, and one of Cuba's very few vegetarian restaurants *(see page 191)*.

Across the road lies **ExpoCuba** ❺ (open Wed–Sun 10am–5pm; entrance charge), a sprawling area of pavilions celebrating Cuba's achievements in science, health, education and the arts.

About 8 km (5 mile) down Avenida de la Independencia from the Parque Lenin turning is the small town of **Santiago de las Vegas**, a sleepy place that wakes up just once a year for the **Procession of the Miracles**. On the eve of December 17, the day of San Lázaro – patron saint of the sick – people come from all over Cuba to the little church of **San Lázaro** at **El Rincón** ❻, just south of town, to pray for help or forgiveness. Thousands of people – a mixture of penitents and those who come just to join in – process slowly through the town to the church, where the pilgrimage culminates with a mass held at midnight. The scenes inside the church are often emotional, with people shouting "¡Viva Lázaro!" "¡Viva Cristo!" Spirits run so high that the security forces always turn out in force in case of trouble. Pope John Paul II gave his penultimate mass here during his visit to Cuba in January 1998.

Otherwise, Santiago de las Vegas is most well known for its Aids sanitarium, which is the largest of its kind in Cuba *(see page 25)*. Perhaps understandably, patients from the institution are often present at the mass in El Rincón church on the Day of San Lázaro.

Just south of here is **El Cacahual**, where Cuban independence hero Antonio Maceo is buried, and where ceremonies were held welcoming back troops returning from Angola at the end of the 1980s.

Fortresses across the bay

From Old Havana, a tunnel dips beneath the bay to the **Castillo de los Tres Santos Reyes Magos del Morro**, which is usually known simply as **El Morro** ❼ (open daily 8.30am–8pm; entrance charge – it costs less if you simply want to walk round the ramparts). This 16th-century fortress, with 3-meter (10-ft) thick walls constructed from blocks taken from Cuba's coastal reef, took more than 40 years to complete. It still dominates the eastern skyline, especially at night when floodlit. The views from here are superb, whether around the bastion's vertiginous ramparts, back toward the city, or out at sea, from where the

The El Rincón procession is a sometimes disturbing spectacle, as many penitents crawl for miles on bleeding knees, or drag themselves by the palms of their hands with a rock or box of stones chained to one ankle to make their progress all the more difficult.

BELOW: the huge statue of Lenin in the Parque Lenin.

LENIN FUE DESDE EL PRIMER INSTANTE NO SOLO UN TEÓRICO DE LA POLÍTICA SINO UN HOMBRE DE ACCIÓN... UN HOMBRE DE PRÁCTICA REVOLUCIONARIA CONSTANTE E INCESANTE   FIDEL

TIP

To get to El Morro you can take a taxi (around cuc$4), or get on any of the buses that run through the tunnel. From El Morro to the Castillo de San Carlos it's about a 20-minute walk. Travel agencies run tours here, as well. The ones that take in the *cañonazo* are particularly popular.

RIGHT: the cannon is fired every evening at 9pm.

main **lighthouse** can be seen 33 km (18 nautical miles) away. It is absolutely stunning at sunset.

The castle was once a vital part of the city's defenses. On the lower level, closer to the harbor, is the **Batería de los Doce Apóstoles** (Battery of the 12 Apostles), with each of its 12 cannons bearing one of their names. In colonial times, these guns would be fired to announce the closing of the city gates – a rite now re-enacted in the neighboring fortress of San Carlos de la Cabaña *(see below)*.

A great chain used to run between El Morro and the Castillo de la Punta in Old Havana. The chain closed the bay to pirate ships in the days when Sir Francis Drake sailed these seas. The pirate Henry Morgan was told by former English prisoners in Havana that he would need at least 1,800 men to take the city – he did not even try. Bizarrely, there are still several pieces of modern artillery directed out from El Morro toward the Straits of Florida, in symbolic defiance against a *yanqui*-inspired invasion.

There are three **museums** at El Morro castle, focusing on navigation, the history of the castle, and on pirates. You will also find one of Havana's most atmospheric restaurants, Los Doce Apóstoles just outside the wall *(see page 191)*.

The **Castillo de San Carlos de la Cabaña** ❽ (open daily 10am–10pm; entrance charge, increased 6–10pm for *El Cañonazo*), was built from 1764–74, after the departure of British invaders. It, too, has two interesting **museums**. One of them documents the fortress in colonial days, when many independence fighters were shot here. A good number of Batista's followers met the same fate after the Revolution in 1959, when Che Guevara used the fortress as his headquarters (the focus of the second museum). In the first year of the Revolution, those found guilty of such crimes as murder and torturing prisoners under the Batista regime were executed here. Bullet holes from the firing squads pepper the walls by the front gate.

At 9pm every evening, the atmospheric ceremony of the **firing of the cannon** (called *El Cañonazo*) is conducted in period military dress, in commemoration of the obsolete practice of closing the city gates. Although nowadays they only fire blanks, the noise is authentic,

Small Town with Big Connections

If you have your own transportation, and time to spare, you might like to make a brief trip to the southwest of Havana (some 37 km/22 miles along the Autopista del Mediodía), to San Antonio de los Baños, which may be the most filmed small town in the developing world. Just 8 km (5 miles) away is the Escuela Internacional del Cine (International Film School), whose students, who come from all over Latin America, and from Asia and Africa, often use San Antonio and its residents in their graduating projects. Gabriel García Márquez is the founder and benefactor of the school, which he has often visited to teach classes in screenwriting. Other notables who have worked with the school include Robert Redford and Francis Ford Coppola.

San Antonio is known, too, for its annual International Humor Festival (in April), and has a small Museo del Humor, which exhibits satirical cartoons. It is also the birthplace of both the composer-singer Silvio Rodríguez (in 1946), whose political lyrics have made him a national icon; and of the late Eduardo Abela (1889–1965), whose cartoon character, El Bobo (The Fool), which appeared in a daily newspaper in the 1930s, created biting social criticism. El Bobo is now the town symbol, standing at its entrance. There is a gallery named after the artist, but it does not contain his works.

and the ceremony is fun, especially as local people often outnumber tourists. Much of the fortress is in a fairly dangerous condition – there are a lot of sheer drops from the high walls, which are neither roped off nor signposted, so take care when exploring. You'll find an excellent restaurant, La Divina Pastora, at the foot of the fortress on the waterside *(see page 191)*, as well as several upscale tourist shops selling arts, crafts and clothes.

The statue by the bay

It's about a 15-minute walk south from the *castillo* to the statue that dominates the bay, the figure of Christ, carved from Italian marble, and very similar to the more famous one in Rio de Janeiro. Sometimes known as **El Cristo de Casablanca**, it was carved by Cuban sculptor Jilma Madra, and inaugurated in December 1958, shortly before the fall of Batista. In the early years of the Revolution the statue was struck by lightning and the head fell off. The government had the figure repaired – to the consternation of some communists who felt it a "waste of the people's money" to repair

a religious monument. The other noticeable structure here is the domed, white national observatory, the **Observatorio Nacional** (no public access).

From the ramshackle little town of **Casablanca**, the best and cheapest way back to Old Havana is by ferry *(lancha)*, which will deposit you on the harbor side at the foot of calles Luz and Santa Clara.

The eastern suburbs

The suburbs east of Havana offer a slice of life you won't see in the city, but if you only have a short time in Cuba you will have plenty to do in Old Havana and Vedado, and if you have longer you will almost certainly be visiting some of the better-known towns on the island. These small towns, although they get a mention, will not be high on most visitors' lists.

If you want to visit **Regla** the best way to get there is by ferry from the foot of calles Luz and Santa Clara in Old Havana. Regla is ringed by heavy industry, but the old town is still quite pleasant, and its main forms of transportation are trucks and horse-drawn carts. The main reason people come here is to visit the early 19th-century **Iglesia de Nuestra**

A marble statue of Christ keeps watch over the harbor.

BELOW: El Morro fortress, built to defend the city.

En route to Regla or Casablanca on the ferry you may see passengers dropping paper into the sea – this means they are hoping to rid themselves of their problems in a Santería ceremony.

Señora de Regla (open daily 7.30am– 5.30pm). This church is dedicated to the black Virgen de Regla, the patron saint of Cuba's sailors. Her counterpart in Santería is Yemayá, goddess of the sea. You will see worshipers making offerings here, many dressed in blue, or wearing blue- and-crystal beads – the colors of Yemayá. Her day is September 8, when there is a procession in her honor. The church also has an altar to Santa Bárbara, twinned in Santería with Changó, god of war and *machismo*. Offerings here are in red, the color of Changó. His feast day is cele- brated on December 4.

Afro-Cuban center

Santería is strong in **Guanabacoa 9** as well, a town renowned in Cuba for its connections with Afro-Cuban religions. Though the outskirts are grim and face- less, the town has an agreeable **plaza** and several interesting churches (in the process of restoration).

The **Museo Histórico de Guanaba- coa** (Calle Martí 108; open Tues–Sat 10am–6pm, Sun 9am–1pm; entrance charge) is best known for its exhibitions on Afro-Cuban cults. There is also lots

about local resistance to the British inva- sion of 1762. Less heroically, Guanaba- coa was a nexus for the slave trade. Wander along **Calle Amargura** (Bitter- ness Street), where slaves were dragged en route to their executions.

The best-known priest in Guanabacoa is Enriquito, whose house may some- times be visited (ask at the museum for directions), but it is a private home, not a museum. It contains rooms devoted to the two main Afro-Cuban religions, San- tería and Palo Monte.

Driving to Guanabacoa, or finding the right bus, is a bit confusing. You could get a taxi if you are interested in finding out more about the Afro-Cuban religions, or include the town on a trip to nearby Cojímar *(see below and page 195)*.

Heading east

The fishing village of **Cojímar 10**, 16 km (10 miles) from Old Havana, is popular for its Hemingway connection *(see page 195)*. Just off the highway before Cojí- mar is the **Villa Pan Americana**, a com- plex of sports facilities, apartments and a hotel built for the 1991 regional games. The volunteers who took on the huge task of building the complex now live in the athletes' apartments, though some are still used by athletes competing at the nearby stadium (Estadio Panamericano).

Across an inlet to the west of Cojímar lies **Alamar**, a suburb built by volun- teers, known as micro-brigades, after the Revolution. Originally planned for 40,000 people, it now has closer to 100,000, mostly in a depressing array of five-story walk-up apartment blocks. Despite or because of the grim sur- roundings, a strong musical culture has sprung up in Alamar. Many young bands rehearse in this dingy neighborhood, which is now home to an annual inter- national rap festival, held in August at the **Casa de la Cultura de Alamar**.

Southeast of here on the *autopista* (Via Monumental) is the suburb of **San Fran- cisco de Paula**, with the Hemingway Museum at **Finca Vigía 11** *(see page 194)*. Close by is **Santa María del Rosario 12**, a lovely place with tall trees,

BELOW: enjoying the Playas del Este.

colonial houses and pleasant inhabitants. The main attraction is the 18th-century **Catedral de los Campos** – best visited on a Sunday afternoon (mass at 2.30pm), the only time of the week when you can be fairly sure of seeing the baroque paintings and statues. Across the shady plaza is the restored **Casa del Conde de Bayona**, once home of the Count of Bayona, a sugar baron notorious for executing a group of rebellious slaves. The site where they were executed is marked on the **Loma de la Cruz** (Hill of the Cross), up a steep street from the plaza. The plain wooden cross was erected as a warning to other slaves, and two flanking crosses were added in 1959 to represent the thieves crucified with Christ.

Playas del Este

Beyond Alamar stretch a series of beach resorts known collectively as the **Playas del Este** (Eastern Beaches). This is where *habaneros* come to enjoy the sea and sand. The closest beach is **Playa Bacuranao**: on a small horseshoe-shaped inlet, it is a favorite with Cuban families and is packed in July and August. Then comes a 16-km (10-mile) stretch of open sea, sand dunes, and coconut palms. The sand starts at **El Mégano** and continues to **Santa María del Mar** ⑬, which has a good beach and is the nicest section of this coast, with a number of seafront hotels. Farther on is **Guanabo**, an old seaside town with a lively beach and a number of wooden bungalows built in the 1920s and 1930s, which are very popular with Cubans.

Farther east lies **Santa Cruz del Norte**, site of Cuba's largest rum distillery (the home of Havana Club). Just inland is the **Central Camilo Cienfuegos** sugar mill, founded by the American Hershey Chocolate Company in 1917, during the sugar boom.

The coast road continues past attractive **Playa Jibacoa**, a good spot for family vacations and with some good walking opportunities; then along the **Litoral Norte** (North Coast) where beach resorts sit amid coastal vegetation. ❑

An impromptu serenade for visitors to Hemingway's memorial in Cojímar.

RESTAURANTS

El Eco-Restaurant El Bambú
Jardín Botánico, Carretera El Rocío Km 3.5, Boyeros
Tel: (07) 754-7278, 549-364
Open: L Wed–Sun. $
Eat all you want for a set price from a huge array of vegetarian dishes, ranging from soups, salads and rice dishes to puddings and fresh fruit juices. Most products grown on the premises.

El Tocororo
Calle 18 and Avenida 3ra, Miramar
Tel: (07) 204-2209, 202-4530. Open Mon–Sat noon–midnight. $$$
Housed in an attractive Miramar villa, with a strik-ing array of Art Nouveau lampshades. There are two dining rooms: one for *criolla* food, one for Japanese dishes, and a tapas bar (till 2am). It's expensive, but excellent. Book ahead.

La Cecilia
Avenida 5ta, between 110 and 111, Miramar
Tel: (07) 204-1562. Open Wed–Sun noon–midnight. $$$
Surrounded by foliage, this relaxing restaurant serves everything from *ajiaco criolla*, a tasty meat and vegetable soup, to grilled sirloin steak. The fish is prepared with subtle seasonings.

La Divina Pastora
Castillo de San Carlos
Tel: (07) 860-8341. Open noon–midnight. $$$
At the foot of the Cabaña fortress, La Divina Pastora offers a stunning view of the Havana skyline. A good place for a meal or a drink before the 9pm *cañonazo (see page 188)*. Among the seafood specialties is fillet of red snapper stuffed with shrimp.

La Terraza
Calle Reál, 161 corner of Candelaria, Cojímar
Tel: (07) 939-232, 939-486. Open 10.30am–11pm. $$$
This old Hemingway haunt serves good seafood: lunch here makes for an excellent day trip. There are views over the rather muddy bay, and photos of Hemingway adorn the walls. Reserve in high season, because it is firmly on the tourist trail.

Los Doce Apóstoles
El Morro Fortress
Tel: (07) 863-8295, 860-8341. Open daily noon–11pm; bar 11pm–2am. $$
Next to the El Morro Fortress and named for its battery, this restaurant serves pork dishes with all the trimmings, though the setting is arguably better than the food.

• • • • • • • • • • • • • •
Price categories are for a meal for one with a beer or mojito. Wine puts the price up.
$ = under $25, $$ = $25–35, $$$ = over $35.

ON THE TRAIL OF HEMINGWAY

Still loved in his adopted country, Papá Hemingway has left a trail of sites connected with his life, including his beautiful estate residence and a monument in the fishing village of Cojímar

Main attractions
HOTEL AMBOS MUNDOS
EL FLORIDITA
LA BODEGUITA DEL MEDIO
FINCA VIGÍA
COJÍMAR

BELOW: Ernest Hemingway at home in Finca Vigía.

For more than 20 years, the Nobel Prize-winning writer Ernest Hemingway lived in and around Havana, drinking in the bars, fishing off the shores, and using Cuba as the background for some of his most famous writing, including *The Old Man and the Sea*. Often known simply as *Ernesto* or *Papá*, he is the Cubans' favorite *yanqui*, his foibles forgiven – even Fidel has sung his praises. It is said that when he went to the Sierra Maestra during the Revolution, Castro took with him *For Whom the Bell Tolls*, Hemingway's epic of the Spanish Civil War, in order to learn about guerrilla warfare.

Hemingway's interest in Cuba began in the late 1920s, when he began crossing the Straits of Florida from his home in Key West on marlin fishing trips. The island's laid-back, sensual atmosphere seemed the perfect antidote to the values of his Midwestern Protestant upbringing, and he soon became a regular in the bars of Old Havana. Returning from the Spanish Civil War in 1938, he moved into the Hotel Ambos Mundos on Calle Obispo; from there he could stroll nine blocks to his favorite bar, El Floridita, cutting a distinctive figure in his cotton shirt, scruffy khaki shorts and moccasins.

Journalist Martha Gellhorn, soon to become Hemingway's third wife, was not content to live in a hotel room. She found a house called Finca Vigía – a former cattle farm on the site of a Spanish fort. The couple bought it in 1940 for US$18,500 cash, and, although Gellhorn later divorced him, Hemingway stayed on at the *finca* for most of his life.

Literary pilgrimages

The world's most famous writers and movie stars made the pilgrimage to his tropical refuge, joining the writer on marlin fishing trips in his custom-made luxury yacht, the *Pilar*. Hemingway may not have always been the most gracious host (one biographer described him as "boastful, lying, obscene, boring, overbearing, ill-tempered, touchy, vindictive and self-righteous"); the opinions of

others were more generous, but few could resist an invitation.

During World War II, Hemingway honed his macho persona by converting the *Pilar* into a gunship and searching the Cuban coast for lone German U-boats (luckily for him, he never found one, although he claimed to have spotted one that submerged before he could approach). He spent a stint as a war correspondent in Europe, then returned to settle into a famous and drunken old age. He became so well-known in Havana that a chorus of "*Papá! Papá!*" greeted him wherever he walked, but strangers approaching him in bars were not always welcome, as the inebriated writer was as likely to punch them as to say hello – though he always apologized afterward.

In the mid-1950s, Hemingway donated his medal for the Nobel Prize for Literature to the Cuban people. It was installed in the Virgin of Charity church at El Cobre, near Santiago *(see page 306)*, and remained there until 1988, when it was stolen; it was quickly recovered however, and is now kept in a Santiago bank vault. He stayed in Cuba until 1960, when illness provoked his return to the US for cancer treatment. This proved unsuccessful and, in 1961, he committed suicide in Idaho.

The Hemingway Trail

There is a well-worn route for Hemingway fans to visit in and around Havana. The best place to start is in the Old City, where the restored **Hotel Ambos Mundos** *(see page 149)* has preserved his room as it was when he wrote *For Whom The Bell Tolls* in the 1930s, and allows visitors to see it for a small charge. **El Floridita** *(see page 158)* bar and restaurant has a Hemingway bust by his favorite chair and serves the writer's own-recipe daiquirí. A sign outside quotes his words "Mi daiquirí en El Floridita." **La Bodeguita del Medio** *(see page 148)*, where he would drink his *mojitos* (a cocktail he helped to popularize), retains more atmosphere than most Hemingway haunts, even if the authenticity of the sign bearing his signature behind the bar is in doubt. The **Marina Hemingway** *(see page 185)* to the west of the city, however, has nothing to do with the writer, although the annual marlin fishing tournament in Heming-

El Floridita, where Hemingway had his favorite daiquirís.

BELOW:
La Bodeguita del Medio will always be associated with the writer.

TIP

Hemingway was oviously
concerned with his
weight. On the bath-
room wall at Finca
Vigía, above the scales,
his varying weight is
recorded beside the
date, rather in the way
that parents note their
children's height on
walls as they grow.

BELOW:
Finca Vigía has
been beautifully
renovated in
recent years.

way's honor is held there in June, when some of the biggest marlin run.

It is well worth hiring a taxi to visit two other Hemingway attractions (some hotels run excursions). The first is the **Hemingway Museum** at **Finca Vigía** (open Mon–Sat 10am–5pm; Sun 10am–1pm; entrance charge) 12 km (8 miles) from Havana city center in the suburb of **San Francisco de Paula**. The house lies at the end of a long, leafy driveway and is surrounded by lush gardens. The views over Havana are splendid.

The mansion looks much as he left it, although it has been meticulously reno-vated (work on the rest of the estate has faltered as the US assistance that made it possible has been withdrawn.) Among the relics are 9,000 books, Hemingway's original Royal typewriter and innumera-ble bullfighting posters and animal heads on every wall – mementos from Spain and Africa. As a precaution against theft visitors can only look in through the open doors and windows, but this is bet-ter than it sounds as you get an excellent view of the large, airy rooms and their contents. Museum attendants treat the objects with great respect, and are

obliged to wear thin white gloves when moving or cleaning them.

Also on display is Hemingway's Mannlicher carbine: with it unloaded, he used to demonstrate to visitors how he one day planned to commit suicide – which, of course, he did.

Close to the main house is a four-story tower, from which the estate gets its name – *vigía* means "lookout." Mary Welsh, his fourth wife, had intended that Heming-way should write on the top floor, but he never liked the tower and used it instead to store his fishing gear. The pool where Ava Gardner swam naked and Gary Cooper once lolled, tanning his famous torso, is still there. Nearby, Hemingway's yacht, the *Pilar* is kept, and carefully guarded, a long way from the sea.

You will see a row of small tomb-stones marking the graves of some of Hemingway's cats – although probably not the six-toed ones that he kept at his Key West home, having been given the original, it is said, by an old sea captain.

Guided tours of the *finca* are available for an extra charge, but are not really necessary. You don't see anything more, and most things are self-explanatory.

Mixed Messages

Hemingway's attitude toward the 1959 Revolution is still hotly debated, with both pro- and anti-Castro adherents claim-ing that he supported them. He had kept a discreet distance from the activist artistic community in Havana, reserving his verdict for private conversations. Biographers agree that Hemingway was heartily sick of the way Batista had been changing Cuba; and the writer's macho instincts were aroused by the drama of the guerrilla war and the characters of Fidel and Che. "This is a good revolution," he wrote to one friend; "an *honest* revolution." When Batista fled, he commented: *"Sic transit hijo de puta"* (There goes the son of a bitch). One of his last comments before he died, however, was that he hoped the US would not push Castro into the communist camp.

The fishing retreat

The second stop on the outer Havana Hemingway circuit is the little fishing village of **Cojímar**, some 10 km (6 miles) east of the city *(see page 190)*. This small community is also well known for another reason: it hit international headlines in 1994 when thousands of rafters *(balseros)* set off from here hoping to catch the Gulf Stream for an easy ride to Florida.

Hemingway kept the *Pilar* moored here, and used the village as the setting for *The Old Man and the Sea*. However, when a film version of the book was made in 1958 (starring Spencer Tracy as the old man), most of the fishing scenes were shot off Cabo Blanco, Peru, since Cuban marlin rarely make dramatic leaps out of the water when hooked.

The palm-fringed village is not particularly attractive, and is now reached via sprawling suburbs, but the center has retained its laid-back Caribbean flavor. A seafront promenade starts at a cube-shaped Spanish fortress, now occupied by the military. Opposite is Cuba's most affectionate memorial to Hemingway: a bronze bust made from boat propellers donated by local fishermen and housed in a circular gazebo.

If you stop to admire the bust (which some people think bears a striking resemblance to Lenin as well as to Hemingway) you are likely to be serenaded by an innovative duo who will make up a song about you on the spot and be grateful for the peso or two you will undoubtedly give them.

Halfway up the main street is **La Terraza** restaurant, which figures in *The Old Man and the Sea* and was Hemingway's local favorite. Today it has been somewhat done up, and does well out of its literary connections. You can eat some excellent seafood here, in a dining room overlooking the sea. Photos of Hemingway fishing cover the wall but, oddly, most of them were taken in Peru. (although there is one picture of him with Fidel). The dark, wood-paneled bar at the front lacks the sea views but has more atmosphere.

Memories of Ernesto

Until a few years ago, no visit to Cojímar was complete without an encounter with Gregorio Fuentes, who died in 2002 at the age of 104. He was Hemingway's fishing guide for nearly 30 years, and credited with being the person who suggested the title *The Old Man and The Sea*. He was also involved in Hemingway's unsuccesssful attempts to hunt down German U-boats.

As a good revolutionary, he later regarded talking to tourists as his patriotic duty, to help Cuban tourism bring in foreign currency. To this end, Gregorio's son took over as his business manager and charged tourists a small fee to talk to the old man.

Fuentes's memories of the long years he spent with Hemingway may have been a little faded, and inevitably became formulaic through constant repetition, but the reservoir of affection was limitless and sincere.

"Of the Americans as a people," he would declare, "there are good and bad. But I have never met a more intelligent man in the world than Ernest Hemingway, nor one more humane." ❏

The late Gregorio Fuentes, pictured in Las Terrazas restaurant.

BELOW: the bust of Ernesto on the seafront in Cojímar.

VIÑALES AND THE WEST

Cuba's westernmost province is one of its most
beautiful, a lush and lovely landscape where
tobacco, bananas and pineapples are grown,
where fields are tilled by ox-drawn plows, and
the white sandy beaches are never far away

Jutting out to the west of Havana, the province of Pinar del Río looks and feels quite different from the rest of Cuba. This is the country's tobacco heartland. Physically, it is dominated by a string of rounded limestone mountains called *mogotes*, around Viñales; in their shadows are lush green tobacco fields – *vegas*. Southwest of the *mogotes* lies the area known as Vuelta Abajo that produces the world's finest tobacco leaves, the dream of cigar connoisseurs from Paris to New York.

The atmosphere in Pinar is several degrees more gentle and relaxed than the rest of Cuba – a fact that the great Cuban intellectual Fernando Ortíz has argued is a direct legacy of the centuries-old tobacco tradition. While eastern Cuba is devoted to sugar cane – a crop whose harvesting is back-breaking work in the fierce Caribbean sun – the cultivation of tobacco is refined, intimate and even elegant. Pinar's plantations are minuscule compared to the endless cane fields of the east, and only a fraction of the numbers of workers are required. Everything is done by hand, from the picking of the leaf to the rolling of the cigars. In some *vegas*, linen nets protect the plants from the sun; in others, harvesters remove their hats, so as not to bruise the fragile, valuable leaves.

Pinar del Río has historically been one of the least-developed provinces of Cuba. For centuries, the central government looked first toward the east (after Havana, that is), and even vacationing *habaneros* avoided Pinar for the beaches of Varadero and attractions of Santiago. One of the Revolution's aims was to bring Pinar more up to par with the rest of the country but rural life is still somewhat reminiscent of the 19th century. Bullock carts are often the main form of transportation and regularly block traffic on highways; the use of oxen and mules for transportation is not exclusive to this region, but Pinar's reliance on them is greater than elsewhere. Thatched *casas de tabaco*, with steeply pitched roofs for drying the leaves, still dot the

Main attractions
LAS TERRAZAS
SOROA ORCHIDEARIO
PARQUE NACIONAL DE LA GÜIRA
PINAR DEL RÍO
VIÑALES
CAYO LEVISA
MARÍA LA GORDA

PRECEDING PAGES:
a view over Viñales.
LEFT: Viñales main
street. **BELOW:**
revolutionary
monument in
Pinar del Río.

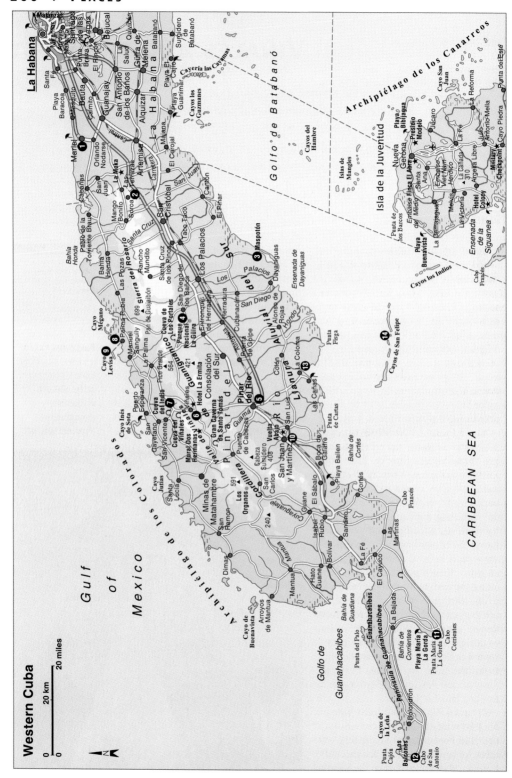

Western Cuba

landscape, although those that were destroyed in the 2002 hurricanes have been replaced by similar sheds roofed with sheets of corrugated iron. You will see traditional palm-thatched cottages – *bohíos*. At a time of severe building shortages, the government began constructing new *bohíos*, using traditional, abundant, natural materials. The villages are small and dreamy, each with a crumbling colonial church, palm-fringed plaza – and inevitable bust of José Martí.

Head west, *compañero*

In its efforts to bring Pinar closer into the national fold, the Castro government pushed through an impressive six-lane *autopista* (highway) from Havana. Today it is hardly used; except for a few trucks and army vehicles, your rental car or tour bus is likely to be the only moving thing on it. Clustered in the shade under bridges are droves of hitchhikers going to buy food in the provinces or visit relatives – be generous with your space since many of them may have been waiting for hours.

Following the highway, the provincial capital of Pinar del Río, 178 km (110 miles) from Havana, can be reached in only three hours. Slower, but more appealing, is the old Carretera Central, a two-lane road that winds through smaller towns and is thick with cyclists. The third and most picturesque option is the rough-and-ready Carretera Norte, which follows the coast. Note that it is considerably easier to get out of Havana and join any of these three routes by first following the coastal road to **Mariel ❶**. During the summer of 1994, *balseros* (rafters) embarked on the hazardous crossing toward the US from all along this coast, in a great refugee crisis that strained political relations between the two countries. Mariel was also the scene of a great exodus in 1980, when more than 120,000 Cubans were allowed to leave, picked up in boats from Miami. This port used to be filled with Soviet ships, and now, after a long hiatus, it is beginning to get busy again, especially as there is a free-trade zone (*Zona*

Franca) for foreign investors. A horrendous cement works rains white powder on the town, which gives it its gray, ashen appearance.

Beyond Mariel, the scene grows more rural. The coast road passes glorious blue seas edged with scrubby beaches, and inland the landscape is agreeably pastoral. Here you will find some of the most accessible sugar mills to visit from Havana, although it is best to see them outside the *zafra* (harvest), which runs from December through May or June. Many roads are unmarked, but local people will give directions. If heading inland, the road from Mariel soon joins the highway or links up with the Carretera Central at Guanajay. Although all Cuban *autopistas* are now pretty well provided with fuel and rest stops, drivers should remember to fill up before heading to the remoter parts of the province.

The verdant sierra

Traveling through the interior, the highways enter the steep hills of the **Sierra del Rosario**. The first detour, just before the provincial boundary, is the biosphere reserve and eco-resort of **Las Terrazas**.

TIP

Just before Artemisa, a large town south of Mariel, you will find the fascinating but unmarked ruins of La Bellona sugar plantation, dating from the 19th century. Walls and columns are spread over a large area, the most identifiable structures being the main house and the slave quarters, which have a tall iron gate and the remains of a watchtower at one end.

BELOW: Las Terrazas is designated a biosphere reserve.

TIP

The area around Soroa and San Cristóbal is the only region in Cuba where grapes – introduced from Spain – are grown for wine production. The industry is still in its infancy, but some of the wines are worth trying.

BELOW: braving the waterfall at Soroa.

(there's a small entrance charge, payable at checkpoints). In 1967 the government built a colony here, on 5,000 hectares (12,300 acres) of land, in an attempt to assist the rural community after indiscriminate tree-felling had all but denuded the countryside. The terraces were created to help prevent further soil erosion. Now run as a tourist complex on principles of sustainable development, the little colony flourishes, its forested terraces tumbling down to a long artificial lake that is lit at night and has a small café suspended over the water on a pier. The community is also the base for several artists who sell crafts and paintings from their workshops. There is also a **museum** of pre-Columbian artifacts. The Hotel La Moka here is a beautiful modern hotel built in traditional Cuban style.

At the **Eco-Center** (Centro de Investigaciones Ecológicas) you can hire guides who specialize in the forest's flora and bird life and will lead you on forest trails. The San Juan River Trail ends at the fabulous **Baños de San Juan** where you can bathe in a deep mountain pool fed by a waterfall. You can also rent bicycles for about CUC$1 an hour.

Just across the provincial border, 8 km (5 miles) from the main highway, is **Soroa ❷** – less a village than a crossroads in the dripping forest (much of the sierra has been declared a UNESCO Biosphere Reserve). Soroa is best known for its **Orchideario** (Orchid Garden; open daily 8am–4pm; entrance charge), maintained behind large gates: on its extensive, pleasant grounds are some 700 types of orchid, more than 200 of them indigenous, and most of them in flower between December and March.

Signposts by the road also direct hikers to a *mirador* (lookout) – a 20-minute walk – and a **waterfall**, as well as the **Villa Soroa-Castillo en las Nubes** complex. This is a good place for a break from the road, with a pleasant dining room (although the food is only average) and views across the sierra to the plains from a sunny, silent terrace. Soroa is now very much a part of the tourist trail but this is still a pleasant place to sit and watch the river and listen to the cicadas – an amazing rattling sound that rolls through the forest like a Mexican wave. Visitors can stay at the Villa Soroa in cabins set in a lush landscape.

West of Soroa, the Carretera Central passes the provincial town of **San Cristóbal**, whose red-tiled roofs and colorful buildings are falling to pieces. As in all such outposts, motor vehicles are few and far between. Slightly to the south, on the railroad line, is **Los Palacios**, and a rough dirt road that heads to the remote and barely populated southern coastline. In the swampy land here is **Maspotón ❸**, where a Club de Caza (hunting club) operates small bungalows. Pigeon and wild duck are common in the winter months, and trout fishing is good year round.

Che's redoubt

Back on the Carretera Central, the route passes the **Presa La Juventud** (Lake of Youth), and there's a detour north to the village of **San Diego de los Baños**. This pretty little town, by the side of a gorge cut by the fast-flowing Los Palacios River, was once famous for its spa. The spa is still there, mainly used by Cuban convalescents, but it is also open to foreign visitors for massages and treatments with volcanic mud and mineral water. There is a milky radioactive pool that glows in the gloom of the domed bath-house, which is said to stimulate the hypothalamus area of the brain and rejuvenate the nervous system. Visitors stay at the delightful Hotel Mirador next door.

The tropical forests of the **Parque Nacional La Güira ❹** can be reached by road, or by crossing the suspension bridge across the river by the spa. This was part of an aristocratic estate in colonial times and still contains a mansion and sculpted garden. The surrounding forest, dotted with lakes, plays host to a rich bird life and is home to the native Cuban deer.

The neighboring **Cueva de Los Portales** was the HQ for the Western Army under Che Guevara during the 1962 Missile Crisis, and was declared a National Monument in 1987. The camping complex here, with a dozen comfortable cabins set among lawns and pines joined by rope walkways, was designed by Celia Sánchez. Neglected for years, it has now been renovated and makes a pleasant, inexpensive place to stay.

Provincial capital

The one exception to the prevailing laid-back atmosphere of the province is the

Cattle egrets are seen all over the province, wherever cattle are kept.

BELOW: graceful statue in the Parque Nacional La Güira.

Polo Montañez

Born Fernando Borrego in San Cristóbal in 1955 Polo Montañez became popular both within and outside Cuba for his *guajiro* (country) music. His first and best-known album was called *El Guajiro Natural* (The Authentic Countryman). Polo joined his father's band when he was 10 years old, and never stopped playing or singing, even when he had to take on a variety of manual jobs to earn a living. He rarely left his Pinar del Río region, and never strayed from his roots. His music was undeniably Cuban, yet it was unlike any other, for he developed his own distinctive style. There was widespread mourning when Polo died following a car accident on his way home from Havana in November 2002. The lively Cultural Center in Viñales, not far from his home town, has been renamed the Polo Montañez Center in his honor.

Guayabita del Pinar is a liqueur specific to the region.

hectic regional capital, **Pinar del Río ❺**. A settlement has existed here since the 1570s, but development really began only after 1774 – comparatively late in the Spanish colonial period. Pinar lacks the clear grid pattern that makes other Cuban towns so straightforward to explore. The streets are unusually narrow and confusing, packed with cyclists. Be warned, too, that for a relatively small place, the town contains an unusual concentration of *jineteros* (street hustlers).

The main street, José Martí, has a number of impressive, if decrepit buildings: the **Palacio Guasch**, dating from 1909, stands out for its fairy-tale Moorish design mixed with various other architectural styles, and appears to owe something to the work of Barcelona architect Antoni Gaudí. It is in a somewhat sorry state, but still houses the **Museo de Ciencias Naturales** (Natural History Museum; open Tues–Sat 9am–6pm, Sun 9am–1pm; entrance charge), which is crammed with stuffed animals and has a curious collection of concrete dinosaurs in the courtyard.

A short walk east is the **Museo Provincial de História** (Calle Martí 58; open Tues–Sat 9am–5pm, Sun 9am–1pm; entrance charge), housed in a colonial mansion and with a collection of local memorabilia ranging from 18th-century furniture to the pistols, radios and rifles of local revolutionary heroes. Next door, the fully restored neoclassical **Teatro Jacinto Milanés** dates from 1845.

More interesting for visitors are two factories in Pinar. Near Plaza de la Independencia, at the eastern end of Martí, on Calle Maceo 157 and Carbada, is the tiny **Fábrica de Tabaco Francisco Donatién** (open Mon–Fri 9am–noon, 1–4pm, Sat 9am–noon; entrance charge), where a constant stream of tourists watch workers rolling a variety of cigars, and where there is also a small shop. South on Isabel Rubio is the **Fábrica de Bebidas Casa Garay** (open Mon–Fri 9am–noon, 1–4pm, Sat 9am–noon; guided tours; entrance charge), which produces a liqueur called Guayabita del Pinar, distilled from sugar cane and the small *guayabita* fruit that grows around Pinar. Tours take you past the vats of liqueur and end up in the gift shop, where the concoction can be tasted and, of course, bought.

Just north of town, the road to the Viñales valley passes the camping resort *(campismo)* of **Aguas Claras**, where comfortable cabins overlooking a swimming pool are surrounded by the lush gardens of a former colonial estate.

The Viñales valley

The touristic core of the province lies north of Pinar in the **Sierra de los Órganos**, a region protected as the Parque Nacional de Viñales and dominated by the bizarre mountains that protrude sheer from the fields on the valley floor. These *mogotes* are fists of hard limestone that were left behind when the softer rock around them eroded over millions of years. In the Jurassic period the *mogotes* were the pillars of vast caves that subsequently collapsed; today, covered in luxuriant foliage, they have the air of overgrown ruins.

From Pinar, a narrow, slippery road with splendid views winds 27 km (17 miles) up into the sierra until it reaches **Viñales ❻**. The local authorities, recognizing the importance of their little tobacco town as a center for this important tourist region, have worked hard to make it appealing to visitors, who used simply to drive on through, having admired the view. Today, the long rows of single-story houses and the porches on which people sit in rocking chairs, have been colorfully painted, and the shady plaza is looking wonderful after recent renovation work, although the church is still in need of some loving care. There are a couple of lively music venues *(see page 211)* and a general air of friendliness. Local residents have discovered the benefits of tourism: Viñales has more rooms to let than any Cuban small town except Trinidad; there were said to be 320 at the latest count.

At the east end of the main street (Salvador Cisneros), nearly opposite the Cupet gas station, is the pretty little **Jardín Botánico** (open daylight hours; donation appreciated). Two elderly sisters and their brother Jesús cultivate a wide selection of flowers and fruits, as well as some oddities, like a tree decorated with beer cans, and another with plastic dolls' heads. They will show you around and tell you the name of everything, before offering you slices of fresh pineapple on their shady porch.

TIP

Severe flooding, a result of a hurricane, inundated much of the Viñales valley in 2003. It's hard to imagine it now, but two people lost their lives, and many lost their livelihoods. The school was rebuilt on higher ground in case such a thing should happen again.

BELOW: the fields are still plowed in an old-fashioned and labor-intensive way.

EAT

Apart from the famous Don Tomás *(see page 211)* and the hotel restaurants, there are no recommended places to eat in Viñales itself. This is because nearly all the *casas particulares* cook excellent food for their guests at very reasonable prices – and some of them mix a mean *mojito*, as well.

BELOW: for local farmers life is hard, but the standard of living is better than in the towns.

There's a little Museo Municipal at the western end of the street (No. 115) in the house of local War of Independence heroine, Adela Acuye (1861–1914). It gamely stays open until 10pm, although it seems to receive few visitors,

A good way to get to know the area is to take the little tourist bus that runs from the main square seven times a day (first bus at 9am, CUC$5). The tour lasts just over an hour and takes in all the main sights; you can get off where you like, and continue on a later bus.

There are three hotels in the area. The **Hotel Los Jazmines** has the most attractive position. The views across the valley are exceptional, from the rooms in the main hotel, the annex, or the terrace, which provides a spectacular spot for the swimming pool. The hotel is a stopping point for tour buses, so the pool isn't as peaceful as it might be, and inevitably a string of vendors have set up stands selling the usual plethora of tourist items, but luckily the parking lot is set slightly behind the main hotel buildings.

The **Hotel La Ermita** is closer to Viñales (a 20-minute walk, above the town to the east). It has more distant views of the valley, but almost all the rooms have balconies facing out to the *mogotes*, as does the swimming pool (which, like that at Los Jazmines, can be used by non-residents for a small charge) and the pleasant, open-air restaurant. At dusk the scenery is particularly stunning: the sun turns brilliant orange as it slides behind the mountains while a thin mist gathers in the valleys, isolating the distant strings of palm trees in a haunting tropical soup.

Agricultural heartland

It is a short drive (or a pleasant walk) from Viñales into the shaded valleys between the *mogotes*, whose rich, red soil is perfect for tobacco growing. Along the isolated tracks, *guajiros* (farmers) cycle past wearing straw hats and puffing huge cigars, or trot past on horseback. In the fields, simple wooden or iron plows are pulled by placid oxen *(bueyes)* instead of tractors, and these animals are often used to pull carts as well. You will see the steep-roofed *secaderos*, sheds in which tobacco is dried, and the small homesteads where local farming families live. Most of the

Insider Knowledge

The Parque Nacional de Viñales has a brand-new Visitors' Center, housed in a bright yellow building just past the Hotel Los Jazmines, about 3 km (2 miles) from Viñales. It offers a limited amount of information on the area's agriculture and geology, as well as guided walking tours (in English if required) into the valley, stopping to visit a tobacco-drying house. It is very convenient if you are staying in the Hotel Los Jazmines, but if you are staying in a *casa particular*, the owner will probably be able to arrange similar walks more cheaply (although you are less likely to get an English-speaking guide). In Viñales, everyone knows someone who can perform such services. If you want to go horse trekking, for example, a guide and a suitable horse will be produced and a price quoted; and if you want to buy cigars, you'll be spoiled for choice farmers here grow a mixture of tobacco, maize, bananas, and pineapples, all on a small scale, and most keep a pig and some chickens, as well as the working *bueyes* and horses.

The **Mural de la Prehistoria**, an enormous, garish painting that covers the flank of the Dos Hermanas Mogote, about 4 km (2 miles) west of Viñales, was commissioned by Castro in the 1960s to portray the emergence of Socialist Man from the primal wilderness. One of Diego de Rivera's students, Leovigildo González, took on the commission, directing dozens of local painters. It is regularly touched up by artists who dangle precariously from the cliff top on rope swings. Close by you can visit the **Casa de las Raíces**, where the garden is full of imaginative carvings made from tree roots and pieces of wood.

A collection of caves

The *mogotes* are riddled with underground rivers and limestone caves. Heading north of Viñales, the road first passes the **Cueva de San Miguel**, a small cave through which you walk to reach **El Palenque de los Cimarrones**, a bar,

restaurant and museum (noon–4pm). A couple of miles farther on, set on manicured grounds amid towering rocks is the **Cueva del Indio** (Indian Cave; open daily 10am–5.30pm; regular tours last 25 minutes; entrance charge) **❼** – so named because the local indigenous Guanahatabey people used it as a cemetery and refuge during the Spanish Conquest. You climb steps to the cave then follow a contorted limestone tunnel down to an underground lake, on which you can take a boat trip (part of the guided tour).

There is a pleasant hotel (El Rancho de San Vicente), with a restaurant and a bar set beside a deep natural pool, with shacks outside selling touristy goods. There's also a camp site, Las Magnolias, and the Cueva del Indio restaurant, where you buy tickets to visit the cave. These eating places are open for lunch only, until around 4 or 5pm.

The road north of Viñales continues through spectacular countryside directly to the coast, ending up at **Puerto Esperanza**, a small, soporific fishing outpost, where benches are laid out beneath palm trees by the mangrove-lined coast. A left turn off this road takes you to the **Cueva**

Socialist slogans now include Raúl alongside his brother.

BELOW: Viñales valley, seen from Hotel Los Jazmines.

The *Guajiro*

A *guajiro* is a Cuban peasant farmer – the romanticized version of the *campesino*, or rural worker. The true *guajiro* has to be country-born and bred, devoted to the land, fiercely independent and firmly set in his ways. Both by tradition and preference, he lives in a *bohío*. These rustic cottages, their roofs thatched with palm leaves, can still be seen throughout the countryside, with rocking chairs tipped up on the front porch, a horse tethered at the door, a television aerial atop the roof, chickens scratching in the yard and a few pigs rooting outside.

The stereotypical *guajiro* is taciturn and mistrustful of outsiders, especially people from the city and farming bureaucrats – the ones who set quotas and prices for whatever they've told him to plant. In recent years, more and more *guajiros* – persuaded by their wives and the state – have joined their land with others to form larger cooperatives. Even so, he's still a *guajiro*, guiding his ox-pulled plow through the fields, dressed like his predecessors in old boots, baggy pants, a long-sleeved shirt and broad-brimmed straw hat; breaking his dawn-to-dusk work day with a big midday meal; relaxing with a cigar and a shot of rum; and occasionally feasting on roast pork accompanied by music.

The first *guajiros* were the tobacco farmers of western Cuba, sons of Spaniards who revolted against the Spanish tobacco monopoly in 1717. Although plantations based on slavery soon dominated Cuban agriculture, they always co-existed with small farms owned and worked by free men. No matter what the crop or where they grew it, these farmers had little in common with the plantation owners, who operated on a totally different scale, with a large workforce of slaves.

Though unsophisticated, the *guajiro* has unwittingly made his contribution to Cuban fashion with the *guayabera*, a white cotton shirt he always donned for a down-home *guateque*, or party. In the 1800s, Cubans rebelling against Spain adopted the *guayabera* for dress parade; in the early 20th century, Havana bohemians took a fancy to the shirt and brought the look into their clubs. The *guayabera* is still the favorite dress shirt of many Cubans – and one that these days is increasingly being bought and worn by visitors.

Typically, the *guajiro* enlivens the *guateque* with a dance that expresses his exuberant energy: called a *zapateo,* it is a toe-and-heel jig that keeps couples hopping around energetically between drinking shots of *aguardiente* (raw rum) and eating hunks of roast pork.

Despite lacking formal education, the *guajiro* brought poetry to the Cuban countryside in the form of the *décima*, which originated in 16th-century Spain. The *décima* consists of 10 octosyllabic rhymed lines, improvized and usually sung in counterpoint, accompanied by three main instruments – a guitar, a *tres* (which is similar to a mandolin) and a lute – with *claves* (wooden sticks) and a dried gourd for percussion.

The songs will usually describe the *guajiro*'s life of joy and pain, trust and deception, success and failure, but they are sometimes witty polemics on a current topic.

Typical of rural Cuba is the *guajira* ballad, first sung by roving troubadours, and much later commercialized for radio. The most famous *guajira* is the one that groups of musicians now play in every square and bar in Cuba where tourists congregate. It is Joseito Fernández's *La Guantanamera*, sung in praise of a girl from Guantánamo, using verse written by independence hero José Martí: "I am a sincere man from the land where the palms grow... Guantanamera, *guajira*, Guantanamera..." ❏

LEFT: a *guajiro*'s life has not changed much for years.

de San Tomás (open daily 9am–5pm; 90-minute guided tour; entrance charge), said to be Cuba's largest cave system. Visitors are provided with headlamps (like miners' lamps) but the lack of other artificial light makes it unsuitable for the claustrophobic.

Two cays on the gulf

A well-signposted road leads westward, passing mangrove swamps on the last part of the journey, to **Cayo Jutías**, a tranquil little sandy beach reached via a long causeway. (There's a gas station at Santa Lucía, just before you get to the causeway.) You pay CUC$5 to gain access. A new *ranchón* (thatch-roofed restaurant) is being constructed right by the shore. Take insect repellent as flying insects can be a nuisance.

Just past the Cueva del Indio, on the road to Puerto Esperanza, is a more oft-traveled route: a turn-off east leads through La Palma to **Palma Rubia** ❽, from where it is a 25-minute boat trip to **Cayo Levisa** ❾: get there by 9.45am at the latest to catch the 10am sailing, or there is another departure at 6pm. This small island has by far the best beaches

in Pinar del Río province, with sparkling white sands. There is a comfortable, unpretentious resort where, thanks to the fishing industry, lobster is the specialty. This is a place to chill out and do little, though there is some good diving – the nearby reef has abundant black coral and other rarities.

East of Cayo Levisa lies a tiny cay with an outsized name, **Cayo Mégano de Casiguas a Paraíso**, which was one of Ernest Hemingway's favorite retreats, and which offers superb scuba diving off the coral reef. Hotels in Viñales can arrange trips to Cayo Levisa, as can the Cubanacán and Havantur agencies in the main street *(see margin)*.

The coastal route heading back to Havana via **Las Pozas** and **Bahía Honda** is often rough, pot holed and narrow, so should be approached with caution. The Sierra del Rosario, Soroa, and Las Terrazas can also be accessed from just east of Bahía Honda. This is a return to more traditional sugar-growing areas, and in the winter harvest time the road can be jammed with trucks. The views of the Caribbean are pleasant, but the beaches are not Cuba's finest, especially since

TIP

The Cubanacán office is at Salvador Cisneros 63, and Havantur at 65, one on either side of the Viazul office.

BELOW: Cayo Levisa is great, whether you want to be lazy or active.

much of the coastline is taken up by mangroves rather than sand. The best of them is probably **Playa Herradura**, some 8 km (5 miles) off the main road, to the north of Cabañas.

The end of the road

Heading west from Pinar del Río, the route passes the town of **San Juan y Martínez** . Between here and **San Luis** is the district of **Vuelta Abajo**, where it is generally regarded that the finest tobacco leaves in the world are grown. Despite its tiny size, the most famous – and therefore the most photographed – field of all is the **Hoyo de Monterrey**.

Increasing numbers of travelers venture west beyond this point. Although the roads are in reasonable condition, invasions of land crabs can cause havoc with your car tires at breeding times (March–April). The Carretera Central leaves the hills for more monotonous terrain. You pass the planned city of **Sandino** – named after the Nicaraguan revolutionary hero, and partially populated by Cubans forcibly transferred from the Escambray mountains during the

1960s for supporting the counter-revolution – and end up at the fishing outpost of **La Fé**.

From La Fé, you can continue west to **La Bajada**, where the road branches south to **Punta María La Gorda** ⓫. This place – Fat Maria's Point – was named for an obviously well-fed Venezuelan girl abandoned here after being kidnapped by pirates. The beach is lovely, but most people come for the diving. There are some sheltered offshore reefs of black coral, some good wrecks to explore, a wide range of marine life, and great visibility. The **International Diving Center** offers a range of dive packages, from a single dive or a night dive to a 10-dive package (costing around CUC$240).

La Bajada marks the beginning of the **Península de Guanahacabibes Biosphere Reserve** and the site of the Guanahacabibes' last stand against the Spanish. At the information center you can arrange guided walks and a tour to Cuba's most westerly point, **Cabo de San Antonio** ⓬. The area has an excellent reputation for bird life, including several rare endemic species. The roadway along the **Bahía de Corrientes** sparkles with fine, white-sand beaches, and dolphins may sometimes be seen in the blue seas of the bay. Beyond this, the Gulf of Mexico stretches into the distance.

Cayos de San Felipe

South of Pinar province these 10 little cays are undeveloped, and a haven for all kinds of wildlife including three species of lizard and a woodpecker that are unique to the islands, and which thrive in the absence of humanity – there is just one tiny fishing community. You get there by boat from **La Coloma** ⓭ (about 20 km/12 miles south of Pinar del Río city), or by taking one of the "eco-packages" available. Most of the latter feature the **Cayos de San Felipe** ⓮ as part of a mountain and sea deal that includes diving and snorkeling and a stay at the Finca La Guabina mountain resort near the Viñales valley, where they breed apaloosa and pinto cubano horses. ❏

Attractive conch shells on the beach – don't be tempted to take them home.

BELOW: Punta María La Gorda in the far west.

RESTAURANTS & BARS

Restaurants

Pinar del Río

Rumayor
Carretera Viñales Km 1
Tel: (082) 763-051
Open daily L & D. **$–$$**
Islazul runs this restaurant, and it's rather a good one. There are various fish dishes if they've run out of the house specialty, smoked chicken (*pollo ahumado*). There's also a late cabaret on weekend nights.

El Romero
Las Terrazas, Autopista Habana–Pinar del Río, Km 51
Tel: (082) 778-600–1. Open daily 9am–9pm. **$**
A vegetarian restaurant in this "eco-community" between Pinar del Río and Viñales. All ingredients are home-grown and organic – and dishes are quite innovative too.

Viñales

Because Viñales is full of *casas particulares* (there are more than 300), which invariably serve guests with good and very inexpensive meals, there are very few restaurants and no *paladares*. The choices are as follows:

La Casa de Don Tomás
Calle Salvador Cisneros, 140.
Tel: (048) 796-300. Open daily L & D. **$$**
A lovely old house in the main street, set in flowery gardens with a vine-draped terrace. The best place to eat is in the patio at the back. The house specialty – *las delicias de Don Tomás* – is a kind of paella, but with lobster. Lots of other choices, too. Always busy.

Palenque de los Cimarrones
Carretera Puerto Esperanza, Km 36, Viñales.
Tel: (048) 796-290. Open daily 11am–4pm. **$$**
You reach the restaurant through the Cueva de San Miguel. You get an Afro-Cuban show with your lunch. Grilled chicken and game are the specialties.

Restaurant Mural de la Prehistoria
Carretera Pinar del Río–Viñales
Tel: (048) 796-260. Open daily noon–7pm. **$$**
The mural may be a bit odd but the food here is great. Charcoal-grilled pork with all the trimmings is the specialty.

Restaurante Cueva del Indio
Carretera Puerto Esperanza Km 38. Open daily 11.30am–4pm. **$$**
Standard *criollo* dishes in a large, functional Palmeres-run restaurant right beside the cave. It can get booked up by tour groups.

Bars

Viñales

Centro Cultural Polo Montañez (Calle Salvador Cisneros, beside the church in the plaza). Named after renowned local singer who died in a car accident in 2002, this place is open all day, serving drinks and snacks, with taped music. Live music, often very good, starts around 10pm and finishes at 1am closing time.

Patio del Decimista (Calle Salvador Cisneros, 102). A lively spot, where you can sit at tables inside or out with a rum or a beer. Live music every night starts at 9pm or 10pm.

El Viñalero (Calle Salvador Cisneros, 105). A very local, friendly spot for a beer or a rum – and you can sit on the terrace and hear the music from the Decimista opposite.

Disco-Bar Cueva de Viñales (Cueva de San Miguel). During the day this is a cool little bar in the cave's mouth; at night (11pm–2am) it becomes a disco.

PRICE CATEGORIES

Price categories are for a three-course meal for one with a beer, or *mojito*. Wine puts the price up:
$ = under $25
$$ = $25–35
$$$ = over $35

RIGHT: La Casa de Don Tomás in Viñales.

SECRETS OF THE CUBAN CIGAR

Thanks to the ideal climate and soil, plus centuries of expertise in cultivating the tobacco crop, Cuba produces the world's finest smokes

The big fat Cuban cigar holds almost as important a role in the national identity as rum and salsa. Tobacco is grown on smallholdings in parts of eastern, central and western Cuba, but the most highly prized comes from the *vegas* (plantations) around the town of San Juan y Martínez and San Luís in the western province of Pinar del Río, in an area called the Vuelta Abajo.

It is this region's leaves – the most important of which are grown under cheesecloth to protect them from direct sunlight – that end up in Havana's cigar factories, to be made into world-famous brands such as Cohiba, Montecristo and Romeo y Julieta. Around 100 million cigars are exported each year, and the industry is one of the island's chief hard-currency earners.

In order to stamp out the black market in counterfeit cigars, official cigar boxes now bear a holographic seal. A box of Cohibas bought on the street may look much like the real thing, with the packaging and cigar bands pilfered from a factory, but the tobacco is likely to be inferior. It's best to buy from an official shop (the best are in tobacco factories), where prices are much higher but still only a fraction of what you would pay abroad.

If you get the chance to inspect the contents of a box before you buy, check that the cigars are of a similar color (the darker the color, the stronger the flavour), and that if you squeeze them they readily spring back into shape and don't crackle.

RIGHT: cigar lengths vary from around 10–20 cm (4–9 inches). Thicker cigars are fuller-flavored and smoother.

BELOW: Montecristo cigars: they are the choice of many cigar enthusiasts all over the world.

ABOVE: painstaking process: the tobacco harvest, which takes place between February and March, is extremely labor-intensive, with the leaves being hand picked in six distinct phases, with about a week between each phase. The finest leaves are in the middle of the plant. The leaves from the top are much more oily, and are generally only used as binders.

BELOW: the Partagás factory: founded in 1845, this cigar factory in Centro Havana is now the largest in the country, producing 5 million cigars a year. You can visit and watch the cigars being made before you buy. Famous brands by other producers include the Cohiba named after the Taíno word for tobacco, and created in the 1960s as largesse for foreign diplomats; and Upmann for Directors, named after an old London bank, which at first imported cigars solely for its directors.

CUBAN CIGAR FACTORIES

Cigars for domestic consumption are made in small-scale factories across the country, while those for export are produced in Havana's large, famous factories such as Partagás and La Corona.

The highlight of a factory visit is seeing a room full of *torcedores* (cigar rollers) dexterously blending together the filler, binder and wrapper leaves. The best rollers can produce as many as 150 cigars a day. All rollers are allowed to smoke as many cigars as they want on the job. To help pass the time and prevent boredom, a lector takes the podium to read from a newspaper or book.

Visitors are often allowed to watch other parts of the cigar-making process, such as the sorting of leaves into their various strengths, and the color grading, banding and boxing of the final product. Before cigars can leave the factory, *catadores* (tasters) smoke random samples from selected batches to ensure their quality.

RIGHT: reformed smoker: Fidel Castro was frequently seen with a cigar in hand, but he gave up smoking them in the 1980s, explaining: "They're good for the country, but not so good for my health." If many people around the world follow his example, the Cuban economy is bound to suffer.

ABOVE: labels and boxes: colorful labels have adorned cedar cigar boxes since the 1830s. Cedar wood is used to keep the contents moist.

BELOW: cigar ambassador: Don Alejandro Robaina is the only living Cuban to have a brand of cigars named after him. Here he is with his precious crop on Las Vegas de Robaina in the province of Pinar del Río.

BELOW: *secaderos:* these thatched barns are where the tobacco leaves are dried, or cured. They are strung up with needle and thread on long poles, and left to dry for up to two months.

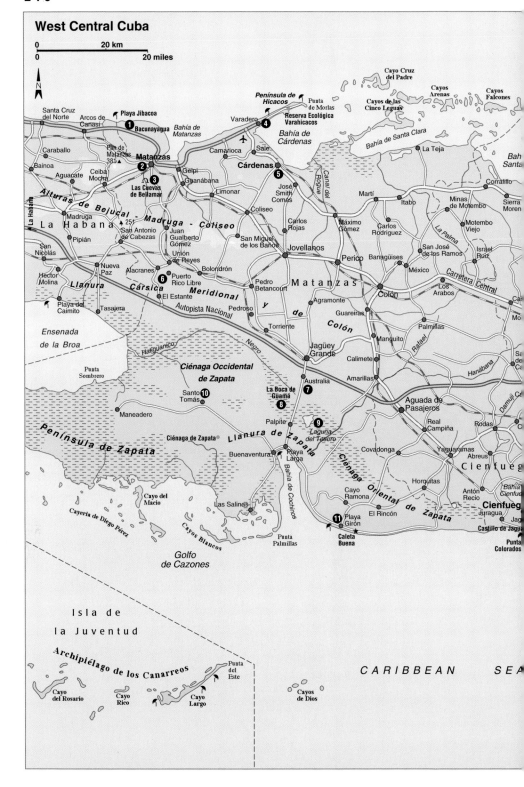

West Central Cuba

0 — 20 km
0 — 20 miles

N

Santa Cruz del Norte
Arcos de Canasí
Playa Jibacoa
1 Bacunayagua
Bahía de Matanzas
Varadero
4
Península de Hicacos
Punta de Morlas
Reserva Ecológica Varahicacos
Bahía de Cárdenas
Cayo Cruz del Padre
Cayos de las Cinco Leguas
Cayos Arenas
Cayos Falcones

Caraballo
Pan de Matanzas 381▲
Matanzas
2
Camarioca
Sale
Bahía de Santa Clara
La Teja
Bah Santa

Bainoa
Aguacate
Ceiba Mocha
3
Gelpi
Guanábana
Cárdenas
5
José Smith Comás
Canal del Roque
Martí
Itabo
Minas de Motembo
Corralillo
Sierra Moren

Las Cuevas de Bellamar
Limonar
Coliseo
Máximo Gómez
Carlos Rodríguez
San José de los Ramos
Motembo Viejo
La Palma
Israel Ruiz

Madruga
San Antonio de Cabezas
Juan Gualberto Gómez
Carlos Rojas
San Miguel de los Baños
Jovellanos
Perico
Banagüises
México

Alturas de Bejucal
La Habana
Pipián
Unión de Reyes
Madruga - Coliseo
Carretera Central

San Nicolás
Nueva Paz
Alacranes
6
Puerto Rico Libre
Bolondrón
Pedro Betancourt
Matanzas
Colón
Los Arabos
Ca

Héctor Molina
Llanura
Cársica
El Estante
Meridional
Agramonte
Guareiras
Palmillas
Mo

Playa del Caimito
Tasajera
Pedroso
Torriente
y
de
Colón
Rafael
Hanábana
Sa Ca

Ensenada de la Broa
Hatiguanico
Negro
Jagüey Grande
Manguito
Calimete
Amarillas

Punta Sombrero
Ciénaga Occidental de Zapata
Santo Tomás
10
La Boca de Güamá
8
Australia
7
Aguada de Pasajeros
Real Campiña
Rodas
Co
Damuj Ce

Maneadero
Ciénaga de Zapata
Llanura de Zapata
Palpite
9
Laguna del Tesoro
Covadonga
Yaguaramas
Abreus
Cienfueg
Bahía Cienfue

Península de Zapata
Buenaventura
Playa Larga
Bahía de Cochinos
Ciénaga
Horquitas
Antón Recio
Cienfueg
Jaragua
Jag

Cayo del Macío
Las Salinas
Cayo Ramona
El Rincón
Oriental
de
Zapata
Castillo de Jagu

Cayería de Diego Pérez
Cayos Blancos
Punta Palmillas
11 Playa Girón
Caleta Buena
Punta Colorados

Golfo de Cazones

Isla de la Juventud

Archipiélago de los Canarreos
Cayo del Rosario
Cayo Rico
Cayo Largo
Punta del Este
Cayos de Dios

CARIBBEAN   SEA

La Habana
Llanura
Cársica
Autopista Nacional

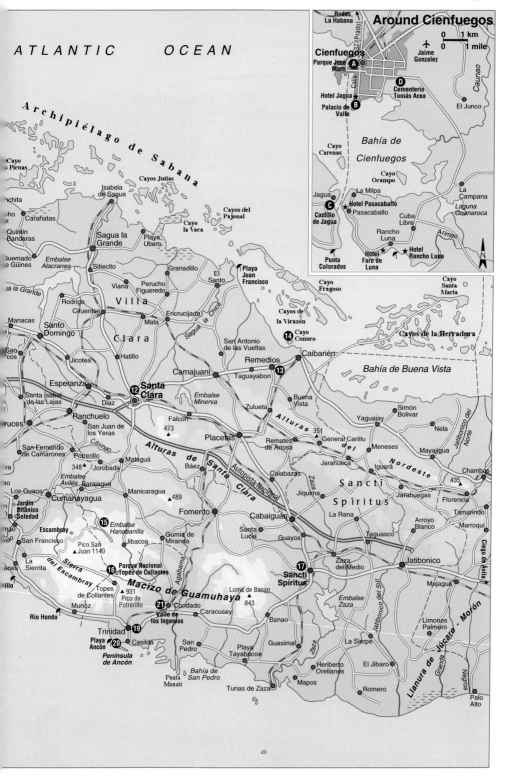

VARADERO AND MATANZAS

Cuba's prime resort for package tourism, Varadero is a world apart from the rest of the island, including the area's own peaceful hinterland and the nearby cities of Matanzas and Cárdenas

The province of **Matanzas** is the largest in Cuba, yet most visitors will never go there unless they are staying in the glitzy beach resort of Varadero. The province couldn't have a grander point of entry than the **Puente Bacunayagua ❶**. This impressive bridge, the highest in the country, spans the 112-meter (370-ft) deep gorge of the Bacunayagua River dividing the provinces of Havana and Matanzas. The Yumurí valley meanders away to the distant mountains beyond. Turkey vultures wind lazy circles above the near-silent gorge. Cicadas sing. Few vehicles pass. There is a small restaurant and café here – an obligatory pit stop for bus parties, and deservedly so: the view is impressive.

City of the slaughter

About 20 km (12 miles) east of here is the provincial capital of **Matanzas ❷**, founded more than 300 years ago. The highway passes right by the city's super-tanker port, capable of receiving 150,000-tonne oil tankers and linked by pipeline to the Cienfuegos Oil Refinery, 187 km (116 miles) to the south.

Matanzas Bay was first navigated by Sebastián de Ocampo in 1509, but the city itself wasn't established until October 1693, when Severino de Balmaseda, the provisional governor of Cuba, traveled from Havana to Matanzas with a team of surveyors to parcel out lots to newly arrived settlers from the Canary Islands. The city's name means "slaughter," and was originally thought to refer to a massacre of a local indigenous tribe, but recent study suggests it had more to do with the killing of herds of pigs kept nearby to resupply ships.

Local farmers started out growing tobacco but by the end of the 18th century they had converted to sugar. Sugar and the slave trade made the city immensely rich, and during the 19th century the local aristocracy became major patrons of the arts. Matanzas developed a rich café society and many poets and artists made their home here. During Cuba's 1895–8 War of Independence, it

Main attractions
PUENTE BACUNAYAGUA
MATANZAS
TEATRO SAUTO
CUEVAS DE BELLAMAR
VARADERO
XANADÚ
CÁRDENAS

PRECEDING PAGES: crocodile in the Zapata peninsula. **LEFT:** Varadero beach. **BELOW:** Puente Bacunayagua.

BELOW: the Museo Farmacéutico in Matanzas has a vast and fascinating array of items.

was the center of a battle between Spanish general Arsenio Martínez Campos, and two of Cuba's most important national heroes, Máximo Gómez and Antonio Maceo. On January 1, 1899, the Spanish Army handed over the town in the **Plaza de la Vigía**, in the center of town – not to the Cubans, but to General J.P. Sanger of the US Army.

The square still has a reminder of that conflict: the **Statue of the Unknown Soldier** – erected in 1919 on the spot where Matanzas was founded. Here, too, is the neoclassical **Teatro Sauto Ⓐ**, which has glorious ceilings and wonderful acoustics. It is open for performances of theater, opera and dance, usually on weekends. In the past such international stars as Sarah Bernhardt (1844–1923) and Andrés Segovia (1893–1987) have performed here and, more recently, the renowned Spanish dancer and choreographer Antonio Gades.

Adjacent to the square is the **Museo Histórico Provincial** in the **Palacio del Junco Ⓑ** (open Tues–Sun 10pm–5pm; entrance charge), which holds hundreds of documents and artifacts relating to the history of Matanzas; slavery in the sugar

plantations is given unusually detailed treatment here.

To the south of the theater toward the river you find the **Parque de los Bomberos** (Firemen's Park), with an elegant neoclassical fire station and a perfectly preserved vintage fire truck. On the same side of the street as the nearby **Galería de Arte Provincial** (open Tues–Sat 10am–6pm; entrance fee) is **Ediciones Vigía**, which produces limited editions of marvelous handmade books: you can tour the workshops (open Mon–Fri 9am–4pm). The street crosses the Río San Juan at the rotating **Puente Calixto García**, a bridge built in 1849. A couple of blocks west of Plaza de la Vigía on Calle 282 stands the neoclassical **Catedral de San Carlos Borromeo Ⓒ** (open Mon–Sat 8am–noon and 3–5pm, Sun 8am–noon), built in 1730, which has been partially restored with money given by a German tourist who fell in love with it on a visit to the city.

A healthy tonic

Perhaps the most important attraction in Matanzas overlooks the main square,

Parque La Libertad: it is the **Museo Farmacéutico**  (Calle 83/Milanés 4951; open Mon–Sat 10am–5pm, Sun 9am–2pm; entrance charge), housed in the three-story dispensary of two 19th-century doctors, Juan Fermín Figueroa and Ernesto Triolet. Considering the shortage of common medications in present-day Cuba, this may be one of the best-stocked pharmacies in Matanzas. Among the most important pieces here are porcelain medicine flasks, hundreds of pharmacy books and a dispensary table that won a bronze medal at the 1900 International Exposition in Paris. Displayed in an adjacent laboratory are ancient utensils, a wood-burning brick oven, and an *alambique* or still, in which water, alcohol and essential oils were distilled for medicinal purposes.

Pop into the **Hotel Louvre** next door – a shadow of its former self but with echoes of a glorious past (it dates from the end of the 19th century). There is a leafy courtyard, a quaint dining room serving good, simple food, and bedrooms with grand old beds and tatty antiques. And don't leave town without visiting the ruined **Ermita de Monserrate** sanctuary on a hill, at the northern end of Calle 306 (Domingo Mujica), which offers a panoramic view of the city and the Yumurí valley beyond.

A slave's cavern

There are many interesting caves in the region. The most important are **Las Cuevas de Bellamar** ❸ (open Tues–Sun 9am–6pm; 45-minute tours every hour; entrance charge), 5 km (3 miles) southeast of Matanzas. After a slave working an open lime pit in 1861 discovered the cavern, 1,000 tonnes of rock had to be broken and extracted to clear the entrance; the work revealed one of the Caribbean's largest and most beautiful underground formations. According to a US traveler, Samuel Hazard, writing in 1897, anyone who hadn't visited the Bellamar Caves hadn't really seen Cuba. This is a slight exaggeration, but the caves are impressive. The Salón Gótico (Gothic Hall), 80 meters (265 ft) long

and 25 meters (80 ft) wide, contains stalagmites with names such as La Mano de la Mujer (The Woman's Hand) and La Capilla de los Doce Apóstoles (The Chapel of the Twelve Apostles). The Lago de las Dalias (Lake of Dahlias), a rocky area covered with water, is famous for thousands of tiny calcite crystals covering its roof, walls and floor. Tours run from Varadero, but if you are coming from Matanzas, and don't have a car, you will need to take a taxi.

The **Vía Blanca** highway powers 32 km (20 miles) eastward from the caves to Cuba's most famous international beach resort, passing towering onshore oil rigs that fly the Cuban and Canadian flags, representing one of the island's joint ventures. At night, the sky is lit up by the eerie orange glow of gas flares.

Varadero

The resort of **Varadero** ❹ is the closest you'll get to finding Miami Beach in Cuba. It is flashy in a Cuban kind of way. Nowhere else on Cuban soil can you find such a high concentration of oceanfront restaurants, nightclubs and luxury hotels. Sadly, nowhere else is the island's "tour-

Stained-glass medio-punto in the glorious but dilapidated Hotel Louvre.

BELOW: visiting the Cuevas de Bellamar.

TIP

Varadero airport is some 25 km (15 miles) from the resort, in the direction of Matanzas. From the UK there are plenty of charter fights from London Gatwick and Manchester, while Martinair flies from Amsterdam, Itu from Leipzig, Air Canada from Toronto and Cubana from Toronto and Montreal.

BELOW: shopping opportunities without leaving the beach.

ism apartheid" more obvious. Indeed, Varadero is the ideal place to vacation if you don't want to meet too many Cubans. Take a leisurely stroll along its palm-fringed, white-sand beach, considered one of the finest in the Caribbean, and you're likely to encounter lots of Spaniards, Italians, Canadians, and Germans – but few local people. This is Varadero's biggest problem: because there are few Cubans, there is very little atmosphere. But if you are looking for a straightforward beach vacation, relatively free of *jineteros*, in a good modern hotel with cable TV; with air conditioning that works; a pool and a jacuzzi; a golf course left over from the 1950s; and restaurants serving pizzas and hamburgers, then this is the place for you. The seas are warm and crystal blue but, really, you could be anywhere in the Caribbean. This is one of the few places in Cuba where women can sunbathe topless. Despite the very open sexuality of Cuba, topless bathing is, perhaps surprisingly, illegal, although it is tolerated in tourist-only resorts like Varadero.

Many package-deal tourists fly directly to Varadero and never leave, so almost the only Cubans they will encounter work on the hotel staff. Foreign hotel firms pay the Cuban Government, on average, the equivalent of US$400 a month for each employee. The government pockets that money and pays the workers in Cuban pesos *(moneda nacional)*. Hotel jobs in Varadero are much sought-after, however, due to the access to tips and the better food they provide. An industrious waiter can make the *peso convertible* equivalent of US$10 a day in tips – which is more than the average monthly salary in Cuba.

The early years

Varadero has been something of a private preserve for much of its history. Local tribes once lived here, but the earliest historical mention of it dates from 1587, when the merchant Don Pedro Camacho began mining salt, both for local use and for Spanish fleets that dropped anchor in Havana.

Throughout the 1600s and early 1700s, pirates preyed on the few inhabitants of the 18-km (13-mile) **Península de Hicacos**, along which Varadero is located. In 1726, a certain José Antonio Gómez

Visiting Varadero

If you are not staying in Varadero but want to check it out there are four buses a day from Havana *(see page 338)*. Taxi drivers hang around the Viazul office trying to tempt you to go with them instead of taking the bus – and if there are more than two of you it is usually a viable way to go. You can also go on a tour bus, which most Havana hotels will arrange. If driving, the divided highway is good (it's 144 km/90 miles from central Havana). You will have to pay a small toll on entry to Varadero (currently CUC$2) at a toll gate that also acts as a checkpoint to ensure that Cubans have an official reason to enter the resort. This strict form of regulation has all but killed the *jinetero* problem in town, but while it has got rid of 95 percent of the prostitutes and hustlers it has also affected the town's ambiance, making it somewhat unreal.

bought the peninsula and used it to produce salt and rear livestock. Thirty-six years later, the Varadero Hacienda – consisting of 1,140 hectares (2,800 acres) of land from Paso Malo to Hicacos Point – was sold to an aristocrat called Bernardo Carrillo de Albornos, whose heirs were still in possession of the land in the mid-19th century.

Varadero's tourist history started in the 1870s, when families from nearby Cárdenas began visiting. In that decade, they built the first palm-thatched frame houses on the northern coast, while the southern coast remained the preserve of fishermen. The beach's fame grew, however, luring visitors from Havana, who in those days arrived by ox cart. The year 1915 marked the inauguration of the Hotel Varadero – the fledgling town's first resort. Three years later, the Cuban Congress passed a law authorizing annual rowing regattas at Varadero Beach, which soon became a highlight of the local social calendar.

A stately pleasure dome

Then in 1926, the chemicals magnate Alfred Irénée Du Pont (who had made his fortune manufacturing dynamite during World War I) scored a real-estate coup with the purchase of 512 hectares (1,265 acres) of prime Varadero property for as little as 4 centavos per sq. meter (11 sq. ft). The lavish vacation home he built, **Xanadú**, is still standing today – one of the few tourist attractions in Varadero worth visiting, the name taken, of course from Samuel Taylor Coleridge's poem *Kubla Khan*. Located right on the beach, the mansion was finished in 1930 at a cost of US$338,000 – an astronomical sum back then. These days, it is a boutique hotel (very popular with golfers) and houses the Restaurante Las Américas, an extremely expensive seafood joint where lobster thermidor costs CUC$35.

But even if you don't eat there, you can see the first floor and visit the bar on the top floor for a sunset drink and a fine view. The mahogany ceilings and banisters are all original, as are the Italian marble floors and the 1932 organ, one of the largest privately built organs in Latin America. Don't overlook Coleridge's poem *(In Xanadu did Kubla Khan a stately pleasure-dome decree...)* reproduced in full on the wall, or the beautiful terrace with a sweeping view of the Atlantic. There is a golf course adjacent, but the small, flat area does not make for a very satisfying game.

Foreign investment

Du Pont, who continued to buy up oceanfront property through the 1930s and 1940s, was not the only land speculator in Varadero. Others invested here, often with the complicity of corrupt Cuban officials or those with Mafia connections. The **Casa de Al**, which evokes those years, is now a restaurant housed in a mansion once owned by Chicago gangster Al Capone.

In 1950, the Hotel Internacional was constructed for US$3 million. That sparked a development boom that continued right up until the 1959 Revolution. Dozens of mansions arose from one end of Varadero to the other, along with golf courses, gambling casinos and

The waters here are warm and crystal clear.

BELOW: Xanadú is now a boutique hotel.

TIP

The poor-quality oil found along the north coast of Matanzas province contains high levels of sulfur, and produces a very unpleasant smell during drilling. If the wind is blowing in the right (or wrong) direction, you can smell it in Varadero.

BELOW: Puerto del Sol Marina in Varadero.

hotels with links to the so-called "Jewish godfather" Meyer Lansky and other notorious figures of organized crime.

That all came to a screeching halt in 1959. A state-approved tourist pamphlet says that two months after Batista's overthrow, the Cuban Government passed Law 270 "proclaiming the people's full right to enjoy all beaches." Even so, for many years the only kind of tourists Castro's regime welcomed were solidarity brigades from the Soviet Union and other sympathetic countries. It was only with the end of aid from the USSR that Cuba began to court large-scale tourism from capitalist countries.

Joint ventures

It was in Varadero that the first joint venture between the Cuban Government and foreign capitalists was inaugurated in 1990 – the US$26-million, 607-room Hotel Sol Palmeras. Since then the same firm, Spain's Grupo Sol Meliá, has built more hotels. As part of its ambitious development program for the area, the Ministry of Tourism has allowed development right to the end of the peninsula (which looks like a giant building site).

Even the old "Campamiento Internacional," where Cuba's youthful pioneers once stayed alongside young foreigners from solidarity brigades, has been bought for development. There are investors here from across Europe, Latin America, the Caribbean, and even China – a Chinese restaurant has recently opened. Problems with cash flow and water supplies sometimes hinder progress.

A break from the sun

Apart from Xanadú, Varadero offers very few sites of historical interest. Visitors with time to spare might like to check out the **Parque de Diversiones** (Amusement Park) at Avenida Tercera between calles 29 and 30. There is a tiny **tobacco factory** on Avenida Primera and Calle 27, and the equally diminutive **Museo Municipal de Varadero** (open Tues–Sat 10am–6pm; entrance charge) on Avenida Playa and Calle 57, which has interesting exhibits of local flora and fauna, and some oddities, such as a two-headed shark. Varadero's municipal park, the **Parque Retiro Josone**, located between calles 54 and 59, has a pleasant flamingo lake where you can rent boats.

Halfway along the peninsula, past the main stretch of tourist hotels, the tiny, 2-sq. km (0.7-sq. mile) **Reserva Ecológica Varahicacos** (open daily 9am–4.30pm) gives some idea of what the peninsula was like before tourism. The Patriarca Playa trail (entrance charge) takes you 300 meters/yds to see El Patriarca (The Patriarch) – a giant endemic cactus. At more than 500 years old, it is thought to be the longest-lived plant in Cuba, and is perhaps the only living thing in the country to have been around in the pre-Columbian age. The aboriginal paintings in the limestone **Cueva de Ambrosio** are interesting. This small cave, discovered in 1961, contains 50 well-preserved pre-historic drawings.

Cárdenas

Rent a car in Varadero and head into northern Matanzas province. The distance is minuscule but the difference in lifestyles is astonishing. Only 15 km (9 miles) south of Varadero, across Cárdenas Bay, is the city of **Cárdenas ❺** (pop. 104,000), founded in 1828. In 1850, Cuba's national flag was raised for the first time here. A plaque commemo-

rating this can be seen on the wall of the Hotel Dominica on Avenida Céspedes. On May 11, 1898, after Spain had been defeated in the Spanish-American War, Cárdenas was shelled by US Navy ships commanded by Admiral William T. Sampson. As in many provincial Cuban towns, traffic in Cárdenas consists of horse-drawn carts rather than cars, which sit in backyards, immobilized by the lack of (or cost of) gasoline.

Cárdenas became the center of world media attention in 2000 as the home town of Elián González, the "tug of love" boy *(see box, page 78)*. The streets of this small dusty town were once filled with his image, but now he has returned to everyday life with his father, it is almost as if the huge media circus never really happened, except that the town now has the **Museo de la Batalla de Ideas** (open Tues–Sat 9am–5pm; entrance charge). Housed in a well-restored 19th-century building, and inaugurated by Castro in July 2001, the six-room museum documents in lively detail the tireless campaign for the repatriation of "Eliancito," as the little boy was known. Exhibits on display include

Rodeos are sometimes held in rural towns in Matanzas province.

BELOW: a display in the Museo de la Batalla de Ideas focuses on the picture that shocked the world.

*A girl's best friend...
Dogs are good
company in the
countryside.*

BELOW: horsemen
on a country road
seem a million
miles from
Varadero.

a striking modern sculpture of José Martí holding a child in his arms.

Cárdenas is also home to the eclectic **Museo de Oscar María de Rojas** (open Tues–Sat 10am–6pm, Sun 9am–noon; entrance charge), named for a local revolutionary hero. Located on the Calzada de Vives, this natural history museum has several exhibition halls devoted to Cuban coins, weapons, shells, butterflies, minerals, pre-Columbian objects, and documents from the various revolutions and wars of independence. At the end of Calle Céspedes is a small **fortress (La Fuerte Roja)**, which is now a café and a popular meeting place for local people.

On Avenida 4 Este is the **Casa Natal de José Antonio Echevarría** (open Tues–Sat 10am–5pm, Sun 9am–noon; entrance charge), the birthplace of the student who was killed in 1957 while leading the attack on Batista's Presidential Palace. The house itself is beautiful, and there is a monument to the student in the park outside, which is also named after him.

The city has a fine cathedral, the **Catedral de la Inmaculada Concepción** (often closed, except for Sunday mass),

on Parque Colón with a statue of Columbus dating from 1858, said to be the first erected in Latin America. There is also a mausoleum in the **Plaza de la Independencia**, containing the remains of 238 patriots who fell fighting Spanish colonialism in the late 19th century.

The quiet hinterland

The province of Matanzas is almost totally dependent on the export of sugar. South of the provincial capital, not far from Cuba's national motorway, is **Puerto Rico Libre ❻** (pop. 1,200), a typical sugar-mill town. The town's name was chosen in 1960, when the newly triumphant Fidel Castro decided to adopt the cause of Puerto Rican independence and make it part and parcel of his revolution. Before that, the place had been known simply as Conchita, after the wife of the American industrialist who was responsible for building the sugar mill where *caña* is harvested for processing and export.

Southeast of Matanzas the potholed Carretera Central offers a route toward Santa Clara that is an alternative to that of the main *autopista*, passing by or through some pretty colonial settlements, like **San Miguel de los Baños** – a delightful old spa town set high in the rolling Matanzas hills. The spa has been forgotten for many years, but there are plans to resurrect it from its sad decay. A once-elegant hotel, the Rincón del Baños, still has a grand air, but is in dire need of restoration.

The road continues through **Jovellanos**, an old slave town with a strong Afro-Cuban tradition, which was named after Gaspar Melchor de Jovellanos, an 18th-century Spanish philosopher and statesman; and on to **Colón**. This is another colonial settlement with a busy main street but otherwise sleepy squares, and some impressive, if crumbling neoclassical architecture.

You then cross over into Santa Clara province. Independent travelers may find it useful to know that Jovellanos and Colón both have a Cupet gas station and both also have peso hotels. ❑

RESTAURANTS & BARS

Restaurants

Matanzas

Matanzas is distinctly lacking in places to eat. The following is the only one that could be recommended.

Café Atenas

Calle 83, 8301, Plaza de la Vigía.

Tel: (0145) 253-493

Open daily 10am–11pm. **$**

Opposite the Teatro Sauto, and with tables out on a patio, this is a pleasant enough stop for good-value pizza, pasta and sandwiches.

Varadero

Resort hotels and villas in Varadero specialize in buffets with lots of fresh fruit and outdoor grills, where you can get lunch without really leaving the beach. The specialty restaurants in the big hotels serve decent food and are open to anyone who wants to try them.

Las Américas

Mansión Xanadu, Carretera Las Américas, Km 4.5

Tel: (0145) 667-750. Open daily noon–11pm. **$$$**

A stylish place for lunch or dinner, with good French food on the menu. Also check out the cool third-floor bar.

Mi Casita

Camino del Mar, between calles 11 and 12

Tel: (0145) 613-787. Open

daily 3–11pm. **$$$**

Intimate, capriciously furnished and specializing in lobster and tasty Caribbean dishes.

Albacora

Calle 59 between 1a and Playa

Tel: (0145) 613-650. Open daily 9am–midnight. **$$**

Excellent seafood is served on a pleasant terrace overlooking the sea (the restaurant's name means swordfish).

Barracuda Grill

Villa Cuba, Calle 58

Tel: (0145) 668-280. Open daily noon–7pm. **$$**

Excellent seafood in a restaurant overlooking the beach. Good for long lunches or very early dinner.

Castel Nuovo

Avenida 1era, corner of Calle 11

Tel: (0145) 667-786.

Open daily noon–10pm. **$$**

Specializes in Italian food including tasty pizzas and good pasta.

El Bodegón Criollo

Avenida de la Playa and Calle 40

Tel: (0145) 667-784. Open daily noon–11pm. **$$**

This restaurant attempts to re-create the ambiance of Havana's Bodeguita del Medio, and serves similar cuisine. The *criollo* food is fine but it's best not to compare the venue with the original. On the other hand, it's cheaper,

and there is a view of the sea.

Esquina Cuba

Calle 36, corner of 1era

Tel: (0145) 614-019. Open daily 10am–midnight. **$$**

A thatched *bohío* in the town center. Serves good *criollo* cuisine with music to match.

Mesón del Quijote

Avenida las Américas, next to El Castillito water tower

Tel: (0145) 667-796. Open daily noon–midnight. **$$**

A jolly, intimate restaurant with a Spanish theme, as you would guess from the name. Well-cooked paella and grilled lobster feature on the menu. Meals are reasonably priced, although lobster always adds to the bill.

Casa de Antigüedades

Avenida 1era, corner of Calle 56, Parque Josone

Tel: (0145) 667-228. Open daily noon–11pm. **$–$$**

International menu and lots of seafood in a neo-colonial villa.

La Campaña

Avenida 1era, corner of Calle 60, Parque Josone

Tel: (0145) 667-224. Open daily noon–11pm. **$**

Traditional Cuban dishes and good desserts.

PRICE CATEGORIES

Price categories are for a three-course meal for one with a beer, or *mojito*.

Wine puts the price up:

$ = under $25

$$ = $25–35

$$$ = over $35

THE ZAPATA PENINSULA

The best-known of Cuba's wildlife havens, the Zapata peninsula is a refuge for many bird and animal species. Nearby Playa Girón earned its place in history during the Bay of Pigs invasion

The half of Matanzas province that lies to the south of the *autopista* from Havana is mainly low, marshy terrain that is primarily a destination for visitors interested in the rich Cuban wildlife to be found here, or those who want to visit the Bay of Pigs for historical reasons. It is not a place where people come to admire the towns or cities. Passing the town of **Torriente**, you come to the main access town for the area, **Jagüey Grande**. This is the heart of the world's largest citrus operation – a 40,000-hectare (103,000-acre) grove of orange and grapefruit trees owned by the Cuban Government and managed by a secretive Israeli firm.

Just south of the *autopista* is the town of **Australia** ⓫, dominated by its sugar mill *(central)*. The mill was Fidel Castro's headquarters during the battle at the Bay of Pigs, and part of it is now a municipal museum, the **Museo de la Comandancia** (open Tues–Sat 8am–noon, 1–5pm; entrance charge). The next long, straight stretch of road leads to the turn-off for the Zapata peninsula, with monuments to the fallen of the Bay of Pigs all along the roadside.

Close by is the **Finca Fiesta Campesina**, a tourist venture with a small zoo, shops, coffee bars, and a small cabin-style hotel, the **Bohío de Don Pedro** tucked round the back of the property. It is an obligatory stop on the Zapata tour, and has surprisingly appealing gardens where you can sip fresh-fruit *batidos* (milkshakes) in the 24-hour bar

and inspect the coffee growing on the hill side. There is even an original kind of lottery where you are asked to bet on which hole a guinea pig will run into on its release. A Cubanacán information office will organize trips to the Zapata peninsula, but these can also be organized in advance at Cubanacán offices in Havana or Varadero.

The Zapata peninsula

The **Península de Zapata**, 156 km (97 miles) southeast of Havana, was named for its similarity to a shoe (*zapato* in

Main attractions
CRIADERO DE COCODRILOS
LA BOCA DE GUAMÁ
LAGUNA DEL TESORO
SANTO TOMÁS
LAS SALINAS
PLAYA GIRÓN
MUSEO DE GIRÓN

LEFT: a flamingo strikes a pose. **BELOW:** rocky coastline in the Bay of Pigs.

The snail kite (Rostrhamus sociabilis) is a raptor that feeds, unsurprisingly, on snails, which they extract from the shells, using their long curved beaks. One indigenous name for them was kiewe balielie (lord of the snails).

BELOW: speedboats make regular trips to the Laguna del Tesoro.

Spanish). An enormous swamp, it has been a refuge, first for indigenous Taíno people, later for buccaneers and charcoal makers. The entire region is now a UNESCO Biosphere Reserve, the **Gran Parque Natural Montemar**.

Most of the Zapata peninsula is barely above sea level and is flooded every year during the rainy season (between June and October). About 30 percent is slightly higher, supporting a wide strip of forest some 16 km (10 miles) from the southern coastline. Other elevated patches of terrain are scattered throughout the swamp, and clumps of trees grow on these patches like tiny islands. The western, triangular part of the Zapata peninsula is entirely unpopulated.

The whole area is described on maps as the Ciénaga de Zapata, divided into east and west, with the Llanura de Zapata in between (*ciénaga* means swamp, *llanura* means plain).

Many narrow, linear canals are visible from the air, connecting lagoons with the surrounding shallow seas. These were all excavated by hand by the desperately poor charcoal makers a century or more ago, to facilitate lumber transportation. There are many hidden sinkholes – so stick to designated trails when walking. Much of the swamp area is covered by a thick mat of peat that acts like a gigantic mattress during the dry season. The underlying hard sediment of limestone frequently shows through, and, below ground, it is eroded into a network of caverns.

The Zapata's forests were once abundant in cabinet-quality hardwoods like ebony, mastic and mahogany. Regrettably, these virgin forests have been thoroughly exploited over the centuries, and even the tallest trees today are only secondary growth. More recent logging has produced unsightly corridors through the forest. Moreover, feral pigs and the introduced white-tailed deer have devastated the plant life of the undergrowth and altered the balance of the forest species. As a result, species that you might expect to grace the forests – like orchids, ferns, bromeliads and vines – are rarities

Crocodile farm

Crocodiles are rare in Zapata. Two species exist – the American crocodile,

and the rarer Cuban crocodile, which is only otherwise found in the Lanier Swamp in the south of the Isla de La Juventud (Isle of Youth), and is under threat there from a small but aggressive cousin introduced from South America. On the road from Jagüey Grande to Playa Larga, just before you reach La Boca de Guamá, is the **Criadero de Cocodrilos** (Crocodile Farm; open daily 9.30am–5pm; entrance charge) where both species can be seen. They used to be held together in the same pits, but hybridized so freely that the Cuban endemic nearly became extinct. Nowadays they are held in separate enclosures.

La Boca de Guamá ❽ is the most visited part of the peninsula, with plenty of tourist facilities. Boats carry passengers from here through a canal to the **Laguna del Tesoro** ❾ (Treasure Lagoon; speedboats every 30 minutes from 9am–6pm; slower ferries run about four times a day). The lake got its name because, it was said, the indigenous Taíno people of the area threw all their valuables into it rather than surrender them to the Spanish. There's a romanticized mock Taíno village at Guamá as well as an interesting Cubanacán hotel complex. Some artifacts have been found, but no gold – it seems that the Taíno had a different idea of treasure from that of the Spanish. Cabins, bridges and piers here are made of coarse wood, in a pleasant, supposedly Taíno-inspired style. Snail kites (*see margin, left*) are abundant, as well as the endemic *manjuarí* (garfish or pike) – its teeth, snout and body are a crude parallel to those of a crocodile, and its lineage goes back some 70 million years.

A birder's paradise

Birds are the main attraction in the peninsula, with a total count of 190 species. Most of Cuba's endemic species can be found here: the bee hummingbird, Cuban parakeet, Gundlach's hawk, blue-headed quail dove, Cuban tody, Cuban trogon, two species of blackbird, two types of woodpecker and a couple of very small owls. Some species, such as the Zapata wren and rail, are unique to

the swamp, while others can be found in few other places – the Zapata sparrow, for instance, is only found here, in Cayo Coco, and the desert area of Baitiquirá, near Guantánamo.

One of the best places for the ornithologist is north of **Santo Tomás** ❿ village. Always let your local guide show you the routes through the seemingly identical 2-meter (6-ft) clumps of sawgrass. The wren is a tiny, drab-looking bird, but an energetic songster; the sparrow isn't dressed to kill either, and barely buzzes or chatters. There is practically no chance at all of seeing a Zapata rail (which is close to extinction), and can pick its way through thickets of near-impenetrable grasses at speed, and only a handful of people have ever glimpsed one. Besides the resident native birds, many migrants show up from October through April: they have flown all the way from the US or Canada. Most are warblers (more than 30 different species), but there are also herons, terns, and several birds of prey.

A trip to **Las Salinas** is well worth making, but you have to go on an organized tour. The scenery is spectacular: flamingos swoop across the milky, salt-

Crocodiles are fascinating – as long as they are at a safe distance.

BELOW: an iridescent *zunzún* – Cuban emerald hummingbird.

A bottlebrush plant
(Callistemon citrinus).
They thrive in the
Zapata peninsula.

water lagoons, and crocodiles meander out across the dirt roads. The area is virtually uninhabited – there are just a dozen or so families scattered here and there who work in the reserve or fish for a living. La Salina is reached via the tiny settlement of **Buenaventura**, just to the west of Playa Larga, at the head of the Bahía de los Cochinos (Bay of Pigs).

Water birds and tropical fish

From **Playa Larga** (one of the landing sites in the notorious 1961 invasion), the road skirts the edge of the Bahía de los Cochinos as it runs south toward Cuba's most famous beach of all, Playa Girón. Some wide canals can be found slightly inland beyond **Los Hondones** (about 10 km/6 miles from Playa Larga) where water birds abound, including coots, gallinules, ducks, whistling ducks, herons, ospreys, jacanas, migratory buntings and peregrine falcons.

Farther along this stretch of road, look out for the many monuments to the Cuban dead of the Bay of Pigs invasion, and stop off at some of the beautiful sinkholes *(cenotes)* surrounded by forest, which are connected to the

BELOW:
scuba diving at
the Bay of Pigs.

nearby sea by underwater tunnels. These flooded caverns in the limestone are full of tropical fish in all colors of the rainbow. The water is crystal clear even deep down, and surprisingly cold. You can snorkel in most of these *cenotes*, which is like swimming in an aquarium.

Sadly, one of the largest and loveliest, the **Cueva de los Pesces** (Fish Cave; open daily 9am–6pm; entrance charge), has been spoiled by over-development. It is well-signposted, and there are restaurants, a bar, and loungers on which you can sit by the lagoon and admire the scenery. You can rent snorkeling gear, and though loud music ruins the ambiance, the swimming and the fish are still lovely. There is an abundance of lizards too, some tame enough to feed under the tables.

The Bay of Pigs

The village of **Playa Girón** ⑪ holds an important place in Cold War history: this was the site of the USA's disastrous 1961 Bay of Pigs invasion. Not far from the palm trees and oceanfront tourist bungalows is a defiant billboard depicting a raised rifle and the words: "Playa Girón

– La Primera Derrota del Imperialismo en América Latina" (The First Imperialist Defeat in Latin America). Less than 100 meters (330 ft) from the landing spot, the **Museo de Girón** (open daily 9am–noon, 1–5pm; entrance charge) was built to commemorate the events of 1961, during which Castro first proclaimed his revolution to be of a "socialist" character. The rather drab-looking museum has some excellent exhibits commemorating the battle that began shortly after midnight on April 17, 1961, when the 2506th assault brigade – a CIA-trained force of some 1,500 mercenaries and Cuban exiles – landed to force the overthrow of Fidel.

However, El Jefe Máximo was ready for them with Soviet-built T-34 tanks and a few T-33 fighter jets, and, after two days of intense air and land battles, the 2506th surrendered. Of the invading force, 107 were killed and 1,189 were taken prisoner. Most of these men were later released back to the States, in return for a US$53-million consignment of medicines and foodstuffs. Castro, who led the people's militia in the battle, lost 161 men and women, aged between 16 and 60 years old (five of these were civilians).

Outside the museum, you can inspect a couple of the Cuban tanks used in the defense. Inside are two rooms full of documents, photographs and weapons and an array of interesting artifacts, among them a 12.7mm Czech-made anti-aircraft battery used to shoot down US planes, and a map showing how the mercenaries sailed from Puerto Cabezas, Nicaragua, to the southern Cuban coast. Their invasion was preceded two days beforehand by a bombing raid aimed at crippling the Cuban Air Force, but it failed in its objective, and only served to put Castro on full alert. You can also see a video compilation of footage from the era (in Spanish only).

Diving and snorkeling

The western side of Playa Girón is a sanctuary for local fauna. You need authorization to go through the gate and follow the old solid-fill causeway that has slowly killed all vegetation. Flocks of rosy flamingos and spoonbills can be seen, feeding in the shallow salty lagoons, alongside other waders such as white ibises, black-necked stilts, sandpipers and plovers.

At Playa Girón itself, you can bathe and snorkel off the beach or at several spots along the shore where the seas are shallow. There are also some good opportunities for deeper scuba diving for those with experience, organized at the scuba center in the Villa Horizontes Playa Larga hotel. Farther out to sea, where the Caribbean shelf sinks vertically to hundreds of meters, you will see rare black corals, spiny oysters, and ocean fish species such as amberjack and little tunny.

A little farther along the bay to the south is another good place to dive, the lovely cove of **Caleta Buena** (entrance charge includes buffet lunch), which is also blessed with spectacular sponges and red coral. Beyond here, a rough road, which should only be negotiated in a four-wheel-drive vehicle, heads east toward the city of Cienfuegos. ❏

A tank at the Museo de Girón that was used to repel the US invasion.

BELOW: a trophy from the Bay of Pigs invasion outside the Museo de Girón.

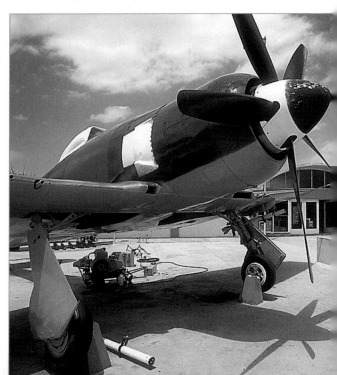

THE ISLAND'S FLORA AND FAUNA

Nature lovers will be delighted with the rich variety of flora and fauna in Cuba. Some of it is easy to find, but you need an informative guide if you want to discover the island's secrets

Cuba is an intensely green island, with a wide range of habitats: from beaches to coastal mangrove swamps, broad plains to rugged mountains, cactus semi-desert to remaining indigenous forests of cedar and ebony. Like many other large islands in the world, Cuba contains a rich collection of rare birds and animals found nowhere else on earth. About half of Cuba's 6,000 species of plants and trees are endemic to the island. Many are directly related to African varieties, apparently having been blown here by strong winds or drifted across the Atlantic on huge rafts made of natural debris thousands of years ago when the ocean was a narrow, embryonic body of water.

Of the animal species, many are believed to have come from from North and South America along an arch-shaped landmass that millions of years ago formed a bridge between the lands. Once Cuba separated from the continents, most species followed a unique evolutionary path and developed into something very different from the ancestors they left behind.

About 350 species of birds can be found in Cuba, more than half of which use the island as a winter resting spot as they migrate from North to South America. There are also 185 species of butterflies, and more than 1,000 species of insects. The Zapata Peninsula and the protected zone of Cayo Coco are among the best regions for wildlife spotting, particularly birds and reptiles, but most parts of the island have their own discoveries to be made.

ABOVE: The *Greta cubana*, an exquisite butterfly, is one of only two clear-winged butterfly species in the world. Its translucent wings are edged in black and rimmed with a bright red band. It inhabits the humid forests near Santiago in Eastern Cuba.

ABOVE: the fragrant white mariposa, or butterfly jasmine, is the national flower of Cuba, even though it is not indigenous to the island.

LEFT: the trogon, or tocororo: with a pagoda-shaped tail, this was chosen as Cuba's national bird, as its coloring of red, white and blue matches the Cuban flag. It still thrives in the forests, where it perches very still for long intervals. However, it is more often heard than seen, shrieking a piercing "to-co-roro" sound.

ABOVE: Cattle egret: wherever there are cattle there are egrets, who feed on the ticks they extract from the animals' hides – a perfect example of an efficiently functioning food chain. You will see many of them throughout Cuba, but especially in the Viñales valley, perching on the cattle's backs, or waiting patiently at their sides.

THE ROYAL PALM – CUBA'S NATIONAL EMBLEM

The stately royal palm tree is not only Cuba's national emblem, it has a wide variety of uses. It rises to 24 meters (80 ft) high, and is a prized resource strictly protected by legislation. Its fronds are used for thatching the roofs of the island's typical *bohíos* (small wooden houses) and the *secaderos* – the huts used for drying tobacco; its bark is also used for cladding the sides of buildings; its seeds are used for animal feed; and bees gather its pollen to make palm honey.

Another fascinating variety of palm tree found in Cuba is the endangered cork palm, a stumpy, prehistoric plant with scrubby fronds that has somehow managed to survive as a relic from the age of the dinosaurs. It can be found now only in a few areas of Pinar del Río province in western Cuba.

ABOVE: Royal palm *(Roystonea regia)*: a tree that is useful as well as elegant and emblematic.

ABOVE: *Crocodylus rhombifer,* known as the Cuban crocodile, lives in the freshwater swamps of the Zapata Peninsula and on the Isle of Youth, but it is threatened by hybridization with the island's other species of crocodile, the more ubiquitous American crocodile.

RIGHT: Cuba is home to three species of hummingbird (two endemics, one rare migrant visitor). You may spot the commonest species, the Cuban Emerald, or *zunzún*, feeding off a flowering bush in a provincial town. But you will have to be luckier, or a dedicated birdwatcher, to see the *zunzuncito* or bee hummingbird *(above)*, the smallest bird in existence, with a length of about 5 cm (2 inches) – bill and tail included – and weighing just 2 grams (0.08 ounces).

ABOVE: Cuban false chameleon *(Chamaeleolis chamaeleonides)*: similar in appearance to a true chameleon, it is long-tongued and slow moving, but it does not have the ability to change color for concealment, and it lives chiefly on a diet of insects and snails, whereas the diet of a true chameleon is more varied, and includes some vegetable matter.

SANTA CLARA TO SANCTI SPÍRITUS

As well as hectares of sugar cane, Cuba's heartland has some lovely towns, such as buzzing
Santa Clara, with its Che Guevara monument, and
the little-visited gem of Remedios, plus stunning
landscapes in the Escambray mountains

East of Varadero begins a fertile green belt of land that produces enough sugar cane to sweeten the entire world. This is Cuba's agricultural backbone: orchards, rice fields, vegetable farms and enormous cattle ranches eat up the remaining terrain and feed much of the island's population.

From Havana or Varadero, the two-lane Carretera Central runs to the region's main cities and innumerable smaller towns: buses, trucks, tractors, carts, cars, bicycles, and animals all share the road, presenting a slow but picturesque parade of life in the countryside. The Ocho Vías Autopista, projected as an eight-lane highway all the way to the eastern tip of the island, is completed only as far as the other side of Sancti Spíritus. Along the way are a handful of CUC-only service stations. These offer gas, oil and air, rest rooms, drinks and food (proper meals in some cases), and usually one or two stores. The busiest are at Finca Fiesta Campesina *(see page 347)*, at the turning to the Zapata peninsula, and at **Aguada de Pasajeros**, where the highway meets the road running south to Cienfuegos and Trinidad.

With a population of 800,000 people, the province of **Villa Clara** runs the gamut of rural backdrops. There are sleepy fishing villages, pretty coves and offshore cays to the north; colonial towns and sugar-cane plantations in the center; the rolling hills of the Alturas de Santa Clara to the east; and to the south, the majestic Escambray mountains.

Santa Clara's old town

Santa Clara ⑫ (pop. 210,000), the provincial capital, lies 276 km (171 miles) east of Havana on the Autopista Nacional, and is well worth visiting. Beyond the suburbs you'll find buzzing, lively streets with a large student population. The center seems relatively litter-free – a startling and agreeable sight to anyone arriving from Havana.

Santa Clara was founded in 1689 by families from Remedios who had been persuaded that legions of demons were afflicting their settlement *(see page 38)*.

Main attractions
SANTA CLARA
TREN BLINDADO
MONUMENTO CHE GUEVARA
REMEDIOS
EMBALSE HANABANILLA
TOPES DE COLLANTES
SANCTI SPÍRITUS

LEFT: Escambray plantation house.
BELOW: the lovely Museo de Artes Decorativas in Santa Clara.

Set in the middle of the island, and being an important center for the sugar industry, the "gateway to the east" was of vital importance during many wars. In 1958, Che Guevara's seizure of the city was the decisive victory in the struggle against Batista: this seminal moment is commemorated at sites across the town, most importantly, in Che's monument and mausoleum *(see page 240)*. It is this that brings most visitors to Santa Clara, but this pretty little city has far more to offer for those with time to spare.

Santa Clara's main square is the delightful, leafy **Parque Vidal** Ⓐ, with a graceful central gazebo used for concerts. A monument marks the spot where Independence hero Leoncio Vidal was killed in 1896, and benches line the promenades that cross and circle the park – in earlier days, a fence separated the inner promenade for whites from the outer area for blacks. Colonnaded buildings from the late 19th and early 20th centuries line the square; they include the **Casa de la Trova**, and the ugly **Hotel Santa Clara Libre** Ⓑ, distinguished by a facade riddled with shrapnel from the 1958 campaign.

On the plaza's north side is the **Museo de Artes Decorativas** Ⓒ (open daily but check hours as they vary; entrance charge), in one of the city's loveliest colonial buildings. Rooms are sumptuously furnished with colonial pieces in many different styles, but dating mainly from the 19th century. On the nearby corner is the lovely **Teatro La Caridad** Ⓓ built in the 1880s, financed by the philanthropist Marta Abreu de Estevez to bring culture to the poor of Santa Clara. Now a national monument, the theater is one of the best-restored and maintained in Cuba.

Perhaps guilt-tripping on their fabulous wealth gained from sugar (and therefore from slavery as well), Marta's parents had earlier established the city's first free clinic and primary school, in 1878. The school, a block behind the theater, was used successively as a convent, a trade school and the incipient Ministry of Education in the early 1960s. Restored as the Restaurante Colonial 1878, with colonial furnishings it now serves simple Cuban food.

Santa Clara's six-block long **boulevard**, running along Calle Independen-

TIP

The views from the rooftop bar of the Hotel Santa Clara, overlooking Parque Vidal, are the best in town.

BELOW: the Armored Train and museum.

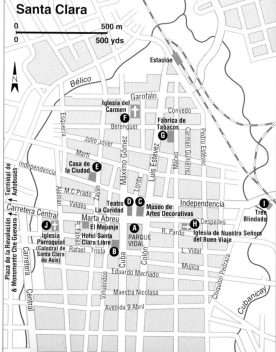

cia one street to the north of the plaza, is an enticing, brick-paved mall with iron grilles, colonial lamps and benches at each crossing. At the western end is the **Casa de la Ciudad** , an attractive old mansion with a motley array of exhibits, where dance classes are sometimes run; and the **Fondo de Bienes Culturales**, where local arts and crafts are sold. From the porches of small houses on any of the streets leading back to Parque Vidal, resident vendors offer paper flutes of freshly roasted *maní* (peanuts), squares of peanut candy *(maní molido)* and guava paste *(guayabate)*.

Farther north, up Calle Máximo Gómez, you reach an attractive church, the **Iglesia del Carmen** . Leaving the church, go left along Calle Berenguer to the **Fábrica de Tabacos**  (open Tues–Sun 8am–noon, 1–4pm; entrance charge) on Calle Maceo, where there is a very good tour as well as opportunities to buy both cigars and rum. Going down Maceo and turning left on Calle R. Pardo you will find the appealing **Iglesia de Nuestra Señora del Buen Viaje** , which is well worth visiting for its hybrid of architectural styles.

The Armored Train

A short walk east along Calle Independencia from Parque Vidal and across the river brings you to the **Tren Blindado**  (Armored Train) and museum (open Tues–Sat 8am–6pm, Sun 8am–noon; entrance charge). This train, loaded with government soldiers and munitions, was sent from Havana to stop the Rebel Army's advance, but was derailed at a critical moment during the battle for Santa Clara in 1958, when it was attacked by rebels with guns and Molotov cocktails. To prevent the men and munitions getting through, Che himself ripped up the lines with a bulldozer, derailing the train, and subsequently winning the battle. Both the bulldozer and the train have been preserved *in situ*.

Artists' hangout

Two blocks west of Parque Vidal, on Calle Marta Abreu, a sign above a brick facade announces **El Mejunje** (open Tues–Sun 4pm–1am). Artists, intellectuals, and bohemians of all ages meet here to sip beer and *infusiones* (herbal teas), to listen to a poetry recital or a musical group, to dance, or just to sit and chat.

Colonial style in the Parque Vidal, warmly illuminated at night.

BELOW: stunning monument to Che Guevara.

The cultural potion is just right for laid-back Santa Clara, and there's no place quite like it anywhere else in Cuba.

A couple of blocks farther along Calle Marta Abreu is the early 20th-century Catedral de Santa Clara de Asís, also known as the **Iglesia Parroquial ⓙ**.

Homage to Che Guevara

Going west from the church, Calle Marta Abreu joins the Carretera Central, which continues west to the *circunvalación* (beltway/ring road). Just south of the junction of the two roads is the **Plaza de la Revolución**, the usual place for revolutionary gatherings. It is dominated by one of Cuba's finest revolutionary statues, the **Monumento Che Guevara**: a giant figure of Che, shown with his arm is a sling – he broke it when he fell from a building during the battle for Santa Clara in 1958. The bronze statue bears the legend "*Hasta La Victoria Siempre*" ("Ever Onward to Victory"), a refrain which appears on many a billboard around Cuba.

Beneath Che's statue is the **Mausoleo** (open Tues–Sat 8am–9pm, Sun 8am–6pm; no cameras; free), where the remains of

Che and 16 of his co-revolutionaries were interred in 1997, after being recovered from Bolivia. The mausoleum, low-ceilinged and made almost entirely of stone, has the look and feel of a cave. By Che's resting place, a lamp casts a light in the shape of a five-pointed star, and an eternal flame (originally lit by Fidel) burns. Few visitors fail to be moved by the aura of reverence. There is also an interesting **museum** (same hours as the mausoleum) featuring revolutionary memorabilia, some primitive broadcasting equipment used at Radio Rebelde, set up by Che at La Mesa mountain station, and some great photographs.

Villa Clara's northern coast

On the province's northwest coast, close to the border with Matanzas province, is the town of **Corralillo**, renowned for the **Baños de Elguea**, natural baths that spew sulfuric mud and carbonic water. The various springs and pools at this large spa help relieve rheumatism, neurological and circulatory pain, minor skin irritations and respiratory distress. Farther east along the coast road, you reach **Sagua La Grande**, which has a Cupet

The Town of Comandante Che

On December 28, 1958, Che Guevara's rebel troops attacked Santa Clara. Two days later, with the aid of townspeople (who braved air raids and snipers to help build barricades and mix Molotov cocktails), the rebels emerged victorious and cut Batista's communications with the east of the island, causing him to flee Cuba on New Year's Eve. Many older Santa Clara residents remember the battle well and will recount fascinating details of the events. To this day, the town remains Guevara's city: his wife, Aleida, is a native of the town; the names of institutions and numerous monuments attest to the affection in which he is held; and now he is even interred here.

When the handless mortal remains of this rebel icon were discovered after a lengthy search in Bolivia in 1997, they were brought to Cuba for burial. His flag-draped coffin lay in state in Santa Clara – the scene of his greatest triumph – for three days, and lines of those wishing to pay their final respects stretched back more than 5 km (3 miles). In the town's Revolution Square, on October 8, 1997, Fidel Castro made a speech as the coffin, and those of six companions from his Bolivian campaign (including one Bolivian and a Peruvian), were laid to rest in the specially constructed mausoleum. It is now a highly revered site, visited by individual Cubans and groups of school children, as well as tourists.

gas station, and is close to the **Embalse Alacranes**, a freshwater reservoir, the second largest in Cuba and renowned for its bass fishing.

Remedios

Some 48 km (30 miles) to the northeast of Santa Clara (heading toward the north coast) is **Remedios ⑬**, a sleepy, engaging little colonial town and the oldest settlement in the province of Villa Clara, dating back to 1578. There has been very little recent urban development here, something the town has in common with Trinidad. While it may not be as picturesque as Trinidad, Remedios scores top marks for its tranquility and lack of tourists.

Remedios did not enjoy an auspicious first 100 years, being ravaged during repeated raids by French, English and Portuguese pirates. If that were not enough, it was subsequently occupied, according to one of the town's pious inhabitants, by "infernal legions of demons," and a number of families decamped to found the settlement of Santa Clara. However, many of the inhabitants ignored their cleric's warn-

ings and stayed put. In the early 19th century, however, the tradition of misfortune continued, and most of Remedios was razed by fire. It was rebuilt around what is now **Plaza Martí**, the town's pleasantly spacious central square.

The most stunning edifice in Remedios is the restored **Iglesia de San Juan Bautista** (usually open Mon–Sat 9–11am, Sun for mass 7.30am, or seek out the church warden at the rear; donations) also known as the Parroquial Mayor, bordering the east side of Plaza Martí. The old church, built in 1692 on the foundations of an earlier one, was severely damaged by a 1939 earthquake, but a millionaire penitent underwrote a 10-year renovation.

The church is a religious treasure: parts of the elaborate cedar-wood altar are carved in Arab style and encrusted with 24-carat gold. The decoration continues along the edge of the mahogany ceiling – which is a breathtaking example of a *Mudéjar*-style vaulted ceiling *(alfarje)*, and was discovered only during the restoration work in the 1940s. The ceiling is particularly rare for its floral decoration. Also overlooking the

Transport in Remedios is a leisurely affair.

BELOW: the spacious Plaza Martí in Remedios.

A poster advertising
The parrandas *festival in Remedios.*

BELOW:
the elaborate
altar in the
Parroquial Mayor.
RIGHT:
the church tower.

square is the attractive but run-down church of the **Virgen del Buen Viaje** (currently closed awaiting restoration), though its interior seems very plain after a visit to the Parroquial Mayor.

On the north side of Plaza Martí is the splendid **Museo de la Música García Caturla** (open Tues–Sat 9am–noon, 1–5pm, Sun 9am–noon; entrance charge), originally the home of Alexander García Caturla, a lawyer who devoted his life to music and became one of Cuba's most famous avant-garde composers. Caturla broke with the conventions of his class in every way. He married a black woman and, after her death, married her sister. His worst crime, though, was his incorruptibility: in 1940, at the age of 34, he was murdered by a policeman he was about to sentence for beating up a prostitute; there are suspicions that there may have been underlying political motives. The museum exhibits Caturla's personal effects, scores, musical instruments and recordings of some of his compositions.

The **Casa de Cultura**, in the former Spanish casino just off the square, and the enormous mansion that is now the **Museo de Historia**, attempt to explain, with mixed success, the folk tales, religious traditions and superstition that mingle in Remedios's bizarre history.

A festival not to be missed

Remedios is famous for its strange and passionate street festivals, known as *parrandas*, which evolved from the percussion street bands, known as *repiques*, that advance through the streets to arouse people for the pre-dawn mass held to honor San Juan de los Remedios on December 24. In the 19th century, this religious celebration developed into a street fair, with costumes, parades, music and food. The fascinating **Museo de las Parrandas** (open Tues–Sat 9am–noon, 1–6pm, Sun 9am–1pm; entrance charge), two blocks off the plaza at Máximo Gómez 71, displays the instruments heard during the celebrations. Neighboring districts (Carmen, identified by a sparrowhawk and a globe, and San Salvador, whose symbol is a rooster) spend the week between Christmas Eve and New Year's Eve competing for best *carroza* (parade float). For months beforehand, artists and engineers secretly plan and build a so-called *trabajo de*

plaza, a great tower of light that represents their neighborhood; it can reach up to 28 meters (90 ft). The *parrandas* start when night falls, with the unveiling of these incredible confections, and continue until dawn, with musicians playing traditional polkas. Paraders carry handmade lanterns and banners, there are tableaus on dazzling floats, and fireworks as thrilling as they are menacing. Nearby Placetas and Zulueta maintain similar traditions. Enjoy the tranquility of Remedios while you can: its days as a sleepy backwater may be numbered, as it has become a picturesque and popular tourist stop on the road to Camagüey Cays.

The northern islands

Ten km (6 miles) northeast of Remedios is the rather run-down fishing port of **Caibarién**, where boats dot the harbor, and almost any local captain will take you out to fish. The wharves and warehouses along the waterfront recall the town's one-time importance as a shipping port. Caibarién has some mediocre beaches, on a promontory jutting out into the sea, and there is also a nautical base

on the bay northeast of the port, where local people practice sailing, windsurfing and kayaking to compete in national and international competitions.

From Caibarién, you can take a boat for the 15-minute ride across to **Cayo Conuco** ⑭. A sagging wooden dock is the landing point on this 145-hectare (363-acre) islet, and a trail leads uphill to one of the most delightful camp sites in Cuba. *Cabañas* (cabins) nestle in the woods, and campers can swim, fish, ride horses, cook outdoors, and enjoy nature: they share the cay with numerous species of animals, including iguanas and *jutías* (a type of rodent), as well as 172 species of plants.

On the coast east of Caibarién, a causeway *(pedraplén)* runs out 45 km (28 miles) to **Cayo Santa María** and the smaller cays closer to shore. All these cays, called the **Cayos de Herradura** are, or soon will be, developed for tourism. Cayo Santa María is an increasingly popular resort. There are already at least a half-dozen hotels distributed among the cays, some of them focused on all-inclusive holidays, and there are plans for many more.

Palm trees and white sands: a Caribbean idyll.

BELOW: Cuban children enjoying the beaches on the north coast.

The Escambray mountains

South of Santa Clara, the scenery of the province folds from pastoral farmland into the Escambray mountains. At **Manicaragua**, the road splits, giving you the option to head straight on to Trinidad or west to the Embalse Hanabanilla and on to Cienguegos.

The **Embalse Hanabanilla** is an enormous reservoir at the top of an 8-km (5-mile) climb from a turning after the village of La Moza. Perfectly located in a gorgeous location by the lake side, with hills all around, is Hotel Hanabanilla. You may decide simply to enjoy the views and the swimming pool, but you can also fish for large-mouth bass, hike through the woods, visit nearby waterfalls, or take a boat across the lake – a trip that is highly recommended for the glimpse it provides of mountain life. Farmers who work small plots along the shore have their own animals, keep bees and grow most of their food – fruit, vegetables and coffee. Bags of beans and jars of honey and royal jelly are sometimes for sale. Coffee is a "state crop" and, legally, only the state can buy or sell the beans, but farmers often ignore the law.

From here you could continue west on winding roads toward Cienfuegos, but our route, for the moment, goes east through the Sierra del Escambray.

Struggle in the Escambray

The majestic Sierra del Escambray is Cuba's second most famous mountain range (after the Sierra Maestra in the Oriente) with its highest peak, the Pico San Juan, topping 1,100 meters (3,700 ft). Even at the height of summer, when temperatures in Trinidad or Santa Clara reach 40°C (100°F), you may still need a sweater here. Some of the heaviest rainfall in Cuba feeds the Escambray's lush jungle, where trees are laden with bromeliads and delicate waterfalls greet you at every turn; look out for the giant umbrella-like ferns, a prehistoric species. This is also an important coffee-growing region. On the lower slopes, jungle gives way to pastures and royal palms.

The Escambray provided a perfect hide-out for counter-revolutionaries in the 1960s. The number of anti-Castro guerrillas, who ranged from hardened CIA-trained fighters to farmers adversely affected by Castro's land reforms, had

TIP

A boat takes visitors across the Embalse Hanabanilla to the Río Negro restaurant. From here, the lake seems as placid as a pond, framed by distant green hills and with a foreground of gaudy bougainvillaea.

BELOW: a pastoral view from Topes de Collantes.

reached an estimated 3,000 by 1962, when the revolutionary government instigated a campaign to defeat the *bandidos* (bandits). Counter-insurgency units combed the area, driving the bands into more and more difficult terrain until they had no option but to surrender or fight. Even so, the last groups were not killed until 1966. (There is a museum about this struggle in Trinidad; *see page 260.*)

Topes de Collantes

If, instead of turning off, you continue south from Manicaragua, the road twists and turns through spectacular scenery, with every bend offering new views of tropical vegetation, interspersed with plantation forests of eucalyptus and pine. Parrots *(cotorras)* and other bird species abound, though casual observers are more likely to hear than see them.

Eventually you come to the undulating, wooded **Parque Nacional Topes de Collantes** ⓰, 770 meters (2,528 ft) above sea level. A wide variety of trees and exotic plants flourish here: as well as pines and eucalyptus, there are cedar and mahogany among others, and orchids enjoy the damp climate.

The unattractive Kurhotel here was originally built in the 1930s as a tuberculosis sanitarium, and later developed for wider health tourism; it still offers good hydrotherapy facilities. Tourists stay either at the Kurhotel or the Hotel Gaviota Los Helechos, which offers air-conditioned rooms, saunas, mineral baths, massages and herbal therapies.

For most visitors, the appeal of Topes lies in the walks, through beautiful scenery, and the exotic **waterfalls** nearby – especially **Salto Vega Grande** and the sweeping, uniquely shaped **Salto Caburní**, a 75-meter (250-ft) fall. This hike involves a fairly testing 6-km (4-mile) round trip; bring plenty of drinking water, sunscreen and swimming gear. Guides are compulsory (CUC$7); if you come here independently, arrange one through the information office at the park entrance (tel: 0142-540231). Many visitors come to Topes on a day trip from Trinidad *(see page 255)*; if you are one of them, you will find the round trip by taxi costs about CUC$25. Havanatur in Trinidad will also arrange excursions (book at least a day in advance; around CUC$25–30).

TIP

Topes de Collantes offers visitors an opportunity to see the national bird, the vividly colored tocororo, otherwise known as the trogon.

BELOW: one of the beautiful Escambray waterfalls.

The burnished-yellow tower of the Iglesia Parroquial Mayor in Sancti Spíritus.

BELOW: Winston Churchill, who visited Sancti Spíritus in 1895.
RIGHT: the Yayabo Bridge.

From Topes the road continues dramatically downhill to Trinidad (22 km (13 miles), with some stunning views of the coastline. If you are driving, be sure to stay in low gear: brake pads can wear out quickly on a hot day *(for Trinidad, see page 256).*

Sancti Spíritus

The Carretera Central and the Autopista Nacional east from Santa Clara cut through the central plains to reach the city of **Sancti Spíritus** ⓱ (pop. 87,400) – capital of the province of the same name. Although the city in no way rivals the splendor of Trinidad, on the province's south coast, it is one of Cuba's seven original *villas* founded by the conquistadors and has a very pleasant atmosphere. The people are friendly, and there is little in the way of *jinetero* (hustler) hassle, since the town is off the main tourist routes. Avoid the ugly, industrial new town and head for the neoclassical **Parque Serafín Sánchez** and the center of the old city to its south.

Serafín Sánchez was an independence hero who died in battle in 1896. His home is now open as the **Casa Museo Serafín Sánchez** (open Tues–Sat 8am–5pm; entrance charge), to the north of the square on Céspedes Norte.

Sancti Spíritus had an unfortunate early history: it had to be relocated from its original site after the area's native inhabitants – a plague of stinging ants – decided to fight off the invaders; and then the new city was twice burned and destroyed by pirates. Therefore, none of this city's historic buildings is as old as those in Trinidad, though it does still have some delights. Chief among them, on the **Plaza Honrato del Castillo** (also called the Plaza de Jesús), is an enchanting church, one of the oldest in Cuba, the **Iglesia Parroquial Mayor del Espíritu Santo**. Originally constructed of wood in 1522, it was rebuilt in stone in the 17th century after its destruction by pirates. The tower was added in the 18th century and the cupola in the 19th. With its rich, burnished-yellow exterior and peaceful location, this is one sight in the city that should not be missed. Although theoretically open Tues–Sat it is often closed, and the daily mass at 5pm or the Sunday one at 9am may offer the best chances of seeing the interior.

A Healthier City

The young Winston Churchill was a visitor to Sancti Spíritus in 1895, when working as a newspaper correspondent. Riding with the Spanish Army he became involved in a skirmish with Cuban independence fighters at Arroyo Blanco, east of the city. He narrowly escaped being shot, and later recalled the experience in his memoirs: "There is nothing more exhilarating than to be shot at without result." Arriving in the city, he was not impressed, dismissing it as "a very second-rate and most unhealthy place." Perhaps he had drunk from the River Yayabo, for years the city's only source of water, despite its impurities. Nowadays, Sancti Spíritus has a modern viaduct, which brings in fresh water from the nearby hills. But there is still a tradition of drinking the river water, filtered of course, and served in a *porrón* – a small earthenware jug. Almost everyone who crosses the Yayabo Bridge stops at a public watering place called El Porrón for a welcome thirst quencher. You're unlikely to face even the danger of a stomach upset here now, let alone yellow fever or bullets.

Also on the square is the small **Museo de la Esclavitud** (open Tues–Sat 9am–5pm; entrance charge), which relates the harrowing experiences of slaves brought to Cuba to work on the sugar plantations. Just to the south (on Calle Plácido) is the **Museo de Arte Colonial** (open Tues–Fri 9.30am–5pm, Sat 2–5pm, Sun 8am–noon; entrance charge), housed in an attractive colonial mansion, and worth visiting for its decor and furnishings alone.

The church, the nearby colonial houses of cobbled Calle El Llano, and the **Puente Yayabo**, the bridge across the Río Yayabo, have all been declared national monuments. This is the only colonial arched stone bridge left in Cuba. Beneath it, the **Merendero el Puente** is an excellent *paladar* on a houseboat, which specializes in seafood.

The sugar plains

Endless expanses of sugar cane surround Sancti Spíritus and supply the Uruguay sugar mill, the country's largest, east of the town. *Bagasse* (residue) from the cane is used in the modern paper mill in **Jatibonico** nearby. Although cane cutting on the flat central plains is largely mechanized today, the *machetero* who fells the stalks with his sharp machete remains the Cuban work hero. Sometimes billowing black clouds can be seen rising from the cane, indicating that it has been burned in preparation for cutting. This process crystallizes the sugar and increases its yield, but also pollutes the atmosphere and blackens the *macheteros* and the machinery – and anything in the vicinity.

Lake-side peace

Cuba's largest man-made lake, the **Embalse Zaza**, just to the southeast of the city, is known for the size and quantity of its large-mouth bass, while the surrounding woods harbor mourning- and white-winged doves, which attract seasonal hunters. There is a hotel here – the Hotel Zara –which will organize excursions for visitors; and there's an international fishing competition held here in September. The reservoir area is also extremely popular with birders, as the mangrove-choked marshes of the River Zaza provide a habitat for large numbers of water birds. ❏

Children try out the urban transportation.

RESTAURANTS

Santa Clara

La Cima
Hotel Santa Clara Libre,
Parque Vidal, 6.
Tel: (0422) 207-548.
Open daily L & D. **$–$$**
On the top floor of the hotel (La Cima means The Peak). The *criolla* food is good enough, the views are great and there is usually live music.

La Concha
Carretera Central,
corner of Danielito.
Tel: (0422) 218-124.
Open daily L & D. **$**
Close to the Che Guevara memorial, this is the best-known restaurant in town. It claims an international menu, but specializes in good pizzas. It can get busy with tour groups at lunch time, when there is sometimes live music.

Remedios

Las Arcadas
Hotel Mascotte, Máximo Gómez, 114 (Parque Martí).
Tel: (0142) 395-144.
Open daily L & D. **$–$$**
The hotel's restaurant ("The Arches") is really the only place to eat in Remedios. The colonial hotel has a modern dining room and serves standard *criollo* food and some meat and fish dishes described as "international." Perfectly pleasant and friendly.

Sancti Spíritus

Mesón de la Plaza
Máximo Gómez, 34.
Tel: (0141) 28-546. Open daily noon–10pm. **$–$$**
An agreeable place, very popular at lunch time, quieter in the evening. The house specialty is *ropa vieja* (literally, "old clothes") – nicer than it sounds: strips of beef stewed with peppers and tomatoes and served with rice. There is also fish on the menu.

Quinta Santa Elena
Padre Quintero, between Llano and Manolico Díaz.
Tel: (0141) 29-167. Open daily 1am–11pm. **$–$$**
Pleasant restaurant in a neoclassical building by the river. You can eat on the terrace, and be serenaded with live music. It's busiest at lunch time. Like the Mesón de la Plaza, it specializes in *ropa vieja*, and also offers fish and, of course, pork.

• • • • • • • • • • • • • • •
Price categories are for a meal
for one with a beer or mojito.
Wine puts the price up.
$ = under $25, **$$** = $25–35,
$$$ = over $35.

CIENFUEGOS AND TRINIDAD

Two historic but very different cities and a splendid stretch of coastline, with one of Cuba's favorite beaches, provide a breath of fresh air after the sugar fields and mountains of the interior

Cienfuegos province, with 326,000 inhabitants, is dominated by green rolling countryside, peppered by small sleepy towns and *bohíos* – palm-thatched cottages. Palm-fringed fields of sugar run down to the Alturas de Santa Clara in the east and the distant blue Escambray mountains in the south. The 1959 Revolution brought change to what was once primarily an agricultural region and it has, around the city of Cienfuegos at least, become highly industrialized: home, even, to Cuba's notorious and still unfinished nuclear power station.

Cienfuegos's past

The road to Cienfuegos city from the *autopista* runs through the small town of Rodas: a pleasant but sleepy place, best known for its Ciego Montenero spring, the origin of most of Cuba's fine mineral water. **Cienfuegos ⑱** (pop. 105,000), is also known as the "Pearl of the South" – though this traditional name is kept alive primarily in Cuban tourist literature rather than on the lips of local people. It's a lovely city with most of its colonial buildings now fully restored.

Europeans first sighted the area in 1494 during Christopher Columbus's second voyage, but no settlement was established until 1819 when Louis de Clouet, a Frenchman who had emigrated to New Orleans, founded the colony of Fernandina de Jagua. It was renamed Cienfuegos the following year in honor of Cuba's Spanish Governor General, who invited further settlers from Louisi-

ana (not, as is sometimes thought, renamed for Camilo Cienfuegos following the 1959 Revolution). In 1869, a group of Cuban nationalists led by Juan Díaz de Villegas rebelled against the Spanish Government, and in October 1895, Major-General José Rodríguez organized the Cienfuegos Brigade, which later played a key role in the battle of Mal Tiempo during Cuba's second War of Independence.

Following the 1959 Revolution, Cienfuegos received massive investment from the Soviet Union, which turned the

PRECEDING PAGES: a view from Trinidad. **LEFT:** Trinidad's Plaza Mayor. **BELOW:** whiling away the day.

A detail on the facade of the ornate Palacio de Valle.

region into a major industrial center. At its height, the province of Cienfuegos had 12 sugar mills which could grind 39,000 tonnes of raw *caña* daily, but many of them have now closed. Likewise, its port – the only deep-water terminal on Cuba's south coast, and home to a sizeable fishing and shrimping fleet – handles around 30 percent of the country's sugar exports. With a little imagination you can appreciate the attempt by its French founders to give the city a certain Parisian feel, with its parks, tree-lined boulevards, and colonnades.

The historic center

The historical center of the city is the **Pueblo Nuevo** district, which is rapidly becoming quite a pleasant shopping center – although only for those who can use convertible pesos. However, there are more CUC stores in Cienfuegos than there are in other cities, and the residents do seem to enjoy a higher standard of living. Most of the city's best buildings are around **Parque José Martí Ⓐ**, the square where the first settlement was founded on April 22, 1819, under the shade of a *majagua* tree. The place

where the tree stood is now marked by a bandstand. There are a series of statues to the city's illustrious citizens, including one to José Martí, guarded by lions, as well as a triumphal arch, inscribed with the date 20 Mayo, 1902 – commemorating the birth of the Cuban Republic.

The square has become a hassle-free zone as Cubans are fined for pestering tourists here. This doesn't seem to deter the more determined, but it does cut down on the nuisance considerably.

The **cathedral**, dating from 1870, dominates the square and has an impressive, but shabby, interior, complete with marble floors. Nearby, on the north side, is the neoclassical **Teatro Tomás Terry** (officially known as the Teatro de Cienfuegos; open daily 9am–6pm; entrance charge), completed in 1895. It was named after a rich sugar baron who arrived in Cuba a poor Venezuelan emigré, and made a dubious fortune by buying up weak and sick slaves, nursing them back to health, and then reselling them at a profit. The ornate interior of the theater is made virtually entirely of precious Cuban hardwoods (a luxury now consigned to the past),

with classical reliefs and nymphs providing some of the decoration. National and local performances are staged here, ranging from the National Ballet to local comedy acts. Adjoining the theater is the pastel-painted, columned **Colegio San Lorenzo**, built in 1927, now a high school. Between the theater and the school is the Café Teatro Terry, with a leafy terrace, and live music from Tuesday to Sunday from 9pm.

On the opposite side of the square, the **Museo Histórico Provincial** (open Mon–Sat 10am–6pm, Sun 9am–1pm; entrance charge) focuses on the city's role in the War of Independence, but you may prefer to go to the **Casa de Cultura**, which occupies the former home of a rich sugar baron on the west side of the square. It's a fine building, with a wide marble staircase and attractive wall tiles. In theory, you can go up the tower, but in practice this is not always so.

Next door is the UNEAC cultural center *(see margin note)*, with a pretty, flower-filled garden with wrought-iron furniture. There's a small movie theater here, and live bands on the weekend.

Also on the square are the **Primero Palacio**, apparently modeled on Havana's Capitolio and now the local government headquarters, and the **Mesón El Palatino**, which has a big wooden bar counter, and tables facing out onto the square.

The streets around the Plaza José Martí hum with activity: particularly traffic-free **Boulevard San Fernando**, where food-standholders, souvenir vendors, flower sellers, boot blacks and other entrepreneurs cash in on Cuba's gradual return to capitalism.

The main street, however, is the broad Calle 37, usually called the **Paseo del Prado** – a more fitting name for the longest boulevard in Cuba. It is bordered by some beautiful but unpretentious colonial buildings, mostly still private residences. South of Avenida 46, just before it hits the waterfront, the street is known as the Malecón. Always busy, and filled with traffic and gossiping crowds, it is the hub of the city's nightlife, most

of which seems to happen around the busy branch of El Rápido. the street is lined with statues, busts, and plaques commemorating Cienfuegos's most notable citizens, as well as yet more impressive colonial houses.

Away from the center

One of Cienfuegos's best-known landmarks isn't in the center of town but at the very end of the Prado. At the south end of the Malecón you reach Punta Gorda, where once-gracious French-style mansions and plantation houses can be found. You can't miss the vast, unattractive Hotel Jagua, formerly a notorious casino hotel run by Batista's brother. It now offers excursions to El Nicho, source of the River Hanabanilla high in the Escambray mountains. However, the main attraction is the adjacent **Palacio de Valle** ❽. This kitsch mansion, done up in Moorish Revival style with a few other styles mixed in for good measure, was commissioned by businessman Aciclio Valle. He brought in craftsmen from Morocco in 1913, and had the building finished by 1917. After the 1959 Revolution, the Valle family fled Cuba, and

BELOW: the Moorish-style Palacio de Valle.

for many years the palace served as a government hotel school. Then, in 1990, the Hotel Jagua, situated across from the Palacio, converted it into an expensive Italian restaurant, which today serves delicious shrimp and lobster dinners and an exquisite *flan* (crème caramel).

Watching the sunset over Cienfuegos Bay from the third-floor balcony of the Palacio is unforgettable (they charge you 2 CUC to go onto the terrace, but this entitles you to a cocktail as well as the view). The resident pianist for many years has been the flamboyant Carmen, who wears glitter make-up and seems to know a song from every country on earth. If you decide to dine here, enjoy an after-dinner sing-along at Carmen's side and finish off the evening at the Hotel Jagua's hilarious drag-show cabaret. Despite these attractions, if you are only in Cienfuegos for a short while, you will be better off exploring the historic center rather than coming out to Punta Gorda.

Around Cienfuegos

The best way to visit the **Castillo de Jagua** on the southern side of the beautiful Bahía de Cienfuegos is to take

a ferry *(lancha)* from a terminal just south of the Parque Martí (Avenida 46, between calles 23 and 25). It departs at 1pm, and returns at 4pm; the journey takes about 45 minutes, and costs just 1 CUC. The colonial fortress was built in the 17th century to defend the area against pirate attacks. The castle is impressive and has a bar and restaurant, but there's not much to it otherwise, except that there is an interesting legend attached: it is supposed to be haunted by a woman in blue.

Alternatively, if you have a car or want to hire a taxi, take the road that follows the eastern side of the bay (buses exist but are not regular or reliable). After about 2 km (1 mile) you pass the **Cementerio Tomás Acea** , an impressive neoclassical cemetery overlooking the bay. You will eventually end up at the ugly, Soviet-built Hotel Pasacaballo – strangely, although it is built directly across the bay from the Castillo de Jagua, all the rooms face the other way.

It does, however, afford excellent views of one of Cienfuegos's most curious sites: the concrete dome of the

TIP

If you want to visit the Palacio or anywhere else that's a bit out of town, do as the Cubans do and take a horse-drawn *coche*. These environmentally friendly people carriers are a cheap and effective way of getting around.

RIGHT: the tower on the Casa de Cultura in Cienfuegos.

Beny Moré

There is a bronze statue on the Prado of Beny (or Benny) Moré, one of the best-loved Cuban musicians, who was born in nearby Santa Isabel de las Lajas in 1919. He got his first breakthrough when he won a radio competition in the early 1940s, and went on to record with the then-famous Trio Matamoros.

Beny (as he is always known) was equally at home with Afro-Cuban music as he was with mamba or the country music known as guajira. He is also much-loved because, when many other musical stars left Cuba after the 1959 Revolution, he remained, although he was already famous in Mexico and much of Latin America, and could have had a good career outside his homeland.

He is particularly honored in Cienfuegos because, at the height of his fame in the 1950s, he chose to make a recording and perform with the little-known Cienfuegos-based Orquesta Aragón and helped them to reach a wider audience. A festival bearing his name is held in the town each September.

Soviet-designed **Juragua Nuclear Power Plant**, known as "Nuclear City." Construction of the US$2.5-billion facility began in 1983, but the twin reactors were only 60 percent complete when the USSR collapsed, and plans for its completion have been scrapped. Gas is now piped down from Matanzas at 30 percent of the cost.

About 6 km (4 miles) east of Pasacaballos, just where the road veers inland, is the Hotel Rancho Luna, a resort popular with Canadian tourists. It has a large pool and sun deck, and looks out on to the beach with its warm, shallow, turquoise-colored sea. The nearby Hotel Faro Luna is smaller but has similar facilities (accommodations in both hotels are only available as part of a package vacation). Non-residents can use the Rancho Luna facilities (including the only good beach close to Cienfuegos) for around 5 CUCs. Scuba diving and snorkeling are also available here. On the way back to town, you pass the **Comunidad Mártires de Barbados**, a collective farm named in memory of 73 Cuban athletes who died in 1976 when right-wing terrorists bombed a Cubana de Aviación jetliner over Barbados.

The road to Trinidad

En route to Trinidad, just north of San Antón and about 18 km (12 miles) east of Cienfuegos, you will come to the **Jardín Botánico Soledad** (open daily 8am–5pm; entrance charge), Also called "Pepito Tey," after the nearby sugar mill, the vast garden is well worth a visit. Established in 1899, it is home to some 2,400 species, including 285 types of palm tree. It was founded by Edwin Atkins, an American sugar merchant; the original aim was to produce more resistant strains of sugar cane, but he gradually became more interested in planting exotic species.

A 30-minute drive out of Cienfuegos, Villa Guajimico offers three-star accommodations in 51 traditional cabins set in lush gardens around a lovely bay. The resort is a dedicated dive center with instructors and all facilities, but also caters for the non-diving traveler looking for peace and quiet. From Cienfuegos, you can also reach Embalse Hanabanilla *(see page 244)* and Santa Clara *(see pages 237–40)* by taking the scenic road via Cumanayagua to Manicaragua, across the foothills of the **Sierra de Escambray**.

The main road between Cienfuegos and Trinidad proceeds south, across a delightful hummocky landscape until it reaches the sea. The road often hugs the shore, pushed close to the sea by the mountains, providing fleeting glimpses of hidden coves and beaches.

At **La Sierrita**, 32 km (20 miles) east of Cienfuegos, you can head inland into the Escambray for one of the most dramatic routes through the mountains to Topes de Collantes, which will take you close to **Pico San Juan**, the highest mountain in the Sierra del Escambray (1,140 meters/3,740 ft). The road surface is poor in places, and the inclines are steep and require concentration, but the views are magnificent. (The more usual route to Topes de Collantes runs north from Trinidad, and is one of the most popular trips from the colonial town.)

Castillo de Jagua on the southern side of the bay can be reached by ferry.

BELOW: a stately avenue in the Jardín Botánico Soledad.

Trinidad's cathedral, officially known as the Parroquial Mayor.

Back on the coast road, you pass several small (and often deserted) beaches, the first of which is **Playa Inglés**, about 48 km (30 miles) from Cienfuegos. The second is **Playa Yaguanabo**, 5 km (3 miles) farther east, where Villa Yaguanabo offers two-story cabins with basic facilities and a restaurant.

Colonial sugar capital

Located in Sancti Spíritus province, 82 km (50 miles) southeast of Cienfuegos, is **Trinidad ⑲**, Cuba's third-oldest settlement and one of the island's jewels. Its red-tiled roofs, pastel-colored buildings, cobblestoned streets, laid-back atmosphere and historic museums make it the main place, outside Havana, that most visitors include on their itinerary.

Trinidad was founded in January 1514 by Spanish explorer Diego Velázquez, at a spot just inland from the Caribbean Sea near the mouth of the Río Arimao. From the outset, Velázquez and his men enslaved the local indigenous Taíno inhabitants but, as they soon began to die from imported diseases and overwork, the colonists started to replace them with slaves, shipped in from Africa.

Throughout much of the 17th century, this area was raided by pirates, who destroyed the provincial capital of Sancti Spíritus but spared Trinidad itself. The town was also a thriving center for smugglers and the slave trade – the source of much of its wealth.

During the boom years of the sugar industry, in the late 18th century, the area around Trinidad became known as the Valle de los Ingenios (Valley of the Sugar Mills), and fabulous plantation houses began to dot the countryside. When Cuba officially abolished slavery in 1880, the practice continued in more subtle forms for several years, even after the 1895–98 War of Independence. Throughout most of the 20th century, Trinidad remained economically tied to the sugar industry, though tourism is now the main source of revenue for the town.

A protected gem

In 1988, UNESCO declared Trinidad and the Valle de los Ingenios a World Heritage Site, but the town had already been recognized as a National Monument back in the Batista years. There are no garish signs or souvenir displays in the

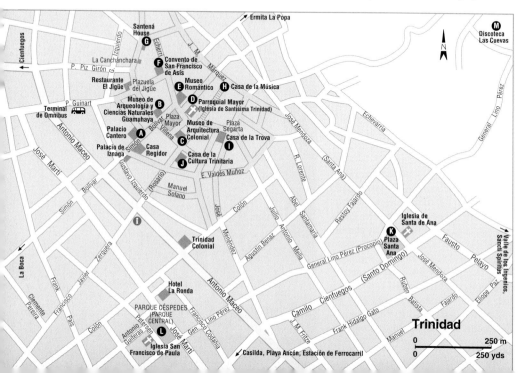

Trinidad

town itself, as these are against the law.

It well deserves the praise heaped on it: painted mahogany balustrades run along the shady colonnades, massive ancient wooden doors open to reveal cool green courtyards beyond, transportation is mainly pony- or mule-driven, and life in the city moves sleepily along. At night, the town is dark, lit only by low lights or the eerie glow of television screens as the inhabitants settle down to watch an evening soap opera or movie – although the sound of music and laughter emanating from one of the bars or the Casa de la Trova indicates that not everybody stays at home at night.

Trinidad's quaintness is much in demand by foreign companies as a TV and movie location, and many magazines have shot fashion features here. However, this is not entirely a "museum city." There is a certain amount of *jineterismo* (hustling), though the colonial center is well policed, which means that the practice is surreptitious.

Exploring the city

Trinidad is divided into the old and new towns. The newer town is built on a grid system and is centered around Parque Céspedes. **Old Trinidad** centers around Plaza Mayor, where the rich built their mansions. The sloping streets all have a central gutter to allow rainwater to flow away easily.

The only way to explore Trinidad is on foot. The streets in the old town are closed to traffic and in other parts of the town they are generally narrow and difficult to negotiate by car unless you know them well. Following a simple walking tour takes three to four hours – museum and lunch stops included – although you may enjoy the town so much that you make it last a few days. Sightseeing is best done in the morning, while it's still fairly cool and the streets are less crowded, or in the early evening, when the buildings are bathed in a delicious, pinkish light.

If you're driving, park on Calle Antonio Maceo, where an attendant will guard your car (and give it a thorough washing too) for CUC$1. Walking up Calle Simón Bolívar you pass several impressive colonial mansions, before reaching the **Palacio Cantero** Ⓐ, one of the city's most exquisite mansions, housing the

BELOW:
a view over the lovely colonial town of Trinidad.

BELOW: the elegant interior of the Museo Romántico.

city's **Museo Histórico Municipal** (open Sat–Thur 9am–5pm; entrance charge), with some fine pieces of colonial furniture and interesting exhibits on the slave trade. There's a Roman-style bathhouse, and a fountain that once spouted eau de Cologne for women and gin for men. However, the finest feature is the square tower, which provides an exceptional view of the whole town – a perfect introduction to the delights of Trinidad, especially in the late afternoon.

Within a few paces of the museum are the **Museo de Artes Decorativas** (open Fri–Wed 9am–5pm; entrance charge) on a site where conquistador Hernán Cortés is said to have lived before departing for Mexico to conquer the Aztecs; the **Casa del Regidor** (formerly the mayor's residence), and **Callejón de Pena**, a street full of private merchants' houses, and a good place to find excellent arts and crafts, particularly lace and woodwork. Be sure to bargain – it is expected.

The heart of the city

One block farther up, you emerge in the splendid yet intimate **Plaza Mayor**, one of Cuba's most photographed sights.

Immediately on your right, the attractive balconied building contains the **Galería de Arte Universal**, with many paintings for sale, although you will find prices cheaper if you buy from artists privately. To your left, another beautiful mansion houses the **Museo de Arqueología y Ciencias Naturales Guamuhaya** ❸ (closed for restoration; due to open in 2008). There are some rather unappealing displays of stuffed animals and birds, and some more interesting items relating to the pre-Columbian past.

Cross the square from the Archeological Museum, past the white wrought-iron benches and small statues, including two bronze greyhounds. On the opposite side, at No. 83, is the former house of the Sánchez family, now the **Museo de Arquitectura Colonial** ❸ (open Mon–Thur and Sat 9am–5pm, Sun 9am–1pm; entrance charge), which tells the history of Trinidad's development with maps and models, showing how colonial craftsmen worked. If you are interested in architecture, ask here about two-hour walking tours of the city (they also arrange visits to the Valle de los Ingenios). Like many buildings in Trinidad, this house, dating

from 1735, was painted yellow rather than white, because white was considered too harsh on people's eyes in the strong tropical sun. When the house was restored in the 1980s, sections of yellow were left as a reminder of its original color.

The museum includes an exhibition of hand-carved doors and windows, gas-lit chandeliers and a stockade built to hold 12 slaves at once. In the shady courtyard is a sundial, an unusual multifauceted shower and even a 19th-century gas generator, made in New York City. A delightful garden is located at the back of the museum.

The huge, cream-colored cathedral standing at the top of the square is the **Parroquial Mayor** ❶ (opening hours vary), begun in 1868. This is the only church in Cuba to have hand-carved Gothic altars, and five aisles instead of three. It was fully restored in 1996, but the church is still unfinished, since its niches remain empty, intended for Italian statues that never arrived.

Elegance and romance

A strong contender for Trinidad's best museum is the bold yellow building with arches located on the same side of the square: the **Museo Romántico** ❸ (open Tues–Sat 9am–5pm, Sun 9am–1pm; entrance charge), housed in a sumptuous mansion that for many years belonged to the Spanish Brunet family. The family, which bought noble titles with its sugar wealth, came to Cuba in 1857, and their 12 children lived in this mansion, along with a number of slaves.

In 1974, the house was turned into a museum, and its rooms were filled with period pieces collected from numerous mansions throughout the city. Here, for example, you can see a priceless 18th-century Austrian writing desk, covered with painted-enamel mythological scenes; a marble bathtub; and a wooden "throne" from 1808 used as a toilet. In the kitchen there is a limestone water filter and a set of beautiful, custom-made porcelain plates and dishes from the 1820s. The upstairs balcony has fine views over the square.

From religion to revolution

Leaving the museum, walk down Calle Echerrí (also called Cristo) to the intersection with Calle Piro Guinart. Here is

Portrait of one of the colonial aristocrats who financed their lavish lifestyles with profits from sugar plantations.

BELOW:
Trinidad bathed in golden light.

TIP

When the original tree in the Plazuela Real del Jigüe reached the end of its life a cutting was taken and replanted, a custom that has continued through the centuries. The present tree was planted in 1929.

BELOW: handmade souvenirs for sale on the Callejón de Pena.

the **Archivo de la Ciudad** (City Archives), recognizable by the colorful coat-of-arms hanging on the facade. Directly in front is the tallest and most famous landmark in Trinidad: the **Convento de San Francisco de Asís ⑥**, parts of which date from 1731. The building was enlarged and embellished in 1809 by a Spanish priest, Father Valencia, but, after the construction of the nearby Parroquial Mayor in 1892, the convent ceased to function, and the building was turned into a barracks for the Spanish Army.

Then, in 1984, in a perverse twist of history, the former convent was turned into the **Museo de la Lucha Contra Bandidos** (Museum of the Struggle Against Counter-Revolutionaries; open Tues–Sat 9am–5pm, Sun 9am–1pm; entrance charge), which concentrates on the campaign to weed out anti-Castro guerrillas in the Escambray mountains during the 1960s. Inside there is a boat in which Cuban exiles came from Florida to destroy the oil tanks at the nearby port of Casilda, and a Russian truck used in the search for counter-revolutionaries in the mountains.

The real beauty of this building, however, has nothing to do with politics. Climb the 119 granite and wooden stairs to the top of the bell tower. Once you've caught your breath, enjoy the view: from here, all of Trinidad is clearly visible, as are the blue waters of the Caribbean and the distant, hazy peaks of the Sierra Escambray. It is well worth the climb.

Cocktails, art and Santería

Walking to the end of Echerri, you reach the area called El Fortuno. In the 18th century it was home to several foreign pirates who were welcomed by the Trinidadians (*trinitarianos* in Spanish), many of whom, indeed, grew rich from smuggling and trading with these disreputable people, who they were supposed to fear. The house at Ciro Redondo No. 261 was said to have been built for a French pirate, Carlos Merlin, in 1754.

At the foot of Redondo, turn left into Calle Martínez Villena, heading toward **La Canchánchara**, a bar with live entertainment, and its own house cocktail, the *canchánchara*, which is made from *aguardiente* (a type of rough rum), lime, honey and sparkling water. It's quiet during the day, but comes into its own at night, and is popular with local people as well as tourists.

On the parallel Calle Vicente Suyama (also known as Calle Encarnación) is a makeshift gallery at No. 39 run by professor of art, Carlos Mata: it's typical of several private galleries that cater specifically to foreign tourists, and which have sprouted up around Trinidad since early 1994, when the government began tolerating certain limited forms of private enterprise.

One block along from La Canchánchara to your right is the spot where, in the early 16th century, the so-called "Protector of the Indians," Bartolomé de las Casas *(see page 35)*, in the presence of Diego Velázquez, conducted the first Christmas mass in Trinidad under a stately old *jigüe* tree: this is the **Plazuela Real del Jigüe**, complete with one of Trinidad's best little restaurants.

The next stop, heading up Vicente Suyama 59, is an authentic **Santería house G**, with Cuban revolutionary posters and an altar complete with a black Madonna. There's also a rock shaped like an egg, inside a pot full of seawater; the whole contraption is covered with fine lace. If you would like to go in, ask for Israel, the Santería priest, who will explain everything. He is very pleasant and knowledgeable and gives an interesting little tour (a donation is appreciated).

East of Plaza Mayor

To the right of the Iglesia Parroquial Mayor, an ancient flight of cobbled steps marks the end of Calle Rosario. At No. 3 is a house built in 1732 for Fernández de Lara, Trinidad's chief inquisitor, who was responsible for upholding Christianity and burning at the stake anyone who disagreed with the Vatican's views. Several people accused of witchcraft and black magic were crucified nearby. Half way up the steps you will find the **Casa de la Música H**, a really lively spot that has live music from early evening until 11pm. The action then moves to a sec-

ond venue at the top of the steps where there are salsa concerts and impromptu dancing until the early hours. The casa also has displays of old instruments, and you can buy a range of Cuban music on CD and tape.

You may hear African music floating down from a nearby terrace: this is the headquarters of the **Conjunto Folklórico de Trinidad**, which has performed Bantu and Yoruba dances all over Cuba and in France, Spain and Germany as well. Like many Cubans, the troupe's 27 members are Santería believers. If you are interested in seeing a practice session, walk half a block east and on your left you will find the entrance to the Conjunto Folklórico. On your way out, leave a small donation.

Slightly farther east is a triangular-shaped plaza – the **Plazuela de Sagarte**, where some of the oldest houses in Trinidad are to be found. One of these is now the **Casa de la Trova I** (open Tues–Sun 11am–2pm, free; Fri–Sun 8pm–midnight, entrance charge), built in 1717 and decorated with murals. It is popular with tourists during the day, but on weekend nights local people take

One of a pair of shapely bronze greyhounds that guard the Plaza Mayor.

BELOW: Trinidad town reverberates with live music.

Elderly local people in Trinidad have seen a lot of changes over the years.

over. Beer can be bought with convertible pesos, and you can sometimes get shots of rough *aguardiente* for a couple of Cuban pesos.

One block down the hill and to your right, you come to **Calle Rosario** again. On the corner at No. 406 is a light-blue house that once belonged to one of Trinidad's sugar barons. Today it is the **Casa de la Cultura Trinitaria** , where dances are held and concerts and plays are performed. Back up the hill, notice the 18th-century walls made from rocks, bricks, bones and bottles of all sizes and shapes and held together with clay, straw, and plaster. The yellow house at No. 79 is the **Casa de los Curas**, the residence for centuries of the parochial church's priests.

Trinidad's other sights

There are two other areas worth visiting outside the heart of the Old Town. A 10-minute walk from the Plaza Mayor, the **Plaza Santa Ana** has a beautiful ruined church of the same name. Also on the plaza is the former Royal Prison (Carcel Real) which is now home to the city's **Centro Cultural**. Here you could catch one of the regular folkloric performances by the Trinidad Folk Ensemble, and there's also a restaurant, a gallery of local art and a store. You may also notice a rare statue of Bartolomé de Las Casas, the Dominican friar who fought for indigenous rights in the 16th century.

To the southeast, the **Parque Central** (also called **Parque Céspedes**) has no stunning architecture but is busy with local life, and has a rather more authentic feel to it. In November, the square is the focus for a week of cultural events and music.

Close to the **Hotel Horizontes Las Cuevas** *(see Travel Tips, page 349)* is the cavernous **Discoteca Las Cuevas** (also called La Alaya) – a series of impressive, lofty caves that have been converted into a nightclub, which is usually empty until 1am, when the other music venues in town close, but great fun thereafter.

Peninsula de Ancón

Some 12 km (8 miles) south of Trinidad lies a spectacular stretch of beach, accessible either by way of **Casilda** or the more scenic route via the small fishing village of **La Boca**, where Trinidad's river disgorges its waters into the sea. The beach here is popular with local people, who can't usually be found at the main tourist resort of **Playa Ancón** , farther out along the peninsula.

Playa Ancón is an excellent long sandy stretch lined with palm trees. The clear blue waters are warm and snorkeling is popular here. Bathers tend to gather on the sections in front of the vast Hotel Ancón and the nearby Hotel Costa Sur, where they can be within easy reach of bars and restaurants. You can use the hotel's sunshades and loungers for a small fee (currently CUC$1).

There used to be a lot of trouble with *jineterismo* (hustling) on the beaches, but the area around the hotels on Playa Ancón is now heavily supervised by hotel security staff. You won't get hassled, but it does seem that the efforts to control the problem have virtually driven local people from the beach.

BELOW: Playa Ancón is the main tourist resort on the peninsula.

Divers can take the trip to **Cayo Blanco**, south of Ancón, from either of the above hotels. The crystal seas and coral make for a fantastic dive (an initiation dive costs 9 CUCs; a full dive for qualified divers costs 30 CUCs, or 35 CUCs at night; costs include all equipment and an instructor/guide).

If you don't have a car, the beach can be reached by taxi (*taxistas* tout for business on the corner of Antonio Maceo and Simón Bolívar). It is also a great cycle ride, with the road following the twinkling waters of the Caribbean. You will notice other beaches as you cycle, narrower than Ancón, and with no facilities except *palapa* palm shade, but equally attractive and often empty.

The bicycle ride is best done fairly early in the morning or in the late afternoon to avoid the sun at its most powerful. Your hotel, or the owner of your *casa particular*, will probably be able to set you up with a bicycle for around CUC$3 a day. Quality varies and they rarely have gears. If you want a newer bicycle, they can be rented from next door to the bus station. Someone will watch your bicycle for you while you are on the beach, for 1 CUC.

Valle de los Ingenios

As you leave Trinidad on Route 12, heading northeast toward Sancti Spíritus, or to join up with the Carretera Central going east, the road passes through the spectacular **Valle de los Ingenios** ㉑ (Valley of the Sugar Mills). Like Trinidad, this lush valley is a UNESCO World Heritage Site. At one point, when it was Cuba's most important sugar-producing region, there were 43 working sugar mills in the valley. However, there was a serious downturn in the valley's economy in the mid-19th century, and then it collapsed completely in 1880 when world sugar prices slumped.

In the rest of Cuba, the more efficient *central* sugar mill was becoming the norm, and the valley's *ingenios* simply could not compete. Many of the magnificent plantation houses and mansions dating from those days are now in ruins, but some still stand, most notably the exceptionally beautiful farm belonging to the Iznaga family, which has been restored. The quaint little **Tren Turístico**, an old steam train, goes from Trinidad station to Manaca-Iznaga (daily 9.30am; CUC$10).

The old steam train that takes tourists from Trinidad to Manaca-Iznaga.

BELOW: the lush and lovely Valle de los Ingenios.

TIP

According to the census of 1795 there were 2,676 slaves in Trinidad. That year, the area's 82 sugar mills produced 680 tonnes of sugar, 1,000 barrels of *aguardiente*, and 700 urns of molasses.

BELOW: the Torre de Manaca-Iznaga. **RIGHT:** pressing sugar cane to make *guarapo*.

Torre de Manaca-Iznaga

You cannot miss the farm, as it is splendidly indicated by the **Torre de Manaca-Iznaga**, 12 km (7½ miles) from Trinidad (open daily 9am–5pm; entrance charge), which rears proudly out of the green cane fields. Legend has it that the tower was built after a bet between two brothers in the family, in which one had to build a tower higher than the depth the other could dig a well. No-one has ever found where the reputed well was dug – so step carefully. You're on safer ground with the tower (designed originally as a watchtower to keep an eye on the slaves working in the fields, and with a bell that summoned them to work), from where there is a magnificent view. Birds of prey circle on the thermals, and a refreshing wind cools you as you climb up above the valley floor.

Down below, local women sell beautiful handmade lace and *guanaberas*, the traditional white cotton men's shirts. The immaculate hacienda (open daily 7am–5pm) below is an excellent place for a meal or a drink of *guarapo*, the freshly pressed sugar-cane juice that is milled by Cuba's only original *trapiche* (sugar press) remaining *in situ*. There are also demonstrations of sugar-cane pressing, in which you can participate, and enjoy the fruits of your labor afterward with a dash of rum. Trips to the *torre* can be arranged through Havanatur and Cubatur in Trinidad.

If you are bound for Santa Clara, you should take the road running north from the Manaca-Iznaga tower to **Güinia de Miranda**. This is a little-used and pot-holed but beautiful route.

The road toward Sancti Spíritus curves and dips across a lovely landscape, passing the heights of the **Alturas de Banao**. Turn left (north) off the highway at La Güira to the Hacienda Los Molinos, an old wooden house where you can rent rooms, and hire horses to follow the various forest trails.

A little farther northeast, turning off at Banao, you can visit an ecotourism center, the **Casa del Guardabosques** (the House of the Forest Guards) in the protected reserve of **El Naranjal** – a diverse mountain forest with 722 species of flowering plants, including more than 60 types of orchid, and rich bird life at most seasons of the year. ❏

RESTAURANTS & BARS

Restaurants

In both Cienfuegos and Trinidad many visitors staying in *casas particulares* will choose to eat there, as the meals on offer are usually good, and inexpensive.

Cienfuegos

Club Cienfuegos
Calle 37, between 10 and 12.
Tel: (0143) 526-510l.
Open daily L & D. $$–$$$
The restaurant in this elegant colonial building serves pretty much the usual *comida criolla* meat and fish dishes, but with a great view over the bay. There is also a cocktail bar and a swimming pool.

Palacio de Valle
Calle 73, corner of calles 2 and 0, Punta Gorda.
Tel: (0143) 551-226/ 553-021. Open daily L & D. $$–$$$
Seafood, including lobster, is the specialty in this extravagant, early 20th-century Spanish-Moorish palace. On the tourist trail, though.

1860
Calle 31, corner of 54
Tel: (0143) 451-020.
Open daily L & D. $$
An elegant restaurant in the Hotel La Unión. Cuban and international cuisine. Not the greatest food in the world, but not bad, and a very pleasant place to sit.

Covadonga
Calle 37 between 0 and 1, Punta Gorda.
Tel: (0143) 516-949.
Open daily L & D. $$
Across from the Jagua Hotel, the Covadonga is famous for its great paella.

La Verja
Avenida 54, 306, between 33 and 35
Tel: (0143) 516-311. Open daily 7.30–10pm. $$
The best place to eat in the center of town, for its shabby elegance and stained-glass *mamparas* more than the Cuban food.

El Polinesio
Avenida 29, between 54 and 56, overlooking Parque Martí
Tel: (0143) 515-723.
Open noon–10pm. $$
Polynesian food in a venue decorated in Polynesian style. Great for people-watching.

Trinidad

El Jigüe
Calle Rubén Martínez Villena, 70, corner of Piro Guinart
Tel: (04199) 6-476. Open daily 9am–10pm. $$
Located in the tiny, picturesque Plaza El Jigüe, a block west of the Plaza Mayor, this restaurant is airy with a pleasant atmosphere and good *comica criolla* at reasonable prices.

El Mesón del Regidor
Calle Simón Bolívar, 424
Tel: (04199) 6-572/6-546.
Open daily 10am–10pm. $$
This restaurant's setting and decor is rather better than the food. The menu offers the usual fare, including grilled steaks and fish.

Trinidad Colonial
Calle Maceo, 402 and Colón
Tel: (04199) 6-473. Open daily noon–10pm. $$
The food does not quite live up to the charm of this lovely colonial mansion, but it is perfectly acceptable. International and Cuban dishes; slow service.

Sol y Son
Calle Simón Bolívar, 283 between Frank País and José Martí
No phone. Open daily L & D. $
One of Trinidad's few *paladares*, this place serves good-value *criolla* food in a colonial house with a jumble of antiques and its own patio. There is often live music, too.

Bars

See the Nightlife section *(page 359)* for suggestions, as the music venues are also bars.

See the Nightlife section *(page 359)* for suggestions

PRICE CATEGORIES
Price categories are for a three-course meal for one with a beer, or *mojito*. Wine puts the price up:
$ = under $25
$$ = $25–35
$$$ = over $35

RIGHT: a beer on the beach at lunch time.

EASTERN LOWLANDS

This region's economic mainstay is agriculture not tourism. While the area is not full of obvious attractions, it is well worth visiting the colonial city of Camagüey, and there are fine beaches along the north coast

The Carretera Central highway continues east from Sancti Spíritus through **Ciego de 85 Ávila province** (pop. 370,000). With its fertile soils and abundant water, this is Cuba's fruit bowl, producing citrus, bananas, and pineapples, in the most productive plantations on the island.

Pineapple town

The provincial capital, also called **Ciego de Ávila ❶**, has little to recommend it apart from the friendliness of its 100,000 inhabitants. The town's original name, San Jerónimo de la Palma, fell out of use long ago, and the present one comes from a 16th-century rancher named Ávila, who cleared the original dense forest here to make a clearing, or "*ciego*." Often called the "Pineapple Town" by other Cubans, its nickname is well-deserved: the pineapple company Empresa Piña, just outside the city, covers fields with the golden Queen of Fruits. Here, a single variety of pineapple, the sweet and juicy *Española Roja*, is grown in vast quantities that still fall short of demand.

Traffic in the town is largely horse-driven, and the longest possible journey by pony trap should only cost a few pesos. The town is built on a strict grid system centered on **Parque Martí**, with the usual bust of the hero, but there are few buildings of note apart from the **Museo de Artes Decorativas** (open daily, variable hours; entrance charge) and the neoclassical **Teatro Principal**

(just south of the square), built in the 1920s by a rich socialite, Angela Hernández Vida de Jiménez, who battled to create a cultural mecca in her home town. She spent 250,000 pesos building this remarkable confection, but, though the theater is still used, her dreams of cultural supremacy for the place have never been realized.

A popular meeting place on the square is the **Casa de Agua** (Water House), which serves free glasses of the local mineral water, as well as home-made *refrescos* (soft drinks) and fruit juices.

Main attractions
CIEGO DE ÁVILA
LOS JARDINES DE LA REINA
MORÓN
CAYO COCO
CAMAGÜEY
CAYO SABINAL
PLAYA UVERO
PLAY LA HERRADURA

LEFT: harvesting pineapples.
BELOW: waves lap the shore of Cayo Coco.

A Cuban fortress

During the first War of Independence in the 1860s, the Spanish colonial government built a string of 43 forts – called **La Trocha** – across the island at this point, so as to cut the rebellious east off from the rest of the island. One of the few remaining forts, the **Fortín de la Trocha**, can be found across the railroad tracks on Calle Máximo Gómez. It now houses an unremarkable restaurant.

Island pearls

South of Ciego de Ávila lies **Júcaro ❷**, a pleasant, if scrappy, fishing village on the coast, and also the point of embarkation for the pristine and enchanting island chain of **Los Jardines de la Reina** (The Queen's Gardens). Visits, which must be organized well in advance, are expensive week-long packages, with accommodations on a floating hotel, the *Tortuga*, moored near Cayo Anclitas. For more information, contact Avalon Outdoor Company (www.avalons.net) or Roxton Bailey Robinson (www.roxtons.com), the only operators who currently have authority to run fishing and diving expeditions here. The 200-km (125-mile)

TIP

The Queen's Gardens are said to have been given their name by Columbus, to honor the Spanish queen, Isabella of Castile.

archipelago has been designated a marine national park and there is a project in the pipeline to get it declared a UNESCO World Heritage Site.

An accent means a lot

Morón ❸, a real country town where people get around on foot, on bicycles or in horse-drawn carts, lies to the north of the province. English-speakers, who tend to ignore the accent on the last syllable (which makes it *mor-ON*), find the name risible. The town's symbol has always been a crowing rooster, representing the people's triumph over arrogant officialdom. In the 1950s, the local citizenry raised money to have the rooster sculpted in bronze as a public monument. Dictator Fulgencio Batista got in on the act and decided to unveil the statue in what would be known as Batista Park. Outraged residents saved their rooster from humiliation by boycotting the inauguration, but the bird was subsequently kidnapped and destroyed by misguided guerrillas.

In the calmer 1980s, Morón's rooster was born anew and placed in the **Parque del Gallo** (Rooster Park), at the

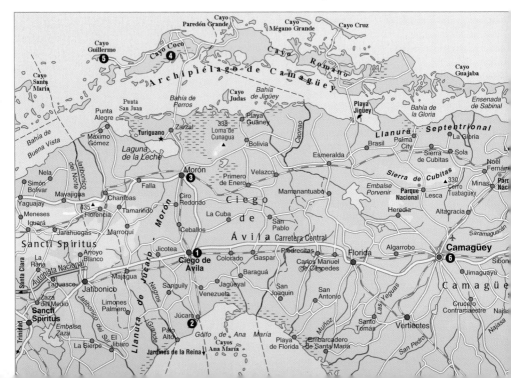

entrance to the town's new hotel, Hotel Morón. In the adjacent tower an amplified recording of jubilant crowing is electronically set to activate twice a day at 6am and 6pm.

North of Morón are popular places for fishing, hunting, and boating: **Laguna La Redonda**, where bass abound; **Aguachales de Falla**, a reserve inhabited mainly by mallards and fulvous tree ducks; and **Laguna de la Leche**, a lagoon milky-white from sodium carbonate deposits that nourish snook and tarpon. The lagoon is Cuba's largest natural reservoir; because of its size and central location, it was strategically important during the 1895 War of Independence: Cuban *mambí* fighters crossed it on numerous occasions to deliver munitions from Camagüey to Villa Clara, thus evading the string of fortifications the Spanish had erected from Júcaro to Morón. On the coast north of the lagoon the **Isla de Turiguano** is devoted to herds of ruddy-coloured St Gertrude's cattle.

The northern islands

Cayo Coco ❹ covers an area of 595 sq. km (230 sq. miles). A 27-km (17-mile) causeway that shoots straight through a mirror of water links the cay to the mainland. It is named, not for abundant coconut groves, as one might suppose, but for a long-legged wading bird, the white ibis, known locally as a *coco*; this, along with the rosy flamingo, is one of the island's more striking inhabitants – although you no longer see flocks of flamingos and other waders that used to feed here. Since the cays in this area were fairly recently settled, wildlife – including 156 bird species, several of them highly endangered endemic species – has had a chance to thrive, and the area is a legally protected zone. However, although hotels have had to comply with ecological provisions, the expansion of the tourist sector is having an impact on wildlife – hotels routinely spray against mosquitoes, for example. Many Cuban ecologists are concerned about the long-term effects of development, especially the way the causeway has obstructed the free flow of currents, leaving the lagoon deficient in some of the essential nutrients required for a healthy ecosystem.

The wild cattle and boar that now roam the cay were imported at some

A rooster is the mascot for the town of Morón.

BELOW: bananas are one of the many crops grown in this fertile region.

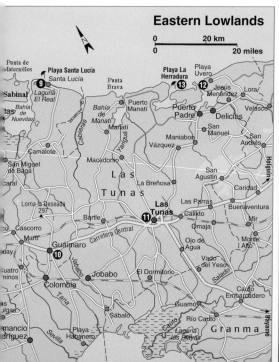

Eastern Lowlands

0   20 km
0   20 miles

TIP

Most Cuban cities are constructed on a grid pattern, but Camagüey is different. What is more, it doesn't have a central square that acts as a focus. A useful reference point is the wide Avenida República, which runs north–south through the city center. The city sights are also somewhat spread out, so the less active or those with little time to spare may find a bici-taxi is a good way to get around without getting too exhausted. Make sure you agree a price before you get in.

BELOW: statue of local hero, Ignacio Agramonte.

point in history, perhaps by passing pirates, but the indigenous iguanas and *jutías* (rodents) were there before them. So were the insects: if you are visiting, it's best to stock up on insect repellent, as the mangrove swamps provide a good breeding ground for these more irksome forms of wildlife.

There are nine beaches of varying sizes on the northern coast. Separated by escarpments, they add up to 22 km (13 miles) of white sand and crystal-clear water. The all-inclusive Hotel Tryp Cayo Coco, a large complex modeled on a colonial township, stands 100 meters/yards in from the shore.

The causeway connecting the cay to the mainland continues west to **Cayo Guillermo** ❺ – also rapidly developing for tourism as a base for scuba diving and fishing – and east to nearby **Cayo Romano** and **Cayo Paredón Grande**, as yet far less developed, with empty white sand beaches.

Camagüey's capital

The province of Camagüey (pop. 750,000), which suffered from severe drought in 2003–4, has its fair share of

sugar-cane fields, but far more important are its cattle pastures, supporting both dairy and beef cattle. *Vaqueros* (cowboys), wearing broad-brimmed hats and dangling machetes, can be seen herding stock from astride their horses, lassos flying. **Camagüey** ❻, the capital of the province, is Cuba's third-largest city (pop. 294,000). It was one of Diego Velázquez's seven original settlements, founded as the Villa of Santa María del Puerto Príncipe in 1514. It was twice moved, and then razed by Henry Morgan and his crew in 1668. It was rebuilt soon after, with a street plan that seems designed to help ambush future invaders: it is a web of unexpected cul-de-sacs.

Unlike the raw farm towns that are the capitals of the adjacent provinces, Camagüey is a place of beauty, culture, and tradition. The old town is a delight: narrow, twisting streets wind from the river, lined by rows of small, rainbow-colored, stuccoed houses, with lush courtyards set back from the street that can be glimpsed through ancient wooden doors. But don't come expecting to find another Trinidad: Camagüey is a large city with a growing tourist reputation.

Honoring famous sons

The city's most famous son, Ignacio Agramonte (1841–73), was the fighting general of Camagüey's rebel forces during the first War of Independence (he died in action in 1873). The **Casa Natal de Ignacio Agramonte A** (open Tues–Sat 9am–5pm; entrance charge) is a museum in the hero's birthplace – a lovely 18th-century mansion, sumptuously furnished with period pieces. The *tinajones* are a prominent feature – round, wide-mouthed earthenware jugs, modeled on the big-bellied jars that came from Spain filled with wines and oils. Cuban versions were created by local potters to solve a pressing problem:

Camagüey had almost no water sources, and rainfall, while abundant, was seasonal. The water supply is more reliable these days, but can still fail, as it did in 2003–4. You still see *tinajones* in the shady courtyard of many Camagüeyan households, and water sellers still ply the streets. Ranging in size from large to enormous, some of the *tinajones* still in use were made more than a century ago. The guides who take you round the house are friendly and thorough, but have only limited English. However, there is much to see that requires little explanation

Near the Agramonte museum, on Calle Príncipe, is the birthplace of a more

You still see some huge tinajones – *earthenware jugs – in Camagüey.*

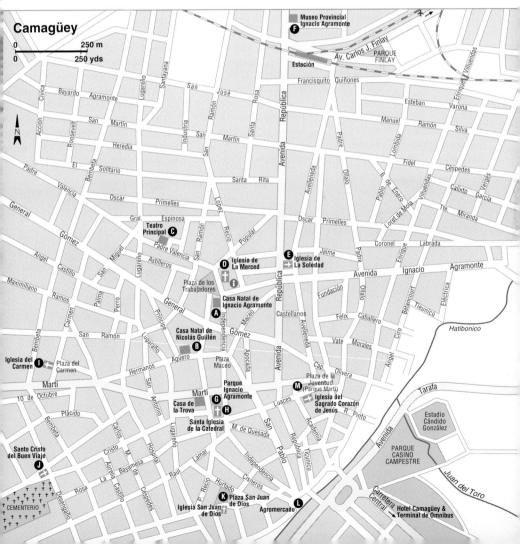

Bronze head of poet, Nicolás Guillén.

BELOW: a statue of a water seller in Camagüey.

recently famous Camagüeyan, the **Casa Natal de Nicolás Guillén** (open Mon–Fri 8am–5pm; entrance charge). The world-renowned writer *(see page 112)* was born here in 1902, and this pleasant little house celebrates his life. There is a small bronze portrait of the poet at the front of the house, and photos and poems on the walls inside. It is more of a cultural center, with a library, than a museum; you are free to wander around but there is not a great deal to see.

More city sights

North of here sits the splendid **Teatro Principal** , which draws the biggest audiences when the Ballet de Camagüey or the local symphony orchestra perform. Calle Padre Valencia brings you back to the attractive 18th-century **Iglesia de La Merced** (opening hours vary), across from Agramonte's birthplace on the **Plaza de los Trabajadores**. Considered one of the most splendid churches in the country when it was first built, La Merced has benefitted from recent restoration: the decorated ceiling is particularly striking. Avenida Agramonte leads you to another important church,

also dating from the 1700s: **Iglesia de la Soledad** . Its red-brick exterior looks unpromising, but inside you are greeted by glorious decoration on the arches and pillars, topped by a splendid vaulted ceiling. Before continuing south to the heart of the city, you can make a diversion north along Avenida República (which becomes Avenida de los Mártires beyond the train station) to the **Museo Provincial Ignacio Agramonte** (open Tues–Sat 10am–5pm, Sun 10am–1pm; entrance charge), with an eclectic collection ranging from stuffed animals to archeological finds. It is best known, though, for its fine-art collection.

Continuing on the route south, you reach **Parque Ignacio Agramonte** , the nearest thing Camagüey has to a main square, though it is too small to fulfill such a role. The dramatic mounted figure of Agramonte is overshadowed by the **Catedral** , which is not as impressive as La Soledad or La Merced, but is still worth a peek. Its wooden ceiling is its best feature. If you ask, you will be allowed to climb spiral steps to the bell tower for a wonderful view over the city (donation appreciated).

Another recently restored, church is the **Iglesia del Carmen** , which lies several blocks west of the square along Calle Martí, on the beautifully restored **Plaza del Carmen**. The plaza is dotted with *tinajones* as well as sculptures of gossiping women, a courting couple, and a man reading a newspaper. While in this area, walk a few blocks south to the **Iglesia de Santo Cristo del Buen Viaje** . The interest here lies mainly in the adjacent **cemetery**, which is one of the finest in the country, and one that is much frequented by local people who like to stroll around, as well as visiting family graves. Running eastward, back toward the center, Calle Cristo has road-side flower-sellers (catering to those needing flowers to take to the cemetery), and a couple of local bars.

Rivaling the Plaza del Carmen for the honor of being the loveliest place in Camagüey is the restored, 18th-century **Plaza San Juan de Dios** , south of Parque Agramonte. Now a national monument, the square is peaceful and surrounded by brightly colored houses with elegant wooden *rejas* (grilles), and tall doors and windows. The plaza is domi-

nated by the **Iglesia San Juan de Dios**, a small, intimate church with a fine mahogany ceiling and altar. Adjacent, in the old hospital, is the local heritage office and a small **museum**. Two of the finest buildings are now restaurants, La Campana de Toledo and the Parador de los Tres Reyes, popular with day-trippers.

Down by the river side

Close by, the farmers' market or **Agromercado** , on the banks of the river, is a great place to appreciate the *agramonteros'* renowned love of good food. In addition to stands selling fresh produce are simple kitchens serving up piping hot meals. It's a lively spot, shaded by palms and tropical foliage, and with vendors noisily hawking their produce. And there's far more produce to hawk than you find in most Cuban markets: piles of glossy mangos, tomatoes and peppers, strings of garlic, and heaps of *mamey* (a root vegetable similar to *yuca*) make it resemble a Mediterranean marketplace.

Backtracking up Calle San Pablo and turning right on Calle Martí you come to the Plaza de la Juventud, to give it the

TIP

The inhabitants of Camagüey are called *agramonteros*, in honor of their city's most famous son.

BELOW: the Plaza San Juan de Dios is a national monument.

Boating on Cayo Sabinal is fun.

BELOW: a tethered *buey* – a working animal.

official name, but local people know it as **Parque Martí **. This quiet square is dominated by the Sagrado Corazón de Jesús, an imposing neo-Gothic church that is currently undergoing extensive renovation work.

Exploring the province

The city of Camagüey is a cultural oasis in an otherwise arid province, where cows seem to outnumber people. Second in size is **Nuevitas ❼**, the Atlantic seaport on the Bahía de Nuevitas. Despite its run-down appearance, Nuevitas is an important trading center for the rural heartland, and several good restaurants have opened here – based primarily on its location close to the causeway to the beautiful **Cayo Sabinal ❽**, a cay to the northwest with more than 30 km (20 miles) of beaches. More hotels are planned, but at present the best place to head for is Playa Los Pinos, where there are basic accommodations and a restaurant. There's a CUC$5 entrance charge to the cay, which is a nature reserve. You may get searched at an overbearing military checkpoint. They're ostensibly looking for drugs but it feels as if they're fishing for bribes. Keep an eye on your stuff and don't be intimidated.

Boats link Cayo Sabinal with nearby **Playa Santa Lucía ❾**, to the east, but the most common route is by road from Camagüey – a journey of 105 km (65 miles) through cattle country. At Santa Lucía, the 20 km (12 miles) of dazzling white sands are still relatively quiet, largely due to the area's isolation. There are half a dozen hotels of varying quality strung out along the main road, and more are planned, but at present there's not a great deal else.

The area is becoming well known for the quality of the diving. Scuba devotees recommend the area for the sheer variety of underwater sites. The Sol Club Santa Lucia incorporates The Shark's Friend International Diving Center, where staff feed sharks. They also offer dives that do not include sharks, for CUC$30 (more for night dives), and boats go out several times a day. Diving is extremely popular here, not only because there is such a variety of marine life, but because of the 33 known shipwrecks just off the coast.

Divers also recommend the coral reef off **La Boca**, a tiny fishing village 8 km (5 miles) west of the main resort. One of the loveliest spots in Cuba, La Boca has a glorious crescent of sand that knocks spots off the strip at Santa Lucía. There are a couple of restaurants specializing, not unnaturally, in seafood. Behind is a lagoon where flamingoes gather.

If you don't have your own transportation you can get a bus from Camagüey or Nuevitas to Playa Santa Lucia; and from here there are (quite expensive) all-inclusive day trips to Cayo Sabinal.

Cattle and more cattle

Traveling eastward from Camagüey along the Carretera Central, you can be in no doubt how the local people make their living. The vast, almost treeless grasslands are virtually empty except for cattle, numerous ranches *(ganaderías)* and the attendant cowboys. The only town before you cross into Las Tunas province is **Guáimaro ❿**, whose main

claim to fame is that it was the site of the assembly which drew up Cuba's first Constitution in 1869.

South of Guáimaro, near the town of **Najasa**, the Sierra Guaicanama-Najasa is the site of the little-visited reserve of **Hacienda La Belén**. The bird life is especially rich, with many species of parrot; there are limited accommodations.

A whistle-stop destination

There is not a lot to detain you in Las Tunas province and most people drive straight through without stopping. The provincial capital, also **Las Tunas ⓫**, does not have a great deal going for it – flying-saucer-shaped water towers are perhaps its most distinguishing feature. Burned down in both wars of independence, it has no colonial landmarks. The main square, Parque Vincent García, is not unpleasant but is spoiled by traffic.

Located close by on Calle Lucas Ortiz is the **Museo Memorial Mártires de Barbados** (open Mon–Sat 10am–5pm; free). It is set in a two-story wooden house, the former home of fencing champion Carlos Leyva González, who was killed with 72 others when a Cuban plane

bound for Barbados was sabotaged by terrorists in 1976. The museum contains documents, photos, and sports implements belonging to all the victims, but especially to Carlos and Leonardo McKenzie Grant, who was also born in the town.

The region's most famous son is El Cucalambé, the pseudonym of poet Cristobal Nápoles Fajardo, whose 19th-century *décimas* (10-line rhyming topical songs) are honored at the annual Cucalambeana Fair, when poets and singers from all over Cuba come for a festival.

The town has a traditional dish, a *caldosa* (stew) of meat and vegetables, which is served in tasty form at Quique Marina, a family-style restaurant on the Carretera Central on the western outskirts. Look for terracotta ceramics dotted about the town – Las Tunas is famous for them.

There is nothing much south of Las Tunas except mangroves and rice farms. On the north coast, near the town of Jesús Menéndez, are two fabulous beaches, **Playa Uvero ⓬** and **Playa La Herradura ⓭**. Both are completely unspoiled, but may not remain so for long. There are two basic hotels here.   ❏

The Spanish name for the prickly pear cactus is tuna, *and it is after this plant that the province is named.*

RESTAURANTS & BARS

Restaurants

All the restaurants listed here are in Camagüey. Elsewhere there is nowhere we would recommend. On the beaches the only places to eat are in the hotels, plus a few snack bars.

Campaña de Toledo
Plaza San Juan de Dios, 18
Tel: (032) 295-888.
Open daily L & D. **$$**
Spanish-style dishes served in a colonial mansion with an attractive patio. Busiest (and most touristy) at lunch time.

Don Ronquillo
Galería Colonial, Calle Ignacio Agramonte, corner República.
Tel: (032) 284-262. Open daily L. **$$**
A cheerfully decorated place, with a terrace and live music. *Comida criolla*, but there is a more varied menu than in many places.

El Ovejito
Calle Hermanos Agüero, between Honda and Carmen.
Tel: (032) 292-524
Open Wed–Mon L & D. **$$**
"The Little Sheep" has a great location on the Plaza del Carmen in a

colonial house with outside tables. As the name suggests, it serves mostly lamb dishes. Nice spot for an early-evening drink, too.

Parador de los Tres Reyes
Plaza San Juan de Dios
No phone.
Open daily L & D. **$–$$**
Traditional Cuban dishes. This is very much a tourist venue, so it's pretty quiet out of season, but a nice place to sit and the food is quite good.

Bodegón Don Cayetano
Calle República, 79 (behind Nuestra Señora de la Soledad)
No phone. Open daily. **$**

Livelier than most, attracting local people as well as visitors. Outside tables and lots to look at on the busy street. Steaks, snacks, and burgers.

Paladar El Cardenal
Calle Martí, 309
No phone. Open daily L & D. **$**
Hearty portions of good *criolla* cooking and a pleasant atmosphere make this well-established *paladar* a popular choice.

● ● ● ● ● ● ● ● ● ● ● ● ●
Price categories are for a meal for one with a beer or mojito. *Wine puts the price up.*
$ = under $25, **$$** = $25–35,
$$$ = over $35.

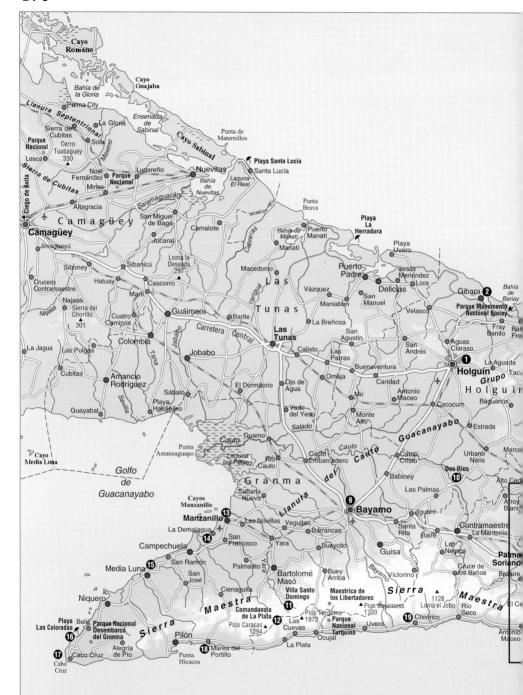

Around Santiago de Cuba

0   10 km
0   10 miles

Holguín

Julio Antonio Mella

Embalse Protesta de Baraguá

Cauto

Bayamo

Palmarito de Cauto

S a n t i a g o   d e

La Prueba

Loma Blanca

▲ 751

La Comunal

C u b a

Los Reynaldos

Costa Rica

Autopista Nacional

San Luis

Alto Songo

Guantánamo

Palma Soriano

Dos Caminos

La Maya

Bellaire ▲ 581

El Cristo

Parque Nacional Gran Piedra

El Aguacate

Niceto Pérez

Carretera Central

El Caney

Cordillera de la   Gran   Piedra

22 El Cobre

Santiago de Cuba

Gran Piedra 1214 ▲ **23**

Aéropuerto Antonio Maceo

Granjita Siboney

24

Parque Baconao

Laguna Baconao

Playa Mar Verde

21

Siboney

26 Valle de la Prehistoria

Reserva El Indio

Antonio Maceo

20

Castillo del Morro

25

★ ★

Sigúa

Baconao

Playa Daiquirí

27

Playa Bacjagua

N

C A R I B B E A N   S E A

A T L A N T I C

O C E A N

aya alavaca

Playa Pesquera

3

Guayacanes

alavaca

Chorro de Maíta

Los Angeles

Punta de Mulas

4

iabon

5 Banes

Cortaderas

Bahía de Banes

Antilla

La Chiva

Cayo Saetía

Playa Corinthia

Bahía de Nipe

Guatemala

7

Herrera

6

Felton

Nícaro

Guaro

Mayarí

Levisa

Cayo Mambí

Cebolla

Cayo Moa Grande

34 Moa

Punta Guarico

Loma de la Mensura 995

Pico del Cristal 1231

El Sitio

Pico del Toldo 1175

Cañete

Sagua de Tánamo

Cuchillas de Moa

Altiplanicie de Nipe

Mayarí

Sierra del Cristal

Santa Catalina

Alturas

Cuchillas de Toa

Playa Maguana

8

Mayarí Arriba

Bayate

Palenque

de

El Yunque de Baracoa

33

Baracoa

32

Punta del Fraile

S a n t i a g o d e C u b a

rito uto

La Comunal

Bernardo

G u a n t á n a m o

To

Baracoa

La Farola

Jamal

Maisí

31

La Prueba

Loma Blanca

Los Reynaldos

Costa Rica

El Salvador

Boquerón

Museo Zoológico de Piedra

Sabanilla

Sabana

Punta de Maisí

Alto Songo

Jaibo

Jamaica

Honduras

Manuel Tames

Pico el Gato 1176

Yumurí

La Máquina

Dos Caminos

El Cristo

La Maya

El Aguacate

Niceto Pérez

28

Guantánamo

Puñales de Caujerí

Sierra del Purial

iago de a

El Caney

Parque Nacional Gran Piedra

Yatera

▲ 747

Cajobabo

Jauco

Punta Caleta

Granjita Siboney

Gran Piedra 1214

Maqueicito

Sierra del Maguey

Central

San Antonio del Sur

Imías

30 Playa de Cajobabo

Siboney

Sigúa

▲ 789

29

Caimanera

Mirador de Malones

Yateritas

Playa Daiquirí

Parque Baconao

Baconao

US NAVAL BASE

Guantánamo

Punta Barlovento

Eastern Cuba

0   20 km
0   20 miles

N

HOLGUÍN AND GRANMA

From the island's top archeological site
to the ragged mountains of the Sierra
Maestra, including the Pico Turquino,
Cuba's highest peak, this region has much to
offer, yet attracts surprisingly few tourists

Havana
CUBA

Often called the "Granary of Cuba" because of its agricultural wealth, the province of Holguín has some 1 million people living within its borders, making it second in population only to Havana province. Its capital city, also called **Holguín ❶**, is the fourth-largest city in Cuba, with a population of 233,000. Along with its agricultural importance, it is a relatively active industrial center and has grown rapidly in recent decades.

The colonial center of Holguín is marked by **Parque Calixto García**, an expansive square built around the monument to the city's most famous independence fighter, General García, who was born in Calle Miró nearby – the house is now a museum. Fronting the square are a striking Art Deco movie house, the local Casa de la Trova, the provincial library, book stores, and art galleries. Most noteworthy is the building known as **La Periquera** (Parrot Cage) – so named ever since Spanish soldiers, in their blue, yellow, and green uniforms, took refuge behind the barred windows during a *mambí* attack in 1868. The building houses the **Museo Provincial** (open daily 8am–5pm; entrance charge), whose prized possession is the *Hacha de Holguín* (Holguín Ax), a pre-Columbian figure of an elongated man carved in polished rock; found in 1860, it has become the symbol of the province. There's a replica in one of the front rooms; ask to see the real one in the main meeting hall. There are also displays on slavery, and all

kinds of historical memorabilia – plenty to fascinate even those who can't read the Spanish explanations.

A half-block south of the square, on Calle Maceo, is the **Museo de la Historia Natural Carlos de la Torre** (open Tues–Sun 9am–10pm; entrance charge), with a fine collection of polymitas, the brightly banded snails indigenous to eastern Cuba; and lots of stuffed animals, including a pair of ivory-billed woodpeckers, now almost certainly extinct. Around the corner, **Parque San Isidoro**, a rather neglected square, is the site of

Main attractions
HOLGUÍN: MUSEO PROVINCIAL
GIBARA
GUARDALAVACA
CHORRO DE MAÍTA
SITIO HISTÓRICO DE BIRÁN
BAYAMO
PICO TURQUINO
MANZANILLO

PRECEDING PAGES: coastal view from El Morro fortress. **LEFT:** Playa Esmeralda. **BELOW:** *bicitaxis* wait for customers.

You may find a rodeo being held in Holguín, where you see this sign.

BELOW: humpbacked hills dot the landscape around Gibara.

the **Catedral de San Isidoro** (1720). Its rough brick arcades harbor birds and figures carved by a local artist; other treasures include the original baptismal font.

Three blocks north of Parque Calixto García, leafy **Plaza San José** is the most picturesque square in Holguín, centered on a ruined church, the Iglesia San José. You'll usually find bicycle rickshaws *(bicitaxis)* parked in the square, offering you a ride to **La Loma de la Cruz** (The Hill of the Cross), Holguín's most visible landmark and a place of pilgrimage. It's not far to walk, but when you get there you must tackle the 468 steps leading up to the 18th-century cross.

On the eastern edge of the city is the enormous **Plaza de la Revolución**, as soulless as most such squares in Cuba. The main feature of interest is the **Mausoleo de Calixto García**, decorated with a vast frieze representing the struggle of the Cuban people from the Conquest to the Revolution. The city's two main tourist hotels, the Hotel Pernik and the Hotel El Bosque, are in the ugly Lenin district, a little way from the center. A more scenic but less convenient alternative, near the airport, is Villa El Cocal, a pleasant villa in lovely gardens. About 10 km (6 miles) southeast of the city is the Mirador de Mayabe, the best accommodations in the area: a collection of cabins on a hill, with a fine panoramic view.

Gibara, a colonial gem

The farther north you go, the better Holguín province gets. **Gibara ❷**, on the coast, 36 km (22 miles) north of the capital, exudes maritime charm and colonial grace. On the road from Holguín you pass through some fabulous scenery with strange, humpbacked hills. Tall hollyhocks line the road to an old iron bridge that crosses the **Río Cacoyoquin** where it empties into the sea. The bridge leads into the town along a shady, seaside drive with a **statue of Christopher Columbus** and a small ruined garrison at the end. A fishing cooperative, the shipyards, and a spinning mill sustain Gibara's population, which numbers more than 16,000.

With terracotta roofs, flowering patios, a weather-beaten church, cobblestoned streets, and harbor fishing boats, Gibara is endlessly photogenic. The restored **Teatro Colonial** (1889) is a lit-

tle masterpiece, but the *pièce de résistance* is the **Museo de Artes Decorativas** (open Tues–Sun 9am–noon, 1–5pm, Thur–Sun also 8–10pm; entrance charge), on the second floor of a magnificent 19th-century mansion. Besides gorgeous *mediopuntos* (Cuba's characteristic, fan-shaped stained-glass windows) and *mamparas* (decorative saloon-style doors), there is a fine collection of furniture and many Art Nouveau pieces. You can climb up to the roof terrace for a view of the town.

There are a few peso hotels and a couple of excellent *casas particulares*. Eating out is easier: the Miramar and El Faro, both on the waterfront, offer meals for *pesos convertibles* and normally have a good choice of seafood.

A controversial monument

There used to be a long-standing debate between Gibara and Baracoa about the exact place where the Europeans first landed in Cuba *(see page 33)*. Nowadays historians agree that the first landfall was made in **Bariay Bay**, east of Gibara. The peninsula has been declared a national monument, **Parque Monumento Nacional Bariay** (open daily 9am–5pm; expensive entrance charge payable at a checkpoint). A **monument**, erected in 1992 to commemorate the 500th anniversary of Columbus's setting foot in America, sits on the tip of Cayo Bariay, within sight of what is almost certainly the flat-topped mountain he mentioned in his logbook. Set in a delightful palm grove, the monument consists of a collection of columns and idols designed to symbolize the meeting of European and American aboriginal civilizations. If you have your own transportation, you can reach the site by driving 7 km (4 miles) north of Fray Benitos, but boat trips are also arranged from Guardalavaca.

Guardalavaca

Farther east, beyond the **Rafael Freyre** sugar mill, with its ancient steam locomotives, lies northeastern Cuba's main resort area, where the sea is a diaphanous blue and the beaches creamy white,

fringed by tropical foliage. First you reach the powdery white-sand beach at **Playa Esmeralda**. A prime attraction here, as well as the beach, is the **Acuario de Cayo Naranjo** (open daily 9am–9pm; entrance charge). You get taken on a speedboat out to the cay, where there are dolphin and sea-lion shows and, on payment of quite a large sum (currently CUC$50) you can swim with the dolphins. There is an excellent seafood restaurant and bar, as well as several hotels, including one of Cuba's most luxurious resorts.

Beyond, **Guardalavaca** ❸ is a quiet resort with a stunning stretch of beach. It has never totally taken off despite great efforts by the Ministry of Tourism, so is greener and less hurried than Varadero. As in Varadero, there are few local people other than those who work in the hotels. The resort may be too low-key for some people, but it is far more scenic than Varadero, with an excellent beach, and it has the advantage of being well placed for exploring some interesting sights. You can rent cars, bicycles, and mopeds, as well as organize boat or bus trips through your hotel, or through the Cubatur office, just behind the commercial center.

Dancers in Holguín's Casa de la Trova.

BELOW: the beach at Guardalavaca.

Gold idol in the
Museo Indocubano.

BELOW: Parque
Monumento
Nacional Bariay, a
monument to the
meeting of two
cultures.

Chorro de Maíta and Banes

Just south of Guardalavaca, the hilly road passes **Chorro de Maíta ❹** (open daily Tues–Sat 9am–5pm, Sun 9am–1pm; entrance charge) the largest pre-Columbian burial ground known to exist in the Antilles. Archeologists' excavations have revealed skeletons of the indigenous Taíno people who inhabited the area from *circa* AD 1000 to the end of the 16th century. A section of the graveyard has been excavated to show how the skeletons were buried. Two of the children wear European jewelry, and the presence of a Spaniard indicates that there must have been cross-cultural relationships in the early years. Over the road is a reconstructed Taíno village, the **Aldea Taíno** (open same hours as above; separate entrance charge) – the most authentic of the country's reconstructed indigenous settlements.

Some of the finds from Chorro de Maíta are on display at the tiny but interesting **Museo Indocubano** (open Tues–Sat 9am–5pm, Sun 9am–noon, 2–5pm, Fri–Sun also 7–9pm; entrance charge) in nearby **Banes ❺**. The utensils and jewelry are made of delicately carved and shaped shells, rocks, bones, ceramic, wood, and metal. The minuscule gold idol of a woman wearing a headdress and offering a bowl is, arguably, a joint Amerindian-Spanish effort, and is one of the few pre-Columbian Cuban gold pieces to have been found.

Banes is a sleepy colonial town and a fascinating relic of US involvement in Cuba. It was once right at the center of the American United Fruit Company's lands and many of the town's wooden buildings show an unmistakable US influence, with their zinc roofs and broad verandahs. Many Jamaicans came here to work in the 1930s, and some people here still speak English.

South of Banes, the road runs around **Bahía de Nipe**. There is a turn-off to **Cueto**, a wild west sort of town where ancient steam locomotives chug right up the main street and *guajiros* (farmers) trot around on ponies. In theory, you can get a bus from here to **Birán**, Castro's birthplace, but in practice the bus rarely runs. If you do not have your own transportation, a taxi from Cueto may be the only answer. The old Castro residence still stands in this tiny community – an elegant,

wooden house with lacy balconies, set by a rippling river. A long avenue of royal palms sweeps up to the front of the pink and yellow house, which is open to the public as the **Sitio Histórico de Birán** (open Tues–Sat 9am–noon, 2–4pm, Sun 9am–noon; entrance charge). There are lots of family photographs on display, as well as domestic items and an ancient Ford (which belonged to his father).

Birán has been entirely reconstructed since the Revolution; the old thatched *bohíos* have gone. The village looks like a second-rate holiday camp, with rows of identical concrete houses, built and furnished by the state. One old farmer still has his original house – a thatched wooden building with pigs scratching around under mango trees. There is nowhere to stay, but friendly local people are happy to accommodate strangers, and older people love to tell stories of the Castro family.

A slave town and the central highlands

Back toward the Bahía de Nipe, **Mayarí** is an industrial town with little to interest travelers, but **Guatemala ❻**, an old slave town right by the bay, is a gem. The sugar mill still dominates the town, but there are plenty of gingerbread cottages, all built by the slaves themselves out of palm timber and driftwood. Each one is delightfully individual, and each a work of art: some have carved wooden gargoyles, others elaborately worked gables, and every house is a different color from its neighbor; the gardens are lush and colorful. Local people proudly show their bar – once an exclusive "whites only" country club but now open to all – selling shots of rough *aguardiente* spirit for around a peso.

At the mouth of the Bahía de Nipe is the 42-sq. km (16-sq. mile) island of **Cayo Saetía ❼**, once the exclusive resort of top Communist Party officials; local people say Raúl Castro used to be a regular visitor. The island is home to deer and wild boar, and a variety of imported animals – ostriches, zebra, antelope – and, although this is a protected reserve, hunting is still allowed

under strictly regulated conditions. It's a delightful spot, with lush vegetation running down to the pristine white sands and one hotel, the Villa Gaviota Cayo Saetía *(see Accommodations, page 352).*

The impressive **Sierra Cristal** mountain range, reaching 1,200 meters (4,000 ft) at Pico del Cristal, rolls through Holguín and Guantánamo provinces. The best place to get close to nature is the pleasant hotel at **Pinares de Mayarí**, established in 1988 to study the mountain ecology of the region, and now run by Gaviota *(see page 369).*

Cuba's great hero of the first *mambí* independence struggle, Carlos Manuel de Céspedes, established his revolutionary government at **Mayarí Arriba ❽** in 1868. The area is covered with coffee plantations established by French planters who fled here in the early 19th century after the slave rebellions in Haiti. From here, a twisting road descends to Cuba's second city of **Santiago de Cuba** *(see pages 293–302).*

Visiting Granma province

Granma province was carved out of the old *Oriente* or Eastern Territory histori-

Indigenous skeleton from Chorro de Maíta

BELOW: the Iglesia de San Salvador, Bayamo.

The digital version of Cuba's only newspaper, Granma, *is published online daily in five languages. For the English version, go to www. granma.cu/ingles.*

BELOW: a reminder that the Revolution has its roots in the past *(ayer means yesterday)*, and is relevant today *(hoy)* and tomorrow *(mañana).*

cally controlled by Santiago de Cuba. The peculiar name, of course, comes from the cabin cruiser Fidel, Che, and their comrades used to sneak into the country from Mexico in 1956 before they took up arms in the mountains. The stunning scenery of the Sierra Maestra is one of the area's main attractions, but so too are the numerous sites linked with the 1950s guerrilla campaign, and with the 19th-century struggle for independence.

Bayamo

Bayamo ❾ (pop. 144,000), the second of Cuba's seven original *villas,* was founded in 1513 by Diego Velázquez. It was located far enough inland to be safe from pirate attacks, and set on the navigable Río Bayamo. This flowed into the **Río Cauto**, the longest river in Cuba and the major transportation route for the eastern end of the island when coastal trade was faster than overland trails. It wasn't until 1902 that eastern and western Cuba were linked by rail through the center of the island, and the Carretera Central roughly paralleling it was only finished in 1932. North of the city, swampland and lakes provided Bayamo's settlers with abundant game and fish. Even today this area, **Los Caneyes de Virama**, is a hunting and fishing reserve where sportspeople can catch duck, ibis, quail, rabbit, or *jutía* (a large rodent) one day and fly-fish for bass the next. The city's location was so strategic that Bayamo became Cuba's smuggling center in the 16th and 17th centuries.

Bayamo is, however, most famous for its role in the Cuban independence struggle. Although it was torched during the war, Bayamo retains its colonial street plan, as well as the horse-drawn buggy. These *coches,* immortalized in a popular song, follow routes from bus and train stations and the civilized Hotel Sierra Maestra.

This quiet, peaceful city is dotted with monuments to the independence struggle. In the main square, **Parque Céspedes**, is the **Ayuntamiento** (town hall) where Carlos Manuel de Céspedes, the rebel president, signed the document abolishing slavery in the liberated zones. This was the first city taken by the rebels, but with the defeat of the independence forces, it was not until 1888 that abolition

came into effect throughout Cuba, by decree of the Spanish Queen. Surrounded by shade trees is a bronze statue of the great man himself.

Across the plaza is the **Casa Natal de Céspedes** (open Tues–Fri 9am–5pm, Sat 9am–2pm, 8–10pm, Sun 10am–1pm; entrance charge), where the campaigner was born in 1819. Built of marble, it emerged unscathed from the independence wars and was for years the local post office. This colonial mansion houses documents and photos on the first floor, with period furnishings and family memorabilia above. It recounts Céspedes's life, from his days as a law student to the rebel presidency.

It seems appropriate that a descendant, Onorio Céspedes, should be Bayamo's historian and director of **La Casa de la Nacionalidad Cubana** (House of Cuban Nationality), situated in a beautifully restored colonial mansion to further historical and cultural research in the city.

A battle cry and anthem

A block from the central square, the **Iglesia de San Salvador** was the church where *bayamese* patriot Perucho Figueredo – like Céspedes, a lawyer and poet – first performed a stirring march for the independence fighters that later became Cuba's national anthem. It was played during the Corpus Christi ceremonies in June, four months before the war began. The church was burned down when Spanish troops re-took Bayamo, and residents, mostly women, decided to torch their own city and flee to the hills. They did, however, save the wooden altar to the Virgen de Dolores, and the stone font at which Céspedes and Figueredo were baptized. Both these artifacts can be seen in the rebuilt church.

Northeast of Bayamo, **Dos Ríos ❿** is one of Cuba's most revered, and least-visited sites. It was here that Cuba's greatest hero, José Martí, met his death fighting for Cuban independence on May 19, 1895, just a month after his arrival at Cajobabo. Dos Ríos was his first battle, and he died without having fired a shot. Surrounded by a lawn scattered with stately royal palms, a stone wall holds a bronze bust of Martí with the inscription; "When my fall comes, all the savor of life will seem like sun and honey." A simple white obelisk marks the spot.

The mansion in which the Casa de la Nacionalidad Cubana is situated was acquired by the state in 1990 and intended originally as a maternity home, before being opened the following year as a research institute.

BELOW: A bust of Carlos Manuel Céspedes, who declared rebellion against the Spanish.

Céspedes and Cuban Rebellion

On the morning of October 10, 1868, Bayamo-born Carlos Manuel de Céspedes rang the great bell at his sugar plantation, La Demajagua, south of Manzanillo. With that stroke he emancipated his slaves and, in the resonant *Grito de Yara* (Cry of Yara), he declared open rebellion against Cuba's colonial rulers, thus beginning the first War of Independence against Spain. As with the US Civil War a few years earlier, emancipation was not the main reason for the war, but it was always an important subsidiary, and became an increasingly necessary weapon. Other landowners were soon to begin freeing their slaves and arming them for battle.

Céspedes's bold action was the climax of 15 years of conspiracy during which he and his friends used Masons' lodges and chess tournaments in Bayamo and Manzanillo as a cover for anti-colonialist plots. He led the rebel forces as President of the Republic in Arms until October 1873, when factional infighting forced him from power. By now almost blind, he accepted his removal with dignity, and retired to San Lorenzo in the Sierra Maestra to teach letters and chess. He had just finished a chess game one afternoon in March 1874 when Spanish troops raided the town and ordered him to surrender. He refused and was shot down.

Into the Sierra Maestra

To experience fully the rugged beauty of the southeastern mountains, the best base is the **Villa Santo Domingo** , south of the road linking Bayamo and Manzanillo on the coast. The mountain road veers off at **Yara**, passing through the small town of **Bartolomé Masó**, on to the **Embalse Paso Malo**, and steeply up into the heart of the sierra.

During the guerrilla war, Santo Domingo was a rebel camp with a mess hall and workshops. Today, these have been adapted for feeding and entertaining campers. Partially hidden in this woody setting are new cabins, each housing two to four people. The Yara River is at hand for swimming, and there are horses for exploring the mountain trails.

Castro's old rebel headquarters in the mountains are at **La Comandancia de La Plata**, just to the south, within the **Turquino National Park** (open from 7am; last entrance 3pm), and not to be confused with the village of La Plata at the foot of the mountains on the coast. A guide is compulsory; you can find one at the park entrance in Villa Santo Domingo. No cameras are allowed; they

will be taken from you and looked after when you're halfway along the trail.

You must also hire a guide at the Villa Santo Domingo to accompany you on hikes up Cuba's highest mountain, **Pico Turquino** (1,970 meters/6,470 ft), in the national park. Both the Comandancia and the Pico Turquino hikes start 3 km (2 miles) from Villa Santo Domingo, up an extremely steep (40-degree gradient) road that finishes at Alto de Naranjo, where there is a parking lot. After that, the trail is exciting and beautiful: between outcroppings of mineral and sedimentary rocks, deep-green conifers stand alongside precious cedar, mahogany, and trumpetwood trees. The slopes are dotted with delicate wild orchids and graceful ferns. Although it can be cold and windy, the temperature rarely drops to freezing and there's never any snow. You can't see anything from the summit of Turquino, but the views from just before it are magnificent.

Other trails and narrow roads link the isolated villages and houses of the sparsely populated mountains. The people of the Sierra Maestra are typical *campesinos*: they keep a couple of cows,

The "liberty bell" at La Demajagua, that launched Cuba's first War of Independence.

BELOW:
mechanized cane-cutting in the Sierra Maestra.

a gaggle of chickens and a few pigs and goats; grow a little coffee and some vegetables for their own use; scrub the laundry on smooth stones *(piedras chinas)* in the nearest stream; cook with wood or kerosene; and those who can, watch television at night (though not everyone has electricity). Rationed staples are brought in monthly. The family doctor makes regular rounds, usually on horseback. In an emergency (and when there's fuel), a jeep ambulance speeds the patient to the nearest clinic or hospital, but pregnant women are checked into special mountain maternity houses.

Liberty bell

Overlooking the Gulf of Guacanayabo, 48 km (30 miles) west of Bayamo, **Manzanillo** ⓮ is the second-largest city in the province. Its fine harbor has also made it the main fishing center and principal shipping terminal for the sugar brought in by truck or rail from the little mill towns farther south. Like Bayamo, Manzanillo is steeped in rebellion, early on as a smuggling port, then during the wars of independence. Cuba's first communist cell was organized in Manzanillo in the 1920s, and the only communist mayor, Paquito Rosales, was democratically elected there in the 1940s. In the same decade, Jesús Menéndez, the incorruptible leader of the sugar workers' union, was assassinated on Manzanillo train station platform. During the 1950s, Celia Sánchez organized an underground campaign here in support of the 26th of July Movement.

Manzanillo seems to turn its back on the port, and the Malecón is often deserted. Attention is focused on the large **Parque Céspedes**, where several colonial buildings show a marked Arab influence – particularly the delightful, brightly colored *glorieta* or bandstand in the center of the square. You still see people play the *órgano oriental*, a type of hand-operated organ brought from France in the 19th century.

Stroll through the dusty backstreets of Manzanillo, which has a pleasantly spacious feel. It is also worth seeking out the **Celia Sánchez Memorial**, with its col-

orful tiled murals of sunflowers and doves, located seven blocks southwest of the main square along Calle Martí. On a hill overlooking the city is Hotel Guacanayabo, another Soviet-inspired eyesore that has little more to offer than a spectacular view.

La Demajagua ⓮ (open daily 7am–5pm), on the coast just south of Manzanillo and connected to the city by a rail spur and a road, is where Céspedes rang the bell to call for independence and the abolition of slavery in 1868 *(see box, page 287)*. The plantation is now a park, with the great bell firmly anchored in a stone wall and a small museum with displays of local archeological relics and some of Céspedes's personal effects.

Past La Demajagua, the road follows the coast through **Media Luna** ⓯, the little town where Celia Sánchez was born in 1920. Her family home at Avenida Principal 111 is now a museum, the **Casa Natal de Celia Sánchez Manduley** (open Tues–Sat 9am–5pm, Sun 9am–1pm; entrance charge). It is somewhat more affluent than others along the main streets, for Celia's father was the local doctor. He was also a follower of José

Celia Sánchez, whose family home is now a museum.

BELOW: the view from just below the summit of Pico Turquino.

An elegant shopping arcade in Manzanillo, with pronounced Moorish influences.

BELOW: detail of an ornate bandstand in Manzanillo.

Martí. In 1953, to commemorate the 100th anniversary of Martí's birth, he and Celia placed a bust of the hero on Pico Turquino. A more explosive commemoration at the time was the attack in July on the Moncada Garrison in Santiago. In the years that followed, Celia Sánchez became a prominent underground organizer and was the first of the underground movement to make contact with Fidel after the landing of the *Granma*. Eventually, she joined the rebel forces and was a part of the revolutionary leadership up to her death in 1980.

Playa Las Coloradas

At **Playa Las Coloradas** ⑯, 20 km (12 miles) south of **Niquero** (which has some interesting French-style plantation houses), is the entrance to the **Parque Nacional Desembarco del Granma** (entrance charge; pay at Playa Las Coloradas). Two km (1 mile) south of the beach here is the starting point of the Rebel Army Trail. You can't miss the life-size replica of the *Granma* at the road side. There's a tiny museum (open Tues–Sat 9am–5pm, Sun 9am–noon; entrance charge) and a boardwalk to the landing site, crossing the mangrove and sawgrass swamps that Fidel, Raúl, Che, and their band waded through after disembarking from the cabin cruiser *Granma* in December 1956 to begin the guerrilla war *(see page 58)*. A monument roughly marks their landing place. The rebels were quickly surrounded by Batista's troops, and were nearly annihilated at the tiny village of Alegría de Pío.

Also within the park is **Cabo Cruz** ⑰, marked by a 19th-century lighthouse and relics from the 5,000 year-old civilization of the indigenous Ciboney. There is a tumbledown fishing village, marking what is effectively Cuba's most southerly point: a pretty place, with gardens overflowing with bougainvillaea. The marine terrace is replete with caverns: fissures in the rocky surface expose drops of up to 70 meters (240 ft) with vertical walls that open into enormous underwater chambers. Fascinating coralline formations and one of Cuba's largest collections of the coveted queen conch hug the rocky shore. Farther out lies the hull of a ship sunk in the 19th century.

The dry surface of the terrace reveals sturdy cacti poking through the rocks. Lizards scuttle underfoot, while cormorants, egrets, and gulls wheel overhead. The Ciboney once lived in the caves along this coast. Their diet consisted of fish, small animals, and native plants; they collected shells and stones to make tools and weapons, and crushed rocks into colored powder for painting. Clearly visible on the walls of several caverns are black and red (sometimes blue and brown) drawings of enigmatic lines, circles, and figures.

The dramatic south coast

Southeast of Niquero you drive through sugar-cane plains and the foothills of the Sierra Maestra before coming to the beautifully sited town of **Pilón**. From here the road hugs the coast, sandwiched between mountains and the Caribbean, all the way to Santiago de Cuba, with some of Cuba's most dramatic scenery along the way. **Marea del Portillo** ⑱, once a small fishing village, is rapidly

being developed as a resort, although the much-vaunted "black sands" of the coconut-fringed beach are actually rather unappealing. Diving is possible off the reef, with shipwrecks and coral caves to explore. There is still some local color, with horsemen mounting their steeds and riding up into the Sierra Maestra. Apart from the usual resort hotel, the village retains a rather sleepy air.

The drive along the south coast to Santiago is one of the most memorable on the island, as you pass through some of the most beautiful countryside in Cuba, with the mountains descending right to the shore. The journey used to be hazardous, due to the terrible condition of the road; it has now been resurfaced, but there are still rock falls, and stones get washed up from the beach, so drive carefully, and always keep an eye out for cows, goats, and other animals. Lastly, there is little in the way of road-side facilities, so fill your tank and take plenty of water and food for the journey.

La Plata (not to be confused with the Comandancia de La Plata inland) is the site of the rebels' first attack on Batista's army on May 28, 1957. A museum (open Mon–Sat 8am–6pm, Sun 8am–noon; entrance charge) in the village focuses on this battle and other aspects of the guerrilla campaign. Nearby, **Las Cuevas** has a pleasant beach, and is the trailhead for the climb up to Pico Turquino from the coast. You can go up Turquino and back from Las Cuevas in a day but it's a tough hike; take plenty of water and sunscreen. The walk to Villa Santo Domingo (charge) is a two- to three-day hike. It is worth contacting the national park's headquarters in Bartolomé Masó (tel: 0123-565349) to ensure there will be a guide available. At **Ocujal** the road passes beneath the mountain.

Uvero, 24 km (15 miles) farther east, is another place where the guerrillas won an important victory. Beyond, the fishing village of **Chivirico** ⑲ is famous for its bat-filled caves, **Las Cuevas de los Murciélagos**, and its **international scuba center**, based at the Hotel Brisas Sierra Mar Los Galeones, one of Cuba's best resorts (an amalgamation of two separate ones), attractive, if rather isolated. Santiago is within easy reach; rental cars are available if you want to drive the coastal route in reverse. ❏

Gardens in the little fishing village in Cabo Cruz are bright with bougainvillaea.

BELOW: the coastline, going toward Santiago.

SANTIAGO DE CUBA

Cuba's second city has a heroic revolutionary
past, beautiful squares, and a vibrant
musical tradition that includes the
country's most vigorous carnival

Nestled alongside a sweeping bay at
the foothills of the Sierra Maestra
mountains, **Santiago** is Cuba's
most exotic and ethnically diverse city.
More Caribbean than Cuban, it is where
many Haitians, both white and black, settled after fleeing the slave uprisings of
their country at the end of the 18th century, bringing with them the cachet of
their French culture. Isolated and remote,
it is Cuba's second-largest city with a
population of 440,000.

Surrounding the city are vast rural
slopes covered with sugar cane and coffee plantations. The city itself has its
share of structural decay, yet it's not
nearly as run-down and dilapidated as
Havana, nor as intense, imposing or con-
gested. Some areas are becoming traffic-
free, and museums, galleries, bars and
restaurants are emerging from *ciudadela*
slums. This process is beautifying much
of the colonial architecture – you'll see
plenty of graceful hanging balconies,
gingerbread latticework, and wrought-
iron gates throughout the city – but Santiago suffered greatly from the privations
of the "Special Period". There is a lot of
poverty here and visitors have to put up
with harassment from hustlers and beggars. For the same reason, crime is on
the increase, and there is more need for
care, especially when walking through
the town alone at night. On the other
hand, most of Santiago's residents are
extraordinarily friendly and helpful.

Santiago is renowned for producing
much of Cuba's most important music,
and this rich musical tradition, mingled
with the remnants of French customs,
gives the city a sensual, somewhat
sleazy, New Orleans-like atmosphere.
Wandering around can be confusing at
times because some of the city's streets
have two or three names, but Santiago is
still ideal for walking and deserves several days exploration.

Bastion of nationalism

Founded by the Spaniards in 1514, Santiago was Cuba's capital from 1524 until
1549. Because of its deep, natural harbor

Main attractions

ANTIGUO CUARTEL MONCADA
PLAZA DE DOLORES
MUSEO BACARDÍ
CASA DE LA TROVA
PARQUE CÉSPEDES
CATEDRAL DE N.S. DE ASUNCIÓN
CASA DE VELÁZQUEZ
CEMENTERIO DE SANTA IFIGENIA

LEFT: Santiago
street scene.
BELOW: view over
the bay.

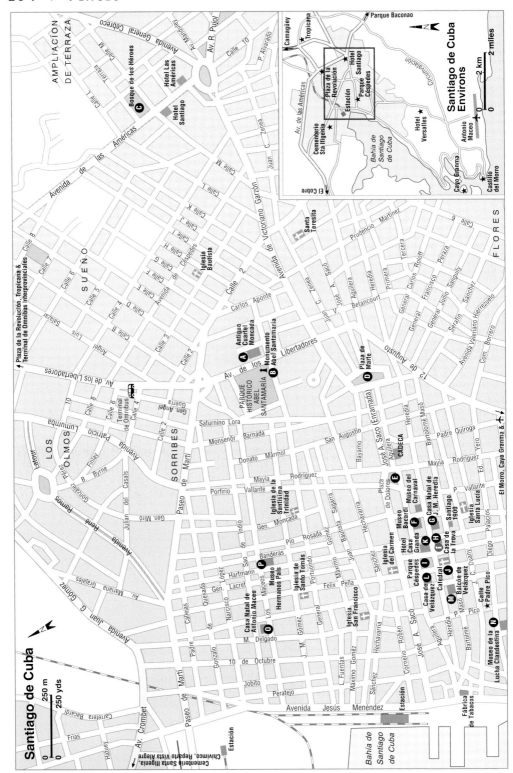

and Caribbean coastline, it also served as the center of the island's prosperous slave trade in the 1700s and 1800s. In 1898, Spain's surrender to the United States took place in Santiago, but then the city gradually slipped into second-class status after the government centered itself in Havana.

Today, Santiago is the island's only official "Hero City," revered for being a bastion of Cuban nationalism and the cradle of the Revolution. It was here, on July 26, 1953, that the Revolution began with the failed assault by Castro and his rebels on the Moncada Garrison, then the second-largest military post in Cuba. It was also here that Castro accepted the surrender of Batista's army in 1959.

Touring the town

The first thing you see when you enter Santiago is the stark **Plaza de la Revolución**, dominated by a vast, equestrian statue: the **Monumento Maceo**. Beneath the monument is a museum containing holograms of revolutionary items connected with the great fighter, one of the major figures in Cuba's 19th-century struggle for independence. The plaza stands at the junction with the Avenida de los Libertadores, a broad street lined with flowering trees and busts of the Moncada rebels.

Here you will find the **Antiguo Cuartel Moncada** Ⓐ (Moncada Barracks; open Mon–Sat 9am–7.30pm, Sun 9am–1pm; entrance charge), which now serves two separate purposes: one half is a school, while the other is a museum dedicated to the Moncada assault and the 1959 Revolution. Inside its bullet-ridden brick walls are revolutionary memorabilia: guns, grenades, documents, photographs, Castro's khaki uniforms and Che Guevara's muddy boots. The museum is visually strong, so non-Spanish speakers can still find a visit enjoyable. Surprisingly, the museum is hardly signposted; you enter by taking a turning left off Libertadores.

Opposite, in a park of the same name, is the impressive **Monumento Abel Santamaría** Ⓑ, a tribute to one of the leaders of the 1953 attack on Moncada. It was Santamaría's job to create diversionary fire at the nearby hospital – a task he performed too well, in fact: unaware that the main assault had failed, he and his men continued firing until the hospital was surrounded. Despite pretending to be patients, the unfortunate rebels were caught and tortured, and most were executed. The park itself is a shady, well-used spot, where plants struggle to survive, boys play baseball, and groups of elderly people take exercise classes.

Toward the colonial center

Walking south from here, you reach Avenida Garzón. If you go left up the avenue you come to one of the city's most modern and most wealthy areas, with the landmark red, white, and blue **Hotel Santiago**. Nearby is a buzzing farmers' market, and, next to the **Hotel Las Américas**, a small, rather neglected park, the **Bosque de los Héroes** Ⓒ, which has monuments dedicated to those who led Cuba's Revolution in the 1950s. Just east of here, flanking Avenida Manduley, is the attractive **Vista Alegre** district.

To reach the old heart of town, how-

The July 26 assault on the Moncada Garrison initiated the Revolution.

BELOW: statue of Antonio Maceo in the Plaza de la Revolución.

ever, turn right and look out for **Hotel Rex**, on the left just before you reach **Plaza de Marte ⓓ**. Now a very basic peso hotel (which does, nevertheless, take tourists), the Rex is only notable as the place where Fidel Castro and his fellow guerrillas ate their last meal before the Moncada Barracks attack in July 1953. From Plaza de Marte, a noisy square where taxis gather, and goat-pulled carts take children for rides at weekends, head down the busy, commercial Calle Aguilera to **Plaza de Dolores ⓔ**, a pleasant, leafy square with lots of benches under the trees, as well as the tables of numerous restaurants lining the plaza. The Cafeteria la Isabelica here is a local institution. Also on the plaza is the popular Taberna de Dolores, which is housed in a cavernous colonial mansion and often has live music *(see page 303)*. In a former church, the Sala Dolores is known for its recitals of choral and orchestral music.

The Egyptian mummy in the Museo Bacardí was bought by Emilio Bacardí, a keen collector, on a visit to Egypt in 1912.

Santiago's museums

Continuing down Calle Aguilera, you come to an imposing provincial government building on the right, oppo-

site the **Museo Bacardí ⓕ** (open Mon noon–9pm, Tues–Sat 9am–8pm, Sun 9am–1pm; entrance charge), Santiago's most interesting museum. It was founded in 1899 by Emilio Bacardí Moreau, a Cuban writer and the first mayor of Santiago, but more famous for his Caney Rum distillery, which was moved to Puerto Rico after the Revolution to produce the re-named and globally popular Bacardi Rum.

The museum contains, on the second floor, some first-rate Cuban art (including works by the talented José Joaquin Tejada Revilla), and some colonial European paintings. On the first floor is memorabilia from Cuba's wars of independence, historic documents, flags, maps, and weapons. There is also a strange section with indigenous artifacts and an incongruous Egyptian mummy, several skeletons from Paracas in Peru, and a shrunken head.

From here it is just a short walk to one of old Santiago's most important and most vibrant streets, **Calle Heredia**, which has a couple of museums worth a quick visit. The most interesting is the small **Museo del Carnaval** (open

BELOW:
the Moncada Barracks is now home to a museum and a school.

Tues–Sun 9am–5pm; entrance charge), where there are some great costumes and *cabezudos* (bigheaded carnival figures) and faded photographs depicting carnival's history. In the courtyard you can watch Afro-Cuban music and dance sessions daily at 4pm – but be prepared to be pulled into the action.

Nearly opposite, the **Casa Natal de José María Heredia**  (open Tues–Sun 9am–6pm; occasional poetry workshops in courtyard; entrance charge) is the birthplace of José María Heredia, one of the first Cuban poets to champion national independence. It's a peaceful, attractive house with original furnishings.

Music on Calle Heredia

Calle Heredia is a good venue for the arts and music. The local office of the **Unión de Escritores y Artistas de Cuba** (UNEAC; Cuban Writers' and Artists' Union) is here, and stages poetry readings, arts shows, lectures, and literary discussions. Another venue is the unprepossessing ARTex shop, which sells various crafts and souvenirs, and hosts good bands in the relaxed atmosphere of the pretty courtyard at the back.

Heredia is famous for its live music, and you may well witness here some of the finest musicians you will hear in Cuba. The most famous venue is the renowned **Casa de la Trova** . This dates back to the 18th century, but underwent a misguided "refurbishment" in the mid-1990s. The place is much less smoky and atmospheric now, but musicians still consider it an honor to be asked to play here – treading as they do in the footsteps of a string of Cuban greats – and so it continues to attract some very accomplished artists. All week long, local musicians perform acts that range from somber Spanish guitar classics to vibrant Afro-Cuban drumming, solo acts to 12-piece bands, trained professionals to talented amateurs.

Not too long ago, most of the musical instruments used by the performers were older than the musicians themselves, and many were held together with tape, wire, and clothes pins. Things have improved of late, especially helped by the money that tourism brings in, even if quality instruments are still in short supply. These days, the venue's clientele consists primarily of tourists, but is still an essen-

Santiago is a city full of music, enjoyed by people of all ages.

BELOW:
Santiago's rooftops against a mountain backdrop.

tial element of any trip to the city. You are not allowed to record the music.

The central square

In the very center of the city is **Parque Céspedes** , a leafy colonial square with a bust of Carlos Manuel de Céspedes at its center. The nucleus of the city, this is where you will find young and old, rich and poor, gathering to exchange news or simply watch the world go by. Teenagers mingle beneath the trees and young couples sit entwined on park benches. It is also a place where you are likely to get a lot of requests for money or soap from the persistent *jineteros* (hustlers) of both sexes who congregate here.

Dominating the park is the **Catedral de Nuestra Señora de la Asunción** (open daily 8am–7.30pm; free) a vast, mainly 20th-century church on the site of the original cathedral, which was built in 1528. There is a good, painted wooden altar, and hand-carved choir stalls, and, it is said, the remains of conquistador Diego Velázquez, though these have never been located. It also contains a small museum (open Mon–Fri 9.30am–5.40pm; entrance charge) entered to the left of the cathedral.

Directly opposite the cathedral is a splendid neo-colonial white building with blue shutters. This is the **Ayuntamiento** (town hall), from the balcony of which Castro announced the triumph of the Revolution on January 2, 1959.

Also on the square is the **Hotel Casa Granda** . Once a high-society spot where the Cuban elite gathered on the rooftop terrace to sip rum, dance, and smoke cigars, the Casa Granda during the 1950s was a sinister place that teemed with US spies and Cuban rebels. One of the hotel's former guests was author Graham Greene, who came here to interview Castro (the interview never took place) and used the setting for a scene in his book *Our Man in Havana*, when his protagonist, Wormold, stayed here. The interior, restored in the mid-1990s, is splendidly grand, and suites have been decked out in golden silk. Breakfast and dinner are taken on the hotel's enormous front patio, which has plenty of character and sufficient distance from *jineteros* on the square. A drink on the roof terrace at sunset is delightful.

TIP

Housed beneath the huge, tiled terrace of the cathedral are a number of small, tourist-oriented stores and a branch of Etecsa (open daily 8.30am–7.30pm) where you can make phone calls, buy phone cards and use the Internet. There's another branch on Calle Tamayo Fleites (same hours).

BELOW: Parque Céspedes, from the terrace of the Hotel Casa Granda.

Cuba's oldest house

In the northwest corner of Parque Céspedes, distinguished by its black-slatted balconies, is the **Casa de Velázquez**  which houses the **Museo de Ambiente Histórico** (open daily 9am–4.30pm; entrance charge). A solid-stone structure with Moorish-style screened balconies, glorious cedar ceilings *(alfarjes)*, floor-to-ceiling shutters, and two lovely courtyards, the house was built between 1516 and 1530 and is said to be the oldest home in Cuba. In the 16th century, Governor Diego Velázquez used the first floor as his office and the upper floor as his residence. Before being turned into a museum, the historic home was a tenement. Among its collection are European tapestries, crystal, paintings, ceramics, and antiques. There is no written information, but the museum staff are helpful. *Peñas* (musical performances) are sometimes held here, and you may hear musicians practicing in the courtyards.

Just behind the square, to the southwest, is the **Balcón de Velázquez**  (CUC$1 to take photos), an open paved area on the site of the first Spanish fort in the city, with good views of the harbor.

Street life

The streets that radiate from the main square are great places to get an idea of Santiago's everyday life. Young men roar around on noisy old motorbikes, belching fumes; men walk along with live chickens under their arms or simply stand on corners, smoking; women wait in long lines at the food markets, and smartly uniformed children scurry to school. Most of the streets are dotted with large, colonial homes that have been turned into overcrowded apartment buildings. Music, both live and emanating from radios, pours out on to the sidewalks from windows left wide open to catch the breeze (no air conditioning here). Dangling above the narrow streets are a tangle of out-of-order neon signs that beckoned shoppers during more prosperous times.

Away from Parque Céspedes

One of the oldest of these thoroughfares is **Bartolomé Masó** (also called San Basilio), a cobblestoned street lined with antique gas lamps, running parallel to Heredia. Look out for the **Restaurante Santiago 1900**, in a grand colonial home

The streets of Santiago are chaotic, packed with pedestrians and traffic.

BELOW LEFT: Santiago street scene, bathed in golden light.

Revolutionary City

Santiago is the place where one feels the strength of revolutionary feeling most strongly. There are good reasons for this, of course: as already mentioned, it was the attack on the Moncada Barracks in 1953 that marked the start of the Revolution and led to the founding of the 26th July Movement; it was here that an uprising, led by Frank País, took place in November 1956, just days before Fidel Castro and his *compañeros* aboard the *Granma* landed at Las Coloradas; and it was from the balcony of the town hall here that Fidel announced the success of the Revolution in 1959. As you enter the city, you are greeted with a sign proclaiming: "Rebelde Ayer, Hospitalaria Hoy, Heroico Siempre" (Rebellious Yesterday, Hospitable Today, Heroic for Ever). Throughout Santiago, the tangible signs of revolutionary fervor are to be seen in the plethora of murals and slogans – more than you will find elsewhere – but the intangible is just as strong: a feeling of local pride and unity. Santiago may have relinquished its guise as Cuba's capital long ago, but its vital role in the island's history is assured.

Los Autos

They haunt the roads of Cuba like ostentatious ghosts of US capitalism: big old Buicks, Packards, Chevys, Chryslers, Studebakers, Hudsons, Edsels, and Fords. It's not known exactly how many antique cars there are in Cuba, but their numbers are estimated to be in the thousands. Since the US trade embargo began in 1961, no new American cars have been exported to the island, and the old ones from the 1940s and 1950s now share the roads with Hungarian buses and boxy Russian Ladas of more recent years.

These flashy US behemoths could once cruise at 160 kmph (100 mph) without a hint of strain. With back seats big enough for six, leather interiors, and two-tone color schemes, they are some of the most powerful cars ever produced by the US automobile industry, the ultimate in conspicuous consumption. In most other countries they would be garage-kept prized possessions, but in Cuba they are everyday transportation work-horses. Many of these gas guzzlers have been turned into black-market taxicabs in order to earn their keep.

Some of the cars are in perfect shape: soaring tail fins that glisten in the sun, sturdy running boards, gap-tooth grillwork, and jazzy hood ornaments polished to perfection. However, these are

usually legitimate taxis, belonging to a state-owned company.

The majority, though, are sorry heaps of metal: bodies wavy from too many putty patches, coated with layers of house paint; electric windows frozen open, and fenders rusted from the salt air. Riding on mismatched tires, they are coaxed into running order by tree-shade mechanics who represent the epitome of Cuban ingenuity. They barter chickens for parts, transplant carburetors from Russian jeeps, and turn water-filled pickle jars into makeshift filters. Wherever you go in Cuba you will see the big old cars with hoods open, and men examining the engines, or lying underneath, spanner in hand. Somehow, they always get them going, even when they have to start the motor with a screwdriver.

During the late 1980s, the Cuban Government began selling some of the old cars to foreign investors. Cuban owners were offered a new Lada or cash for trade. However, following the collapse of the Soviet Union, the Ladas became difficult to get hold of, and Cuba's classic-car racket faltered. In fact, many Cubans had proved reluctant to part with their old, much-loved vehicles.

Although a blatant symbol of Yankee imperialism, these antique autos are very much part of Cuban history. During his first few years in office, Castro cruised around in a luxurious Oldsmobile, and Batista before him did the same. A museum in Old Havana *(see page 150)* is dedicated to famous old cars (including Che's Chevy), and there's another auto museum located in Baconao Park, east of Santiago.

One reason why there are so many of these old autos in Cuba is that during the years when Hollywood stars and Mafia hoods treated Havana like their own personal playground, they liked to have a state-of-the-art car waiting for them when they got there. So, for young men with a sense of adventure, driving the lovely machines down to Miami and shipping them over to Havana became a very popular way of earning some spare money. ❑

ABOVE: some of the old cars have become taxis.
LEFT: an impressive gas guzzler.

that once belonged to Emilio Bacardí. With a series of balconies set around a courtyard with a central fountain, and furnished with 19th-century antiques and crystal chandeliers, it retains some of its original elegance. It's a better spot for a drink than a meal, however *(see page 303)*. The Rum Factory at No. 358 is closed at present but its atmospheric little bar remains open. The street leads down to Avenida Jesús Menéndez and Parque Alameda, flanking the harbor.

Off to the left, before you reach the harbor, is one of the prettiest streets in the city, **Padre Pico**, which climbs to the top of a steep hill southwest of Parque Céspedes, in the **Tivolí district**. The streets here are lined with 16th-century houses that were once home to prosperous French refugees fleeing the slave rebellion in Haiti.

At the corner of Padre Pico and Santa Rita is the **Museo de la Lucha Clandestina**  (Museum of the Underground Struggle; open Tues–Sun 9am–5pm; entrance charge), a lovely mustard-yellow colonial mansion with fine views of the city, reached via a slope fringed with bougainvillaea. It is dedicated to the heroes of the 26th of July Movement. In 1956 one of Castro's guerrillas fire-bombed the Batista police headquarters that was housed here, but it has since been beautifully restored.

Fidel Castro lodged in a house opposite when he was a student at Belén College here in the 1940s.

Farther south, on Calle Rabí, is the Casa de las Tradiciones, a great place to come at night for authentic *trova*, and a lot more local than the Casa de la Trova.

The broad, dusty promenade by the seafront is not particularly scenic, but you may want to venture down here to visit the cigar factory, the **Fábrica de Tabaco Cesár Escalante** (open Mon–Fri 9–11am, 1–5pm; entrance charge).

Santa Ifigenia

You will also cross this district en route northwest to the **Cementerio Santa Ifigenia** (open daily 8am–6pm; entrance charge includes a guide), but you are advised to pick up a cab or a horse and cart. Once segregated by race and social class, the cemetery has both massive mausoleums and unpretentious graves. Carlos Manuel de Céspedes, Emilio

There are numerous casas particulares (private houses that rent rooms) in Santiago. Look for a sign like this outside a building.

BELOW: an elderly resident and local family group.

The Bacardí family tomb in Santa Ifigenia Cemetery.

BELOW LEFT: the guard at Martí's tomb is changed every half hour.
RIGHT: the impressive Martí mausoleum.

Bacardí, and Cuba's first president, Tomás Estrada Palma, are among the famous figures buried here. Buena Vista musician Compay Segundo, who was brought up in Santiago, lies in the pantheon here, but his remains will soon be moved to a private grave.

The tomb to receive most visitors, though, is that of the patriot José Martí, whose marble vault has the figures of six women carved around the outside bearing the symbols of Cuba's provinces. Buried within the mausoleum is earth from each of the Latin American countries inspired by Martí to assist in the independence struggle; their names are inscribed on wall plaques. The national flag is draped over Martí's sarcophagus, which is so positioned as to catch the sun throughout the day. Accompanied by martial music, a uniformed armed guard is changed every half hour. The remains of 38 of the Moncada rebels are also buried here, in a special wall just inside the cemetery entrance.

Back to the center

You could ask your cab driver to return to the center via the **Casa Natal de** **Antonio Maceo** (open Mon–Sat 9am–5pm; entrance charge), at Calle Los Maceos, a modest house where the great man, nicknamed the Bronze Titan, was born. It exhibits photos, personal possessions, and Maceo's battle flag.

From here, you can walk along Calle General Banderas where there is a museum dedicated to two of Santiago's revolutionary heroes, the **Museo Hermanos País** (open Mon–Sat 9am–5pm; entrance charge). Frank País was a poet, teacher, and army rebel who led the 26th of July Movement in Oriente. His younger brother, Josué, was also active in the movement. Both were gunned down in the street in separate incidents in 1957, and their boyhood home is a national shrine.

Close by, on **Calle Félix Peña** is the 18th-century **Iglesia Santo Tomás**. Also worth a visit is the **Iglesia de la Santísima Trinidad**, five blocks east, on Moncada, but it is often closed, so do not make a special journey. Now you could wander along Santiago's main shopping street, Calle Saco (also known as Enramada), or return to Parque Céspedes for a cooling drink. ❑

RESTAURANTS AND BARS

Restaurants

Santiago is a great place for bars and nightspots, but not so good when it comes to restaurants. Below are a few of the choices *(and see Around Santiago chapter for nearby options).*

Casa Granda
Hotel Casa Granda, Parque Céspedes
Tel: (0122) 686-036
Open daily L, D. **$$**
An elegant venue in Santiago's most atmospheric hotel. Eat in the dining room, out on the broad terrace, or in the rooftop bar/restaurant. International-style food and pleasant, if not very rapid, service.

Café Palmares
Calle M, corner of Avenida de las Américas.
No phone. Open daily early till late. **$**
Average food, but live music and lots of atmosphere in this popular courtyard restaurant near the Meliá Santiago Hotel.

La Taberna de Dolores
Plaza de Dolores (Calle Aguilera)
Tel: (0122) 623-913. Open daily B, L & D. **$**
Set in an attractive colonial building. The *comida criolla* is fairly standard, but the patio is pretty, the music and the cocktails are good, and it's a real local place. Gets busy in the late evening, as it seems to be everyone's favorite spot.

Los Vitrales
Hotel Versalles
Altura de Versalles, Km 1
Tel: (0122) 691-016
Open daily 7am–10pm. **$$$**
A pleasant restaurant, and worth making the short trip from the center of town if you are not staying at the hotel.

Santiago 1900
Calle Masó (San Basilio), 354, between Pío Rosado and Hartmann.
Tel: (0122) 623-507. Open daily L & D. **$**
In a beautiful mansion that was the Bacardí family home. There's a great courtyard with a fountain, an upstairs patio, and a rather dim though elegant dining room. There is often live music, too. Unfortunately the food really isn't very good and they tend to run out of things, especially if they have been catering for a group.

Zunzún
Avenida Manduley, 159, corner of Calle 7, Vista Alegre
Tel: (0122) 641-528. Open Mon–Sat L & D, Sun L only. **$$$**
Marble floors, crystal chandeliers, and attentive waiters. Such elegance is rare in Santiago, and so is the menu. Both meat and fish are prepared with panache, and the lobster is excellent.

Bars

Santiago bars and clubs are pretty much interchangeable, so some of these venues are also mentioned in the Nightlife section *(see page 359).*

Bello Bar (Hotel Meliá Santiago, Avenida de las Américas, corner Calle M). A quiet bar on the hotel's 15th floor, with wonderful panoramic views. **Café de Ajedréz** (Chess Café, Plaza Céspedes). A good local bar (small and easy to miss). Great coffee all day; music at night. **Casa de la Trova** (Calle Heredia, 208). There's always music here, afternoon and evening, and drinks are not expensive. **Patio de ARTEX** (Calle Heredia, 304). Rum, beer, coffee. and snacks in the patio behind the ARTEX shop, with two daily sessions of live music.

RIGHT: on the balcony of La Taberna de Dolores.

AROUND SANTIAGO

Several interesting trips can be made from Santiago de Cuba, including one to the spectacular Morro Fortress, to El Cobre, the island's most holy Catholic shrine, an historic coffee plantation, and some great beaches

Main attractions
BASÍLICA DEL COBRE
CASTILLO DEL MORRO
CAYO GRANMA
LA GRAN PIEDRA
CAFETAL LA ISABELICA
GRANJITA SIBONEY
VALLE DE LA PREHISTORIA

LEFT: the Basílica del Cobre.
BELOW: a detail of Castillo del Morro.

Within easy striking distance of the capital are several sights that shouldn't be missed. A rental car provides the most convenient way of exploring these, but they are also accessible either on public transportation or by hiring a taxi for an individual trip or for the day – make sure you strike a deal and agree an itinerary before you set off.

Most sights are located east of Santiago. West of the city you'll find a scattering of pleasant beaches, such as **Playa Mar Verde ⑳**, not to mention the stunning drive along the coast into Granma province.

A Spanish fortress

To the south of the city, perched above Santiago Bay, is the Spanish fortress known as **Castillo del Morro ㉑** (open daily 8am–8pm; entrance charge). A taxi from Parque Céspedes will cost CUC$10–12 for the round trip. Construction work on this stunning fortress began in 1638, to a design by a specialist Italian architect, Juan Bautista Antonelli, son of the man who built El Morro in Havana.

It was destroyed in 1662 by English forces commanded by Sir Christopher Myngs, an expedition in which the pirate Henry Morgan took part, and rebuilt between 1690 and 1710. It has an elaborate labyrinth of drawbridges, moats, passageways, staircases, and barracks, all executed with marvelously precise angles and a geometric beauty – many people think it is more impressive than Havana's fort. Its dark, dank inner cells,

complete with built-in iron shackles, once housed African slaves in transit, and a small chapel still contains a wooden cross carved by a 16th-century Spanish artist. Look out for the contraption that was used to haul mighty stone balls up from the store to the cannon above. There's a *cañonazo* (firing of the cannon) every evening at sunset. The views across the bay and along the coast are splendid at any time of day. You can have an excellent lunch here *(see page 309)* or just buy snacks or drinks (and souvenirs, of course) from the stands outside.

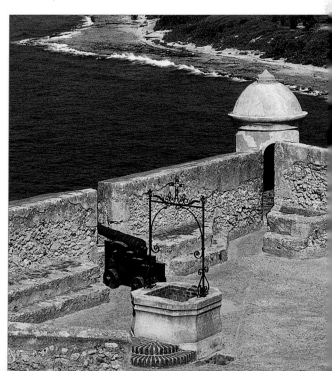

You can get a ferry to Cayo Granma from the Ciudamar pier.

BELOW: flower seller on the road up to El Cobre.

The ferry boat to **Cayo Granma** – a small island community that lies just inside the mouth of the Bay of Santiago – departs from the Ciudamar pier 1.6 km (1 mile) along the coast from the small beach at the foot of El Morro (you will see it signposted as you drive up to the fort on the Carretera del Morro). Ferries, costing a few centavos, depart roughly every hour throughout the day and follow a roundabout route linking the island with several little communities on the bay shores. Ferries also depart from Punta Gorda on the bay, about a CUC$6 taxi ride from the center.

The island was formerly called Cayo Smith, for the wealthy English slave trader who once owned it, but the name was changed after the Revolution.

Cayo Granma today has about 4,000 residents, some of whom still fish and build boats for a living, although most commute by ferry to factory and office jobs in Santiago. Since there are no cars or hotels on the island, it has a tranquil and old-time atmosphere. It has a beautiful beach, a small park where local people gather for games of dominoes, a school, a few stores and a good seafood restaurant *(see page 309)*. Many residents offer rooms, and the island makes a pleasant, relaxing place to spend a night – it also feels a very long way indeed from the bustle of Santiago.

Virgin or Goddess?

Of all the monuments in the Santiago region, the most famous is the shrine to the Virgen de la Caridad del Cobre, 19 km (12 miles) northwest of the city. The **Basílica del Cobre ㉒** (open daily 7am–6pm; free) is named for the first open copper mine in the Americas, which supplied the ore for Havana's artillery works, the largest in the New World, around 1600.

Although the mine was producing copper until a few years ago, the place has long been identified with an object that some people believe is far more precious, which three young men found floating in the Bay of Nipe off Cuba's northern coast, in 1608. This is a 30-cm (1-ft) tall wooden statue of a mestizo (mixed-race) Virgin carrying the infant Christ on her left arm, and holding a gold cross in her right hand. At her feet was the inscription, *Yo soy la Virgen de*

la Caridad (I am the Virgin of Charity). Legend has it that she had been floating for almost 100 years, since an indigenous chieftain – who had been presented with the statue by the conquistador Alonso de Ojeda in 1510 – had set her adrift to protect her from the evil intentions of other less Christian native *caciques* (chiefs).

Through the years, the Virgin has been invoked to protect freedom, perform miracles, offer consolation, and heal the bitterness of battle. In 1916, at the petition of veterans of the War of Independence, the Pope declared her the patron saint of Cuba. The Virgin's sanctuary, Cuba's only basilica, was inaugurated on her saint's day, September 8, in 1927. Pope John Paul II visited the basilica during a trip to Cuba in 1998, and there is a bust of him outside the main door.

On the hilly drive from Santiago you will pass flower sellers offering blooms that people buy as gifts for the Virgin. From a distance, the cream-colored church, surrounded by bougainvillaea, looks stunning against the wooded slopes behind. Inside, the nave rises in arched vaults above stained-glass windows set high on the side walls. Above the altar is an air-conditioned niche that holds the diminutive figure of the Virgin, dressed in a gold-encrusted satin gown and wearing a replica of the coronation crown presented on her saint's day in 1936.

The Virgin is displayed to worshipers during mass, then the figure is rotated so that it can be seen only by climbing stairs above the Shrine of Miracles, where grateful believers leave braces, crutches, flags, armbands, coins, medals, locks of hair, and other *ex-voto* offerings. There is even a piece of the Berlin Wall, and the athletic shirt of the famous Cuban 800-meter Olympic gold medalist, Ana Quirot. It is said that the mother of Fidel and Raúl Castro laid an offering here for the safety of her boys when they went off to fight in the Sierra Maestra. Well, that worked.

Thousands of worshipers flock to the church on her saint's day every September 8, for the Virgin is also worshiped in Afro-Cuban religions as Ochún, the magnetic and sensual goddess of love and rivers in the Santería religion. El Cobre attracts hoards of persistent touts and beggars. Visitors should be careful if they are carrying valuables, and be firm when refusing to buy miniature statues of the Virgin (unless, of course, you really want one).

From the basilica you can see the **Monumento al Cimarron**, a sculpture commemorating a revolt by African slaves forced to work in the copper mines. If you feel like a steep hike to the statue, you will be rewarded with stunning views.

Gran Piedra

The highway east of Santiago, which follows the Caribbean coastline, is a marvelous road that slips between the sea and a rocky cacti desert with the blue-green mountains beyond. An 80,000-hectare (200,000-acre) area here, the **Parque Baconao**, has been recognized as a biosphere reserve by UNESCO.

Thirteen km (8 miles) into the mountains there is a well-marked turn-off to **Gran Piedra ㉓**, taking you from dry and dusty desert into cloud-capped mountains shrouded in rainforest, up a

Ernest Hemingway donated his Nobel Prize to the Virgen de la Caridad, but unfortunately it was stolen from the Shrine of Miracles. It was soon recovered but is now safely stored away.

BELOW: the Virgen de la Caridad is an object of veneration.

Sorting through coffee beans, one of the crops that helped make Cuba wealthy in colonial times.

BELOW: a sheltered bay in Santiago province.

long access road that looks like a testing site for land mines (under-powered or overloaded cars may struggle to get up the slope). Each twist and turn in the road reveals a new vista across the mountains, and local people gather by the road to sell delicious fruit and scented flowers. At 1,300 meters (4,300 ft) above sea level, you come to the Gran Piedra (Great Rock) itself, with fabulous uninterrupted views across the mountains and out to sea, where even the lights of Jamaica can be seen at night – if there's no cloud, that is: sadly, there often is. It's ideal for what Cubans call *montañismo* or climbing. Most people visit for the day, but visitors can stay at the Villa Gran Piedra, an "ecolodge" with comfortable rustic cabins along the edge of the mountain ridge and unbeatable views. There is a CUC$1 charge to climb the steps to the Gran Piedra.

Close to Gran Piedra, the **Jardín Ave de Paraíso** (Bird of Paradise Garden; open Tues–Sun 8.30am–4.30pm; entrance charge) should not be missed. First planted in 1960 to provide flowers for hotels, celebrations, and formal presentations, the gardens are beautifully land-scaped and the flowers are breathtaking, especially the brilliant *ave de paraíso* for which the garden is named.

Coffee and rebellion

In a lovely spot a mile or so along a dirt road east of La Gran Piedra, the **Cafetal La Isabelica** (open daily 8am–4pm; entrance charge) is one of the area's few relics of the plantation era. This 19th-century estate, now under UNESCO protection and containing a museum, gives an insight into what life on a coffee plantation was like. The house originally belonged to a family of French descent, refugees from Haiti's slave rebellion (1789–1804). It is said that the plantation was named for the owner's mistress, an enslaved woman whom he later married.

Down the mountain, and back on the main highway is **Granjita Siboney** ❷❹ (open Tues–Sun 9am–5pm; entrance charge), the farmhouse where Fidel Castro and other rebels planned the 1953 attack on the Moncada Barracks in Santiago *(see page 295)*. It has been converted into a museum, with some classic examples of revolutionary hagiography – the most sacred relic may be the check from the Santiago restaurant where the *compañeros* had their last supper before the failed assault, but there is also the usual collection of bloodstained clothing. The weapons were hidden in a well in the garden. The road along the coast is peppered with monuments to those who died at Moncada.

Back to the coast

About 2 km (1 mile) away the village of **Siboney** ❷❺ has a pleasant, although not outstanding, beach, as yet undeveloped for tourism and much used by local families. **El Oasis** a little farther on is an artists' colony with a store just off the road. Just after El Oasis, another excellent small beach, **Playa Bucanero** is well developed as a tourist resort. The Club Bucanero Hotel caters mostly to German and Canadian package tourists. The next turn-off, heading inland, brings you to **La Poseta**, a large natural pool fed by an underground spring.

Rather spoiled by tourism, it has a barbecue and bar, whose loud music ruins the atmosphere.

One unmissable site for anyone interested in Cuban kitsch is the **Valle de la Prehistoria** ㉖ (open daily 8am–5pm; entrance charge), located some 24 km (16 miles) east of Santiago. This dinosaur theme park was created in 1983, but the collection of life-sized models of brontosauri, tyrannosauri, and other mammals from the Pleistocene Era has certainly attracted more visitors since the worldwide success of the film *Jurassic Park*. Children love it and adults usually find it entertaining as well. There is also a good little museum here, the **Museo de Ciencias Naturales** (open Tues–Sun 8am–4pm; separate entrance charge), packed with interesting facts on local flora and fauna.

The **Museo Nacional de Transporte** (open daily 8am–5pm; entrance charge), up a left-hand turning a little farther to the east, is also definitely worth visiting for its collection of vintage cars – including the Cadillac that belonged to the renowned Cuban singer, Beny Moré – and the display of more than 2,000 miniature cars.

History was made on the coast south of here. Not, for a change, the history of political movements or ideologies, either. The name says it all: **Villa Daiquirí**, for the daiquirí was invented here (originally as a type of anti-malarial tonic for local miners), even if it was "perfected" in Havana's El Floridita bar.) Unfortunately, neither Villa nor Playa Daiquirí are accessible to visitors, having been taken over by the military as a center of relaxation for their personnel.

Beyond, the delightful **Playa Bacajagua** ㉗ is home to the **Reserva El Indio**, an ecoreserve with marvellous walks and bicycle tours. Accommodations can be found in 20 comfortable cabins, and there is a decent restaurant as well as a small beach. The best place to aim for, however, is **Playa Cazonal**, though the shallow water makes for limited swimming. Just beyond lies **Laguna Baconao**, a lagoon surrounded by hills. There's a restaurant, a couple of boats and a small crocodile enclosure, but few signs of activity.

The paved road ends by the lake. Beyond lies a restricted military zone – do not go any farther. ❏

The Villa Daiquirí has another historical connection, too: it was on Daiquirí Beach that Teddy Roosevelt and his Rough Riders came ashore during the Spanish–American War of 1898.

RESTAURANTS

Restaurants

Casa de Pedro El Cojo
Sigua
Tel: (0122) 356-210
Open daily, all day. **$**
The "House of Pedro the Lame" is just outside Sigua, directly south of La Gran Piedra. It is a pleasant thatched-roofed restaurant *(ranchón)* that serves fish (mostly) with the usual accompaniments. Compay Segundo entertained friends here in his latter years, and there is an Eliades Ochoa song of the same

name on a *Best of Buena Vista* album.

El Morro
Carretera del Morro, Km 9
Tel: (0122) 691-576
Open daily 9am–9pm. **$$**
This popular place serves what is probably the best *criolla* cooking you will find in the Santiago area, with a varied menu that includes spicy shrimps and lobster. It's right next to Castillo del Morro with cracking views of the coastline. It's busiest at lunch time, when booking is advisable.

El Cayo
Cayo Granma
Bahía de Santiago
Tel: (0122) 641-528
Open daily noon–7pm. **$**
This pretty little blue-and-white building right by the water houses Cayo Granma's only restaurant. You can eat good *criolla* food here – mainly fish – in pleasant surroundings. Booking at lunch time is a good idea because it gets busy.

Hotel Villa Gran Piedra
Gran Piedra
Tel: (0122) 686-147 and 651-205. Open daily D only. **$**
The restaurant in this "ecolodge" is open to non-residents as well as

guests, and serves traditional Cuban food.

La Rueda
Calle Montenegro s/n
Siboney
Tel: (0122) 039-325
Open daily 9am–9pm. **$**
The food is pleasant enough and the service is friendly, but the main reason this little café/restaurant is well known is as the birthplace of Buena Vista musician, Compay Segundo.

• • • • • • • • • • • • • •
Price categories are for a meal for one with a beer or mojito. Wine puts the price up.
$ = *under $25,* **$$** = *$25–35,* **$$$** = *over $35.*

BARACOA AND THE FAR EAST

The US military base of Guantánamo is synonymous with the "war against terror," but it is the lush mountain landscape, the pristine beaches and the laid-back town of Baracoa that draw visitors to the east

T he main reason most visitors venture east of Santiago de Cuba is to visit Baracoa, the most popular destination in the region, which has been opened up to tourism. If you want to go straight from Santiago to Baracoa, there is a daily Viazul bus (tickets available from Cubatur on the corner of Heredia and Parque Céspedes). The 4½-hour journey down the road called La Farola is delightful; views are splendid and bends are tortuous, so it's preferable to have somebody else doing the driving.

However, there are a few other places of interest in the surrounding area for those who have rented a car and want to explore at leisure.

Guantánamo

To get to **Guantánamo** ㉘ you take the Autopista Nacional from Santiago, then, after about 15 km (9 miles) go east on the Carretera Central. The road then becomes motorway again about 20 km (12 miles) before Guantánamo.

There's no immediately obvious reason to make the trek from Santiago to Guantánamo. The city is not particularly pretty, nor is it a great cultural center. It seems to have two rather unfortunate unofficial emblems. One is a depot crammed with rusting buses that have no fuel. The other is an apartment tower that was to be a showcase of efficient, prefabricated architecture. Eighteen stories of apartment units were to be built in Santiago, then assembled in Guantánamo. But local people had to lower their

expectations, along with their building: there was a shortage of cement and of diesel for trucks carrying the few prefab pieces being made, so the would-be landmark had to be topped off at 12 stories.

Not everything is so grim, however. City life revolves around **Parque Martí**, a pleasant leafy square shaded by laburnum trees (glorious in March), and with an attractive golden-colored church, the 19th-century **Iglesia Parroquial de Santa Catalina**. It's worth at least spending an hour exploring the streets around the main square. There are some

Main attractions
GUANTÁNAMO US BASE
LA FAROLA
BARACOA
RÍO YUMURÍ
EL YUNQUE
PLAYA MAGUANA

LEFT: lazy day on the Río Yumurí.
BELOW: Guantánamo transport.

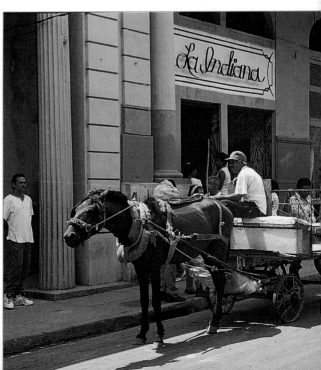

TIP

The only way across from the Cuban Guantánamo to the American is by swimming, avoiding sharks and, some say, gunshots; the US State Department has declared that Cuban troops have endangered, and even killed, swimmers by shooting at them. The Cuban Foreign Ministry countered that it was *soldados norteamericanos* who fired the shots.

BELOW:
driving over
La Farola, en
route to Baracoa.

attractive old houses on calles Pérez and Calixto García, north of Parque Martí, while Los Maceo, one block east, is buzzing with shoppers. Seek out the unusual **market**, a neoclassical structure occupying an entire block.

Caimanera and the base

The only reason most people come here is for a view of the controversial US naval base, one of the last vestiges of the Cold War, and the place now best known as the site of the infamous Camp Delta, where men suspected of terrorist involvement are detained in conditions that have aroused widespread disquiet.

Travel agents often don't explain that the city of Guantánamo itself offers no views of the base, which actually extends to the south of the city. If you want a glimpse of it, there are two options open to you. The first and most difficult option is to pass through marshland and two Cuban military checkpoints, to **Caimanera**. You need a pass, however, to get through the military checkpoint. The necessary papers can be obtained from the Ministry of the Interior (MININT) office on Calle José Martí

in Guantánamo but independent travelers will find it difficult and very time-consuming to get hold of one. Visitors staying at the Hotel Caimanera on a pre-booked itinerary through a tour agent get a pass included in their booking. The hotel has a three-story observation tower overlooking the **US Naval Base** ㉙. A billboard in the town proclaims "Caimanera: The First Anti Imperialist Bunker of Cuba."

From far away, it is hard to believe the world came close to nuclear war over Nikita Khrushchev's project to put nuclear missiles in Cuba in 1962, with Castro grumbling about "Cuba, the little sardine" and "the satiated shark, the United States." But from the balcony of Caimanera's school, the closest observation point, it all begins to seem real. Looking at the no-man's land and watching the jeeps and troops on the move beyond, you can almost hear Kennedy saying: "It shall be the policy of this nation to regard any nuclear missile launched from Cuba as an attack by the Soviet Union on the United States, requiring full retaliatory response on the Soviet Union."

On a sultry afternoon nowadays, Caimanera hardly looks like it's on a state of alert. Families spill out of their small cinder-block houses on to narrow sidewalks to play dominoes on folding tables. Even the occasional North American tourist is offered a glass of rum. But look up: on all sides of town are the omnipresent tunnels where residents are to go in case of an emergency.

Los Malones

For the average visitor, the best view they will get of the US base is from the **Mirador de los Malones**, off the Baracoa road about 24 km (15 miles) east of Guantánamo. You can arrange a visit by purchasing a pass at one of Santiago's central travel agencies, ideally a couple of days in advance. You must arrive at the military checkpoint between 10am and 2pm. For a reasonable fee, a guide will meet you at the checkpoint and accompany you into the Cuban military zone that surrounds the base and then along a bumpy dirt track to the lookout point. If you don't have a car, you will have to take a taxi, but drivers will pick you up from downtown Guantánamo. You will be shown a model of the base, and given a few vital statistics before climbing the stairs, where a telescope allows you to pick out vehicles and people moving around, and spot the US and Cuban flags flying by the perimeter fences. It may seem strange that tourists are able to do this, but visits provide much-needed income for local operators. There is even a restaurant and bar, called La Gaviota (The Seagull).

Up into the mountains

You could make a detour into the mountains northeast of Guantánamo, toward Palenque, where the village of **Boquerón** is home to the **Museo Zoológico de Piedra** (Stone Zoo; open daily 7am–6pm; entrance charge), the handiwork of Ángel Iñigo, a coffee farmer who has carved over 100 animals out of the limestone on his land. Some large sculptures are carved *in situ* from outcrops or large boulders, others from smaller rocks lifted

into position, and all stand amid a beautiful garden. Almost all were carved from pictures in books: Ángel has never seen most of the animals he has so faithfully sculpted. The zoo is now run, and the more recent figures carved, by Ángel's eldest son, Angelito. From here, access is prohibited, and you must retrace your steps to Guantánamo and the Baracoa road beyond (where you would have taken the Mirador de los Malones turning if you chose to get a glimpse of the US base at Guantánamo).

Along the coast

The road east out of Guantánamo passes pleasant little farming communities and beaches at **Yacabo Abajo** and **Imías**. **Playa de Cajobabo** ㉚, next along the coast, is a place of great historical importance as it was here that José Martí and Máximo Gómez came ashore to begin the fight against the Spanish in 1895. However, it is not a particularly interesting beach destination. From here, the road divides, turning north to Baracoa, and east to **Punta de Maisí**.

Few people will take the road to Maisí. It is in poor repair, and to attempt a trip

A road sign warns that you are approaching Camp Delta.

BELOW: a creature in the Stone Zoo, Boquerón.

US Guantánamo

The naval base sits in the southeast corner of Cuba, an enclave of US military might, occupying 116 sq. km (45 sq. miles) of Cuban territory. For decades, it has been one of Uncle Sam's most-favored ports, known to sailors as Gitmo.

Founded in 1898 after 600 US Marines landed here to fight in the Spanish–American War, the base was formally established in 1901 by a Cuban constitutional document known as the Platt Amendment. Until 1959 it was a good-time assignment where sailors overindulged in cheap rum and accommodating women. Saloons and brothels dotted the streets of nearby Guantánamo city.

Following Castro's takeover, brothels and bars were closed, commerce between the Americans and Cubans forbidden, and security on the base tightened considerably. Many Cubans still worked there, but had to get a bus then walk through the gate after vehicular traffic was prohibited.

Surrounded by barbed wire, Gitmo is an isolated installation guarded by 500 Marines. About 8,000 people live here, including civilians and military families. It contains housing, a school, health spa, a movie theater, a shopping center, and a McDonald's. Children watch Saturday-morning cartoons picked up by satellite from US television networks, and military planes fly in with supplies.

Servicemen stationed on the base conduct defense exercises, maintain warships and monitor Cuban airspace. Rifles slung over their shoulders, they patrol the perimeter, which is mined with explosives. Though neither the US nor the Cuban government will confirm the figure, it is estimated that about 100 Cubans a year enter the base illegally by swimming through the shark-infested waters or jumping the fence. Dozens of these asylum seekers have died in the attempt. In the early 1990s, the camp held Haitian refugees who fled their country after a military coup, and in 1994 it became a temporary refugee center for thousands of Cuban rafters who had been picked up at sea by the US Coast Guard.

As Cuba poses little military threat to the US, the base had little strategic value except as a thorn in Castro's side, until 2002, when it became the site of the now-notorious Camp Delta, the subject of international controversy, which holds people suspected of belonging to al-Qaeda or the Taliban.

Since 1960, Castro has not cashed any of the annual US$4,085 rent checks issued by the US Treasury, as to do so would acknowledge the legitimacy of the base. Guantánamo, according to Castro, is "a dagger plunged into the heart of Cuban soil," but it remains in US hands until the two countries reach an agreement to end the arrangement, or the US unilaterally decides to abandon the base. In 2005, a US$12-million wind project was completed, with four turbines that will supply a quarter of the power needed by the base. In the same year, the US announced that defense contractor Halliburton is to build a new detention facility and security perimeter around the base. It seems that the US has no intention of leaving any time soon. ❑

LEFT: Camp Delta inmates.
ABOVE: a lookout at Los Malones.

requires a good four-wheel-drive vehicle and a skilled driver, not to mention a strong nerve, as it bends higher and higher up the stone mountain terraces. It passes through dry, scrubby desert land with dramatic mountain scenery rising to the north. The vast limestone terraces are full of caves with stalactites and stalagmites. Below the coffee-growing town of La Máquina, the village of **Maisí** ③ sits on a wide coastal plain of dry shrubby vegetation and cacti. Cuba's most easterly point consists of a lighthouse and a few shacks. This is a military zone and you may be denied access.

Instead, take the route heading north (inland) from Cajobabo to Baracoa – along the hair-raising but well-maintained road over the mountains. Known as **La Farola** (The Beacon), it twists through some fearsomely acute bends. The crash barriers are disconcertingly broken through in places and warning notices appear regularly – "Caution: 72 Accidents on this Bend So Far." The risk is compensated for by the wonderful scenery: magnificent mountain vistas, wild jungle, coconut groves, and coffee and cocoa plantations. You will be approached by vendors of wonderful fruit and snacks, such as *cuchuruchos*, grated, flavored coconut neatly encased in palm leaves, but if they offer you anything made of polymita snail shells, say no, as they are endangered and protected by international law.

Cuba's first town

Some believe that Columbus landed at **Baracoa** ㉜ on October 27, 1492, and stayed a week, but it is far from certain. The explorer was in fact looking for the Orient, but no matter: he found the *oriente* (East) of Cuba. "A thousand tongues would not suffice to describe the things of novelty and beauty I saw," he later recalled. The town nestles beneath El Yunque – a flat anvil-shaped mountain that was described by Columbus in his log *(see page 33)*.

Baracoa certainly was Cuba's first town, founded by Diego Velázquez in 1512, and was also both the first capital of Cuba and the starting point for the Spanish conquest of the rest of the island. Three years later, Santiago, and finally Havana, took over the role as capital. Baracoa then remained an isolated town

Baracoa has become a popular tourist destination.

BELOW: view over Baracoa after a tropical storm.

"This is the last church in Cuba to be renovated," said an elderly lady, mopping the church floor after rain flooded through holes in the roof. "We are farthest from Havana, so it takes a long time for money to get here."

BELOW: a boy sneaks a peek between murals in Baracoa.

right up until La Farola was built in 1962; prior to that, access was possible only by sea.

Even the most rigid travelers can find themselves staying for more than a week in Baracoa as they succumb to the gentle, old-world atmosphere of this Caribbean frontier town, with its neat lines of one-story, pastel-colored houses with red-tile roofs and lush vegetation.

The streets, impossibly picturesque in the late-afternoon light, are absolute heaven for photographers. This laid-back air is a result primarily of Baracoa's isolation – face to the sea and back to the mountains, with Havana 1,070 km (670 miles) away. Some things are changing, however. While Baracoa is still well away from the main tourist trail, word is spreading fast that the town's combination of friendly people, attractive scenery, and a distinctive cuisine make it a great place to spend some time. The Cuban tourist industry has finally taken note of the constant stream of visitors to Baracoa, and new hotels are being planned.

The best place to get an overview of Baracoa is from the gardens of the Hotel El Castillo *(see page 354)*, on a cliff overlooking the town. This building was originally a castle, built in 1770 to keep out the British; it later became a prison, and more recently a hotel. You need to climb a long flight of steps or a steepish slope to reach the hotel and gain glorious views of the town, the bay, and the unnervingly short runway of Baracoa's tiny airport on the far side of it.

Baracoa life

Life in Baracoa revolves around leafy **Parque Independencia**, where legend has it that the indigenous chief Hatuey was burned alive by Spanish conquistadors *(see page 35)*: the supposed spot where he died is marked by a bust, directly opposite the entrance to the **Catedral de Nuestra Señora de la Asunción** (open daily noon–6pm; free) although his death is more likely to have occurred in Yara, near Manzanillo. The church was built in 1805, replacing the original, destroyed by pirates in 1652. It is sadly in need of renovation, but mass is still held here. What is believed to be Columbus's Cruz de la Parra *(see box opposite)* is kept inside.

It is at this point that the town's two

main streets, Maceo and Martí, merge. It is along these streets that everything in Baracoa happens. Check out the very small but very lively **Casa de la Trova**, at Antonio Maceo 149, which normally gets going at about 10pm and is a popular gathering place. In neighboring **Plaza Martí**, each Saturday is "La Fiesta" – a lively affair with loud street music and plenty of rum, roast pork, and snacks for sale. Farther along Maceo (at No. 124) is the **Casa de la Cultura**, where there are exhibitions of modern art by local artists, and regular live music.

The Malecón

Baracoa doesn't show its best face to the sea. The **Malecón**, Baracoa's seafront boulevard, is lined with tattered apartment blocks, and sees surprisingly little action. As you drive into town you pass the small but well-preserved **Fuerte Matachín** (1802), which houses a small **Museo Municipal** (open daily 8am–noon, 2–6pm; entrance charge). Outside the fort is a chunky statue of Columbus and a large wooden cross (but not the one he is said to have brought here from Spain). The museum contains a mini-

mum of revolutionary wonders, offering instead a mixture of displays on the indigenous Taíno people, local history, and a few Baracoan characters.

One of these was La Rusa, founder of a well-known hotel farther along the Malecón (you can't miss it, it's bright yellow). La Rusa was a Russian woman who abandoned the Soviet Union in the 1950s, came to Cuba and ended up supporting the rebels. Fidel and Che both stayed here, and guests fight over the rooms where they are said to have slept.

At the the western end of the Malecón, close to the bus station, is **La Punta** fortress, now a restaurant, with a statue of a defiant-looking Hatuey outside. From here there is a great view of the bay, on the far side of which is a good hotel, the Porto Santo, and a small airport (two flights a week to Santiago).

Baracoa's past

If you climb a flight of steps on the inland side of Antonio Maceo toward a neighborhood called Reparto Paraíso, you will pass the outdoor El Ranchón disco, then walk along pretty, rural tracks lined with little houses in lush gardens, with

Baracoa's cathedral, in the Parque Independencia, is in a state of disrepair.

BELOW LEFT: a monument to Columbus on the Malecón.
BELOW: the wooden cross, kept in the cathedral.

A Cross Debate

In Baracoa almost every resident can, and will, tell you the story of the Cruz de la Parra (Cross of the Vine), fashioned from hardwood, which Columbus reputedly brought from Spain and planted here. It vanished and was later found amid the backyard blackberries of a colonizer's house in 1510. This historic cross survived pirates, fires, vandals, and other hazards, although relic-hunters have chipped away at the edges. Standing 1 meter (3½ ft) tall, it is now kept safe in the

cathedral, with its edges encased in metal. That, at least, is the story. But did Columbus really bring the cross? The church maintains he did. So does Alejandro Hartmann, director of the Museo Matachín of local history in Baracoa. But a host of scholars disagree. Everybody has a conflicting notion – and everyone can back it up with data. The latest carbon-dating tests appear to indicate that Baracoa's wooden cross was planted in Cuban soil in the late 15th century, which supports one strand of the Columbus theory, but it is made of a hardwood native to Cuba, not Spain. So the mystery deepens, but the cross is still revered.

*Close to the mouth of
Río Yumurí is
the Tunel de los
Alemanes (German
Tunnel). This impres-
sive natural rock for-
mation, through which
the road runs, is so-
called because, in
pre-revolutionary
times, a German
family lived closed by,
and charged
drivers of motor- and
horse-drawn vehicles
for passing through.*

children playing, goats roaming, and
chickens pecking in the dust.

The **Museo Arqueológico** (open officially 9am–6pm but hours may vary;
donations) is tucked away up a narrow
path, its reception area a small thatched
hut. The outdoor part of the museum is a
re-creation of Taíno society, the indoor
section, in the Cueva del Paraíso, contains objects found in and around
Baracoa, including a skeleton of a chief
called Guaramá. The story is that he was
murdered by a single blow to the head,
dealt by the man whose wife he had
stolen. There is also a replica of the Taíno
tobacco idol, found nearby in 1903, and
said to be the most important in the
Americas. The original is in Havana's
museum of anthropology (*see page 176*).

Excursions from Baracoa

Going east from Baracoa through the
small settlement of Jamal, there are some
beautiful (and gentle) walks through
countryside where the crops are a mixture of bananas, coffee, cocoa and
avocados, where pigs snuffle in the
undergrowth and chickens roam. Nearby
lies the small beach of Playa Barriguá –

its fine, gritty sand is not the greatest, but
it is a lovely, deserted spot, fringed with
tropical vegetation.

The Río Yumurí is the next port of
call, and a boatman is usually available
to take visitors on a short trip. The green
river is delightful, flowing between high
cliffs, and you may be lucky enough to
see and hear Cuba's national bird, the
trogon (also known as the *tocororo*).

Baracoa's horizon is dominated by **El
Yunque** ㉝ (The Anvil) looming at 560
meters/1,800 ft, to the west of the town.
Archeologists have found shells and skeletons left by the Taíno people who, during
the conquest, took advantage of the mountain's cliffs and natural lookout points, as
did anti-Spanish rebels during the 19th
century. Many caves in the mountains
contain pre-Columbian paintings.

The slopes are cloaked in virgin rainforest, part of which is protected by the
rarely visited **Cuchillas de Toa** mountain reserve. This is one of the wildest
regions in Cuba, with excellent potential
for hiking and some wonderful flora,
such as wild orchids. The Hotel El
Castillo runs excursions here, including
white-water rafting trips on the River

BELOW LEFT:
coconut milk is
used in local
dishes. **RIGHT:**
cutting sugar cane
is hard work.

A Regional Cuisine

In Baracoa you can buy local specialties like tamales – made not of boiled
corn, as in the rest of Cuba, but mashed plantains, stuffed with spiced
meat, wrapped in a banana leaf, and roasted over a fire. Baracoan food is
very different from that of the rest of the country, with a greater use of
spices and specialties such as coconut and chocolate. Food is cooked in
coconut oil and *lechita* (coconut milk), giving the whole town a heavenly
smell when the cooking starts in the evening.

Other local dishes include *bacón* (a plantain tortilla filled with spicy
pork), and *tetí* – a bizarre type of small red fish that are caught in the river
estuaries between August and December;
they have a gelatinous protective wrapping,
which dissolves upon reaching fresh water,
and are tasty when eaten raw or in omelets.
Rice is colored yellow with annato seeds
while "Indian bananas" are boiled in their
pink skins and dressed with garlic and lime
juice. The Casa del Chocolate at Antonio
Maceo, 121 is a Baracoa institution known
for its hot chocolate. It is currently closed for
long-term restoration.

Toa. You can climb El Yunque in a couple of hours; bring plenty of water and good footwear, as the path can get muddy and slippery. A guide is compulsory. The path runs from Campismo El Yunque, near the base of the mountain, but you can also rent horses and hire guides for the trip at Finca Duaba, just outside Baracoa, along the Moa road.

The Finca, which, like Hotel El Castillo, is part of the Gaviota chain, has a restaurant that serves Cuban food, and organizes demonstrations showing how local crops, such as cocoa and bananas, are cultivated.

From honey to chocolate

Legend says that those who sleep in Baracoa's **Bahía de Miel** (Bay of Honey) will never want to leave. Disappointingly, the city beach, at the eastern end of town, is gritty and gray, and the sea rather muddy. Most people prefer to swim in the cool mountain rivers or in the sea northwest of Baracoa. The best beach, and one of the finest in Cuba, is **Playa Maguana**, 22 km (14 miles) from the town, where there is a good hotel *(see page 355)*. A coral reef ensures that the

3 km (2 miles) of sugar-white sand is lapped only by gentle waters.

Closer to Baracoa is **Playa Duaba**, near the mouth of the Duaba River; you can swim in either fresh or salt water.

Cubatur in Baracoa (Calle Martí, 181) can organize excursions of the area led by knowledgeable local guides, who can incorporate interesting additions, such as visits to cocoa farms. Here, you can learn how the cocoa pods are harvested and transformed into a variety of delicious products including chocolate.

The road northwest from Baracoa takes you into Holguín province, along a dramatic route that skirts the mountains and the sea. It is rough going in the early stages, with many potholes, so allow three hours for the drive to **Moa** ❸. Unless you are a metallurgist, you won't want to spend much time in Moa. This is mining country, with possibly the world's largest reserves of nickel and cobalt. Nickel production is an important industry, but one that results in belching chimneys and polluted seas and rivers washing up against blackened hills. Most people, however, return to Santiago full of the joys of Baracoa. ❏

The polymita snails of eastern Cuba are an endangered species.

RESTAURANTS & BARS

Restaurants

Guantánamo

La Cubanita
Calle Martí, 864. No phone.
Open daily L & D. **$**
A great little *paladar* serving well-cooked *comida criolla*.

Baracoa

El Castillo
Calle Calixto García,
Lomo El Paraíso.
Tel: (021) 645-165.
Open daily L & D. **$$**
The Hotel El Castillo restaurant has a varied menu of local dishes,

including spicy soups, and prawns and fish cooked in coconut-milk sauce. The three-course set menu costs cuc$12.

Finca Duaba
Carretera Mabujabo, Km 2.
Tel: (021) 645-206. **$$**
The *finca* is a farm, not far from town, and the restaurant serves good barbecued meats.

La Colonial
Calle Martí, 123.
Tel: (021) 643-161. Open daily D only. **$**
A delightful *paladar*. Two small dining rooms and an interior patio lively

with caged birds. The menu may include swordfish, octopus, and lamb, depending on what's available on the night.

Porto Santo
Carretera del Aeropuerto.
Tel: (021) 645-105. Open daily L & D. **$$**
A hotel restaurant with an international menu and a barbecue, located just outside Baracoa.

La Punta
Malecón s/n.
Tel: (021) 645-224.
Although currently closed for restoration La Punta, within the walls of one of Baracoa's three forts, has always enjoyed a good reputation.

485 Aniversario
Calle Antonio Maceo, 139
Tel: (021) 63-446. Open daily all day. **$**
Basic but well-cooked food in the town center.

Bars

Baracoa

Casa de la Trova (Maceo, 149). Lively at night; open during the day. **Casa de la Cultura** (Maceo, 124). Music most nights. **Café El Patio** (Maceo, 120). Pleasant courtyard bar.

• • • • • • • • • • • • • • •
Price categories are for a meal for one with a beer or mojito. Wine puts the price up.
$ = under $25, **$$** = $25–35,
$$$ = over $35.

SOUTHERN ISLANDS

Most important are the Isle of Youth, with good diving, caves with indigenous paintings, and the prison where Fidel Castro was once incarcerated, and Cayo Largo, with its sugar-white beaches

L ocated off the main island's south coast, each of the islands of the Archipiélago de los Canarreos has its own distinct personality. Isla de la Juventud (Isle of Youth) is relatively undeveloped and cheap, with a colorful history as a pirate refuge, home for US settlers, and prison camp for revolutionaries; Cayo Largo, on the other hand, is one of the most pricey and commercialized places in all of Cuba; other cays, like Cayo Rosario, are just virgin specks of sand wallowing in the blue Caribbean.

The real Treasure Island

Isla de la Juventud, the largest by far of Cuba's subsidiary islands with an area of 3,020 sq. km (1,180 sq. miles), lies to the south of the mainland, and can be reached either by plane from Havana or by the catamarans or ferries that depart from the port of Surgidero de Batabanó. The latter is a time-consuming option, and one that is usually only undertaken by travelers with time to spare *(see margin tip on page 324)*. Accommodations for visitors are concentrated in Nueva Gerona, the capital, although the Hotel Colony on the southwest coast is a popular base for divers, and the best spot on the island.

Over the centuries, the island has seen immigrants from Spain, England, Scotland, China, Japan, Jamaica, the Caymans, and the USA, and it has had a similarly varied history in terms of the names it has been given. Indigenous peoples called it Camarcó or Siguanea, but Christopher Columbus renamed it La

Evangelista when he landed here in 1494, on his second voyage to the New World. By the 17th century it was known as Isla del Tesoro (Treasure Island) because of the pirate treasure allegedly buried here (thus inspiring the name, at least, of Robert Louis Stevenson's classic adventure tale, published in 1883). By this time, the Spaniards, who finally got around to colonizing the island in the 1840s, had renamed it Colonia Reina Amalia. Later names include: the Isla de los Deportados, when it became a dumping ground for criminals and rebels

Main attractions
ISLA DE LA JUVENTUD
NUEVA GERONA
MUSEO DE LA LUCHA CLANDESTINA
PRESIDIO MODELO
COCODRILO
PUNTA DEL ESTE
CAYO LARGO
CAYO ROSARIO

PRECEDING PAGES: idyllic island beach. **LEFT:** repairing fishing nets. **BELOW:** Nueva Gerona harbor.

TIP

Hydrofoil tickets to the island (along with tickets for the connecting bus) have to be bought in advance at Havana's main bus terminal and, at the time of writing, return tickets are not available. If you have your own transportation you could try driving to Surgidero de Batabanó and booking there, but tickets are often sold out in advance. If you want to visit the islands, it is advisable to fly.

BELOW:
a youthful smile
on the Isle of Youth.

deported from the mainland; La Siberia de Cuba, in recognition of the isolated prison where Castro and others spent several years in the 1950s; Isla de las Cotorras (Isle of Parrots), as the habitat of the brightly colored birds that are still the trademark of the island's bottled water; and, until 1971, Isla de Pinos (Isle of Pines). Finally, it acquired its present name in the 1970s, a symbol of the influx of young people to the island.

An island education

In 1971, Cuba began taking students from countries in the Developing World and educating them for free on the island, thus hoping to spread solidarity for the Cuban Revolution across the undeveloped world. At its height, the program included 60 boarding schools with 150,000 students. The flow of foreign students has dwindled, due to economic difficulties in Cuba and political changes in their own countries.

The last foreign students completed their studies in 1996, although the schools still remain. Today, around 77,000 people live on the island, almost half of them in the capital, Nueva Gerona.

Town with a *yanqui* touch

The point of arrival on the island is invariably **Nueva Gerona ❶**, which looks a little like a small village in the USA's West at the turn of the 20th century: the older houses are wooden, with spacious, columned verandas, shuttered windows, and carved doors with brass knockers. The similarity is no accident, since many of the town's first pioneers came from the US in the early 1900s, lured by unscrupulous US land dealers.

It was these midwesterners who planted the island's first citrus groves, which now cover some 25,000 hectares (62,000 acres). Along the river-side road is a wooden bungalow built by a Swedish-American family whose last surviving member lived there for 60 years before finally returning to the US. Her parents, like hundreds of other Americans, believed the island would soon become another state in the Union by vote of the US Congress. They built houses and planted orchards in places they named McKinley, Columbia, Westport, and San Francisco Heights. They spoke English, worshiped a Protestant God and were buried in the **Cementerio Americano**,

maintained today as a historical site. The starkly simple headstones – most of them dating from 1905 to 1925 – contrast sharply with the mausoleums, statues, and vaults that decorate the **Cementerio Católico** in town.

Cayman and Jamaican islanders added their Caribbean English to that of the Americans in those early years, while a sizeable group of Japanese settled as farmers. This mix, together with Spanish merchants, Chinese storekeepers, and Cuban landowners, provided a lively diversity in island life.

Getting around the town

Today, downtown Nueva Gerona consists of an eight-block grid, so everything is within easy walking distance. This area has stores and eateries (mostly snack places, though El Corderito restaurant serves decent meals). There are also a couple of night spots: Los Luceros, by the river, is a popular open-air cabaret venue that attracts a mostly young crowd; and Disco Calle 24, an indoor spot with dim lights and loud music that also appeals mainly to a younger set.

Calle 39, the main street of downtown Gerona, has been radically refurbished with pretty pink tiles and fresh coats of paint on every building. The street runs south from the always empty La Cubanita Hotel – which still denies access to foreigners despite the lack of a Cuban clientele – and along one side of **Parque Central** (also called Parque Guerrillero Heróico on some newer maps). In the square stands the island's oldest church, **Nuestra Señora de los Dolores**, a typical Latin-American colonial-style church, which was built in 1929.

At Calle 39, between calles 24 and 26, is Ecotur, the main agency that runs tours of the island (tel: 0146-327101). The staff are very helpful and all tours to the southern (military) zone *must* be booked through them. A tour guide is compulsory, to get past the military checkpoint. You will need to rent a car to get there, in most cases. Tours are best booked well in advance, as is car rental, as there are only a couple of four-wheel-drive jeeps available (try Havanautos, on the corner of Calle Martí and Calle 32).

Opposite the church is the **Ayuntamiento** (town hall), formerly the Spanish military commander's HQ. During the 1895–98 War of Independence, the square was the scene of a thwarted uprising led by a beautiful young rebel girl. She was later imprisoned in Havana, rescued by a US journalist and then smuggled to the United States to promote Cuba's freedom – along with the interests of the Hearst press.

The **Academia de Ciencias y Planetario** on Calle 41 (open Tues–Sat 9am–5pm; entrance charge) covers natural history and archeology, and is worth visiting for the replica of the Punta del Este cave paintings *(see page 328)* if you don't have the time to see the real thing. On the corner of calles 24 and 45 is the local **Museo de la Lucha Clandestina** (open Tues–Sat 9am–5pm; entrance charge), devoted mainly to the underground campaign in the run-up to the Revolution. *El Pinero*, the ferry boat that carried Fidel Castro and his fellow revolutionaries back to the mainland after their release from prison, is now just a

Working in the cane factory in Nueva Gerona.

BELOW: Nuestra Señora de los Dolores in Nueva Gerona.

rotted hull on the river bank between calles 26 and 28. You may be surprised to see a nearby statue of a cow: it is dedicated to **Ubre Blanca** (White Udder), a local cow who broke world milk-production records.

Memories of Cuban Siberia

If you travel a few kilometers east of town, on the road to Playa Bibijagua, you can't miss the **Presidio Modelo ❷** (Model Prison). It was built between 1926 and 1932 using the plans from a prison in Joliet, Illinois, to house Cuba's hardest cases – most famously Fidel Castro and other revolutionaries after the failed attack on the Moncada Barracks in 1953. As political prisoners, Castro and his *compañeros* fared a good deal better than the common inmates. They were housed in the hospital wing, where they studied, trained, and imposed their own group discipline without much interference from the Batista-appointed prison officials.

The prison was closed in 1967. An impressive **museum** (open Tues–Sat 8am–4pm, Sun 8am–noon; entrance charge), which includes Fidel Castro's (rather comfortable) old cell, recounts the prison's grim past.

Cuba's 19th-century revolutionary hero, José Martí, also spent time on the island in 1870, when he was awaiting deportation to Spain for expressing anti-colonial ideas. For a few months between his grueling prison labors and his exile, Martí stayed at the **Finca El Abra** (open Tues–Sun 9am–5pm; entrance charge), a country estate where the Sardá family nurtured him back to relative health. The farm is located just off the road to the Hotel Colony, near marble quarries – the source for the floors, facades, and carved objects seen all over the island.

A spa town

La Fé ❸, southeast of the island capital, used to be the market town for the surrounding farmlands. The shady main plaza is no longer a farmers' market, but the presence of a radio station, public library, post office, and telephone company make this an important point of communications. The ruins just off the square are what is left of an old hotel. In the early 20th century, La Fé was a well-known spa resort: the medicinal springs

BELOW:
the Presidio
Modelo is now
a museum.

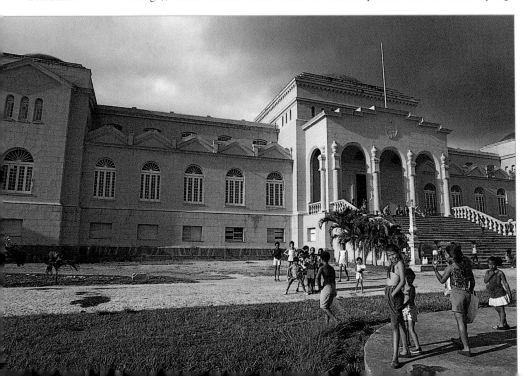

are located nearby, close to the deteriorating hotel and baths.

La Fé is far more attractive than Nueva Gerona, with green parks and tree-lined streets (although, of course, they eventually lead out to barren-looking prefab housing blocks). Not far from the center of town is **La Cotorra** spring, in a perfect little park enclosed by an iron fence with a ceramic parrot *(cotorra)* at the gate. This is the spring that supplies the island's bottled drinking water. It is also the best place on the island to have a close look at some brilliantly colored parrots, who screech at visitors from their cage perches.

Pirates' Coast

From La Fé and Nueva Gerona, roads lead west to the **Hotel Colony** ❹ on **Ensenada de la Siguanea** (Siguanea Sound). For years the only luxury hotel on the island, the Colony was completed at the end of 1958, just in time for the rebels to take it over. The bay here is picturesque but too shallow for good swimming – the pool is the best place for that.

Across the bay, though, is **Cabo Francés**, with the spectacular scuba sites of the **Costa de los Piratas**. At more than 50 marked sites, divers can see coral of every shape, size, and color, giant sponges, tropical fish, and crustaceans, underwater caves, tunnels, and rock formations. The site is of particular interest as it contains the sunken remains of a great sea battle between the pirate ships of Thomas Baskerville and the Spanish fleet. And near Punta Francés are three Spanish galleons lying together.

The international scuba center at the Hotel Colony *(see page 355)* provides the boats, scuba gear, and monitors for diving – usually an all-day trip, moving from site to site and with a buffet lunch aboard. It also provides special diving packages to the Pirates' Coast. There is an international marina here, too, as well as plenty of opportunities for deep-sea fishing trips.

The south coast of the island, from **Punta Pedernales** in the west to **Punta del Este** in the east, is breathtaking.

However, the entire area inland of Cocodrilo and nearby **Caleta Grande** is a military zone and definitely off limits unless you pre-arrange a visit with Ecotur in Nueva Gerona *(see page 325)*.

This beautiful area is practically uninhabited except for the little town of **Cocodrilo** ❺, settled by English-speaking Cayman islanders at the beginning of the 20th century. Their descendants speak a lilting Caribbean English, though this is beginning to die out as younger generations slowly adopt Spanish. There are numerous magnificent beaches, as yet untouched by tourism and development, but accessible on day trips.

The blue-green water and fine white sand along this coast are backed by thick forests of pine and hardwoods. The region is separated from the north by the mosquito-ridden **Ciénaga de Lanier** (Lanier Swamp) – and this geographical isolation once made the area a plunderer's paradise, especially for lumbermen who felled trees and shipped logs to all the ports of Cuba and the Caribbean. Reforestation has fortunately been a priority since the early 1960s. The Isle of Youth and the Zapata peninsula (on the

Playing for guests at the Hotel Colony.

BELOW: bicycles are the usual form of transportation.

Sea turtles sometimes get caught in fishing nets – not all are released in time.

BELOW:
ancient Ciboney pictographs.

mainland) are the only places in the world where the endangered Cuban crocodile can be found.

Close to Cocodrilo there is a **marine science station** (open daily 9am–5pm; entrance charge) which is breeding native turtles for release into the wild. It may have as many as 6,000 turtles in captivity at one time.

Indigenous cave paintings

Punta del Este ⑥, in the southeast corner of the island 60 km (37 miles) from Nueva Gerona, is beautiful. Except for the ferocious mosquitoes, it is altogether magnificent. It is so far mercifully free of intrusive tourist development, and likely to remain so as long as the restrictions on entering the zone are in place.

Just inland from a sparkling, pristine beach is a series of mysterious **caves** where the indigenous Ciboney inhabitants painted pictographs 3,000 years ago. The caves are one of the most important archeological finds in the Caribbean, first explored by the Cuban anthropologist Fernando Ortíz in 1922. The main cave is considered the Ciboneys' Sistine Chapel. It is a single spacious chamber with a

fairly low ceiling containing seven natural vaults and more than 200 drawings of circles, arrows, triangles, and serpentine lines. The whole is a great red and black mural which is believed to represent a lunar calendar, including human figures and animals in the world the Ciboney knew and imagined.

Coral reef

From the top of the headland above the caves, a long coral reef is visible about 3.5 km (2 miles) offshore. Blue waves crash against the coralline wall in a spray of foam that rolls onto the inner lagoon. The calm, nearly transparent water affords a marvelous view of the seabed – a clean, sandy plain rippled in undulating zigzag crests like tiny dunes. At some points, a fine celgrass carpets the sea floor, revealing queen conch shells, with their shiny pink mouths; large king helmuts shaded from dark brown to lustrous cream; and conical top shells. Starfish adorn the sandy bottom, on which white coral appears in a thicket of gorgonians, with delicate hands and multiple fingers swaying in the water.

Snorkelers can explore this far, but full diving gear is needed if you want to swim through the coralline wall into the extraordinary reef garden, formed of the most varied green, white, yellow, violet, and pink corals surrounded by a nearly transparent liquid mass. These corals are found only where the sea is less than 100 meters (330 ft) deep and where the temperature never drops below 19°C (68°F). At a deeper level, squirrelfish, hogfish, barracudas, and sharks may be spotted.

Cayo Largo

East of the Isle of Youth, a myriad of tiny cays lies scattered in a wide arc. Most are uninhabited and inaccessible from the mainland. All have delicious beaches of white powdery sand and magnificent diving amongst the coral and the shipwrecks: the Nueva España treasure fleet that went down in 1563 on the reefs somewhere between Cayo Rosario and Cayo Largo provides just a fraction of the more than 200 known wrecks in this

area. So far, all but one of these dream islands are undeveloped and only accessible by boat. Plans are afoot to develop Cayo Rico, just west of Cayo Largo, but nothing has happened there yet.

The only cay currently geared to tourism is **Cayo Largo**, which has 27 km (17 miles) of white beaches, but is no more than 3 km (2 miles) wide at any point. The cay is accessible by plane from Havana or Varadero, and the easiest way to visit is on a day trip organized by one of the tour agencies in Havana *(see page 369)*, which includes transfers and lunch.

In 1985, before Cuba plunged into schemes to attract international tourism, the slogan for this pristine island was "Thus it all began." Then came the building boom, the package tours, and the airport disco reception with watery rum cocktails. Even the boat trip to swim and lunch at lovely **Playa Sirena** has been over-commercialized, and tourists are charged a fortune. An indication of its international tourist status is that, like Varadero, Cayo Largo accepts euros.

Still, Cayo Largo remains popular with travelers looking for sun, sea, and sand, and not much else – anyone at all interested in Cuba or Cubans would be better off going elsewhere.

Getting away from it all

There is, however, an escape: from Cayo Largo, you can take day trips to nearby islets that have no tourist installations at all. But you cannot travel between Cayo Largo and Isla de la Juventud by boat or plane, so you won't be able to "island hop" and visit both places on one trip.

Other accessible places include **Cayo Iguana**, inhabited by hordes of these friendly reptiles (which can also be seen on the main island). **Cayo Rosario**, west of Cayo Largo and almost as large is a crescent-shaped beach, backed by high sand dunes. It is enclosed by a sandbar that forms a natural lagoon of clear blue water over fine pearly sand, with minuscule shells of deep pink piled in the ridges of the sea bed, creating a wavy texture. The calm water is lovely for gentle swimming. The cay also has a freshwater river. For the time being at least, the only inhabitants are the large iguanas and other, more elusive wild animals and birds that exist in this sensitive environment. Long may it last. ❏

TIP

Cayo Largo suffered badly from Hurricane Michelle in November 2001, but fortunately it seems to have recovered.

BELOW: one of the glittering white beaches on Cayo Largo.
FOLLOWING PAGES: a Cuban serenade.

INSIGHT GUIDES

TRAVEL TIPS

CUBA

TRAVEL TIPS

T RANSPORTATION

GETTING THERE AND GETTING AROUND

By Air

The availability of flights to Cuba and the airlines in service are subject to change, so always check. However, most visitors book their flights through a travel agency, which should be aware of the current situation. **Cubana de Aviación**, the national airline, flies scheduled and charter routes between Cuba and other cities in the Americas and Europe, serving primarily Havana. Most flights are positively no-frills, but for many visitors Cubana flights provide the cheapest, quickest and easiest route into Cuba. The airline has suffered from a poor safety record in the past, but this has improved since it began upgrading its fleet, replacing old Russian aircraft with Airbus on international flights.

From Europe

Cubana (www.cubana.cu or www.cubajet.com) operates flights to and from: London (Gatwick), Paris, Moscow, Madrid, Las Palmas (Canary Islands), and Rome. Flights from London (twice weekly) usually make a stop in Holguín.
  Air France (www.airfrance.com) has scheduled flights to Havana; travelers from the UK have to break their flight in Paris.
  Iberia (www.iberia.com) also has scheduled flights, and UK travelers have to change in Madrid.
  Virgin (www.virgin-atlantic.com) operates direct flights twice a week from Gatwick to Havana. These are more expensive than those with a stop in Europe. Flight time from London on a direct flight is about 9 hours.

There are various **charter flights** from Gatwick, Luton, Stansted, Manchester, and other regional airports in the UK to Havana, Varadero, and Holguín. The Dutch charter airline **Martinair** (www.martinair.com) flies from Amsterdam to Havana, Varadero, and Holguín. These flights are usually booked through package-tour operators.

From Latin America and the Caribbean

Cubana flies to and from: Buenos Aires, São Paulo, Santiago de Chile, Kingston (Jamaica), Mexico City, Guatemala City, Caracas, Panama City, Bogotá, and Lima.
  Many Latin American and Caribbean airlines also serve Cuba, with scheduled and charter flights available. **Mexicana** (www.mexicana.com) flies between Mexico City and Havana, and there are also frequent flights from Cancún and Mérida in Yucatán. There are regular connections between Havana and various Central American cities on the Costa Rican airline, **Lacsa** (www.lacsa.com); and **Air Jamaica** (www.airjamaica.com) flies to Havana.

From Canada

Cuba is accessible by air from Montreal, Toronto, and Ottawa. **Cubana** runs scheduled flights from Montreal and Toronto, while **Air Canada** (www.aircanada.ca) and **Royal Airlines** (www.royal.ca) fly from Toronto to Havana, Varadero, Santa Clara, Holguín, Cayo Coco, and Ciego de Avila. Direct flight time from Montreal to Havana is 4 hours; 3¾ hours from Toronto. There are also charter flights from Ottawa.

From the US

In 1998, the US State Department resumed daily charter flights between Miami and Havana (these were suspended in February 1996) but these are very strictly regulated by the US State Department. They are intended solely for Cubans visiting relatives and for those US citizens who meet Treasury Department requirements (such as accredited journalists, diplomats, or family members traveling for proven emergencies). Those with their visas already in order can buy air tickets from **Marazul Tours**, Tower Plaza Mall, 4100 Park Avenue, Weehawken, NJ 07087, tel: 800-223 5334 or visit: www.marazultours.com. There is often a long waiting list to travel on these flights, and US currency restrictions apply.
  Although there are no flights to take tourists from the US, Americans keen to visit Cuba sometimes travel via Canada, Cancún, Jamaica, or Nassau, although the latter is not recommended as there is a US customs office there with the aim of sniffing out Americans returning from Cuba.
  Cuban officials do not stamp the passports of US – or any other –

Tourist Cards

Remember to keep your tourist card in a safe place as you will need to surrender it when you leave the country. Visitors may also be required to produce their tourist card, along with their passport, when changing traveler's checks, booking into a *casa particular* or a hotel, if traveling independently.

travelers they simply stamp their tourist cards. US visitors are welcome as long as they steer clear of "subversive" activities.

Airline Offices

In Havana, international and domestic airline offices, as well as some tour operators, are all located on La Rampa – a stretch of Calle 23 running between Calle M and the Malecón, in Vedado.

On Departure

If you do not have a transfer to the airport as part of your vacation deal, you should take a taxi. Buses exist, but they are not a reliable option. Allow at least 45 minutes for the trip from Old Havana to the airport.

Be at the airport at least 2 hours before an international flight; security and customs checks can be lengthy.

Airport departure tax for international flights is CUC$25, which *must* be paid after you have checked in, in cash, in *pesos convertibles*. You can exchange the necessary amount of foreign currency into CUCs at the airport, but this can be time consuming and best not left until the last minute.

By Sea

People traveling on chartered (or private) yachts arrive by sea. There is no ferry service, and few cruise ships make Cuba's harbors a port of call. A few cruise lines are now stopping in Cuba, ships dock at the Terminal Cruceros in Havana.

GETTING AROUND

From Havana Airport

José Martí International Airport, tel: (07) 33-5666 for international flight information; (07) 452-589 for domestic flights. Most international flights operate from Terminal 3, where there is a 24-hour tourist information desk (tel: 07-66-6101 or 66-6112, but phones are rarely answered), numerous car-rental desks, bars, restaurants, and an exchange desk. Some charter flights use Terminal 2.

Tourist taxis are always available at the airport: the fare is around CUC$20–25 with Cubanacán *(see page 369)* or Havanautos, which have desks in the terminal; other companies, such as Panataxi, Taxi OK, and Gaviota, are somewhat cheaper. (The airport is about 18 km/11 miles from central Havana.)

Drivers from the various taxi companies gather at the terminal and hustle for your custom. It is illegal for **unlicensed cabs** to drive tourists to or from the airport, and the police keep an eagle eye out for offenders.

By Air

Flying is the most convenient way to travel for anyone with limited time and a desire to see various corners of the island. Most services originate from Havana. The national airline, **Cubana** (www.cubana.cu), has regular scheduled flights to 13 Cuban cities from the capital. New destinations are being added all the time, so check with your tour operator or with the airline.

The addresses of Cubana offices are as follows:

Havana: Calle 23, 64, corner of Infanta, Vedado, tel: (07) 836-4950, 834-4446.
Baracoa: Calle Martí, 181, tel: (0121) 42171.
Bayamo: Calle Marti, 58, between Parada and Rojas, tel: (0123) 423916.
Camagüey: Calle República, 400, corner of Correa, tel: (0132) 291338, 92156.
Ciego de Avila: Calle Chicho Valdes, 83, between Maceo and Honorato Castillo, tel: (0133) 325316.
Holguín: Edificio Pico de Cristal, Calle Libertad, corner of Martí, 2nd Floor, Policentro, tel: (0124) 425707, fax: 024-468111.
Santiago de Cuba: Calle Enramada, corner of San Pedro, 673, between Heredia and Bartolome Masó (San Basilio), tel: (0122) 651577–9, fax: (0122) 686258.
Varadero: Avenida 1era, corner of Calle 55, tel: (0145) 611823, fax: (0145) 614855.

Aerocaribbean and **Aerogaviota**,

Public Transportation

Fuel shortages have prompted drastic cuts in inter-urban and inter-provincial public bus services. Many Cuban cities rely on horse-drawn carts that use the same urban routes buses once used to follow. You will also see open-backed trucks, sometimes with a tarpaulin "roof," carrying passengers in many towns.

In Havana, thousands of Chinese-made bicycles have been introduced, but there are many more non-cyclists who wait two hours or more for a bus every day. In some places, it is mandatory for Cuban state-owned cars and trucks to pick up hitchhikers; but the farther you go into the countryside the fewer vehicles you see. Tourists are not obliged to pick up hitchhikers but it is rather churlish not to. What is more, local people often make good company and can be very helpful in giving directions on Cuba's poorly signposted roads.

two smaller lines, operate charter flights to Cayo Largo, Cayo Coco, Cayo Santa María, and other popular tourist destinations.

The Aerocaribbean office in Havana is at Calle 23, 64, corner of Calle P, Vedado, tel: (07) 879-7524, 870-4965. The Aerogaviota office is at Avenida 47, 2814, between calles 28 and 34, tel: (07) 203-0686, 203-0668.

For most visitors, however, especially those who do not speak Spanish, it is better to purchase tickets for domestic flights from a hotel reception desk or a recognised travel agency *(see page 369)*. They do not charge commission for making the airline booking.

Puncture Repairs

The nearest petrol station may be able to help if you have a flat tire. Otherwise, ask around for the local *ponchera*. Since self-employment was legalized, many Cubans have set up puncture-repair workshops. Most of these deal mainly with bicycle tires, but many can handle car inner tubes.

By Bus

City buses, known as **guaguas**, are crowded and uncomfortable, but they are cheap and traveling on them does help to immerse you in local life (take care of your valuables). Long-distance buses, on the other hand, are a good, and relatively inexpensive, way of getting around the island.

Viazul is a highly recommended CUC-only bus service offering fast, comfortable, air-conditioned vehicles, with toilets, and plenty of luggage capacity, that operate between the major centers. From Havana to Santiago there are four buses a day, but the best one is the **express**, the overnight service that leaves Havana at 6.15pm, as it takes 12 hours, and stops only once, in Camagüey. The other services take just under 16 hours (although that is still often faster than the train).The cost is the same whether you take the express or not: currently CUC$52 single. There are four Viazul buses a day from Havana to Varadero (3 hours), two a day to Viñales (3½ hours), and two a day to Trinidad (just under 6 hours), as well as many other destinations, including a direct service from Viñales to Trinidad, and from Santiago to Baracoa. Be sure to wear something warm as the air conditioning on the bus is fierce.

The Viazul station is by the city zoo on Avenida 26 and Zoológico, Nuevo Vedado, tel: (07) 881-1413, fax: (07) 883-6092, e-mail: viazul@transnet.cu; www.viazul.com.

Provincial offices are at:
Varadero: Calle 36 and Autopista Varadero, tel: (045) 614886.
Viñales: Salvador Cisneros, 63, tel: (08) 793195.
Trinidad: Pirojial, 224 between Antonio Maceo and Gustavo Izquierdo; tel: (04199) 2660.
Santiago: Avenida Libertadores, 457, tel: (0122) 628484.
Camagüey: Carretera Central s/n, corner Perú, tel: (032) 270395.
At busy times of year, and on popular routes, it is a good idea to reserve your ticket in advance. It is

sometimes easier to do this through a **Cubatur** office (in most towns) or, in Havana, through the **Infotur** office at Calle Obispo 524.

You will pay a deposit and receive a voucher, which you then exchange for a ticket at the bus station. You still have to turn up about 45 minutes in advance, but it's a safer bet than lining up for a ticket without a reservation.

There are also long-distance bus services run by **Astra** (Terminal de Omnibus Nacional, Avenida de la Independencia and 19 de Mayo, near the Plaza de la Revolución, tel: 07-870-3397), but they are slower and less comfortable, and there are no printed schedules. There are not many tickets available for *pesos convertibles*. These are the buses used by Cubans, who have to join long lines to book tickets and you will have to do the same and hope for the best.

Tour Buses

Hotels can book reasonably priced excursions to a wide range of tourist destinations on modern, comfortable air-conditioned buses. Tourist agencies will also book tours, contact: Cubanacán, Cubatur, and Havanatur *(see Tourist Agencies, page 369)* for more details.

By Train

The Cuban railroad was the first in Latin America, but it may be the last in efficiency and comfort today. Trains are crowded and services have been reduced – almost all are now locals that stop at every station. All are achingly slow and prone to breakdown. Except on the so-called Havana–Santiago Express (which averages 18 hours traveling time), little or no food or water are to be had, so remember to take provisions with you.

Seats on Cuban trains are always booked well in advance with long waiting lists. However, there are always seats reserved for those paying in CUCs. For peace of mind, you ought to try and book your ticket a day in advance, and you should arrive at least an hour before departure to check in, and before 7pm if taking a night train: unassigned seats will be re-allocated to those on the waiting list if you have not confirmed that you are traveling.

In Havana buy your tickets at window 1 in the main hall of the Estación La Coubre, Avenida del Puerto y Ejido, tel: (07) 860-3163/64/65. You must pay in cash,

in CUCs, and bring your passport. The trains leave from the main station, Estación Central de Ferrocarril. Advance tickets are sold until two hours before departure at the office of Ferrocuba on the corner of Arsenal and Avenida de Bélgica; open Mon–Fri 8am–5pm; for ticket information, call: (07) 861-4259 or 862 4888.

At many provincial Ferrocuba offices (in the train stations) the staff are not really accustomed to dealing with foreigners and tend to take the same unhelpful (or downright rude) attitude they inflict on fellow Cubans. They are also unlikely to speak English. Persist if you are told that there are no seats: it is unlikely that this is the case if you are paying hard currency. Unfortunately, it is only too common in Cuba that a firm *"No hay"* (there aren't any) is simply a way of asking for a bribe. If the worst comes to the worst, try offering CUC$1 to see if that helps.

Fly/Drive

Cubanacán *(see page 369)* operates several fly/drive options from airports in Havana, Varadero, Camagüey, Holguín, and Santiago de Cuba. It is convenient because your car is waiting for you when you arrive, and the negotiations have been done in advance.

Driving

Increasingly, tourists are getting around Cuba by car. This gives the greatest degree of independence, and allows you to reach corners of the island that otherwise would be hard to get to in a short time.

Cuban highways and secondary roads are fairly well maintained, except for the potholes. Otherwise, driving is safe and Cubans are ever helpful with directions – even though they are often vague when it comes to distances. Away from the cities, you won't find traffic congestion a problem: sometimes you may travel miles without seeing another vehicle – even stretches of the *autopista* can be completely empty.

Car Rental

Current rental charges range between CUC$45 and 100 per day, depending on the vehicle, plus a deposit of CUC$200–300. The fee and deposit must be paid in advance (cash, non-US credit card, or traveler's checks). Unlimited mileage is included but insurance and fuel are extra. The tank should be full when you start (check that it is – it's a common scam for staff to underfill it) and you will be charged 95 cents a liter (correct at the time of going to press). Remember to return the car empty – there are no refunds.

There are two grades of insurance: Grade A at around CUC$12 per day covers theft only, Grade B at CUC$15 per day covers all risks except loss of radio and spare tire. Additional drivers are charged at a flat fee of CUC$12–15 each, or CUC$3–5 per day.

Be sure to check the car carefully for damage and scratches. Draw attention to anything you find, and insist any damages are noted on the paperwork. Be warned that car-rental agents have all kind of ruses for not returning the full deposit. Whatever you do, be sure to take out the maximum insurance cover possible, it is well worth the extra cost, in case of even minor scrapes or mishaps.

If you are involved in an accident or have something stolen from the car you must report this to the police and be sure to get the right paperwork *(denuncia)* or you will not be able to claim insurance in Cuba or at home. Be aware that the business at the police station will be time consuming and take many hours.

Cars can be rented through the desks of the major hotels in Havana, Varadero, Cienfuegos, Trinidad, Camagüey, Holguín, and Santiago de Cuba. The main rental company is **Transtur**, whose head office is at Calle L, 456, between 25 and 27, opposite the Havana Libre, tel: (07) 55-3991, fax: 835-3727; e-mail: comercial@ transtur.cu; www.transtur.cu. They also rent out multipurpose vehicles and cars with drivers. Others include:

Panautos, airport: tel: (07) 33-0306; Vedado: tel: (07) 55-3286, 55-3255/6.

Cubacar, airport: tel: (07) 33-5546 and offices in major hotels.

GranCar, tel: (07) 57-7338; Varadero: tel: (0145) 66-7175.

Havanautos, tel: (07) 835-3141/42, www.havanautos.cubaweb.cu.

Gas (Petrol)

Buying gas used to be a nightmare in Cuba. It still is for most ordinary Cubans, at least for those who have no access to CUCs. Tourists and anyone else with convertible currency, however, can now make use of the **Cupet** gas stations, which you will find in all the main towns and, increasingly, in smaller provincial towns all over the island. Cupet stations normally offer minimal mechanical back-up, as well as snack bars. Most are open 24 hours.

Private Cars & Taxis

You may prefer to let someone else do the driving. One way Cubans are making CUCs now is by driving visitors around (though the many crackdowns have hit unlicensed drivers hard). Some charge a flat rate for a half or a whole day of sightseeing or for a particular excursion, for example from Havana to Varadero or Havana to Viñales and back. The price should be considerably less than the cost of an organized tour with a state agency, especially if two or more of you are traveling together. Always agree a price before you set off.

It is even possible to organize a car and driver for a week – as long as you are prepared to pay for all their food and lodging.

It will not always be apparent, but some private taxis are licensed and some are not – depending on whether the driver pays the hefty license fee-cum-tax imposed by the government. As you walk around the streets of Havana and other towns and cities you will constantly be asked if you want a taxi – most of these will be private operators, legal or illegal.

It is supposedly illegal for private taxis – legal or illegal – to ferry passengers to any airport or to Varadero, the Eastern Beaches (Playas del Este) or any other tourist resort. A Cuban caught doing this will be heavily fined and may lose his license – even his car, if it's not a first offense. Hence, some "street" taxis will now refuse to take you to these destinations.

Note that if you find a private driver willing to take the risk, and are stopped by the police, you too could end up spending several hours at a police station while the paperwork is done – though it will be the Cuban who suffers in the end.

Several state companies provide a

taxi service, the main ones being: **Turistaxi**, tel: (07) 33-55341, 33-6666; **Havanataxi**, tel: (07) 53-9086; and **Taxi OK**, tel: (07) 877-6666, which are comfortable and air-conditioned. You can call them or pick them up from designated ranks (usually outside hotels, and tourist haunts such as major museums). **GranCar** tel: (07) 33-5647, operates a taxi service in the shiny old vintage cars that all visitors appear to love.

The cabs run by **Panataxi** (tel: (07) 55-5555, 55-5456) are cheap, friendly, reliable, and metered (starting at CUC$1, then CUC$1 per kilometer).

Coco-taxis

These are the little round, yellow taxis that are fine (and fun) for short distances, although there is no room for luggage. They charge 50 cents a kilometer.

Bici-taxis

These little rickshaw-type vehicles, drawn by bicycles, can be fun and are inexpensive – but agree a fare before you start. They are not really supposed to take tourists, but they do, especially outside Havana.

Horse Carriages

In some provincial towns horse-drawn carriages (often just called *coches*) provide an inexpensive taxi service, and are widely used by local people.

Cycling

Cycling is the way many Cubans get around, and if you want to cycle while you are here you will certainly have no trouble finding someone to mend a flat tire *(see box opposite)*. There are cycle lanes on all roads outside towns. Bring a strong lock with you, and be careful where you park, or you may find yourself going home without your bicycle.

ACCOMMODATIONS

HOTELS AND CASAS PARTICULARES

Looking for a Hotel

Many of Cuba's tourist lodgings have been, or are in the process of being, upgraded – and so are their prices. Foreign tour operators and hotel chains pay about half the listed price for groups of 15 or more, giving them space for the attractive packages of which the vast majority of tourists take advantage. The price categories given here reflect the rack rate an independent traveler will pay for a room. Be aware, too, that low-season prices can be considerably lower than those provided here.

   Tourist hotels are run by a variety of tourist enterprises, and it is possible to ascertain the standard of the hotel from the name of the enterprise that manages it. For example, hotels run by **Islazul** tend to be two-star or three-star, while those run by **Gran Caribe** or **Cubanacán** are often four-star. In the popular resorts, there are hotels run by foreign companies, such as **Sol**

Cuban Addresses

A few points on understanding addresses in Cuba. An address written as (e.g.) Calle Martí 65, esq. Céspedes means it is at 65 Martí Street on the corner of (or intersection with) Céspedes Street. Similarly, Calle Martí 65, entre 9 y 11 means it is at 65 Martí Street between streets 9 and 11. You will also see (e.g.) Avenida 1era or Avenida 5ta, which mean 1st Avenue or 5th Avenue. Piso 1º or Primero Piso means first floor. We have used the anglicized form in our listings, but you will encounter the Spanish form in written material in Cuba.

Meliá (from Spain). Sol Meliá accommodations may be booked from the UK, tel: 0808-234 1953.

   Most rooms have private bathrooms, but even in a three-star hotel you may occasionally find there's no hot water. You can expect air-conditioning in rooms, but in a two-star establishment you may just get a fan *(ventilador)*.

Campsites

Campsites are operated by **Campismo Popular** in every province. Campers sleep in a hut *(cabaña)* more often than in a tent. Group showers and latrines prevail. The majority of these sites are designed for Cuban tourists, and are closed out of the peak vacation months of July and August. However, a few sites are used for international tourism and are open all year round. These places have better amenities, such as flush toilets and hot water. The international sites include:
● **Aguas Claras**, near Pinar del Río.
● **Villa Santo Domingo** in the Sierra Maestra, in Granma province.

   Reservations can be made directly with **Cubatur** on arrival *(see page 369)* or, even better, booked from abroad through a specialist tour operator.

Private Rooms
(Casas Particulares)

For many years, it was illegal to rent private accommodations in Cuba, but this was, nonetheless, widely practiced and universally tolerated. The government decided to legalize the practice in 1996, but imposed rules, which are fairly strictly enforced.
● *Casas particulares* should display a blue sign, shaped rather like an anchor, on the front door.

● It is illegal for a Cuban to rent an entire apartment – but people do.
● It is illegal to rent more than two rooms – but people do.
● It is illegal to let unless you register with the government and pay hefty taxes – but people do.
● Cuban hosts must fill out a form with visitor's details, which you sign, and the host presents this to the police the following day. Note that you can now put a legally registered *casa particular* on your tourist card as your official place of residence in Cuba.

   There are now literally thousands of *casas particulares* in Havana and hundreds in provincial towns, especially in popular spots like Santiago, Trinidad, Viñales, and Baracoa. The internet is great for finding them: some even have their own websites. One useful site is www.casaparticularcuba.org.

   You may be approached by agents for people with rooms to let (they take a commission from the owner). Otherwise, ask around: taxi drivers are good sources of information. Not everyone who lets rooms is honest, and you should be careful with money and valuables. The best way to find a good *casa particular* is by recommendation from a fellow traveler.

Taking Priority

A number of hotels in the Cubanacán and Islazul chains are currently being used to accommodate patients and medical teams in the Operación Milagro scheme. The website: www.cubahotelbookings.com will inform you which are unavailable at the time of your visit.

OLD HAVANA

Hotel Ambos Mundos
Calle Obispo, 153, at the corner of Mercaderes
Tel: (07) 860-9529/9530
Fax: (07) 860-9532
Elegant, nicely renovated, old-style hotel (where Ernest Hemingway stayed). The lovely views are lost to many guests since most rooms are windowless (although they are air-conditioned). Nice ground-floor piano bar and a rooftop bar with stunning city views. **$$$**

Hostal Conde de Villanueva
Calle Mercaderes, 202, between Lamparilla and Amargura
Tel: (07) 862-9293
Fax: (07) 862-9862
E-mail: comercial@cvillanueva.co.cu
In the heart of Old Havana this is a specialist cigar-smokers' hotel (there's a giant model cigar in the lobby and rooms are named after tobacco plantations but there are three non-smokers' rooms as well). Small and atmospheric, with a beautiful colonial patio. It has its own cigar bar and Cuban restaurant. **$$$**

Hotel Florida
Calle Obispo, 252, corner of Calle Cuba
Tel: (07) 862-4127
Fax: (07) 862-4117
E-mail: reservas@habaguanexhflorida. co.cu
Bang in the busy heart of Old Havana, this restored colonial building centers on a lovely courtyard. Rooms have air conditioning, minibar, 24-hour room service, safe, and satellite TV. **$$$**

Hostal Los Frailes
Calle Teniente Rey, 8, between Oficios and Mercaderes
Tel: (07) 862-9383
Fax: (07) 862-9718
E-mail: comercial @habaguanexhfrailes.co.cu
A small, attractive restored colonial hotel in the center of Old Havana – this one with the gimmick of having its staff dress up as

Franciscan friars. It has 22 comfortable rooms with air conditioning and private bathrooms. The standard rooms (**$$**) have no windows. Junior suites do, and just tip over into the quoted price category. **$$$**

Hotel Inglaterra
Parque Central (Prado, 416)
Tel: (07) 860-8595/96/97
Fax: (07) 860-8254
E-mail: reserva@gcingla.gca.cma.net
A cool, gold and white lobby, a lovely 24-hour café-bar, with live music from the grand piano or a (rather deafening) mariachi band. The restaurant next door is beautiful, gently lit by chandeliers and stained glass, but the food doesn't live up to the decor. The small rooftop bar holds a salsa cabaret every night except Tuesday (entrance charge). The interior rooms tend to be rather stuffy but are at least quiet, while those with balconies looking out over the Parque Central or the Gran Teatro, next door, are light but noisy. You should try to specify what kind of room you would like when you book; they're all the same price. **$$$**

Mercure Sevilla
Trocadero 55, corner of Prado
Tel: (07) 860-8560
Fax: (07) 860-8575
E-mail: reserva@sevilla.gca.tur.cu
The renovated Sevilla has a wonderfully Spanish ambiance. Cool, tiled lobby and delightful blue-tiled patio café complete with fountain. The ninth-floor restaurant, in what used to be the ballroom, has spectacular views – and the food, once average, is now very good.

NH Parque Central
Calles Neptuno and Prado (Paseo de Martí)
Tel: (07) 860-6627
Fax: (07) 860-6630
E-mail: reservations@nh-hoteles.cu
It has a rooftop pool, a jacuzzi with sterling views, a gym, and numerous

bars, cafés, and restaurants. The food is good in the extremely formal ground-floor restaurant. Some renovation work going on at the time of writing. **$$$**

Hotel Raquel
Calle Amargura 103, corner of San Ignacio
Tel: (07) 860-8280
In a beautifully restored Art Nouveau building, with a gorgeous lobby and some stunning stained glass, the 25-room Raquel is a real treat. There's a little gym and sauna, too, and it has the only kosher restaurant in Havana. **$$$**

Hotel Santa Isabel
Calle Baratillo, Plaza de Armas
Tel: (07) 860-8201
Fax: (07) 860-8391
E-mail: comercial@habaguanexhsisabel.co.cu
A beautiful, renovated colonial palace, right in the heart of Old Havana. A vision in turquoise and stone with a lovely courtyard. Five-star, popular with the business market. Excellent restaurant. One of the nicest hotels in the city. **$$$**

Telégrafo
Prado 408, corner Neptuno
Tel: (07) 861-1010
Fax: (07) 861 4741
E-mail: reserva@telegrafo. co.cu
This hotel first opened in 1860, and re-opened in its present form in 2001. Very smart and efficient, the decor mingles the old with the new, with a state-of-the-art restaurant set amid the bare brick arches of the original building. **$$$**

Beltran de Santa Cruz
Calle San Ignacio 411, between Muralla and Sol
Tel: (07) 860-8330
Fax: (07) 860-8383
E-mail: reserva@bsantacruz.co.cu
A lovely 18th-century building, with beamed ceilings, stained glass, and blue-painted balconies. Eleven air-conditioned rooms and a friendly atmosphere. **$$**

Hotel el Comendador
Calle Obrapía, corner of Baratillo
Tel: (07) 867-1037
Fax: (07) 860-5628
E-mail: reservas @habaguanexhvalencia.co.cu
Small, attractively restored colonial house in the heart of Old Havana (linked with Hostal Valencia). Quiet, with attractive air-conditioned rooms (with hairdryers) and a tapas bar on the ground floor. **$$**

Hotel Plaza
Agramonte, 267, Parque Central
Tel: (07) 860-8583
Fax: (07) 860-8591
E-mail: reserva@plaza.gca.cma.net
Favored by European tour groups, the Plaza has a grand columned lobby, while the café-bar on the ground floor has a fountain, and is full of parrots and palms. The hotel has three rather mediocre and over-priced restaurants, but breakfast on the roof terrace is undeniably pleasant, and the bar serves decent sandwiches. Rooms are on the poky side, looking out to the street or inner courtyards. All have delicate stained-glass windows and tasteful prints. **$$**

Hostal del Tejadillo
Calle Tejadillo 12, corner of San Ignacio
Tel: (07) 863-7283
Fax: (07) 863-8830
E-mail: cubacon@enet.cu
Thirty-two rooms set around two plant-filled courtyards. There's an air-conditioned restaurant and bar, plus babysitting, and laundry facilities. Rooms have minibars, safe, telephone, cable TV, and fans (no air conditioning). **$–$$**

PRICE CATEGORIES

Price categories indicate the cost of a double room in high season:
$ = under $80
$$ = $80–150
$$$ = $150–250

TRANSPORTATION

ACCOMMODATIONS

ACTIVITIES

A – Z

LANGUAGE

Hostal Valencia
Calles Oficios and Obrapía
Tel: (07) 867-1037
Fax: (07) 860-5628
E-mail: reserva@habagua
nexhvalencia.co.cu
The hotel has just 11
rooms and three suites, in
a beautifully restored
colonial mansion, centered
around a glorious vine-
draped courtyard with a
pleasant café-bar. There is
also a decent Spanish
restaurant, La Paella (see
page 164). Rather noisy in
the early morning, but the
rooms are delightful, with
original colonial features.
Staff are very friendly, too.
The Valencia is popular and
usually booked up well in
advance. If you can't get a
room, try its sister hotel, El
Comendador (see page
341). **$$**

Casas Particulares

Most casas particulares in
Havana charge about
CUC$30 per night,
regardless of whether one
or two people share the
room. Breakfast is usually
extra (typically CUC$3 per
person) and is usually large
and very good – fresh fruit,
fruit juice, coffee, and eggs
any way you want them.
Eugenio Barral
San Ignacio 656, between Jesús
María and Merced
Tel: (07) 862-9877
Quiet, clean and friendly,
with antique-furnished
rooms. Excellent
breakfasts.
Fefita y Luís
Aguacate 509, 4th floor
Tel: (07) 867-6433
Two rooms. Centrally
located, and the owners,

the food, the views of Old
Havana and the comfortable
beds are all wonderful.
Shared bathroom.
Casa Humberto
Compostela 661, between Luz
and Sol
Tel: (07) 860-3264
Two large air-conditioned
rooms with private
bathrooms, and breakfast
served on a shady terrace
outside your door. One tiny
double room on the roof,
where there's a huge
terrace, with hammocks,
for all guests' use. Run by
a pleasant young couple,
Humberto and Miladys.
**Rafaela y Pepe – Los
Balcones**
San Ignacio 454, between Sol and
Santa Clara
Tel: (07) 867-5551
Two comfortable air-
conditioned rooms, with

balconies, share a
bathroom in a friendly
house full of antiques,
plants, and bric-à-brac. The
owners are the parents of
Eugenio Barral (see
previous entry).
Juan y Margarita
Obispo 522, between Bernaz and
Villegas
Tel: (07) 867-9592
A light, two-bedroomed
apartment with bathroom.
No kitchen but the
living/dining room has a
fridge and television.
Extremely central.
Colonial Maritza
Luz 115, between San Ignacio
and Inquisidor
Tel: (07) 862-3303
Two double rooms in a
beautiful colonial house
near the harbor, with an
internal patio. Private
bathrooms.

CENTRO HABANA AND VEDADO

Hotel Habana Libre
Calle L between 23 and 25, Vedado
Tel: (07) 834-6100
Fax: (07) 834-6366
E-mail: tryp.habana.libre@solmelia.com
A time capsule of 1950s
design for decades, the
Libre is – after a US$20-
million refurbishment – just
another high-rise modern
hotel. It is, however, far
more pleasant and
comfortable than before.
Rooms are spacious and
comfortable. The higher up

you go, the more expensive
the room because of the
views. The hotel has a pool,
several decent bars
(including the rooftop Bar
Turquino) and restaurants, a
branch of the Banco
Financiero Internacional,
and a range of shops. **$$$**
Hotel Meliá Cohiba
Paseo and Primera, Vedado
Tel: (07) 833-3636
Fax: (07) 834-4555
E-mail: melia.cohiba@solmelia.com
Cuba's first five-star hotel,

opened in 1995, on the
seafront. It's not pretty, in
architectural terms, but it is
luxurious, the service is
excellent, and most of its
460 rooms have sea views.
Filled to bursting with
restaurants, cafés, bars,
nightclubs, and shops, as
well as a gym, a business
center and, of course, a
swimming pool. Some
rooms are equipped for
visitors with disabilities.
$$$

Hotel Nacional
Calle O and 21, Vedado
Tel: (07) 836-3564–67
Fax: (07) 836-5171
E-mail: reserva@gcnacional.gca.tur.cu
Once Havana's top hotel,
and still pretty classy. The
rich and famous of the
city's golden age in the
1940s and 1950s used to
stay here – you can see
their pictures in the
corridors and the Bar of
Fame. The neoclassical
building is undeniably
elegant. There are beautiful
tropical gardens, tennis
courts, and two pools – can
be used by non-guests
(CUC$15, but you get
CUC$15-worth of food and
drink). There are lovely
views along the Malecón,
and the Cabaret Parisien is
the next best thing to the
Tropicana. **$$$**
Hotel Deauville
Calle Galiano and Malecón, Central
Havana
Tel: (07) 338-812–3 and 866-8812
Fax: (07) 338-148
E-mail: reservas@hdeauvil.hor.tur.cu
Long used by tour groups,
the Deauville has been
refurbished although it still
looks a bit grim from the
outside. Rooms are
comfortable but TVs, lamps,

BELOW: the neoclassical Hotel Nacional in Vedado.

showers, etc. tend not to work. There is, however, a wonderful rooftop pool and breakfast is good. The hotel is situated on the fringe of a rough part of Central Havana, but it is pleasant to wake up to the sound of the sea crashing on the Malecón. **$$$**

Hotel Habana Riviera
Paseo and Malecón, Vedado
Tel: (07) 836-4051, 334051
Fax: (07) 833-3739
E-mail: reserva@gcrivie.gca.tur.cu
Built by Mafia boss Meyer Lansky, it is rather over-shadowed by the Meliá Cohiba next door. However, it has an excellent swimming pool, and some rooms with sea views. The lobby retains a 1950s appearance and atmosphere, and there's the lively Copa Room cabaret. Good value. **$$**

Hotel Presidente
Calzada and Avenida de Presidentes, Vedado
Tel: (07) 838-1801
Fax: (07) 33-3753
E-mail: comercial@hpdte.gca.tur.cu
Restored hotel with an impressive marble-floored lobby, filled with antiques. About half the 160 rooms

have sea views; some rooms are rather small. The pool is beloved by *jineteras* (hustlers) and the music tends to be loud. **$$**

Hotel Victoria
Calle 19, 101, corner of M, Vedado
Tel: (07) 333-510, 333-625
Fax: (07) 333-109
E-mail: reserva@victoria.gca.tur.cu
A quiet, unassuming, classically elegant hotel in a good position, but with only 31 rooms, the Victoria is usually booked up. The restaurant is average, favoring seafood. There is a small pool, a business center, and a bar that serves excellent coffee. **$$$**

Hotel Bruzón
Calle Bruzón, 217, between Pozos Dulces and Boyeros
Tel: (07) 877-5682
Basic rooms. Near the Plaza de la Revolución and convenient for the bus station, but inconvenient for the rest of the city. **$$**

Hotel Colina
Calle L between 27 and 27 de Noviembre (also called Jovellar), Vedado
Tel: (07) 334-071, 553-077, 662-065 and 836-4071
Fax: (07) 834-4104

E-mail: reservations@colina.hor.tur.cu
Good views from the higher floors, especially of the university next door. Rooms are comfortable, but aging equipment tends to fail. Noisy, but all the rooms have private bathrooms and air conditioning, and there's a great-value buffet breakfast. **$$–$$$**

Hotel St John's
Calle O, 206 between 23 and 25, Vedado
Tel: (07) 833-3740
Fax: (07) 833-3561
E-mail: reserva@stjohns2.hor.tur.cu
Budget hotel, but it is pleasant with a small rooftop pool. Well situated off La Rampa (Calle 23), a stone's throw from the Malecón. Some of the rooms have sea views. There's a quirky bar, Pico Blanco, which features a nostalgic little cabaret act. **$$**

Casas Particulares

Armando Gutiérrez
Calle 21, 62, between M and N Vedado
Tel: (07) 832-1876
mobile 0589 -25186
E-mail: abelcodina@yahoo.es

A comfortable and spacious air-conditioned room with private bath, a terrace with great views, and friendly English-speaking owners.

Casa de Aurora Ampudia
Calle 15, 58, between M and N, Vedado
Tel: (07) 832-1843
Awkward to find, on a small spur of Calle 15 off Línea, a block from the Malecón. Ask taxis for the former Japanese Embassy *(Embajada Japones antigua)* – the house is next door. Right in the heart of Vedado, it is noisy but convenient and lively. Aurora, the owner, is friendly and seems to know everyone in Havana. She warmly welcomes all visitors and loves British guests.

Casa de Luís Quintana y Mirta Miranda
Avenida de Independencia (Galiano) 408 between San Rafael and San José
Centro
Tel: (07) 863-1242
A double room in the heart of bustling Central Havana, run by a hospitable family. Meals served.

AROUND HAVANA

Miramar

Hotel Meliá Habana
Avenida 3ra, between 76 and 80, Miramar
Tel: (07) 204-8500
Fax: (07) 204-8505
E-mail: melia.habana@solmelia.com
Highly recommended large modern hotel (409 rooms, including a number of suites) offering smooth service and all-round excellence. Rooms with ocean views, five restaurants, three swimming pools, private beach, and a business center. **$$$**

Carrusel Bello Caribe
Calle 158 and Avenida 31,
Tel (07) 863-9555, 833-9906–9
Fax: (07) 833-0566
E-mail: aloja@bcaribe.cha.cyt.cu
New Cubanacán hotel by the Palacio de Convenciones. Several

bars, restaurants, and good modern facilities in general. **$$**

Chateau Miramar
Calle 1era between calles 60 and 70, Miramar
Tel: (07) 204-1953
Fax: (07) 204-0224
e-mail: eservas@chateau.cha.cyt.cu
This is promoted as a "boutique hotel", which is pushing it a bit, but it is small by Miramar standards – 97 rooms, 27 of them with sea views. And it is right by the sea. It has a saltwater pool and a good restaurant. **$$**

Hotel Comodoro
Calle 84 and 3ra, Miramar
Tel: (07) 204-5551
Fax: (07) 204-2089
E-mail: reservas@comodor.cha.cyt.cu
A resort complex that mainly deals in all-inclusive vacations. There are 371 rooms and 163 bungalows,

all airy and pleasant. Excellent swimming pool, and small private beach. Transfers three times a day to Old Havana. **$$**

Hotel Mirazul
Avenida 5ta, 3603 between 36 and 40
Tel: (07) 204-0088/5551
Fax: (07) 204-0045
E-mail: hotelmi@net.cu
A pleasant small hotel in an old mansion, with individually decorated rooms and a garden café. Restaurant, sauna, and room service 7am–midnight. No pool. Book well in advance. **$$**

Playas del Este

There are many hotels here, of which the following are only a selection; all are adequate, none is outstanding.

Hotel Club Atlántico
Avenida de las Terrazas, corner of Calle 11, Santa María del Mar
Tel: (07) 797-1085–7
Fax: (07) 796-1532
E-mail: reserva@complejo. gca.tur.cu
Bright and airy hotel on the beach with 150 air-conditioned rooms. Two pools and excellent sporting facilities. **$$$**

Hotel Blau Club Arenal
Laguna Itabo between Santa María del Mar and Boca Ciega
Tel: (07) 797-1272
Fax: (07) 797-1287
E-mail: reservas@arenal.get.tur.cu
The best of the Eastern

PRICE CATEGORIES

Price categories indicate the cost of a double room in high season:
$ = under $80
$$ = $80–150
$$$ = $150–250

Beaches' uninspiring choice of hotels, a peaceful place set on an island amid mangroves slightly back from the beach. There are 166 rooms, including 62 junior suites. Also a huge pool, pleasant gardens, and a thatched-roof bar/restaurant. Excellent value. **$$**

Villa Los Pinos
Avenida de Las Terrazas 21, between 4 and 5, Playa El Mégano, Santa María del Mar
Tel: (07) 797-1361 and 797-1269
Fax: (07) 797-1524
E-mail: reservas@complejo.gca.tur.cu
Another good choice, offering privacy in two-, three- and four-bedroom villas built in pre-revolutionary

times. Most have their own pools, and there are tennis courts on-site. **$$–$$$**

Hotel Gran Vía
Avenida 5ta, corner of 462, Guanabo, Habana del Este
Tel: (07) 796-2271 and 796-2186
Modest but airy rooms by the main road. The restaurant is adequate and inexpensive. **$**

Villa Marina Tarará
Vía Blanca Km 19
Tel: (07) 971-462
Fax: (07) 971-333, 971-500
A quiet, out-of-town hotel in a gated community (you have to sign in at the main gate) on tiny Tarará beach. Cosmopolitan atmosphere due to the number of boats (especially American)

coming and going. Accommodations in two-bedroom apartments, many of which have been renovated. There's a pleasant marina-side restaurant and bar. Pool. Cable TV. But it is out of town and sometimes hard to get taxis, especially at night. Currently used for Operación Milagro. **$**

Hotel Miramar Islazul
Avenida 9, 478, corner 7B, Guanabo
Tel: (07) 796-2507–9
Twenty-four modest but pleasant rooms, with balconies that face the sea. **$**

Villa Loma
Via Blanca Km 65, Playa Jibacoa, Santa Cruz del Norte
Tel: (0692) 85-316 and 85-343

The hotel sits on a little hill (*loma* means hill) above the beach and has good sports facilities for guests. The complex is actually a collection of bungalows, accommodating 40 people in total. Ecological trips can be arranged and it is a pleasant family place to stay. Closed during 2007. **$**

Villa Playa Hermosa
Avenida 5 and 470, Guanabo
Tel: (07) 796-2774
Thirty-three pleasant rooms in a single-story building with Spanish-style arches. There's a swimming pool, and it's not far from the beach. Cheerful atmosphere; popular with Cubans. **$**

VIÑALES AND THE WEST

Las Terrazas

Hotel la Moka
Complejo Turístico Las Terrazas, Autopista Habana–Pinar del Río, Km 51 (take this turn, then it's 8 km/5 miles farther on)
Tel: (082) 778-600–1 or (07) 204-3739 (in Havana)
Fax: (082) 778-605
E-mail: reservas@commoka.get.tur.cu
A beautiful hotel in Spanish-Cuban style in this purpose-built eco-complex. Forest trees pierce its split levels and patios. There are light, airy rooms in the main hotel, little cabins by the lake, and a few simple rooms in wooden huts in Baños de San Juan 3 km (2 miles) from the main hotel. Swim in the waterfall-fed pool, hire a bicycle, or spend time in the nearby artists' colony. **$**

Soroa

Villa Soroa
Carretera de Soroa Km 8, northwest of Candelaria
Tel: (085) 3534, 53512, 53556
Fax: (085) 53861
Forty-nine pleasant cabins and eight villas *(casitas)* with good facilities in stunning landscaped gardens, plus a large pool. The houses are well equipped with everything from kitchens to VCRs or

DVD players. There are five bars and three restaurants, one poor, one mediocre – the hilltop Castillo de Las Nubes – and one good (serving *paladar*-style food). If you want to visit and swim but don't want to stay, it's only an hour's drive from Havana, and makes a pleasant daytime excursion (there are lockers for storing clothes). **$**

San Diego de Los Baños

Islazul El Mirador
Tel: (082) 778-338
A lovely canopied hotel on a hill by a rolling river and virgin rainforest, with just 32 rooms. Serves the spa next door, which offers medical and cosmetic treatments using its volcanic, mineral-rich waters and mud. Pleasant restaurant and a pool-side barbecue area. **$**

Pinar del Río City

Hotel Pinar del Río
Calle Martí Final and Autopista, at the eastern entrance to the town
Tel: (082) 755-070–4
Fax: (082) 753-460 or 754-449
The staff are friendly, but don't expect a particularly appealing ambiance in this concrete monolith. There

are 136 rooms and 13 cabins, all fairly simple. Mediocre food and shops. The pool is popular with local people. **$**

Villa Aguas Claras
Carretera de Viñales Km 7.5, just north of Pinar del Río
Tel: (082) 778-427
Fifty pleasant cabins with private bathrooms, grouped around a swimming pool in acres of gardens and woods, including indigenous fruit trees. This is described as a *campismo*, but accommodations are comfortable. Horseback riding and hiking can be organized. **$**

Islazul Vueltabajo
Calle José Martí, 103
Tel: (082) 755-363
Renovated with 39 pleasant, air-conditioned rooms in a pastel-pink colonial mansion. **$–$$**

Viñales

Hotel La Ermita
Carretera la Ermita, Viñales, Km 2
Tel: (048) 796-071 or 833-4042
E-mail: laermita@laermita.co.cu
Just above the town of Viñales, nicely situated at the edge of the valley. La Ermita is a modern hotel of Spanish colonial design with 62 rooms ranged around a good-sized swimming pool. Some

rooms have been renovated. Balcony rooms are the nicest, but there are great views from almost all rooms, especially lovely at dawn and sunset. Decent restaurant, and a good barbecue restaurant by the pool. Tennis court. Non-guests can use the pool for a small charge. **$–$$**

Hotel Los Jazmines
Carretera Viñales, Km 25
Tel: (048) 693-6205
Fax: (048) 693-6215
A handsome, colonial-style hotel in a magnificent setting at the top of a hill above the town, with the Viñales valley unfolding beneath. Vine-draped gardens, large, deep swimming pool, periodic pool-side cabaret, children's playground, and recreation hall. There are 62 rooms in the main building and 16 cabin-style rooms in an annex – most with balconies, and offering gorgeous views. Horseback riding and other excursions available. **$–$$**

Hotel El Rancho San Vicente
Carretera Puerto Esperanza Km 33
Tel: (048) 76-201, 76-221
Fax: (048) 796-265
E-mail: rrp@sanv.co.cu
Seven km (4 miles) north of Viñales, close to the

Cueva del Indio, with 20 air-conditioned cabins in a pleasant landscaped setting. Swimming pool; spa treatments available (the algae-rich mud is said to alleviate rheumatism). Restaurant, cafeteria, bars, table games, viewing room. **$**

Cayo Levisa

Hotel Cayo Levisa
Tel: (07) 66-6075 or (07) 833-4042 in Havana
Fax: (07) 833-3161
Resort and diving center, with 40 thatch-roofed, rustic, but air-conditioned, cabins with porches, gathered beside the beach. Water sports, bar, excellent "international" and seafood restaurant; massage facilities. **$$**

María La Gorda

María La Gorda
Tel and fax: (082) 77-8131
E-mail: recepcion@mlagorda.co.cu; comercial@mlagorda.co.cu
A wonderful, small-scale resort popular with divers, in the far-western region of Cuba. It's a peaceful place, set amid semi-deciduous woodland – wake up to the sound of songbirds, and wander the 100

meters/yds to the beach. There are 55 rooms, of which the 20 newish cabins are the best option. **$–$$**

Casas Particulares

Pinar del Río

Eloina Arteaga Gonzales
Calle Isabel Rubio, 14, Apto 4, between Martí and Adela Ascuyz
Tel: (082) 5063 (neighbor)
A kind lady, whose house is right in the center of town.
Casa Pepe
Carretera Soroa Km 5
No phone
Air-conditioned room, comes highly recommended.

Viñales

There are more than 300 *casas particulares* in this little town. Most of them offer excellent food. If you get one on the south side of the main street, Calle Salvador Cisneros (left side, coming from Pinar del Río), you get great views of the *mogotes*.
Casa El Cafetal
Calle Adela Azcuy Norte, s/n
Tel: 01522-39137 or (048) 793-314 (neighbor)
A pretty house set in lush gardens. Señora Marta Martínez is an agreeable hostess.

ABOVE: Hotel Los Jazmines in Viñales for a room with a view.

Casa El Campesino
Calle Salvador Cisneros, 202-A
Tel: (048) 793-369
Just off the main road as you enter Viñales, this is a small farm, with chickens clucking on the porch and a pig tethered at the back. Host, Zenobio, will teach you how to roll a cigar. María, his wife, will provide excellent meals.
Eloy Hernández Rodríguez
Calle Salvador Cisneros, 198
Tel: (048) 793-263 (neighbor)
Quiet, pleasant house, one of the first as you enter the town, and surrounded by coconut palms.

Villa Los Reyes
Calle Rafael Trejo, 134
Tel: (048) 695-225
E-mail: yarelis@pnvinales.co.cu
The hosts, Esthelita and Yoan speak English and offer a double room in a lively house, and meals if required.
Villa Tinguillo
Calle Sergio Dopicp, 30
Tel: (048) 695-158
Set back from the main road this pleasant house offers quiet accommodation in a large twin-bedded room. Good evening meals on can be provided.

VARADERO AND MATANZAS

Varadero

Superclub Breezes Varadero
Avenida Las Américas Km 3
Tel: (045) 667-030
Fax: (045) 667-005
E-mail: reservationmanager@breezesvaradero.cyt.cu
A rather pretentious, all-inclusive resort, with 100 rooms and 170 suites. Beautiful gardens, and facilities include a gym, water sports, and a complete scuba program. Not for families. **$$$+**
Meliá Las Américas
Autopista del Sur, Km 7
Tel: (045) 667-600
Fax: (045) 667-625
E-mail: melia.las.americas@solmelia.com

Next to the Du Pont mansion (Mansión Xanadú) and beside the golf course. Has a fabulous lobby with art, palms, and colored glass, pleasant sun deck and a good stretch of beach. With 340 rooms, including suites and bungalows. **$$$+**
Meliá Varadero
Ctra. de Las Morlas
Tel: (045) 667-013
Fax: (045) 667-012
E-mail: melia.varadero@solmelia.com
Next to the shopping mall and convention center this is another hotel in the Spanish-run Meliá chain, with a spectacular seven-story spiraling atrium with parrots and trailing vines, and even glass elevators.

There are 483 rooms and seven suites, all with balconies, most with sea views. **$$$**
Paradisus Varadero
Punta Francés
Tel: (045) 668-700
Fax: (045) 668-705
E-mail: paradisus.varadero@solmelia.com
The most luxurious and expensive all-inclusive resort on the peninsula, with bungalow-style accommodations and a spacious layout. It's relatively secluded, as it's surrounded by the Reserva Ecológica. 421 suites in two-story bungalows, with sea or garden views. And there are all the facilities you would expect. **$$$+**

Sol Sirenas Coral
Avenida Las Américas and Calle K
Tel: (045) 668-070
Fax: (045) 668-076
E-mail: sol.sirenas.coral@solmelia.com
A 660-room all-inclusive upscale resort: the Sol Sirenas and the Sol Coral. Good for families. **$$$**
Arenas Doradas
Km 17 and Autopista
Tel: (045) 668-150–6
Fax: (045) 668-159
316 rooms in two-story

PRICE CATEGORIES

Price categories indicate the cost of a double room in high season:
$ = under $80
$$ = $80–150
$$$ = $150–250

chalets set in tropical gardens by the beach, east of the Sol Palmeras.

Sol Elite Palmeras
Autopista del Sur Km 8
Tel: (045) 667-009
Fax: (045) 667-209
This was Varadero's first joint venture with Spanish investors, dating from 1990. It has a slightly dated feel and a bustling, family atmosphere. There's a touch of the jungle, complete with tropical birds, in the lobby, and a thatched bar on an island in the swimming pool. This is one of Cuba's largest hotels, with 375 rooms, 32 suites, and 200 bungalows, laid out in a horseshoe shape. **$$–$$$**

Hotel Cubanacán Tuxpán
Avenida Las Américas
Tel: (045) 667-560
Fax: (045) 667-561
With 235 rooms, attractive Mexican decor (design is based on Mayan pyramids) and an informal atmosphere, the hotel is known for its fitness facilities: it has an enormous swimming pool, massage and gym, and what is claimed to be the biggest jacuzzi in the Americas – in addition, of course, to the beach. The bars, restaurants, and outdoor grill offer good food and service. **$$$**

Mansión Xanadú
Avenida Las Américas Km 8.5
Tel: (045) 668-482, 667-750, 667388
Fax: (045) 668-481
E-mail: hotelsales@cubaism.com
The swish mansion built for industrialist Irenée Du Pont in 1930, who made the peninsula effectively his own private resort when he bought up most of it in 1926. The property was nationalized after the Revolution, but retains most of its original fittings. Great for golf fans, as you get free green fees on the course it overlooks; and you've got use of the swimming pool at the neighboring Meliá Las Américas. There's an excellent bar upstairs, with a fine view of the peninsula. Restaurant

serves international cuisine (about CUC $30–50 a head including wine). Only six rooms, so book at least a month in advance. **$$$+**

Cuatro Palmas
Avenida 1era and Calle 61
Tel: (045) 66-7040
Fax: (045) 667-583
The complex consists of a hotel on the beach side of Avenida 1era, and villas across the road. The villas provide less-expensive accommodations. Both are designed with Spanish-type arcades and galleries that offset the blight of the Atabey and Siboney hotels up the hill. Helpful staff and a good atmosphere.

Gran Caribe Club Barlovento
Avenida de la Playa between calles 13 and 14
Tel: (045) 667-140
Fax: (045) 667-218
Located on the seaside promenade in downtown Varadero, the Barlovento has 171 attractive rooms and a large pool, and does a great breakfast. Convenient for downtown restaurants, cafés, and shops. **$$**

Los Delfines
Avenida 1era, between 38 and 39
Tel: (045) 667-720
Fax: (045) 667-737
www.cubahotelbookings.com
Small Islazul hotel in a colonial-style building, right on the beach in downtown Varadero. Friendly and pleasant but currently booked exclusively by an Italian tour operator. Check the website to see if it has returned to the open market. **$$**

Hotel Pullman
Avenida 1era, between 49 and 50
Tel: (045) 667-161
An attractive Islazul hotel, resembling a frosted white castle, with a pretty interior patio, and near the sea. It has a friendly atmosphere – more Cuban than most hotels in Varadero. It's small and gets booked up, so book in advance. **$$**

Super Club Puntarenas
Avenida Kawama, Final
Tel: (045) 667-120–4
Fax: (045) 667-074
E-mail: reservation@rlparad.gca.tur.cu
At the "unfashionable"

western end of the beach. The hotel, built in the early 1990s, offers accommodations in two eight-story towers: 518 rooms on the upper seven floors, above the recreational and service facilities. There are swimming pools and an enormous sun deck. **$$**

Hotel Acuazul
Avenida 1era and Calle 13
Tel: (045) 666-7132
Fax: (045) 666-7229
Located a couple of blocks from the beach. Basic, but friendly. It has a small pool, bar, and disco. **$**

Hotel Herradura
Avenida de la Playa between calles 35 and 36
Tel: (045) 613-725
Fax: (0145) 667-496
An apartment-hotel right by the sea, curved like a horseshoe. It has 78 double rooms in 33 apartments, which means that tenants share the other apartment facilities. This can be awkward if sharing with strangers, but fine if four people are traveling together. Some rooms have TVs. **$**

Hotel Dos Mares
Corner of Calle 53 and Avenida 1era
Tel: (045) 612-702
A pleasant building in Spanish *Mudéjar*-style, in downtown Varadero, one block from the beach. The Dos Mares has just 36 rooms, with two suites for families with children. It has a seafood restaurant and a solarium. Not the usual Varadero hotel. **$**

Villa Tortuga
Calle 7 between Avenida 1era and Camino del Mar
Tel: (045) 614-747
Fax: (045) 667-485
A pleasant complex of scattered villas, with 79 rooms (no TV or telephone), close to the beach. Tennis court, bicycles, mopeds, and cars for rent. Friendly staff and good food. Good value for money. **$**

Matanzas

Most visitors come to Matanzas on a day trip, either from Havana or, more often, from Varadero.

There is currently only one hotel in the town itself and that may be closing temporarily for renovation. Two more hotels are located on the road some way outside town. There are several good *casas particulares*, however; the two listed at the end of this section are recommended, but they will happily direct you to others if their rooms are occupied. Or look for the blue "anchor" signs on house doors.

Canimao Hotel
Carretera de Varadero Km 3.5
Tel: (045) 261-014
Located on a picturesque bend of the Canímar River on the road to Varadero, with rooms gathered around a swimming pool (which can be used by non-guests). Spacious lobby, with bar, comfy chairs and birds in cages. Comfortable rooms, hot water but normally there's no water at all at night (check when it's likely to go off, or shower early). There are two restaurants, a pool-side bar, and evening entertainment ranging from salsa lessons to Mr Canimao contests. **$**

Hotel Louvre
Parque de la Libertad
Tel: (045) 244-074
A crumbling old colonial mansion in the main square. Bags of atmosphere in the antique-furnished rooms. Don't rely on it being open, however, as it may be closed for much-needed renovation when you want to visit. **$**

Villa El Valle
Tel: (0145) 253-300
The hotel is 7 km (4 miles) northwest of Matanzas, in woodland in the Valle del Yumurí. It has 42 rooms, some with shared bathrooms. Swimming pool, bowling alley, gym, massage facilities, horseback riding, and lovely walks. Offers a therapy regime and workshops, but did not accept any bookings in 2007. Check before you go because it is possible it is being used for Operación MIlagro, although this is not made clear. **$**

Casas Particulares

Matanzas

Colonial Alma
Calle 83, between 290 and 292
Tel: (045) 247-810
Two rooms (one double, one triple) both with private bathrooms, in an attractive colonial house with a large terrace. Friendly host.

Breakfast and evening meal are available.
Hostal Colonial Azul
Calle 83, between 290 and 292
A near neighbor of the Colonial Alma, which shares the same telephone number. There is just one large room to rent in another atmospheric colonial house in the center of the town.

ZAPATA PENINSULA

Boca de Guamá

Villa Guamá
Laguna de Tesoro, reached by boat from La Boca de Guamá
Tel: (0459) 5155
Mosquitoes are a big problem here and the disco is very noisy, but slap on the insect repellent, and when the last tourist leaves at dusk it becomes a place of peace and loveliness. It is a replica of a pre-Columbian village, with thatched-roof *bohíos* built on wooden bridges over a lake to lodge guests. Cabins have modern amenities and there are restaurants and a pool. You can watch flocks of wild parrots descend to feed on the nectar of the bottle-brush trees. The village was Fidel Castro's idea (in the early 1960s) and he was once a regular visitor. Staff say that he always used to sleep in cabin No. 33. The establishment has been renovated. **$**

Playa Larga

Villa Playa Larga
Tel: (0459) 7206/7225
An unenthralling facility with large but basic cabins, by a small beach on the eastern edge of the village. It is popular with local people during the summer. The restaurant has a very limited menu (there's a better Palmares-run restaurant opposite) and there is little to do, though it's well placed for exploring the Zapata peninsula, which is the reason people come here. **$**

Jagüey Grande

Bohío de Don Pedro
Autopista Nacional Km 142
Tel: (0459) 2825/3224
E-mail: sistema@cienaga.var.cyt.cu
One km (½ a mile) south of the Jagüey Grande highway junction, on the road to Australia and Playa Larga. This is a small, rustic complex with large log cabins that have palm-thatched roofs. Cabins have their own bathroom, TV, fan, and fridge, and there's a small family-run restaurant (Just down the road, the state-run Finca Fiesta Campesina serves good *criollo* food.) Mosquitoes can be a problem in summer, so remember to bring repellent and cover your arms and legs at night. **$**

Playa Girón

The beach and the facilities here are much better than at Playa Larga. There is a scuba center, which offers initiation dives. The diving is superb, with sponges and red coral.
Villa Playa Girón
Tel: (0459) 4110
A beach resort with 292 rooms in rather ugly concrete cabins and a couple of equally unprepossessing blocks. But there's a pool, two bars and four restaurants, offering the usual fare; bicycles and mopeds to rent, and guides can be arranged for visits to the local area. All in all, quite a pleasant place to stay if you're not too fussy about the architecture. **$**

SANTA CLARA TO SANCTI SPÍRITUS

Corallilo

Hotel and Spa Elguea
Circuito Norte, Corallilo
Tel/fax: (0422) 686-298 and 686-292
This Islazul-run spa hotel has 99 air-conditioned rooms with bath, TV, telephone, and refrigerator. The waters, and the mud, are reputed to be a rich source of minerals, and good for all kinds of ailments. There's a pool, massage facilities, tennis courts, and motorbike rental, in case you want to get to the beach. **$$**

Embalse Hanabanilla

Hanabanilla Hotel
Southwest of Manicaragua
Tel: (0422) 204-3449 or 491-125
E-mail: concuba@enet.cu
An unappealing concrete Soviet creation, but with a breathtaking setting on Lake Hanabanilla, at the end of a 8-km (5-mile) hill, in the Escambray mountains south of Santa Clara. The lake is stocked with large-mouth bass and the hotel has its own dock and boats. There are 125 comfortable, air-conditioned rooms, a disco, well-stocked games room, 24-hour bar, and a lovely big pool. The restaurant specializes in lake-caught fish and will gladly cook and serve your catch. It's a good base for hiking, boating, and horseback riding, and there are waterfalls and caves to explore. **$–$$**

Remedios

Hotel Mascotte
Máximo Gómez, 114 (Parque Martí)
Tel: (042) 395-144
Fax: (042) 395-723
E-mail: mascotte@civc.inf.cu
A wonderful 19th-century mansion offering comfortable, no-frills accommodations, in ten airy, high-ceilinged rooms. Some rooms have French windows opening onto balconies. The food is good and there's bags of nostalgia. The only hotel in Remedios. **$–$$**

Santa Clara

Hotel Santa Clara Libre
Parque Vidal, 6
Tel: (0422) 207-548
Fax: (0422) 205-171
Fairly basic accommodations: the 159 rooms in the ten-story hotel have a shower and radio, but not all come with air conditioning. It's not a particularly attractive building, but conveniently sited on the main square, although it is not always easy to park nearby. There are good views from the top-floor restaurant (which also serves a decent breakfast), and from the rooftop bar. Rooms on the upper floors also have pretty good views. The hotel was home to Che Guevara and many of his men after the battle of Santa Clara; its facade is still pock-marked by shells fired during the 1958 battle. **$**

PRICE CATEGORIES

Price categories indicate the cost of a double room in high season:
$ = under $80
$$ = $80–150
$$$ = $150–250

Hotel Horizontes Los Caneyes
Circunvalación and Eucalypto
Tel/fax: (0422) 218-140 or
(07) 334238 (in Havana)
On the main *autopista* a mile or so west of the Che Guevara monument, this motel was designed to resemble an Amerindian settlement. The conical thatched-roof huts contain 95 comfortable, spacious rooms, with hot water, TV, refrigerators, and air conditioning. The garden setting is delightful. The pool provides the focus, with a bar, disco, and a restaurant overlooking it – the food isn't great. Those who wish to hunt can make use of the Los Caneyes hunting lodge, and bass fishing in the Alacranes dam, Cuba's second-largest reservoir. There is also a hairdresser, massage, and shops. There are buses and taxis into town, and car rental can be organized. Excellent value. **$–$$**

Hotel La Granjita
Carretera Maleza Km 2.5
Tel: (0422) 218-190
Fax: (0422) 218-149
E-mail: aloja@granjita.vcl.cyt.cu
Cubanacán's renovated villa hotel. It lies in the northeastern outskirts of Santa Clara, and has 80 rooms with balconies or terraces in thatched cabins in a garden setting, with bars, a pool, and a children's playground. **$–$$**

Cayo Santa María

Meliá Cayo Santa María
Jardines del Rey
Tel: (0422) 350500
Fax: (0422) 350505
E-mail:
melia.cayo.santa.maria@solmelia.com
Resort hotel on a developed

cay to the north of Villa Clara province, linked to the mainland by causeway, but also accessible by air. There are 360 rooms in bungalows set in 12 hectares (30 acres) of grounds by a gorgeous white beach. A choice of restaurants, buffet and à la carte, and all the usual Meliá resort facilities and services. Aerogaviota flies there from Havana for day trips. **$$$**

Sol Cayo Santa María
Tel: (0422) 351-500
Fax: (0422) 351-505
E-mail:
sol.cayo.santa.maria@solmelia.com
A smaller sister resort to the Meliá Cayo Santa Maria, offering all-inclusive deals. There are 298 rooms in two-story buildings. There is a choice of restaurants and bars, beside the pristine white beach. **$$**

Sancti Spíritus

Hotel Plaza
Parque Serafín Sánchez
Tel: (0141) 27-102
Fax: (0141) 26-940
Renovated, and now run by Cubanacán, this small former peso hotel is in the center of Sancti Spíritus. Lovely colonial architecture with a distinctive blue facade and a central garden courtyard. There are 29 large and airy rooms with bathrooms, air conditioning, and satellite TV. There's also a restaurant and a 24-hour snack bar. **$**

Hostal Rijo
Calle Honorato, 12
Tel: (0141) 285-882
A 16-room hotel in a well-restored 19th-century mansion that belonged to a

renowned local doctor, after whom it is named. Comfortable rooms, meals in a pretty courtyard, and a central location make it an ideal choice. **$–$$**

Villa Islazul Rancho Hatuey
Carretera Central, Km 384
Tel: (0141) 28-315
Fax: (0141) 28-830
A modern complex in landscaped grounds on a hill about 5 km (3 miles) north of town. Accommodations are in two-story apartments around a pool and sun deck. All rooms have TV, air conditioning, and bath. Half-board only. **$$**

Villa Los Laureles
Carretera Central, Km 383
Tel: (0141) 27-016 or 27-345
Fax: (0141) 23-915 or 23-913
A former peso hotel, run by Islazul, now accepting foreign visitors, located about 6 km (4 miles) from town. Clean and friendly; the 70 rooms have air conditioning and their own bathrooms, but there isn't always hot water available. The video bar, favored by local people, is noisy by day, the disco noisy at night. There are two restaurants, and a pool with a bar. **$**

Hotel Zaza
Embalse Zaza (southeast of Sancti Spiritus)
Tel: (0141) 28-512
Overlooking the reservoir *(embalse)*, this hotel is a bit run-down, concrete-built, and outwardly unattractive, but the staff are extremely friendly and helpful, rooms are comfortable, and there's a pool. Fishing and boating trips can be arranged here. It is sometimes busy with tour groups. **$**

Casas Particulares
Sancti Spíritus

Señora Heriberta Díaz
Adolfo del Castillo
Avenida de los Mártires, 6 and Tello S
No phone
Air-conditioned rooms in an attractive and friendly colonial home. Hot water.

Remedios

Hospedaje San Carlos
José A. Peña, 75, between Maceo and La Pastora
Tel: (042) 395-624
A friendly option, with air conditioning, a bathroom shared between two rooms, and great meals. Near the main square.

Hostal Villa Colonial
Calle Antonio Maceo, 43 between General Carrillo and Fé del Valle
Tel: (042) 396-274
An attractive house with a separate living room and entrance for guests, and a host family that could not be more helpful.

Santa Clara

The best street for *casas* is Calle Bonifacio Martínez, four-and-a-half blocks south of Parque Vidal.

Hospedaje Laura Torres
Calle Bonifacio Martínez, 4
Tel: (0422) 203481
E-mail: lauratg@correo.unam.mx
Clean and quiet.

Casa de Rosalía Reyes
Calle Bonifacio Martínez, 8
Tel: (0422) 202466
Also clean, quiet, and recommended. CUC$20.

Casa de Orlando García
Rolando Pardo 7 (half a block east of Parque Vidal)
Tel: (0422) 206761
This is another good option. Shared bathroom.

CIENFUEGOS AND TRINIDAD

Cienfuegos

Palacio Azul
Calle 37 between calles 12 and 14
Punta Gorda
Tel: (0143) 555-828/9
Only seven rooms, in a beautiful, pale-blue

neoclassical mansion built in the 1920s and converted into a hotel in 2003. Three rooms have their own balconies, with great views, and all have air conditioning, TV, and a minibar. There's also a

small restaurant. A bit isolated, but has a lot more charm than the Jagua (*see below*). Good value. **$**

Hotel Jagua
Calle 37, 1, between calles 0 and 1a, Punta Gorda
Tel: (0143) 551-003

Fax: (0143) 551-245
E-mail: reservas@jagua.co.cu
Located 3 km (2 miles) south of the heart of the city, this was once a notorious casino hotel run by Batista's brother. Externally, it's monolithic

and ugly, but the 145 large, airy rooms have air conditioning, TV, and good bathrooms. There's a large pool, but no beach, and a tacky cabaret show if you feel so inclined. $$

Hotel Boutique La Unión
Calle 21, corner of 54
Tel: (0143) 551-020
E-mail: comercial@union.cfg.cyt.cu
By far the most attractive option in town, this huge, converted mansion has interior patios, a pretty pool, and comfortable rooms with antique furnishings. Staff are friendly, too. $$
The following are all across the bay, southeast of the town and have been listed in the order in which you come to them, driving from Cienfuegos.

Rancho Luna Hotel
Carretera Rancho Luna Km 16
Tel: (0143) 548-012
Fax: (0143) 548-131
E-mail: rancholuna@ranluna.co.cu
Set on its own small beach 10 miles (16 km) southeast of Cienfuegos, Rancho Luna has motel-type cabins with a total of 222 rooms. There is a large pool and sun deck, and it looks out on to a small beach with shallow water. There is a choice of restaurants, a cafeteria, bar, medical post, and shop. Also keep-fit classes. Rancho Luna runs the car-rental agency for Cienfuegos. Usually booked by Canadian package-tour groups.$

Hotel Faro Luna
Carretera de Rancho Luna Km 18
Tel: (0143) 548-139 or 548-034
Fax: (0143) 548-062
E-mail: aloja@fluna.cfg.cyt.cu
A rather run-down Cubanacán motel by a rocky beach across the bay, with 14 terraced rooms, a pool, shop, taxis, plus a babysitting service. Again, Canadian groups are the main clients, along with those here on dive packages. $

Hotel Pascaballo
Carretera Rancho Luna Km 22
Tel: (0143) 548-013
Fax: (0143) 548-002
E-mail: director@pasacab.cfg.cyt.cu
The bluff at the mouth of the harbor, opposite the

Jagua fortress, deserves better than this rather ugly concrete block, whose 180 rooms face away from the bay. Facilities include a cafeteria, bar, saltwater pool, medical post, and shop, but no beach. The hotel is popular with Cubans in summer, and the disco draws crowds from Cienfuegos at weekends. The hotel is 25 km (15 miles) southeast of Cienfuegos. There is a ferry from the harbor downtown, and the hotel has its own boats. Otherwise the most reliable transport into town is by taxi. $

Trinidad

Iberostar Grand Hotel Trinidad
Calle José Martí y Lino Pérez (Parque Céspedes)
Tel: 34-902-995555 (bookings line in Spain)
www.gran-caribe.com
A hotel in a gorgeous renovated colonial building with a green-and-white facade. Just 36 standard rooms and four suites. Elegant and comfortable but no swimming pool or external patio. No children under 15 years old. $$$

Hotel Las Cuevas
Finca Santa Ana
Tel: (04199) 6133
Fax: (04199) 6161
E-mail: reservas@cuevas.co.cu
In a lovely spot overlooking the town. The hotel has 110 rooms in individual, simple but clean cabins, with private bath, phone, and radio. There is a swimming pool and bar, two restaurants, and a disco/nightclub with live entertainment most nights in a nearby cave – hence the hotel's name. Prefers half- or full-board. $$

Hotel La Ronda
Calle Martí, 238 (Parque Central)
Tel: (04199) 2248
E-mail: hotelsales@cubaism.com
This 100-year-old hotel has been taken over by Cubanacán, and offers budget-price basic rooms. The hotel is undergoing a building renovation, which should be complete at the end of 2007. $

Playa Ancón

Playa Ancón is 13 km (8 miles) from Trinidad. Good choice for a beach vacation but if you have only a few days in Trinidad it is preferable to stay in the town itself.

Hotel Ancón
Carretera María Aguilar
Tel/fax: (04199) 612-327
E-mail: reservas@ancon.co.cu
The three-star Ancón has undergone extensive renovation, having been badly hit by Hurricane Denis in 2005. It remains, however, a rather unattractive five-story block, albeit with a great location, right on the beach. Rooms are air-conditioned with bath and radio. There are several bars, a swimming pool, and bicycles for hire. $$

Brisas Trinidad del Mar
Península Ancón
Tel: (04199) 6500
Fax: (04199) 6565
E-mail: reservas@brisastdad.co.uk
The most attractive of the Playa Ancón establishments, this all-inclusive hotel has 240 rooms in two- and three-story houses around a central pool – and its very own bell tower. Popular with French and Dutch package-tour groups, it offers dance classes and beach volleyball. Ideal for families, with a children's program. Good water sports, including scuba lessons. Tennis court and gym. $$

Hotel Costa Sur
Playa María Aguilar
Tel: (04199) 6174
Fax: (04199) 6173
The three-star Costa Sur is smaller and cheaper than the Ancón (above), but in a similar, rather unattractive, building. However, it has its own private beach and offers scuba diving. There is a swimming pool and rifle range. The air-conditioned rooms and cabins have bathtubs and radios. $–$$

Guajimico

A resort on the coast between Cienfuegos and

Trinidad, specializing in scuba diving, with trained instructors.

Villa Guajimico
Carretera a Trinidad Km 42, Municipalidad de Cumanayagua
Tel: (0142) 540-946–7
Fifty-one small, but very attractive *bohíos* (traditional bungalows), all with private bathtubs and air conditioning, in an attractive resort. Fourteen dive sites, 10–15 minutes from shore. Scuba diving twice a day: one morning dive that returns to shore for lunch, and one afternoon dive. Dive gear available for rent. $

Casas Particulares

Cienfuegos

Armando y Leonor
Avenida 56, 2927 Altos, between 29 and 31
Tel: (0143) 516-143
E-mail: casamistad@correodecuba.cu
In a central location just off Parque José Martí, this lovely old building has a well-stocked bar, a pretty courtyard, and private bath with hot water.

Carmen y Felipe
Avenida 60, 4703 between 47 and 49
Tel: (0143) 512-885
Large, kitsch pink room with a small balcony and good bathroom. Lovely, friendly hosts serve great supper and breakfast. Good value, and very handy if you have come by bus as it's close to the bus station.

Hostal Bahía
Avenida 20, 3502 Altos, corner Calle 35, Punta Gorda
Tel: (0143) 515-263
Mobile: 528-24133
If you're going to stay in Punta Gorda this is by far the most attractive option. Located about 10 minutes' walk down the Malecón, this is a splendid old

PRICE CATEGORIES

Price categories indicate the cost of a double room in high season:
$ = under $80
$$ = $80–150
$$$ = $150–250

ABOVE: inside the Casa Colonial Muñoz in Trinidad.

colonial house right on the seafront. Two large rooms overlooking the sea. There is a patio terrace, hot water, and a well-stocked refrigerator in each room.

Trinidad

There are numerous *casas particulares* in Trinidad, some excellent, some less so, but most perfectly acceptable. If you're driving, beware of people who stop you on the approach road, telling you the road's been closed, and offering to guide you round the obstruction – it's

a scam to earn commission for finding you a room. If arriving by bus, you will find people outside the terminal offering rooms.

Araceli Reboso Miranda
Lino Pérez, 207, between País and Calzada
Tel: (04199) 3597
Two large rooms with a roof terrace. Good meals.

Casa Font
Gustavo Izquierdo, 105, between Simón Bolívar y Piro Guinart
Tel: (04199) 3683
One of Trinidad's most stylish *casas*, with crystal chandeliers and stained-glass *mamparas* (swing doors). Reserve in advance.

Casa de Carlos Zerquera
Fernándo Hernández, 54
Tel: (04199) 3634
Two excellent rooms in a beautiful colonial building dating from 1808. English and French spoken.

Casa Colonial Muñoz
Calle José Martí, 401, between Fidel Castro and Santiago Escobar
Tel: (04199) 3673
Two large double rooms in a lovely, breezy colonial house, with *mamparas*, built in 1800, right in the center of Trinidad. There's hot water, and Julio speaks English. Book in advance.

Casa López-Santander
Camilo Cienfuegos, 313, between

Jesús Menéndez and Julio Antonio Mella
Tel: (04199) 3541
Two rooms in an attractive home dating from 1916 with a porch and striking neoclassical facade. Two blocks from Plaza Santa Ana; less than 10 minutes' walk to the Plaza Mayor. Parking, and pleasant patio area.

Dr Rogelio Inchauspi Bastida
Calle Simón Bolívar, 312, between Maceo and Martí
Tel: (04199) 4107
In the house of the former Spanish Consulate. Friendly service and excellent food. Popular, so be advised to book in advance.

Hospedaje Yolanda
Piro Guinart, 227, between Izquierdo and Maceo
Tel: (04199) 3051
Nice rooms in a huge, busy house. The room on the top floor has views down to the coast. Opposite the bus station.

Hostal Julia Ramírez
Simon Bolívar, 554, between Rita María Montelier and Juan Márquez
Tel: (04199) 3485
E-mail: ch190302@hotmail.com
One room only, with private bathroom, in a fine colonial house, with antique furniture and a mango tree in the patio. Book early.

EASTERN LOWLANDS

Cayo Coco

Meliá Tryp Cayo Coco
Tel: (0133) 301-300
Fax: (0133) 301-386
E-mail: tryp.cayo.coco.@solmelia cuba.com
Modeled as a simulated colonial township, this 508-room complex is just 100 meters/yds in from a glorious white-sand beach. At the center is the airy town hall, with a colonnaded portico, tiled floors, and a central patio where the computerized reception facilities are located. Accommodations are in terracotta tile-roofed buildings of two or three stories, and named for the flower planted in front of

each one, such as *azucenas* (madonna lilies) *mariposas* (butterfly jasmine), *claveles* (pinks), and so on. Italian, continental, seafood, buffet, barbecue, and criollo specialties are served in six pleasantly designed restaurants. There are facilities for all the usual water sports. Trips offered by catamaran to outlying islands are not always well organized. **$$$**

Cayo Guillermo

Riu Villa Vigía
Tel: (0133) 301-760
Fax: (0133) 301-748
An imposing-looking all-inclusive hotel set amid gardens. **$$**

Villa Cojímar
Tel: (0133) 301-712
Fax: (0133) 301-727
E-mail: alojamiento@cojimar.gca.tur.cu
An attractive, if somewhat run-down 212-room Gran Caribe hotel consisting of bungalows set among lawns and gardens. Lovely beach and excellent diving. **$$**

Ciego de Ávila

Hotel Ciego de Ávila
Carretera de Ceballo Km 2.5
Tel: (0133) 225-772
The usual Soviet-designed monolith, run by Islazul, but with 143 air-conditioned rooms and a pool. Located 3 km (2 miles) north of the center. Popular with tour groups. **$**

Hotel Santiago-Habana
Calles Honorato Castillo and J Agüero
Tel: (0133) 227-262
A renovated former peso hotel in the center of town. 76 air-conditioned rooms with private bathrooms; those at the front have balconies. Basic but acceptable. The tiny La Cima disco attracts a local crowd at weekends. **$**

Morón

Hotel Carrusel Morón
Avenida de Tarafa
Tel: (01335) 2230 or 3901
Fax: (01335) 2133
A two-star modern hotel on the outskirts of this small, dusty town. The 144

rooms have all the usual facilities: air conditioning and private bathrooms. Suites have their own balconies. The hotel has two restaurants (including a recommended seafood restaurant), three bars, pool, tennis courts. **$**

Camagüey

Hotel Colón
Avenida República, 472
Tel/fax: (0132) 254-878
A small, elegant, if slightly jaded, colonial hotel in downtown Camagüey, with a lovely columned lobby, old wood-topped bar, and a stained-glass window picturing Christopher Columbus landing in Cuba. Rooms are simple and can be noisy, but have TV and air conditioning, and there's a decent breakfast served. **$**
Gran Hotel
Calle Maceo, 67 between Agramonte and Gómez
Tel: (1032) 292-094, 292-314
Fax: (0132) 293-933
E-mail: reservas@hgh.camaguey.cu.
A restored hotel, established in 1939 in an 18th-century mansion, right in the heart of Camagüey. Rooms surround a central patio with a fountain. The elegant Salón Caribe restaurant on the fifth floor offers the best views in town (apart from the cathedral bell tower). **$**
Hotel Horizontes Camagüey
Carretera Central Km 4.5
Tel: (0132) 287-267

Fax: (0132) 287-180
E-mail: eva@hcamaguey.hor.cu
Ten km/6 miles out of town. Rooms are shaded by arched colonnades with views over lush, quiet gardens, and have air conditioning. There is a large, pleasant pool, two restaurants, and two bars. Has been used for Operación Milagro program so check beforehand that it has re-opened. **$**
Hotel Isla de Cuba
San Esteban (Oscar Primelles) 453 and Popular
Tel: (0132) 291-515, 292-248
Centrally located budget hotel; air conditioning and private bathrooms. Good restaurant serving Cuban food. **$**
Hotel Plaza
Van Horne, 1
Tel: (0132) 282-413
A recently renovated hotel (opposite the train station), with pleasantly restored original Victorian features, a short walk from the center of town. Friendly staff. **$**

Florida

Hotel Florida
Carretera Central, Km 536
Tel: (0132) 53-011
Located 48 km (30 miles) northwest of Camagüey. Convenient if you want somewhere to stay late at night, and don't have the energy to continue to Camagüey itself. It has 74 rooms with air conditioning and private bath. Though set in pleasant gardens,

you may find the noisy pool intrusive. At weekends, the hotel is a popular spot for wedding parties from Camagüey. Accommodations are only average, but inexpensive and the staff are friendly. **$**

Santa Lucía

This resort is small so it's not hard to find any of the following places; they are all strung out along the beach. With 31 shipwrecks offshore, Santa Lucía is gaining a reputation as one of the best diving centers in Cuba. Currently catering mainly to Italian and Canadian tour groups. More developments are planned on the stretch of beach toward La Boca.
Gran Club Santa Lucía
Tel: (0132) 336-109 or 336-265
Fax: (0132) 365-153
E-mail: aloja@clubst.stl.cyt.cu
Efficient, all-inclusive villa complex with 252 rooms, set on a broad stretch of the beach. **$$**
Club Amigo Caracol
Tel: (0132) 365-158 or 336-403
Fax: (0132) 365-307
Accommodations in this renovated all-inclusive resort is in 150 bungalows, in tropical gardens, with all the usual facilities. **$$**
Club Amigo Mayanabo
Tel: (0132) 365-168
Fax: (0132) 365-176
All-inclusive hotel set 100 meters/yds from the beach, with 213 rooms and 12 suites in two blocks

between pool and beach. Quieter than the other hotels and with a somewhat older clientele. Currently being used for Operación Milagro. **$$**
Hotel Las Brisas Cuatro Vientos
Tel: (0132) 365-120
Fax: (0132) 365-142
E-mail: aloja@brisas.stl.cyt.cu
Next to the Gran Club Santa Lucía, the all-inclusive Las Brisas has 315 rooms, of which two dozen have sea views, the rest garden views. Loads of entertainment on offer, from dance classes to "theme nights," and a disco. **$$$**

Casas Particulares

Camagüey City

Alex and Yanitze
Calle Ramón Guerrero, 104, between Espinosa and Primelles
Tel: (032) 297897
A friendly and attentive couple offer a large room with a big modern bathroom. Good breakfast and evening meals.
Los Vitrales
Calle Avellaneda, 3, between Gómez and Martí
Tel: (032) 295-866
Two large rooms in a colonial house with a friendly, English-speaking host.
Milagros Sánchez
Calle Cisneros, 124, corner Raúl Lamar
Tel: (032) 29-746
Very central, rather kitsch, with a cool, tiled courtyard.

HOLGUÍN AND GRANMA

Holguín City

Hotel Pernik
Plaza de la Revolución and J Dimitrov, Reparto Pedro Díaz Cuello
Tel: (0124) 481-011, 481-081
Fax: (0124) 481-667
E-mail: reservas@hotelpernik.cu
With 200 rooms, a reasonable if unexciting restaurant, large pool and huge lobby, the four-star Pernik is the biggest and best place to stay in

Holguín. There is a car-rental desk. **$**
Mirador de Mayabe
Loma de Mayabe
Tel: (0124) 422-160, 423-485
Fax: (0124) 425-498
E-mail: mayabe@islazul.hlg.tur.cu
An attractive, Islazul-run villa in a rather isolated but attractive spot 10 km (6 miles) southeast of Holguín. Popular with honeymooners. Accommodations are in cabins scattered among

trees. There is a splendid view of the valley from the terrace pool, 2 rustic restaurant and a famous beer-drinking donkey. **$**

Mayarí

Villa Pinares de Mayarí
32 km (20 miles) south of Mayarí
Tel: (0124) 533-08 or 53-308
Sitting at 600 meters (2,000 ft) above sea level, between Holguín and Moa, this small, peaceful

complex comprises 28 log cabins in a woodland setting. There's a pleasant bar-restaurant, a swimming pool, gym, and tennis courts. Visitors can rent

PRICE CATEGORIES

Price categories indicate the cost of a double room in high season:
$ = under $80
$$ = $80–150
$$$ = $150–250

TRANSPORTATION

ACCOMMODATIONS

ACTIVITIES

A – Z

LANGUAGE

mountain bikes, and the hotel will book excursions to the Mensura National Park, which is excellent for hiking and birding. **$$**

Guardalavaca/ Playa Esmeralda

As in Santa Lucía, the hotels in Guardalavaca are all strung out in a line along the beach. You won't have any trouble finding them.

Atlántico Guardalavaca
This encompasses four separate sections, including the Hotel Guardalavaca and Bungalows Villa Turey (both set back from the beach), and Villas and Hotel Atlántico set on the beach, which are the better options.
Tel: (0124) 30-180
Fax: (0124) 30-200
E-mail: comercial@clubamigo.gvc.cyt.cu
or ventas@clubamigo.gvc.cyt.cu
The Atlántico Guardalavaca itself is a Cubanacán-run resort hotel in the center of Guardalavaca, complete with diving center. **$$$**

Bungalows Villa Turey
Tel: (0124) 30-195
Fax: (0124) 30-444
E-mail: comercial@clubamigo.gvc.cyt.cu
Part of the Hotel Guardalavaca complex offering accommodations in small villas. **$$$**

Hotel Guardalavaca
Reservations through the central agency.
Tel: (0124) 30-121
Fax: (0124) 30-265
E-mail: rpublic@clubamigo.gvc.cyt.cu
The hotel, run by Cubanacán, consists of a moderately priced, conventional hotel (with 225 rooms) and a clutch of budget *cabañas* down the road. **$$$**

Las Brisas Guardalavaca Resort
Tel: (0124) 30-218
Fax: (0124) 30-162
E-mail: reserva@brisas.gvc.cyt.cu
Probably the best of Guardalavaca's resorts, comprising hotel and villas, with 230 rooms in the hotel and 200 in the villas. The hotel part is popular with honeymoon couples, the villas with families. The

hotel section is more lively, but ask for rooms away from the disco. Good facilities, including water-sports center, pool, disco, tennis courts, bicycles for hire, and several restaurants and bars. **$$$+**

Paradisus Río de Oro
Tel: (0124) 30-090
Fax: (0124) 30-095
Email: jefe.ventas.pro
@solmeliacuba.com
One of Cuba's most luxurious resorts and the best hotel in the Guardalavaca/Playa Esmeralda area. All-inclusive, tasteful, and expensive. **$$$+**

Villa Don Lino
Playa Blanca, 8 km (5 miles) north of Rafael Freyre and about 24 km (15 miles) west of Guardalavaca
Tel: (0124) 30-310, 30-259, 30-307
Simple cabins overlooking a small beach, with Playa Blanca beach nearby. There's also a saltwater pool and a restaurant. Fine for a spot of isolation. **$**

Sol Río de Luna y Mares
Playa Esmeralda
Tel: (0124) 30-030
Fax: (0124) 30-035
E-mail: sol.rio.luna.mares@
solmelia.com.
A large (445-room) hotel, set in gardens in the Marine Park Bahía de Navajo, with excellent facilities, particularly for water sports, and several good restaurants. **$$$+**

Cayo Saetía

Villa Gaviota Cayo Saetía
Tel: (0124) 96-900, 96-957
A secluded resort on a pristine beach. There's a great variety of flora and fauna in the area. The hotel offers snorkeling, jeep safaris, and horseback riding. **$$**

Bayamo

Hotel Royalton
Calle Maceo, 53
Tel: (0123) 422-224, 422-268
Fax: (0123) 424-792
E-mail: hroyalton@islazul.grm.tur.cu
A small hotel, built in the 1940s in traditional style, right on the main square. Just 33 rooms (including

three suites and one ground-floor room with special facilities for the disabled). No-frills rooms, but all with air conditioning and private bath. The hotel offers accompanied tours to the Sierra Maestra mountains. **$**

Villa Bayamo
Carretera de Manzanillo Km 5.5
Tel: (0123) 423-102
Fax: (0123) 424-485
A good, inexpensive choice if you don't mind being slightly out of town. This attractive hotel, in a former holiday center for the military, has a garden and a nice pool. **$**

Manzanillo

Guacanayabo
Avenida Camilo Cienfuegos, southwest of the town center
Tel: (0123) 54-012
Fax: (0123) 34-139
Yet another Soviet-inspired concrete nightmare, with 112 rooms, but at least it has a pool and a spectacular hill-top view of the fishing port. **$**

Marea del Portillo

This is a dark-sand beach on the south coast, with two hotels that are part of the same resort, catering for package tour clientele. All-inclusive deals, with facilities for horseback riding and hiking in the mountains, diving, sport-fishing, boat trips, etc. Cars and mopeds can be rented and there is plenty of evening entertainment.

Hotel Farallón del Caribe
Tel: (0123) 597-008–9, 597-080–4
E-mail: comercial@hfarcar.cyt.cu
This excellent, 140-room resort hotel, set a couple of hundred meters/yards back from the beach, is the more luxurious and expensive of the two hotels here. Owned by Cubanacán, it is popular with Canadian tourists. Lovely views of the mountains. All-inclusive. **$$**

Hotel Marea del Portillo
Tel: (0123) 594-201–3, 594-004
Fax: (0123) 594-134
E-mail: comercial@hfarcar.cyt.cu

Somewhat run-down, but right on the beach, this low-key 70-room facility built in the 1980s has had more bungalows added recently. All-inclusive. **$$**

Chivirico

The following is an all-inclusive resort that's a good place to get away from it all.

Brisas Sierra Mar Los Galeones
Playa Sevilla, 65 km (40 miles) west of Santiago de Cuba, 12 km (8 miles) east of Chivirico
Tel: (0122) 29-110 and 2-115
Fax: (0122) 29-116
Inaugurated in 1994 by Fidel Castro himself, this four-star Andalusian-style resort is located on a lovely (man-made) sandy beach at the foot of the Sierra Maestra mountains. It used to be two separate resorts, one large, one small, but has become one, with 234 rooms in total, some in bungalows. A variety of eateries, including a vegetarian restaurant; fitness center, shopping mall, freshwater pool, art gallery, games room, video room, disco, and cabaret cover most needs on the spot. There are lots of water sports on offer, as well as tennis and volleyball, and a golf course nearby. There are dance classes and Spanish classes, and a special children's program, too. **$$**

Casas Particulares

Holguín

Oneida Parra
Calle Miró, 56 between Arias and Aguilera
Tel: (0124) 424-255
Right in the center of the city; inexpensive and with air conditioning.

Sr Evaristo Bofill and Sra Mirtha Lago
Calle Luz Caballero, 78, between Miró and Morales Lemus
Tel: (0124) 427-097
A large apartment and a spacious room, both with balconies, only two blocks from Parque Peralta. Hospitable couple, but they don't serve meals.

Villa Liba
Calle Maceo, 46
Tel: (0124) 423-823
Air-conditioned triple rooms with private bathrooms; 250 meters/yds from the Loma de la Cruz. Patio.

Bayamo

Sra Dolores Marson Sosa
Pío Rosado, 171, between Capote and Parada

Tel: (0123) 422-974
The accommodations come highly recommended.

Gibara

Hostal Vitral
Calle Independencia, 36
Tel: (0124) 34-469
Superb, clean colonial house; all of the rooms come with private bathrooms. This is

considered to be one of the best *casas particulares* in Cuba. Reserve in advance to avoid disappointment.

La Casa de los Amigos
Calle Céspedes, 15, between Peralta and Luz Caballeros
Tel: (0124) 34-115
E-mail: lacasadelosamigos@yahoo.fr.
Modern and stylish with a big courtyard; French cooking and French spoken.

Manzanillo

Montell's House
Mártires de Viet-Nam, 49, between Caridad and San Silvestre
Tel: (0123) 55-332
A welcoming place on the Celia Sánchez memorial staircase. Adrián and Tonia are helpful and the rooms are well-appointed and comfortable. A great roof terrace for views of the bay.

SANTIAGO DE CUBA

Balcón del Caribe
Carretera del Morro, Km 7
Tel: (0122) 691-011 and 691-506
In a nice spot by the sea next to Santiago's Morro Castle, 10 km (6 miles) from the center of town. The hotel, with 72 rooms and 24 *cabañas*, is largely unmodernized but has a pleasant atmosphere, and there's a little cabaret. It is handy for the airport, but it's also under the flight path. **$**

Hotel Casa Granda
Parque Céspedes
Tel: (0122) 686-600 and 653-021
Fax: (0122) 686-035
E-mail: recep@casagran.gca.tur.cu
Overlooking the main square, this landmark hotel is Santiago's nicest. Built in

1914, it has been completely renovated. The interior is splendidly grand, with suites decked out in golden silk. There is a broad terrace bar overlooking the square. The fifth-floor bar offers fine views over downtown Santiago, and is great at sunset. **$$**

Gran Hotel Escuela
Corner J.A. Saco and Hartmann
Tel: (0122) 653-020/653-028
E-mail: gh@ehtsc.co.cu
Clean, central, and cozy. The 15 rooms are plain but quite large. The *escuela* in the name means that it is a hotel school where tourism students train – as they are usually enthusiastic,

the service, and the food, are usually very good. **$**

Las Américas
Avenida de las Américas and General Cebreco
Tel: (0122) 642-011, 687-225–6
Fax: (0122) 687-075
E-mail: jcarpeta@hamerica.hor.tur.cu
Opposite high-rise Santiago de Cuba, Las Américas has 68 rooms. Its restaurant is mediocre and the pool is small, but there's usually a pleasant, buzzing atmosphere; the cabaret is popular. **$**

Imperial
J.A. Saco, 251
Tel: (0122) 627-710
A couple of blocks north of Parque Céspedes, this former peso hotel has 47 basic, fan-cooled rooms. **$**

El Rancho
Alturas de Quintero, Km 4.5
Tel: (0122) 633-280
Located near the university, about 5 km (3 miles) north of the city center, El Rancho has 30 very pleasant *cabañas* and there is a magnificent view from the thatched-roof restaurant. **$**

Hotel Libertad
Aguilera, s/n, between Serafín Sánchez and Pérez Carbó, on Plaza de Marte
Tel: (0122) 628-360
E-mail: reservas@libertad.dstgo.islazu.tur.cu
Hotel with a total of 40 air-conditioned rooms with private bathtubs and satellite TV, unfortunately only half of the rooms have windows. There's a bar and small restaurant, which serves food that is not too bad by Santiago standards. **$**

Hotel Meliá Santiago de Cuba
Avenida de las Américas and Calle M
Tel: (0122) 687-070
Fax: (0122) 687-170
E-mail: melia.santiago.de.cuba@solmelia.com
Spectacular red, white, and blue modern building with glass-front lifts, but rather soulless inside. With 270 spacious rooms, 34 suites and a conference room, it's popular with business guests. Four restaurants, three pools and a lavish cabaret/nightclub. **$$**

Hotel Carrusel Versalles
Alturas de Versalles, Km 1
Tel: (0122) 691-504 and 686-245
Fax: (0122) 686-039
E-mail: comercial@versall.scu.cyt.cu
Just outside the city, a pink and white stuccoed gingerbread house of a hotel in lush gardens. There are 61 rooms and one suite, all with garden views from their balconies. Air conditioning, satellite TV, two restaurants, two cafés, two bars, large pool and separate children's pool, nightclub, and sporting facilities. **$$**

Villa Gaviota
Avenida Manduley, 502 and Calle 19, Vista Alegre
Tel: (0122) 641-346, 641-370, 641-598
Fax: (0122) 687-218
E-mail: reserva@gaviota.co.cu
A complex of 47 rooms in

BELOW: the Casa Granda, Santiago's loveliest hotel.

PRICE CATEGORIES

Price categories indicate the cost of a double room in high season:
$ = under $80
$$ = $80–150
$$$ = $150–250

13 well-designed villas in the quiet, leafy district of Vista Alegre, not far from the Meliá Santiago and Las Américas hotels. Visitors can rent just one bedroom or a complete house. There is a swimming pool up the road for the use of residents. **$**

Hotel San Juan
Carretera de Siboney, Km 1.5
Reparto Vista Alegre
Tel: (0122) 687-200–1
Fax: (0122) 687-017
E-mail: jcarpeta@sanjuan.co.cu
On the outskirts of town, 3.5 km (2 miles) from Parque Céspedes, this motel is set in lush gardens on historic San Juan Hill – the scene of the final battle in the War of Independence. Pleasant rooms, good restaurant,

large swimming pool, shallow pool for children. **$–$$**

Hostal San Basilio
Calle Masó 403, between Rosado and Valiente
Tel: (0122) 651-702
Santiago's only "boutique" hotel, this pretty, pastel-green place is very close to Parque Céspedes. It takes its name from the old name of the street (and one that many people still use). Just eight rooms with air conditioning and TV. There's a restaurant on site. **$$**

Casas Particulares

Dr Armando Carballo Fernández
Calle San Félix (Hartmann), 306, between Havana and Trinidad

Tel: (0122) 628-643, 624-961 (neighbors)
A whole family of kind and friendly doctors own this house right in the center of the city. Accommodation has private bathroom; air conditioning.

Adela Díaz
Calle Heredia, 374, corner of Reloj
Tel: (0122) 652-696
A very central house offering a large room with refrigerator, fan, air conditioning, and separate private bathroom; and an extremely friendly, hospitable hostess; plus there's parking nearby on Plaza de Dolores, for a small daily fee.

Casa Mundo Raimundo Ocaña y Bertha Peña
Calle Heredia, 308, between Pío Rosado and Porfirio Valiente

Tel: (0122) 624-097
E-mail: co8kz@yahoo.es
Two rooms with small private bathrooms and air conditioning in a nice old house which also has a pleasant little patio. Evening meals are available upon request. Very central location, close to the Casa de la Trova and other music venues.

Dulce María Rodríguez Corominas
Calle Masó (San Basilio) 507, between Reloj and Clarín
Tel: (0122) 623-016
Another good, centrally located choice. Just one spotlessly clean, air-conditioned room to rent, which has a double bed, private bathroom, and a very agreeable and helpful hostess.

AROUND SANTIAGO DE CUBA

Gran Piedra

Hotel Villa Gran Piedra
Tel: (0122) 686-147 and 651-205
An "eco-lodge" with comfortable rustic cabins set along the edge of the mountain ridge (*gran piedra* means large rock). The views are absolutely wonderful when the weather is fine. There is also a café, a restaurant, and a souvenir shop on the road beneath the rock. Has been used for

Operación Milagro in the past but should be open to guests. **$–$$**

Hotel Carrusel El Saltón
Carretera a Filé, Contramaestre
Reservations through
www.cubahotelbookings.com
Northwest of El Cobre, deep in the Sierra Maestra. There are 22 rooms in wooden cabins set by a mountain lake fed by waterfalls. Originally an anti-stress center, still offering sauna and massage facilities. You

can take jeep trips to Saltón from Santiago. **$**

Guantánamo

Hotel Guantánamo
Calle 13 Norte, between Ahogados and 1 Oeste
Tel: (0121) 381-015, 381-025, 381045
Fax: (0121) 382406
The standard provincial monstrosity, run by Islazul, overlooking Plaza Marina Grajales. Has 124 rooms with good facilities that are

at least comfortable and inexpensive, plus 24-hour café, two restaurants, and a pool. Helpful at arranging excursions. **$**

Hotel Caimanera
Caimanera, Guantánamo Bay
Bookings only by e-mail:
hotelsales@cubaism.com
A perfectly adequate hotel but off the beaten track. It usually only takes small groups and is only interesting if you want an arranged trip for a view of the base. **$**

THE FAR EAST

Baracoa

Hotel El Castillo
Calixto García, s/n, Loma el Paraíso
Tel: (0121) 644-165
Fax: (0121) 645-223
E-mail: castillo@enet.cu
High on a cliff overlooking the town, this was one of Baracoa's three castles, built in 1770 to keep the British out. It later became a prison. It is hard to resist staying here: it has just 34 air-conditioned rooms, a gorgeous pool with a barbecue bar, lovely gardens, and an excellent

restaurant; and offers the best views of the town and El Yunque mountain. Great value. Reached by a steep flight of steps or curving drive. **$**

Hostal La Habanera
Maceo, 68, corner of Frank País
Tel: (0121) 645-273, 645-225
This ten-room hotel with an ochre-facade in the center of town has recently been taken over by Cubanacán and well-renovated. It is spruce, there's cable TV and air conditioning in the rooms, and the beds are comfy. Can be noisy at

night as the Casa de Cultura next door has loud music – but it's very atmospheric. **$**

Hotel Porto Santo
Carretera del Aeropuerto
Tel: (0121) 645-105, 645-106
Fax: (0121) 645-223
E-mail: reservasps@gavbcoa.co.cu
Three km (2 miles) from town, close to the airport. Beautiful location on a terraced hill with lush foliage, birds, and steps leading down to a small private beach across the harbor from Baracoa. With 60 rooms and three suites,

and a small but pleasant pool. Car and moped rental. **$**

Hotel La Rusa
Máximo Gómez, 161
Tel: (0121) 643-011
Fax: (0121) 642-337
An aristocratic Russian who fled the revolution in her own country and lived to see another on her adopted island, founded this 12-room hostelry near the waterfront. Now run by Cabanacán, the low-rise yellow-painted La Rusa is popular with independent travelers. **$**

Villa Maguana
Carretera a Moa
Tel: (0121) 645-165, 645-106
A lonely but beautiful villa with just four rooms by a spectacular white-sand private beach, 20 km (12 miles) north of Baracoa. There is a restaurant and a barbecue. The renovated villa belongs to the Gaviota chain (like the Hotel El Castillo).**$**

Casas Particulares

There are plenty of *casas particulares* in Baracoa, and most of them serve excellent evening meals with a Baracoa flavor – which means lots of fish and sometimes a coconut sauce. Among the best are:
Casa Colonial El Mirador
Calle Maceo 86 between 24 de Febrero and 10 de Octubre

Tel: (0121) 642-647
E-mail: joan@toa.gtm.sld.cu
Run by Antonio and Iliana, this is a hospitable, airy house with a balcony overlooking town, close to the main square. Antonio speaks good English.
Carmen Vernier Rodríguez
Calle Martí, 98, between 10 de Octubre and 24 de Febrero
Guantánamo
Tel. (0121) 645-31
A quiet colonial house in the center of Baracoa on one of the two main streets.
Isabel Castro Vilato
Calle Mariana Grajales, 35
Tel. (0121) 642-267
An agreeable hostess and a nice colonial house with a garden. If Isabel has no room available she will recommend someone else who may be able to accommodate you.

ABOVE: El Castillo's pool area and gardens, in Baracoa.

SOUTHERN ISLANDS

Isla de la Juventud

Hotel Colony
Carretera de Siguanea, Km 46
Tel: (0146) 398-181–2
Fax: (0146) 398-420
E-mail: reservas@colony.co.cu
On the southwest coast, 42 km (26 miles) from Nueva Gerona. Facilities are good and improvements and renovations are underway. There are around 80 air-conditioned rooms, some in cabins. The only reason to come to this hotel, which is miles from anywhere and surrounded by swamp and mangrove, is to dive. There is some of the best diving in Cuba here (if not the best) and the beach is pleasant (but bring insect repellent). There's an international scuba center, and the hotel also provides diving packages. There is also an international marina, which provides deep-sea fishing trips. **$$**
Hotel Rancho
Carretera La Fé, Km 3, on the way to the airport, less than 3 km (2 miles) south of Nueva Gerona
Tel: (0146) 323-035
Fax: (0146) 323-657

Refurbished in colonial style. Rooms set around a courtyard with a fountain and vines hanging from wooden beams. Hot water and air conditioning; pool and restaurant. **$$**
Villa Gaviota
Autopista Gerona–La Fé, Km 1.5
Tel: (0146) 323-256
Fax: (0146) 323-657
The complex has 20 rooms in modern bungalows, a decent swimming pool and views. A salsa band plays in the afternoons and evenings. **$**

Cayo Largo

All the hotels on the island flank the beach on the south side of the island. Reservations are best made as part of an inclusive package from the mainland.
Hotel Barceló
Tel: (0145) 248-080
Fax: (0145) 248-088
E-mail: reservabarcelo@cayolargo.co.cu
A large resort complex that opened in 2004, with 306 rooms in the main hotel building and bungalows. All-inclusive packages.
$$–$$$

Hotel Isla del Sur y Complejo de Villas
Tel: (0145) 248-160, 248-111
Fax: (0145) 248-201
E-mail: reserva@isla.cls.tur.cu
Includes the Hotel Isla del Sur and three villa complexes: Villa Soledad, Villa Coral, and Villa Lindamar. All inclusive.
$$–$$$
Sol Club Cayo Largo
Tel: (0145) 248-60
Fax: (0145) 248-265
E-mail: jefe.reservas.scl @solmeliacuba.com
This four-star, all-inclusive hotel is right on the beach. Water sports, nightly cabaret, sauna, Jacuzzi, massage, gym, scuba center, children's facilities, honeymoon specials. **$$$**
Sol Pelícano
Playa Lindamar
Tel/fax: (0145) 248-333
E-mail: jefe.reservas.spl @solmeliacuba.com
Good family hotel. All-inclusive. **$$–$$$**

Casas Particulares

Isla de la Juventud

Odalis Peña Fernández
Calle 10, 3710, between 37 and

39, Nueva Gerona
Tel: (0146) 322-345
Friendly place, with good home cooking, Odalis knows a lot about the island and can make suggestions for unusual excursions or find transport.
Joel Díaz Prout
Calle 49, 2214, between 22 and 24, Nueva Gerona, No phone
Very friendly, with an airy balcony.
Maggie
Calle 39, 816, between 8 and 10
Three blocks north of the Hotel Cubana. Comfortable house.
Nora Rodríguez
Calle 8, 4932, between 49 and 53
Tel: (0146) 321-722
Unpretentious room with its own entrance and private bathroom in the house of loud and friendly Nora, 10 minutes' walk from center. Huge meals available.

PRICE CATEGORIES

Price categories indicate the cost of a double room in high season:
$ = under $80
$$ = $80–150
$$$ = $150–250

A CTIVITIES

THE ARTS, FESTIVALS, NIGHTLIFE, SHOPPING AND SPORTS

THE ARTS

Museums

The colonial mansions and public buildings clustered around the historic centers of Cuba's older cities are now mostly museums. Whatever their theme, they are often worth seeing for the beauty of the buildings themselves.

The main museums in tourist centers charge an admission fee of 1–3 CUCs, but the cost is higher in some of Havana's top attractions, such as both branches of the Museo de Bellas Artes (although a combined ticket is available), and the Museo de la Revolución.

Exhibits are generally labeled in Spanish, though sometimes shortened notes are given in English. The most popular museums usually have at least one guide who speaks English and sometimes French.

Opening hours are notoriously erratic, and buildings can be closed for renovation work. Many museums close on Monday or Tuesday, and some open only for the afternoon on Sunday – the current opening times of all the major museums are given in the main text.

Music

Cubans are crazy about music. It blares from every window and accompanies every activity. Rumba, son and its derivative salsa, trova ballads and nueva trova political songs, jazz, country and classical can be heard and seen on TV, along with modern, US-influenced rap and hip-hop, especially popular with younger Cubans. There is always some group performing live, but sadly many are obliged to play for tourists in their hotels rather than in local nightspots.

One Saturday of each month (usually the third, but check when you visit) the **Noche Plaza** is held in Havana's Plaza de la Catedral. It's a fantastic festival of music, song and dance which brings in musicians from across the island, and occasionally beyond. You can't miss them – just follow the crowds.

Son, bolero and **salsa** are everywhere, but never better than at the Casa de la Cultura de La Habana Vieja at Calle Aguiar, 509 (see Nightlife, page 358).

Most of the bars and tabernas of Old Havana feature live (some-times residential) bands (see Nightlife, pages 357–9).

Jazz has deep roots and Cuban musicians are creative interpreters. The genre is at its most exciting when the best Cuban and international jazz musicians gather in the capital for the Havana International Jazz Festival in late November to early December (see Festivals, page 357).

The national **opera** company is based at the Gran Teatro, off the Parque Central. Performances are posted on notices on the columns outside, or call the theater, tel: (07) 861-3077 and (07) 552-946.

With fantastic acoustics, the church of **San Francisco de Asís** in Plaza San Francisco is a great venue for classical music. Tickets are available from the venue and recitals are usually held at 5pm or 6pm.

Dance

Cubans dance from the moment they can walk and, to Westerners, it seems they all have an innate rhythm, impeccable footwork and the endless energy expected of a pro. Perhaps that is why Cuba's professional groups are so good, and have become internationally recognized.

Afro-Cuban Dance

Now internationally renowned, **Clave y Guaguancó** was founded to keep Afro-Cuban dance and music alive, concentrating mainly on rumba, son and danzón. They sometimes perform in Callejón de Hamel (between Aramburo and Hospital, Centro Habana) on Sunday noon–3pm.

Art in Havana

In terms of art treasures in Cuba, Havana has the lion's share – in particular at the Arte Cubano section of the **Museo Nacional de Bellas Artes** (see page 160) which has the most representative collection of 20th-century Cuban art. The **Casa de las Américas** at Avenida 3era and Calle G, Vedado, has an interesting collection of Latin-American art, and the **Galería Habana**, Linea, 460, between calles E and F, Vedado has lively and well-displayed Cuban contemporary works. **Galería UNEAC**, Calle 17 corner of Calle H, Vedado, has exhibits by contemporary Cuban artists (in official favor). **Calle Obispo** in Old Havana is home to a number of galleries/sale rooms for contemporary art. Others are dotted all around the old town.

For information on buying contemporary art and taking it out of the country, see Export Procedures on pages 360–1.

Clave y Guaguancó give live open-air performances every other Wednesday from 5pm, at the Hurón Azul, UNEAC, calles 17 and H, Vedado; at El Palenque, Calzada and 4 Vedado Saturday 2pm; and at El Callejón, Hamel, Centro Habana, Sunday noon–3pm.

The **Conjunto Folklórico Nacional de Cuba** (Calle 4, 103, between Calzada and 5ta, Vedado, tel: (07) 830-3939, 830-3060, 831-3467) hosts rumba performances on the patio every Saturday. The box office opens at 2pm on Saturday before the 3pm performance; there is often a line, so you need to be there early. You can also book a course of dance lessons here (same numbers as above, or go in person).

Tango

Tango is not indigenous to Cuba, of course, but it can be found here. The best place for tango classes and some excellent performances is Caserón del Tango, Calle Jústiz, 21, between Baratillo and Oficios, tel: (07) 861-0822. It's a lovely colonial mansion near Plaza de Armas in Old Havana, where a multitude of tango-based activities run by the National Association for the Promotion of Tango take place.

Ballet

The **National Ballet of Cuba**, currently directed by Alicia Alonso, is world-famous for its fluid grace. The company is often on tour, nationally and abroad, but when they are at home they perform at the **Gran Teatro**, Paseo de Martí, 458, corner San Rafael (Parque Central), tel: (07) 861-3077/78; or the **Teatro Nacional de Cuba**, Paseo and Calle 39 (Plaza de la Revolución), tel: (07) 879-6011. The company's ballet school is based at the Gran Teatro, and during the day you can see the young students rehearsing (also see Festivals below).

The **Museo De La Danza** covers all aspects of the history of dance with special emphasis on ballet. It is at Línea, 365 and G, Vedado, housed in an elegant building that is worth a visit in itself. Open Tues–Sat 11am–6.30pm.

Modern Dance

Cuba's impressive **Contemporary Dance Company** (Danza Contemporánea de Cuba) performs both avant-garde and traditional choreography. Its base is the **Teatro Nacional de Cuba**, Calle Paseo and 39 (Plaza de la Revolución).

Cinema

Both Cuban and foreign films run in public movie houses. Most overseas films tend to be at least a couple of years old, often more. Movies are often put on only at weekends or on selected evenings – other than in the main cinemas in Havana, such as those in Vedado, including the Yara, opposite the Habana Libre, and the Charles Chaplin, farther along Calle 23. These same cinemas tend to show the pick of the films during the annual **New Latin-American Film Festival**, which is held in the first two weeks of December and draws stars, directors, critics and film buffs from around the world. In 2008 the festival will have been running for 30 years. The Teatro Karl Marx is the venue for some high-profile screenings.

Theater

Café Teatro Bertold Brecht, Calle 13 and I (near Línea), tel: (07) 329359. Stages satirical comedy that pokes gentle fun at the system; very popular, there is always a long line. Tuesday 8.30pm.

Teatro Guiñol, calles M and 19, Vedado, tel: (07) 832-6262, stages contemporary youth theater.

Teatro Nacional de Cuba, Paseo and Calle 39 (Plaza de la Revolución), tel: (07) 879-6011. There are three auditoria, where experimental and children's theater is staged, as well as ballet performances.

Festivals

In addition to the festivals mentioned above, all Cuban provinces celebrate a **Culture Week** (Semana Cultural) once a year, with music, dance, arts and crafts and local culinary traditions.

Havana International Jazz Festival in late November to early December, has been running since 1978, organized by Chucho Valdés. The festival is based in the Teatro Nacional de Cuba but venues include the Teatro Amadeo Roldán and Teatro Karl Marx, where major performances take place, and there are impromptu performances along the Malecón.

The **International Ballet Festival** in the first 10 days of November has been running since 1986, and draws companies from Cuba and abroad. Most performances are held in the

Gran Teatro or the Teatro Nacional but there are various other venues.

During the **Varadero International Music Festival** in November, operatic and choral groups and the National Symphony Orchestra play with visiting ensembles.

Havana now holds its **carnival** in August – dates have changed over the years. It was moved from February (the traditional month) to November to coincide with the anniversary of the foundation of the city. The venue is the Malecón, where flamboyant parades are held throughout the day and night.

Santiago de Cuba holds a lively carnival in late July. Again, not the traditional pre-Lent celebration, but one that grew out of traditional summer festivals. Varadero has a less spirited festival, with tourist participation, in January and February.

At all these events, popular Cuban bands often play for free, and there are fairgrounds and attractions. For most Cubans, though, the food fairs at which basic staples like rice and bananas are sold from the back of trucks at very low prices are the main attraction.

The **comparsas** or street dances of Cuba's carnivals are as colorful and symbolic as the floats. In Havana and Santiago, neighborhood comparsa groups have rehearsals at least once a week during the year, and you may be lucky enough to come across one in full flow.

A less well-known festival, **Las Parrandas**, takes place in certain towns and villages of Villa Clara province, in the week between Christmas and New Year – most famously at Remedios. For a description of this wild and colorful event, see page 242.

see page 242.

NIGHTLIFE

Every hotel in Cuba has one or more bars and many also have programmed entertainment at night, often focused around the swimming pool; this may come in the form of anything from salsa classes to silly competitions. Most large hotels have their own disco and cabaret.

If you want to be more adventurous, ask around for the best local peña, disco or cabaret, where you will be able to pay in pesos and drink rum and dance alongside the locals. Local discos are obviously at their liveliest at weekends, but don't normally get going until 11pm or even later.

TRANSPORTATION

ACCOMMODATIONS

ACTIVITIES

A – Z

LANGUAGE

What's On

Havana's nightlife scene is constantly changing. It is well worth asking in music stores, and asking waiters and taxi drivers, for venues. The weekly magazine *Carteleras* (free in most hotels) has a reliable "what's on" section. *Guía La Habana* (also free) is a monthly publication that may also be useful. The list below offers a selection of venues.

The beach resort of Varadero has abundant discos and night-time shows and cabarets, but you will find by far Cuba's best and most varied nightlife in Havana.

1830
Malecón, 1252, right by the Miramar tunnel
Tel: (07) 55-3090
Outdoor dancing to live music. Expensive. Open 10pm–2am.

Atelier
Calle 17, corner of Calle 6, Vedado
Tel: (07) 830-6808
Recently refurbished basement club. Daily 10pm–4am. Shows start at 11.30pm, followed by a disco.

Casa de la Amistad
Paseo 406, between 17 and 19, Vedado
Tel: (07) 830-3114–15
Music in the evenings, usually *son*. The best nights are Tuesday and Saturday. Mon–Fri 11am–midnight. Sat till 2am. Sunday afternoon.

Cabaret Parisién
Hotel Nacional, calles 21 and 0
Tel: (07) 333564
If you can't be bothered to trek to the Tropicana, this show in the Nacional is the best alternative. Open Fri–Wed 9pm–2.30am; show starts at 10pm.

Café Cantante Mi Habana
Teatro Nacional, Paseo and 39, Plaza de la Revolución
Tel: (07) 879-0710
The program varies: sometimes disco, live music of all kinds (usually at the weekend), or stand-up (in rapid Spanish). Afternoon and evening performances. It's a small, lively basement venue and quickly fills up. Open daily till 5am.

Café de Paris
Calle San Ignacio, 202, corner of Obispo
Live and lively music every night.

Café Taberna "Amigos del Benny"
Calle Mercaderes, 531 and Teniente Rey (Brasil)
Tel: (07) 861-1637.
A restaurant and bar, with live music from 8pm – good-quality *son* and mambo.

Casa de la Cultura de La Habana Vieja
Calle Aguiar, 509, between Amargura and Brasil (Teniente Rey)
Tel: (07) 863-4860
Starting around 8pm, nightly performances are held either in the lovely theater or outdoors in the churchyard. Large crowds, mostly local people, gather to listen – the atmosphere is enchanting.

Casa de la Música
Avenida de Italia (Galiano), between Neptuno and Concordia, Centro Habana
Tel: (07) 862-4165
Salsa, *songo* and rock bands. There are matinee slots for young up-and-coming bands and prime evening slots for the big guns, when you can pay CUC$20 or more for a ticket (but usually it's far less). Performances start around 11pm.

Casa de la Trova
Calle San Lázaro, 661, between Gervasio and Belascoain
Tel: (07) 879-3373
Local musicians show up for informal jam sessions. You may hear anything from ballads to tango, but traditional *son* is the most common.

La Cecilia
Calles 5a and 110, Miramar
Tel: (07) 204-1562
Music and dancing to a salsa orchestra. Open Thur–Sun 9.30pm till late.

Pico Blanco
Hotel St John's, Calle 0, 206, between 23 and 25, Vedado
Tel: (07) 333740
Live bolero till 1am followed by a disco. Fantastic views over Vedado. Open every night 9am–3am.

Delirio Habanero
Teatro Nacional, Paseo and 39, Plaza de la Revolución
Tel: (07) 873-5713
Piano bar and salsa. Cooler and quieter than the Café Cantante Mi Habana downstairs. Great views over the Plaza de La Revolución. Open Tues–Sun 6pm till late.

Jazz Café
Galerías del Paseo
Paseo, corner of Avenida 1era, Vedado
Tel: (07) 862-6401
Famous jazz club, frequented by Chuchó Valdés. Live music in the evening (two sets, 8pm and 11pm). New groups and lots of improvisation. Good food

El Gato Tuerto
Calle 0, 14, between 17 and 19, Vedado
Tel: (07) 866-2224.
A refurbished club near the Hotel Nacional. Major artists, mostly bolero. Open daily till 6am.

Club Havana
Calle 5A, between 188 and 192, Reparto Flores, Miramar
Tel: (07) 204-5700
Social and sailing club with café-bar, piano bar and live music and dancing. Friday and Saturday karaoke 10.30pm–1am.

Hurón Azul (UNEAC)
Calle 17 and H, Vedado
Tel: (07) 553112
Headquarters of the Cuban Union of Artists and Writers, and mainly a Cuban hangout. Boleros on Saturday night, rumba and Cuban *nueva trova* (a kind of melodic folk music) on Wednesday evening (5–8pm), and *son* on Sunday evening (5–8pm).

Club Imágenes
Calzada 602, corner of C, Vedado
Tel: (07) 33-606
Differing types of entertainment: live bolero, *son* and traditional music, plus soft piano sounds. Open Tues–Sun 10pm–3pm.

Club Karachi
Calle K, between calles 15 and 17, Vedado
Tel: (07) 832-3485

BELOW: the sign of good music.

Mostly Cuban clientele. Recorded and live music; a show at midnight. Open Tues–Sat till 3am and Sun afternoon.
Opus Bar
Calzada and Calle D, Vedado
Housed in the elegant and newly restored old School of Music. Live music, cocktails and snacks. Open 3pm–3am.
Patio de María
Calle 37 between Paseo and 2, near the Teatro Nacional
Tel: (07) 810722.
A popular and more alternative venue, serving a mix of rock and salsa – mainly at weekends, as well as poetry readings and workshops. Open till midnight.
El Polvorín
By the Twelve Apostles restaurant at the foot of El Morro, this is a funky disco bar and salsa venue with an excellent outdoor terrace in an historic setting. You can sip *cuba libres* among the big guns that face out over the bay toward the golden strip of the Malecón. Popular with hip young Cubans and tourists. Open daily 9pm–3am.
La Red
Calle 19, 151, corner of Calle L, Vedado
Tel: (07) 832-5415
A mainly Cuban club. Live music – usually salsa, sometimes pop, reggae, even excellent Cuban rap, most nights, usually around midnight.
Salón Rosado de la Tropical
Avenida 41 and 46, Miramar
Tel: (07) 206-1281–2
Formerly the Salón Rosado Benny Moré, this is the best live salsa venue in Cuba. A big, no-frills outdoor arena. The best (and lesser-known) artists play here.
Club Tikoa
Calle 23, 177, between calles N and O, Vedado
Tel: (07) 830-9973
Salsa rules in this lively disco favored by Cubans. Admission 2 CUC. Open daily 10pm–4am.
Tropicana
Calle 72, 4504, between 41 and 45, Marianao
Tel: (07) 267-1717
This overblown 1950s show is the most elaborate and impressive of Cuba's cabarets *(see page 184)*. Any hotel tourism bureau will book seats for you but the show is expensive – CUC$65–85 – and drinks are expensive, too. They move the show into the old disco if it rains. Open till 2am. (Santiago has its own version of the Tropicana cabaret.)
Bar Turquino
Hotel Habana Libre, calles 23 and L, Vedado

Tel: (07) 334011 and 834-6100
Disco on the 25th floor, with occasional live salsa from top groups. Open daily 10.30pm–3am.
La Zorra y el Cuervo
Calle 23, between N and O, Vedado
Tel: (07) 833-2402
Famous jazz club in a La Rampa basement (look for the UK-style red telephone box at the entrance). Live music from 11pm. Open daily, 9.30pm–2am.

Nightlife Outside Havana

Just about every Cuban town has a **Casa de la Trova** (a traditional Cuban-style music hall), and/or a Casa de la Música. A few of these, and other venues worth mentioning, are:

Santiago
Casa de la Trova
Calle Heredia, 208, between San Pedro and San Félix
Tel: (0122) 652689
One of the most famous *casas* in Cuba. There always something going on, and most of it is excellent. Open Tues–Sun, afternoon and evening.
Casa de las Tradiciones
Rabi, 154, Tivoli
Tel: (0122) 653892
Smaller and more intimate than the Casa de la Trova, and very much a local venue.
Patio de ARTex
Calle Heredia, 304 between Carnicería and Calvario
Tel: (0122) 654814
In the patio behind the ARTex store you will often hear excellent music, with late-afternoon and evenings sets. Dance, or just have a drink and enjoy the music.
Tropicana
Autopista Nacional Km 1
Tel: (0122) 642579
Not quite up to the standard of its famous Havana namesake, but for old-style cabaret with plenty of glitz and glitter, it's pretty good.

Trinidad
Casa de la Música
On the steps by the Plaza Mayor. Music and dancing till the early hours.
Casa de la Trova
Calle Echerrri, 29.
Can be great or average. When its good, it's very good.
Palenque de los Congos Reales
Calle Echerri, corner Menéndez.
Son and salsa nightly on a small patio; has a lively following.
Las Ruínas de Sagarte
Calle Jesús Menéndez
Great Afro-Caribbean music and dance in a ruined building, until 2am.

Holguín
El Guayabero
Calle Maceo, between Frexes and Martí
On the main square. Lively and fun, with a mixed Cuban and tourist crowd. Mainly *son* and bolero. Open Tues–Sun.

Baracoa
Casa de la Trova
Calle Maceo, 149, between Ciro Frías and Pelayo Cuervo
Tiny, traditional place with great entertainment. Plenty of local people. Tourists very welcome.

Manzanillo
Carlos Puebla
Calle Masó, corner of Merchán
Traditional and welcoming place on the corner of the main square. Very few tourists. This region is in the heartland of *son*.

Bayamo
La Bayamesa
Calle Maceo, 111, between Marmol and Martí
Tel: (0123) 425673
Another lively place in the heartland of *son*. Open Tues–Sun.

SHOPPING

What to Buy

Nobody goes to Cuba for the shopping. In fact, one of the most striking things for most visitors is the lack of consumer goods – along with the lack of advertising. However, two of the things that Cuba is most famous for – Cigars and rum – are easy to find and make the best gifts to take home. Most countries have import limits on both, which travelers should check out beforehand: the standard limit is 50 cigars and two liters of rum. Both items can be purchased in the big hotels or tourist stores, or directly from the cigar factories and rum distilleries that offer tours.

Pages 360–1 lists some recommended places to buy cigars, whereas rum can be bought just about everywhere. Habana Club is the best: the cheapest variety of this brand is the three-year-old white rum; the most expensive (and this only means about cuc$12) is the *añejo siete años*; in between come the *añejo cinco años* and the *añejo reserva* – these three are all dark rums. Cuban coffee is well worth purchasing, too; Cubita, Turquina and Hola are the best brands. Try the **Casa del Café** on Calle Baratillo, between Obispo and Jústiz.

If you love chocolate, go to the **Museo del Chocolate** on Calle Mercaderes (really just a café and store) where excellent pure chocolate can be purchased.

If you fall under the spell of Cuban music, as most people do, you will almost certainly want to splash out on a few **CDs**. Many hotels have a reasonable selection, but keep an eye open for **ARTex** stores, which tend to have a better-than-average choice *(and see panel below)*. Many of the groups that serenade you in Old Havana and elsewhere have their own CDs for sale. The recording quality is not the best, and the music may not sound quite as good once you get it home but they can make good, nostalgic mementos.You can also pick up wonderful old **records** cheaply from street vendors – if you still have an old-fashioned record player to play them on. They may not be in tip-top condition, but you can find great classics if you are prepared to look.

Handicrafts tend to be of mixed quality in the state-run stores, but the legalization of private enterprise has meant that many Cubans have started painting pictures and making things such as jewelry, embroidery, ceramics, leather goods and musical instruments.

Foreign interest in Santería and other Afro-Cuban religions has also spawned the proliferation of souvenirs related to these cults, from the colorful necklaces associated with Santería to sculpted figures of the gods *(orishas).*

Secondhand **books** and fascinating **newspapers** and **magazines** from the pre- and early revolutionary era are worth looking out for, too. Across Cuba you will find people selling books in the street or from the front of their houses. The biggest collection is to be found in the market in the Plaza de Armas in Old Havana (Wed–Sat 9am–6pm).

While many **peso book stores** are depressingly empty of new titles, books that are of obvious interest to tourists are being published for sale in CUC stores. The range of titles is improving, but the stock is often dominated by illustrated books about Cuba and Havana, expensive reprints of old Cuban revolutionary volumes (collected speeches of Che Guevara or the works of José Martí, etc.) and a limited number of novels by "safe" authors in Spanish (García Márquez is a favorite).

Export Procedures

Visitors who wish to buy Cuban art should note that they need an export permit. State-run stores and galleries will issue this permit automatically.

You also need a permit if you buy a work of art from a street market, or an artist – no matter how inexpensive. Sometimes, the artist will issue a permit, but otherwise you must go to the **Registro Nacional de Bienes Culturales** (National Registry of Cultural Goods) at Calle 17, 1009, between calles 10 and 12, in Vedado, and allow a minimum of three or four days for processing. The permit costs around CUC$20 and is good for up to five artworks. It is important to get a permit, otherwise Cuban Customs will confiscate your purchases at the airport. This is also true for antiques and antiquarian books, over 50 years old.

Buying Cigars

Cigars can be bought on any visit to a factory, such as the **Fábrica de Tabaco Partagás** just behind the Capitolio in Havana *(see page 169).* Outside Havana, there's the **Fábrica de Tabaco Francisco Donatién** in Pinar del Río; numerous opportunities on *vegas* (tobacco plantations) in and around Viñales; and the **Fábrica de Tabaco César Escalante** in Santiago, as well as many other places. Hotel cigar stores all have large humidors and usually well-informed staff; and their cigars are often cheaper than in the factory stores. The cheapest place to buy cigars is at the airport, though the selection is smaller. The Casa del Habano, attached to the Hostal Conde de Villanueva, Calle

Where to Buy Crafts, Books and Music in Havana

Arts and Crafts

One of the best places for crafts in Cuba is the **Feria de Artesanía**, on Calle Tacón, by Parque Céspedes, a block and a half east of Plaza de la Catedral (Wed–Sat). You will find jewelry, leather goods, carved wooden items and more. You are expected to haggle. There are smaller, cheaper versions of this market on Calle Simón Bolívar, just off Parque de la Fraternidad (near the Capitolio); and the Feria del Malecón on the Malecón and corner of Calle D, a few blocks east of the Hotel Riviera.

The **Palacio de la Artesanía**, an attractive colonial building on Calle Cuba 64, Old Havana, has a good selection of crafts, CDs and other items that make good souvenirs and mementos.

Books

Stalls sell second-hand and antiquarian books, including many with revolutionary and political themes, at a market on the Plaza de Armas (Wed–Sat). Prices are fairly high, but there is a good choice. If you are looking for something specific, it's always worth asking around; even if a vendor does not have the book to hand, they may well be able to track down a copy for you if you can wait a day or two.

The book stores worth checking out include the following:

● **La Librería Anticuaria El Navío**, Calle Obispo, 119, between Oficios and Mercaderes, is one of many very fine, decidedly up-market stores that are springing up all over the restored old town. Selling expensive rare books, first editions and old postcards, the prices are steep, but it's great for a browse. If you buy, remember that export procedures apply to books over 50 years old.

● **La Moderna Poesía**, at the top of Obispo, just off Parque Central. This was the most famous peso book store in Havana, but became a dollar, now a CUC, store.

● **La Internacional**, opposite La Moderna Poesía. Part of this store is CUC only, but attached is an excellent second-hand book store, selling a mixture of old university textbooks and an eclectic mix of fiction, often in quite old editions, and sometimes in English.

● **Librería Bella Habana**, in the Palacio del Segundo Cabo (Instituto del Libro), Plaza de Armas. This store has an extensive choice.

Music

Cassettes and CDs are available all over town. Most hotels have a good selection, as does the **ARTex** store on Calle 23 and L (opposite the Habana Libre). There are ARTex stores throughout Cuba. The music store in the **Palacio de la Artesanía** at Calle Cuba 64 in Old Havana is good, too. The **Museo Nacional de la Música**, on Avenida de las Misiones, currently closed for renovation, has a store selling an excellent selection of CDs, and knowledgeable staff.

Mercaderes, 202, between Lamparilla and Amargura, is an excellent cigar store.

In Centro, there's the **Tienda Romeo y Julieta**, at Calle Belascoaín, 852, between Peñalver and Desagüe, and in Miramar, **La Escogida**, a fine cigar store, is housed in the **Hotel Comodoro**, on Avenida 3ra, corner of 84; and the **Casa del Habano**, Calle 5ta, 1407, corner of 16, is a small, but good cigar store.

Don't be tempted to buy cigars on the street. Every hustler has a tale ("I have a friend who works in the factory, etc."), but almost all the cigars they offer you are fakes made from cheap tobacco or even banana leaves.

You can take up to 23 cigars out of the country without an official receipt. Otherwise, keep both copies of your official receipt (one copy will be retained by customs on your departure). You should always keep cigars in your hand luggage when you leave the country.

General Shopping

The shopping scene in Havana was transformed in the 1990s. The main commercial streets of the pre-revolutionary era are now gradually coming to life, with new and more up-market stores opening all the time. Habana Vieja tends to have smart, expensive stores, geared specifically at tourists, in the renovated streets; in the warren of old, unrenovated streets there is little for anyone to buy.

Old Havana

Habana 1791, Calle Mercaderes, 156, between Obrapía and Lamparilla, sells its own original brands of colognes in gorgeous old-world bottles of heavy glass and sealing wax, beautifully packaged in pure linen bags. One interesting fragrance for men is a woody cologne made from tobacco. The store will mix bespoke fragrances and offer prices well below what you would expect to pay in Europe or North America. Also sells aromatherapy oils and products.

One interesting development is the re-opening of once famous department stores such as **Harris Brothers** on Avenida de Bélgica (Monserrate), 305, between O'Reilly and Progreso (open daily 9am–9pm). For clothes, food and more.

Centro Habana

The main shopping streets of Centro Habana are **San Rafael**, **Neptuno** and **San Miguel**, where you will see many familiar names over the store fronts – from Western Union to Woolworths, Hotpoint and Philips. The area has changed little since the 1950s, except that the stores have little to sell – most are almost completely empty, or have windows filled with pitiful offerings. There are long lines, however, outside the **Tiendas Panamericanas** CUC stores.

La Época department store, Avenida de Italia (Galiano) and Neptuno, is good for children's and women's fashion.

El Palacio del Tabaco, Reál Fábrica de Tabacos La Corona, Calle Agramonte (Zulueta), 106, between Refugio and Colón, sells fine Corona cigars from the factory.

La Vajilla, on Avenida de Italia (Galiano) and Zanja, is a state-run antiques store of enormous prices (they're in pesos). You have to root about a bit but there's often a gem or two to be found by the intrepid (open Mon–Sat 10am–5pm).

Vedado

Calle 23, particularly **La Rampa** – the section that runs from the Hotel Habana Libre down to the Malecón – was once the hub of Havana's life; the street itself is inlaid with coloured panels by famous Cuban artists. The **Habana Libre Hotel** has various stores selling basic medicines, snacks, coffee, etc. (Be warned that the hotel is a hotspot for hustlers, black marketeers, prostitutes and illegal cab drivers.) There is a small craft market at Malecón and D selling similar things to the big market in Old Havana.

The **International Press Center**, on the corner of La Rampa and Calle O, hosts exhibitions by Cuban artists, and has a store where you can buy newspapers, magazines and books (particularly political titles), and a photo center. You can get good, cheap photocopies here.

There is an extensive shopping complex under the Focsa Building – a giant boomerang-shaped edifice that spans calles 13 and 15, and M and N. On the Malecón and Prado (opposite the Hotel Cohiba) there is a glass-fronted shopping mall. The top-floor supermarket sells fresh foods, such as Cuban cheeses, unusual cuts of meat, and breads that are often hard to find outside the Diplotienda in Miramar.

Sala Contemporanea – a gallery selling Cuban arts and crafts – is at Calle 3a and G, Vedado (open Mon–Fri 10am–5pm).

It's a Dog's Life

Opposite the Hotel Meliá Cohiba in Vedado is a large shopping mall that includes Havana's first pet store. In 2001, when it opened, its stock consisted solely of dog beds and squeaky toys, but it has now expanded its range. There's now a second one, a "canine and feline beauty store" at Calle Obispo, 410 in Old Havana, although it does not seem to do a roaring trade. Pet food has been unavailable due to a government ban, officially implemented as a precaution against foot and mouth disease. Suspicious animal lovers claim that it is really a measure to put an end to wealthy, pampered pooches, which enjoy a more privileged lifestyle than their peso brethren. Either way, the cost of giblets has risen 500 percent in the *agromercados*. Strangely, you will also see pedigree puppies being sold, alongside caged birds, on street corners in Old Havana.

Between M and N, still on La Rampa, the **Pabellón** is an entertainment and computer center belonging to the Union of Young Communists (UJC).

Calle 23 continues west through a mainly suburban area until it meets the corner of Calle 12, where there is a busy little area of cinemas, stores and restaurants.

Pan de Paris, Línea and 8 (next door to the Cine Línea) is a French-owned patisserie selling the best bread in Cuba, baked using imported French flour.

Hotel Nacional, Calle O and 21, Vedado, has a few small stores. The best is the **Casa del Habano**, which sells a wide range of cigars, most of which can be bought individually as well as in boxes. The Nacional also has a very good swimwear store by the pool.

Hotel Meliá Cohiba, Paseo, between 1ra and 3ra, Vedado, has a mall along one side of the hotel selling everything from children's toys to imported liquors at good prices. Inside the hotel, there is a store selling good (mostly imported) jewelry, ceramics, clothes and one of the best cigar stores in Havana (closed Sunday).

The **Galerías Amazonas**, Calle 12, between 23 and 25, Vedado, is a small mall of stores near the Chaplin Cinema selling wines, liquors and handmade chocolates, and has one of the few good bakeries in Cuba. **Tienda Brava** sells men's designer clothing. All are open daily.

Miramar

Behind the Russian Embassy, rows of advertising billboards herald the former **Diplotienda** on Avenida 3ra and Calle 70. The store is now open to anyone who has CUCs and can afford to shop there; in fact, most buyers are Cubans, not foreigners. It has the widest range of food of any store in Cuba, but it is still very limited and dreadfully expensive. There's a small **Diplo Electrica** next door which sells electrical goods.

Other popular shopping centers in Miramar are the huge **5 Y 42** complex on Avenida 5ta and Calle 42, which has a bakery/patisserie and stores selling clothes, fabrics, shoes, electrical goods, cosmetics – you name it – plus a handful of cafés and snack bars.

Those looking for computer supplies should check out **Tecún**, just around the corner on Calle 42.

There is another popular CUC shopping complex at the former **Hotel Sierra Maestra** near the mouth of the bay at Avenida 1era, between calles 0 and 2.

Havana's *haute-couture* **Maison** on Calle 16 and Avenida 7ma (tel: 07-204-1546, 1548) has a series of smart boutiques selling Cuban

BELOW: Cuba has ideal conditions for windsurfing.

fashions and antiques. There are also regular fashion shows, which are very entertaining.

Le Select, Avenida 5ta and 30, is another new department store, noticably up-market, with an amazing foyer with marble statues and chandeliers. There's a fantastic (by Cuban standards) delicatessen that sells caviar and smoked salmon, a lovely bakery, men's and women's fashions, lingerie, even bridal hire. All very un-Havana. Rather snooty staff. Closed Sunday.

Hotel Comodoro, Avenida 3ra, corner of 84, has a good selection of stores including quality women's fashions (Guess, Versace, Mango) and **La Escogida**, a fine cigar store *(see page 361).*

SPECTATOR SPORTS

Italian **cyclists** pedal the Vuelta a Cuba island tour every February, and teams from many countries regularly compete on the island.

Anyone interested in attending sports events should contact their nearest Cuban tourist office or you could check the website of the National Institute of Sports, Physical Education and Recreation (INDER), www.inder.co.cu, but it is sometimes out of date.

Estadio Latinamericano
Calle Zequiera 312, Cerro.
Tel: (07) 870-6526.
Baseball, Cuba's favorite game, is played in this stadium five days a week. Your hotel should be able to give you exact details. The stadium accommodates around 55,000 spectators, and is about a 10-minute taxi ride from Old Havana.
Estadio Panamericano
Cojímar
Built for the 1991 Pan-American Games the stadium, to the east of Havana, is now used mostly for soccer matches. The stadium has a capacity for 34,000 spectators.

ACTIVE SPORTS

Beach resorts usually have facilities and qualified instructors for a wide range of water sports. Some hotels also rent out bicycles and mopeds, but supplies vary, and sometimes there is a clampdown, when the facility disappears altogether.

Cuba runs many sports-based tours and vacations centered, for example, around **baseball** (Oct–May) or the Girardo Córdova Cardín Tour,

the annual winter **boxing** tournament in which Cuban boxers compete for a place on the national team. For more information, visit the state-sponsored website at www.cubasports.com (in Spanish and English) or e-mail: info@gocubaplus.com (information), sales@gocubaplus.com (bookings).

Serious runners come for the **marathons** – such as the one held in Varadero in November – but Cuba's heat takes its toll. There are many specialized sports tours available: cycling, fishing, birding, etc. that can be arranged via an agency in your home country, or online. Cuba is especially well organized for scuba, snorkeling and sailing, and these are best arranged through a dedicated travel agency.

Cubanacán's UK subsidiary has a series of package tours that include scuba diving, deep-sea fishing, birding, hiking, horseback riding, kayaking, cycling and mountain biking. Contact them at Cubanacán UK Ltd, Unit 49, Skylines Village, Docklands, London E14 9TS, tel: 020-7536 8175, e-mail: reservations@cubanacan.co.uk.

In Canada, Cubanacán can be contacted at 372 Bay Street, Toronto, Ontario, tel: (416) 601-0343, and 1255 University Suite 211, Montreal, Quebec H3B 3B2, tel: (514) 861-4444. See under separate activity headings for alternative contact details.

Horseback Riding

Viñales and Trinidad are the main sites for horseback riding in Cuba. In the former, treks can be arranged through the hotels Los Jazmines and La Ermita *(see page 344),* or privately in the village itself (the owners of most *casas particulares* will know someone with horses for rent, who will accompany you on a trek). In Trinidad, you can tour the Valle de los Ingenios *(see page 263)* on horseback. Ask at the local Cubanacán office, or at your hotel or, again, ask the owner of a *casa particular*, who will probably be able to help.

Hotels in Varadero and other resorts will also be able to arrange treks. Or, if you want a full riding holiday, check www.captivatingcuba.com.

Golf

Cuba has two professional golf courses open to foreign visitors.

The **Havana Golf Club** (tel: 07-33 8820, 07-33 8918), also known as the "DiploClub" in Boyeros, is 30 minutes from the city center. The course is currently 9 holes but it's hoped to increase to the full 18 holes at some point. The clubhouse has a pool, bowling alley, two bars and a restaurant which looks over the course. Hire of clubs, personal caddies, trainers and balls are all available at day rates. Closed Mondays.

There is also the **Varadero Golf Club** (tel: 045-668482, fax: 045-668481, e-mail: info@varaderogolfclub. com), an 18-hole course that covers a narrow 3.5-km (2-mile) strip of land and is the usual venue for international events. The course, which abuts Varadero beach, was designed in 1927 for millionaire Irenee Dupont, and the clubhouse is next door to the former Dupont mansion (Mansión Xanadú), where golfers (and others) may stay. Clubs, caddies, trainers and balls can all be hired.

Fishing

Deep-sea fishing is available at any of the 12 marinas around Cuba's coasts, principally at;
Aquaworld Marina Chapelín
Carretera Punta de Hicacos, Varadero, www.aquaworldvaradero.com. Good, safe fishing boats can be hired from 25 CUC. Fishing is bait, spin, trolling or fly. Fish are shark, snapper, bonefish, striped bass and tuna. Fish as large as 70-kg (150-lb) sailfish and tarpon, and 225-kg (500-lb) marlin, black marlin and wahoo are to be caught here.
Marina Hemingway
There is an international sport fishing competition here at the end of May, named after Ernest Hemingway. Deep-sea fishing trips can be arranged through Cubanacán Náutica, Avenida 5ta, and Calle 248, Santa Fé, Havana.
Marina Tabará
Cubanacán Náutica, Vía Blanca Km 18, Tarará, Habana del Este. A popular fishing area where boats can be hired and trips arranged.

There are also great opportunities for fly fishing in the **Zapata peninsula**. Contact a specialized agency, such as Angling Direct Holidays, www.anglingdirectholidays.com.

Rafting

While Cuba has few big rivers, there is some white-water rafting, notably on the Río de Aguas Blancas and the Río Toa (both in Guantánamo province). For details of rafting packages, contact CubaFun at e-mail: info@gocubaplus.com.

Scuba Diving

Diving is extremely popular along Cuba's stunning coastline. In Cayo Coco, Cubanacán Náutica has **Blue Diving Centers** in Hotel Meliá and Hotel Tryp, and in Cayo Guillermo in Hotel Meliá and Hotel Sol Club, e-mail: bluediving@bluediving.com. Protected by a barrier reef, Cayo Largo has numerous great diving sites. Packages can be arranged through WoWCuba, e-mail: wowcuba@enet.cu, with accommodations at the Villa Marinera or Sol Club Cayo Largo. Dives in María La Gorda, Playa Girón and elsewhere can be arranged through Cubamar, www.cubamarviajes.cu.

Rock Climbing

This sport is mainly located on the limestone crags called *mogotes* in the Viñales valley. The *mogotes* offer fantastic climbing and the sport is becoming increasingly popular. Best months are from October to April, when it is not too hot or too wet. The Hotel Jazmines *(see page 345)* is the central venue. Check the informative website www.cubaclimbing.com, which offers a quote from Castro: "The Revolution was the work of climbers and cavers."

Trekking

There are great opportunities for trekking in Cuba, but you really do need to go with a guide. It is possible to arrange local guides but it is probably best to go on an organized trip that will offer the kind of experience you want.

Pico Turquino in the Sierra Maestra is a favorite trekking destination. At 1,975 meters (6,749 ft) it is the highest peak in Cuba. The landscape is stunning and there is good bird life to spot while you catch your breath. Try a dedicated agency such as Andean Trails, www.andeantrails.co.uk.

Cycling

Cycling in Cuba is seen more as a way of getting around than a sport – it's a very good means of transport for visitors, and essential for most Cubans – but if you want to take it seriously there are numerous opportunities to embark on a Cycle Cuba vacation. These are usually organized as a means of fundraising for various charities, Just type "Cycle Cuba" into your search engine and you will be spoiled for choice.

Birding

Birding is good all over the island but tours tend to concentrate on the Zapata peninsula where thousands of migratory birds nest each winter *(see page 000)*. Other good spots are the Sierra Maestra mountain range where trekking (with a guide only) is centered around the Saltón region, the Península de Guanahacabibes in the far west, Cayo Coco, the mountains around Baracoa in the east of the island, and the Sierra Najasa region of Camagüey.

Birding tours can be arranged in the UK by Cuba Welcome, tel: 020-7731 6871, www.cubawelcome.com, or through Cubanacán UK Ltd, Unit 49, Skylines Village, Docklands, London E14 9TS, tel: 020-7536 8175, e-mail: reservations@cubanacan.co.uk.

Environmental Issues

Cuba has a good record for environmental awareness and has done much to protect and preserve the island's natural attributes. But there is, inevitably, a conflict between conservation and providing the facilities needed for the tourist industry – which is the country's main source of income. For example, hotels in certain areas must be allowed to spray against mosquitoes, even though this kills many insects that feed the indigenous and migratory birds.

"Ecotourism" is an expression that is bandied about a great deal these days, and one that is difficult to define, as it is used to cover a wide range of activities and intentions, from wilderness adventures to volunteering for activities that promote economic opportunities for local communities. And it is sometimes misused simply to promote vacations in places of natural beauty.

We should all be aware that the infrastructure put in place to cater for our needs can have an adverse affect on a country's ecosystem, and anyone engaged in any kind of outdoor pursuit should behave responsibly, and be aware that their activities could potentially cause damage. Care should be taken at all levels, from avoiding touching coral when diving to staying on designated paths when hiking, or simply taking all your rubbish home with you.

A – Z

A HANDY SUMMARY OF PRACTICAL INFORMATION, ARRANGED ALPHABETICALLY

A dmission Charges

There is an admission charge for most museums, galleries and other places of touristic interest. It is generally CUC$1–3. A few places, such as the Museo de la Revolución in Havana, charge CUC$5. In many places, you pay extra if you are going to use a camera, and quite a lot extra to use a video camera.

B udgeting for Your Trip

A good hotel in Havana will cost around CUC$160 for a double room in high season (see page 340), but there are cheaper options, and almost anywhere outside Havana is cheaper. You can choose to stay in casas particulares, where you will, on average, be charged CUC$25 (less outside Havana), with breakfast costing around CUC$3. Eating out is rarely very expensive. About CUC$25 per person in a smartish restaurant, but there are many restaurants and paladares, where you can eat well for around CUC$15 or less. If you are going to drink wine, this puts the price up quite a lot. In a bar, beer costs around CUC$1.50, mojitos CUC$3–6, depending on the location.

Car rental is expensive, around CUC$50 a day (see page 338). Taxi fares are reasonable: you can get to most places in Havana for CUC$5. Long-distance bus fares are reasonable, the longest journey you could make would be Havana to Santiago, currently CUC$51. As there are not many consumer goods for sale you are unlikely to spend a great deal on shopping.

Business Hours

Most **banks** open Mon–Fri 8.30am–3pm. Most Cuban **offices** open around 8.30am–5 or 6pm, often with a break at lunch time. But it is not rare for offices, even those serving the public, to close early because of blackouts, shortages and transportation problems.

Farmers' markets open early, from around 7am or even earlier, and close when traders decide to leave – usually between 4 and 6pm.

CUC retail stores (previously dollar stores, and still often referred to as such) are opening all over Cuba; most open Mon–Sat 10am–5pm but may stay open later.

CUC supermarkets usually open Mon–Sat 9am–6pm and Sun 9am–1pm. Tourists may be asked to show their passport at the diplomercado, near the Russian Embassy in Havana's Miramar suburb. One of the city's original dollar supermarkets (before the embargo on the US$), popular with expats, the "diplo" sells fresh meat and vegetables and household supplies. It is open Mon–Sat 9am–7pm. Many of the bigger stores open 9am–9pm.

C hildren

Cubans love their own kids and take them everywhere with them, so they are fascinated by foreigners who do the same. Your children will be pampered guests at any hotel and the employees will quickly learn their names and interests. The beach resorts all have supervised activities for them, and family rates are offered during the low season.

Climate

Cuba has a subtropical climate, with an average annual temperature of 25°C (77°F). The mean relative humidity is 77 percent during the dry season (Nov–Apr) and 82 percent during the wet season (May–Oct).

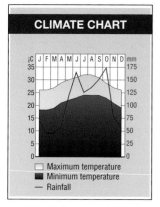

CLIMATE CHART

☐ Maximum temperature
■ Minimum temperature
— Rainfall

The sun seems to shine all the time in Cuba, but temperatures are most definitely higher during the rainy "summer" season than in the drier "winter" months. Those who are not accustomed to melting temperatures would do well to avoid visiting the island in July and August – when most Cubans spend every spare moment either on the beach or in the shower.

While the rain of the wet season is not often more than an inconvenience – torrential showers can be replaced by sun within the space of half an hour – the late summer is also hurricane season.

Therefore, the best time to visit Cuba is from November to April, after the hurricane season is over and before the hot, muggy summer months arrive. To avoid high-season prices and crowds, visit in November or from February–April.

Crime and Safety

Crime is undoubtedly on the increase in Cuba, but it is still low by Latin American standards. Indeed, in comparison with most of the countries from which they come, visitors will find Cuba reassuringly safe. However, bag snatching and pickpocketing are not uncommon, particularly in the poorer sections of Havana and Santiago.

In the summer of 1999, after a rapid increase in crime, Fidel Castro announced a serious crackdown. Hundreds of extra police were drafted in and black marketeers, prostitutes and petty criminals were arrested by the thousand. Consequently, the crime wave has abated, but it has not been wiped out completely. The streets feel much safer, but visitors should still take sensible precautions. Leave travel documents, large banknotes and ostentatious jewelry in your hotel, and keep a firm grip on your camera and on any bag you decide to carry.

Violent crime is rare, but there have been some incidents that have landed tourists in hospital. Most of these occurred when people tried to fight off muggers – DON'T.

Although Havana is still considered to be safer than most cities, some areas – such as the darker streets of Old and Central Havana – should be avoided after dark, even if you are in a group. Be sensible and take the same precautions you would in any large, unfamiliar city, and at night keep to busy and well-lit streets (admittedly, not always easy with blackouts and complete lack of street lighting in some places).

There is much less crime outside the capital, but in Santiago you must take the same precautions as you would in Old or Central Havana.

Loss of Belongings

In case of theft, you should immediately report the crime to the nearest police station. Make sure you ask for the case report (*denuncia*) to back up any insurance claim on your return home. This may take time, but is essential if you intend to make a claim. The Cuban firm **Asistur** (tel: 07-866-8339) can help with cash advances and replacement of documents.

You should report lost or stolen passports to your embassy or consulate, which can issue emergency papers to get you home.

Customs Regulations

Tourists may bring in, duty-free, personal effects – including medicine for their own use or as gifts – cameras, tape recorders, MP3 players, personal computers, cellular phones (mobiles), sports and camping equipment. All of these items should in theory be listed on a customs declaration form on arrival. Customs inspections are random.

Visitors importing electrical items as gifts – TVs, kitchen equipment, etc. – should note that 100 percent duty is payable. Certain items, mainly video recorders, modems, and photo-copying equipment and supplies, are restricted: you may bring them in only for accredited people such as journalists and approved organiza-tions. Such items will be confiscated by customs until the necessary paperwork from the Ministries of Foreign Relations and Communi-cations are presented.

D isabled Travelers

Travelers with disabilities may find getting around Cuba quite difficult. Some modern hotels have facilities, but older hotels and other buildings do not. Streets and sidewalks are narrow, and wheelchair ramps do not exist. Public toilets (and those in restaurants and bars) are not adapted for people with disabilities. On the positive side, Cubans are extremely helpful and will come to the assistance of anyone who appears to need it.

E lectricity

Both 220 and 110 volts are used, but 220 is more common. Electric outlets usually take plugs with two flat prongs but you may find some that take round prongs. It's best to come prepared with adaptors and transformers so as not to be caught out – they are inexpensive and can be bought at the airport before you travel. Power cuts are less frequent than they were, but not uncommon.

Embassies and Consulates

Havana

Canada: Calle 30, 518, corner of 7ma, Miramar, tel: (07) 204-2516.
Germany: Calle 13, 652, corner of B, Vedado, tel: (07) 833-2539, 833-2569.
UK: Calle 34, 702, corner of 7, Miramar, Havana, tel: (07) 204-1771.
Italy: Avenida 5, 402, corner of 4, Miramar, tel: (07) 204-5616.
Netherlands: Calle 8, 307 between 3 and 5, Miramar, tel: (07) 204-2059.
Spain: Cárcel 51, corner Zulueta, Habana Vieja, tel: 866-8025/8029.
United States: (Interests Section): Calzada, between L and M, Vedado, tel: (07) 833-3551–9, also toll-free: 1-866-374-1769.

Emergencies

The general number to dial for emergencies is **116**, for police, fire or ambulance. However, this is a relatively new system that does not function in all parts of the country, and where it does, you may not get through to an English-speaking person. **Asistur** is often a visitor's best bet. The Havana office is at Prado 208, tel: (07) 866-8339, and there are branches in tourist centers all over the island. Hotels are also able to help with medical emergencies.

G ay and Lesbian Travelers

The hardline Cuban policy on homosexuals has lessened in recent years (sex between consenting adults was legalized in 1979) and there is generally a more tolerant attitude *(see page 24)*. It is still not the most gay-friendly place to visit, however, although there is a growing number of openly gay people – mostly in the capital and in some small, laid-back places such as Viñales and Baracoa.

H ealth and Medical Care

No health certificate is required of visitors unless they are arriving from areas where cholera, smallpox or yellow fever exist, in which case they must show a certificate of vaccination against those diseases. However, it's a good idea to be up-to-date with tetanus, typhoid and hepatitis A vaccinations. There are no malarial areas in Cuba, but dengue fever, although it has been virtually eradicted through determined fumigation measures, may still occur. There is no vaccination, so do all you can to prevent mosquito bites – use a DEET-based repellent, and cover up in areas where mosquitoes are prevalent. The fever is spread by the *Aedes aegypti* mosquito which, unusually, tends to bite during the day rather than at night. The illness presents with flu-like symptoms and, while usually mild, can be serious.

On the whole, biting and stinging insects, and bugs in general, are not a great problem in Cuba.

Common medicines – such as aspirin and basic stomach remedies – can be bought in hotels, but it's sensible to bring a small supply with you. More specialized items can usually be bought over the counter without prescription from CUC pharmacies, but these outlets are uncommon outside the capital. In Havana, there are good ones at the **Camilo Cienfuegos Hospital** on Línea and Calle L, and at the **Cira García Hospital** in Alamar (in Habana del Este). Of course, if you use prescription medicines, you should bring a supply with you.

To avoid upset stomachs and diarrhea – the two main complaints suffered by tourists – drink bottled water and eat lightly. Be sensible about over-exposure to the sun.

Medical Services

All hotels have a first-aid post of sorts, and the larger hotels will have a resident doctor or nurse,

plus transportation to take a patient to the nearest clinic or hospital. Unless you fall ill in a remote rural area, as a foreign visitor you will be treated in a CUC-only hospital or a special tourist clinic (run by Servimed).

Most doctors and some nurses speak at least a little English, but hardly anybody is multilingual. The Cuban health-care system is free and readily available to all Cubans, but medicines are in short supply except in facilities that cater to CUC-paying foreigners.

I nternet

Many of the large tourist hotels have Internet access and in some (the Inglaterra and the Nacional in Havana, for example) it is available to non-guests. Most towns have a branch of Etecsa (the telephone and communications company) which offers Internet facilities. Be aware, though, that telephone lines can be slow and unreliable, so it's always worth writing long e-mails on Word and saving them to a pen drive/memory stick in case the connection breaks. Lines may also be down completely and access unavailable.

Using the Internet is quite expensive: a user card costs CUC$6 and gives only one hour's access, although this does not have to be used in one sitting.

L anguage Courses

The University of Havana, the University of Santiago de Cuba and the Central University in Santa Clara offer intensive Spanish-language programs for foreigners and a range of specialized courses and seminars for Spanish-speaking foreigners. Low-cost lodgings and meals as well as field trips are usually part of a student package. Travel agents dealing with Cuba have these schedules, as do Cuban consulates.

M aps

The best road map of Cuba is Guía de Carreteras by the Directorio Turístico de Cuba (on sale in Cuba for CUC$6). Freytag and Berndt's Kuba/Cuba (1:250,000) is less up-to-date but has useful city plans. Individual city-centre maps of larger cities cost around CUC$1–2. Hotels and book stores in Havana and Santiago sell reasonable maps; however, they may not always be in stock when you want them.

Media

Newspapers and Magazines

The printed media of Cuba is extremely limited due to paper shortages and governmental control. Newspapers are posted on kiosks for the general population to read, and you sometimes see vendors wandering the street with copies to sell. The only daily paper is the Communist Party organ, *Granma*, which mainly offers an update on solidarity, trade and agriculture and provides interesting rather than scintillating reading. This is published weekly in Spanish, English, French, German and Portuguese. Tourists are more likely to find the international edition in hotel stores, but street sellers often have English-language versions.

The long-established magazine *Bohemia* offers general features, and there are various other special-ized Cuban publications on sale at CUC newsstands in hotels and airports. Four- and five-star hotels (particularly in Havana) often carry foreign publications from *Time* to *Cosmopolitan*.

Television

Cuban national television is broad-cast on two local channels (2 and 6), with approximately six hours of programming a day. National and international **news** is reported on two half-hour programs. **Sports** events – especially baseball, boxing and soccer – are often covered live. Other shows include officials and specialists speaking at length and **music** of all kinds in concerts or videos. Foreign **movies** (usually American), seven a week, are shown on Thursday, Friday, Saturday and Sunday. Action movies are most popular, but a recent crackdown on violence and sex has resulted in an increase of "family" movies. **Soaps,** usually Brazilian, Mexican or Cuban,

Traveler's Checks

Traveler's checks can be cashed at the front desk of most tourist hotels – except for American Express, and others issued in the US, which are not accepted because of the US economic embargo. You should, in theory, be a guest at the hotel, but not all reception staff enforce this rule. The cashier at the Hotel Inglaterra in Havana, for example, will cash checks for non-guests. CADECA branches cash traveler's checks but you need the issuer's receipt.

Banks

Banco Financiero Internacional

Open Mon–Fri 8.30am–3pm. You can get cash on a credit card here, if it's not from a US bank. In **Havana**, there are branches inside the Hotel Habana Libre; at the corner of Línea and O, Vedado (near Hotel Nacional), also open on Sat 8.30am–noon; at the Plaza de la Revolución; in Old Havana at Oficios, 200 (near Plaza de San Francisco); and at Calle 18, 111. In **Santiago de Cuba**, there is a branch on Felix Pena (also called Santo Tomás), 365, north of Parque Céspedes.

Other branches in Cuba: **Camagüey**: on Independencia. **Guardalavaca**: at Hotel Atlántico.

Holguín: at Calle Libertad, 56.
Matanzas: on Calle Medio, at the corner of 2 de Mayo.
Varadero: Avenida de la Playa and Calle 32.

Banco Metropolitano SA

The branch on the corner of Línea and M, in Vedado, Havana, deals in foreign currencies (cash on credit cards, traveler's checks, etc.), and has shorter lines than the Banco Financiero).

Banco Nacional

The branch next to the Cubana office on La Rampa (Calle 23) in Havana cashes traveler's checks and gives cash on credit cards.

are extremely popular. North American soaps and series are also screened.

Tourist hotels all have satellite TV with more than 20 channels.

Radio

Just about everybody in Cuba has a stereo, and loud music is a constant background sound wherever you go. Apart from local stations, radios pick up waves from Miami, Jamaica and the American Forces Network at Guantánamo Base.

Radio Reloj (Clock Radio) gives round-the-clock news on AM, to the infuriating background noise of a ticking clock; **Radio Havana Cuba** broadcasts news and features on short wave, where the **BBC** also comes through, though the reception is poor (early morning on 6195, 8–10am on 15220, 10am–1pm on 17840, and mid-afternoon till late in the evening on 5975).

Voice of America broadcasts from 6pm on 7070, short wave. **Radio Martí**, Voice of America's Spanish-language propaganda service, broadcasts from Miami, and often changes its frequencies to avoid jamming, but without much success.

Money Matters

The **Cuban peso** *(moneda nacional* or *peso cubano)* divided into 100 **centavos**, is the official currency. Until November 2004 US dollars were widely used, but since the new ruling the only currency generally used by foreigners now is the *peso convertible* (CUC), which is roughly equivalent to the US dollar, although a 2005 re-evaluation of the *peso convertible* has affected currency

exchange. Euros can be used in the large resorts: Varadero, Cayo Largo, Cayo Coco and Santa Lucía.

Some people find it useful to change a small amount of foreign currency into Cuban pesos (the exchange rate is CUC$1 = CUP24) for use on public transport (fares on most urban routes cost between 40 centavos and one peso), in cinemas, when shopping for fresh fruit at farmers' markets, and when buying food and drink from street vendors. You can make domestic phone calls using the peso phones, saving yourself a lot of money, so you may also want to have a few 20-centavo coins for call boxes. However, many old peso phones have been replaced with new phones which take only cards.

But you won't need many *pesos cubanos;* you can usually buy street food, for example, with *convertibles,* and will be given the change in *cubanos.*

Changing Money

You can change foreign currency into *pesos convertibles* at government-licensed CADECA booths and some large banks *(see box above),* and it is wise not to attempt to do so elsewhere. There is no black market. Branches of CADECA are fairly widely scattered. In Old Havana, they can be found on Calle Obispo and Calle Oficios and elsewhere, and in Vedado there is one on La Rampa (Calle 23) and one on the corner of the Malecón and Calle D. Every sizable town has at least one – ask at your hotel. CADECAs change traveler's checks but you must produce the original purchase receipt as well as your passport.

Change foreign currency into convertible pesos at the CADECA booth at the airport when you arrive. Bring sterling or euros if possible, as a 10 percent commission is charged on dollars. Remember to keep enough convertible pesos to pay the 25-CUC departure tax, but don't take them home with you except as souvenirs, since they are not, in fact, convertible currency, despite the name. The only place you can exchange them back into another currency is at the airport in Havana, but it is unwise to count on this as there may be delays and the exchange desk, although theoretically open 24 hours, may not be.

Credit Cards

Access/MasterCard, Visa and other credit cards are welcome at most hotels, and some of the old dollar restaurants and stores (now CUC establishments), provided they have been issued outside the US, so American Express is no use.

Credit-card operations in Cuba do not always run smoothly. The centralized computer system often fails, going down for hours at a time; this affects every credit-card machine in the land, and you will not be able to use your card at all while the system failure lasts.

A credit card can also be a useful backup if you need cash in an emergency: cash can be withdrawn against a credit card at branches of the Banco Financiero Internacional, and at CADECAs, but an 11 percent

Public Holidays

January 1 Liberation Day, commemorating the guerrillas' triumph over Batista.
May 1 Labor Day, celebrated with workers' parades.
July 25–27 A three-day holiday celebrating July 26, 1953, the date of the attack on the Moncada Garrison in Santiago, recognized as the start of the Revolution.
October 10 Celebrating the start of the War of Independence against Spain in 1868.
In addition to these official public holidays, there are innumerable other important dates which are commemorated, including:
● **January 28** The birth of José Martí (1853).
● **April 19** The victory at the Bay of Pigs (1962).
● **Second Sunday in May** Mother's Day
● **October 8** Death of Che Guevara.

TRANSPORTATION
ACCOMMODATIONS
ACTIVITIES
A – Z
LANGUAGE

commission rate is currently being charged, which makes it an expensive transaction. There is also an increasing number of ATMs in Havana – for example, at the CADECA office in Calle Obispo, available when the office itself is closed – each site should give the location of others in the area. Be warned that there are almost no opportunities to withdraw cash against Cirrus or Switch cards, and that these transactions are best done in Havana and Santiago.

Cash

While traveler's checks are a safe way to carry money, you should always try to have a good supply of cash with you, particularly if you head out of the city. Not all provincial hotels will be able to cash traveler's checks for you.

Getting change from big bills is often difficult, so it is worthwhile keeping a stock of 10s, 5s and single notes in your wallet. Try to get as many small-denomination bills as possible when you change foreign currency, and always try to break big bills when you are staying at city hotels, where they are more likely to have a better supply in their tills. If your hotel can't help, you may have to go to a bank; most banks will change big bills for you. You will normally have to show your passport if you produce a 50- or 100-CUC bill in a Cuban store.

The UK Foreign Office warns that the wider use of the convertible peso (CUC) has meant an increase in the number of forged CUC banknotes of all denominations but in particular 100-CUC notes.

Be careful, too, when you pay for something, that the change you are given is in CUCs not *pesos cubanos* – the notes look extremely similar.

Postal Services

Every rural town has a post office, and major cities have a central post office with municipal branches. You can buy stamps (*sellos*) here for pesos. In hotels, you will be charged the same price, but in CUCs. Some stamps are not glued, so you have to ask for a dab of glue at a post office.

Postcards and letters to Europe cost 75 cents. Domestic delivery is slow, but usually faster from city to city than within the same city. Postcards and letters to Europe and the Americas sometimes only take a fortnight but may take a month or more, even via airmail.

Mother's Day (second Sunday in May) is the one day of the year when

ABOVE: Internet access and public phones in a street kiosk.

cards and telegrams are delivered on time all over Cuba. For a week or so ahead of the mailing deadline, cardboard boxes labeled by province are stacked in the lobby of the larger post offices so senders can drop in their addressed and stamped cards. The boxes are flown to the provincial capital to be sorted and then dispatched – and they are sure to reach mother on her day.

Religious Services

The government blunted the influence of the Catholic Church in the early 1960s, but never cracked down on it completely. Since the Pope's visit to Cuba in 1998 there has been a resurgence of Catholic practice – and a seeming relaxation of hostility from the government. Mass is still said in churches throughout the island. Your hotel tourism bureau can direct you to the church of your choice, but service times vary.

In Havana, times of mass in the **cathedral** in Old Havana are posted at the entrance. The **Jewish synagogue** at Línea and Calle M holds services and has a library. The **Methodist church**, a block away from the Habana Libre Hotel at calles 25 and K, lays on social activities as well as services, and has a small guesthouse. **Catholic churches** are open all over the island and anyone can walk in at any time to have a look or attend mass.

Student Travelers

There are no official discounts or special deals for student travelers in Cuba, but discounts on accommodations, museum entrance fees, etc. are offered in some places to

holders of ISIC cards (International Student Identity Cards). Check their website: www.isic.org.

Telecommunications

The Cuban **local telephone service** has undergone a complete overhaul and it is now possible to make crackle-free calls right across the island (sometimes). Certain exchanges have been set up for satellite communications and are rented in CUCs. These work fairly efficiently.

Local and international telephone calls and faxes can be made through the operator from your hotel room (or sometimes through hotel reception). However, calls can also be made far more cheaply from public phones. For international direct dial, key in 119, followed by the country code and the number.

Buying and using phonecards (*tarjetas*) can be quite confusing. There is a variety of cards on offer, but they cannot all be used on all public phones – and it isn't immediately obvious on which phones they can be used. The best and cheapest cards to get are the **Propia** cards priced in *pesos cubanos* – those priced in CUCs are international and will route your calls through the US, making a local call extremely expensive. Propia cards give you a personal code which you input before using a phone. They can be bought at branches of Etecsa and cost 5 or 10 *pesos cubanos*.

Peso convertible cards, for international calls, can also be bought at ETECSA offices and at hotel reception desks, and come in denominations of 5, 10 or 20 CUCs. Local calls cost about 5 centavos a minute, calls to other provinces cost about 35 centavos a minute.

TRANSPORTATION

Collect calls *(reverse charge/ cobro revertido)* can be made from a regular Cuban line (as found in most homes) to the US, Canada, the UK, Mexico, Puerto Rico, Portugal, Spain and Italy, but they are prohibitively expensive. You cannot make a collect call from a hotel or a public phone.

International calls are expensive: CUC$2 a minute to the US and Canada; CUC$5 a minute to Europe and the rest of the world (and even more if you call from a hotel).

Given the unpredictability of postal services, many Cubans use **telegrams**, sent from the post office, as a fast and fairly inexpensive way of communicating to other parts of the island. CUC payment is the general rule.

It is possible to hire cellphones (mobiles) at **Cubacel**. The head office is at Centro de Negocios Miramar, Edificio Santa Clara, corner calles 3 and 78, tel: (07) 5264-2266; www.cubacel.com; and there is an office at Havana airport. Phones cost around CUC$5 a day to hire. Call charges are high, about 70 cents a minute for local calls, rising steeply for calls outside Cuba. As with your own cellphone if used abroad, you pay for incoming as well as outgoing calls. The bill must be paid by cash or credit card. A deposit is refunded when the phone is returned and the bill has been paid. You can use your own cellphone in Cuba (where there is a signal) but costs are prohibitively high.

Telephone Codes

Phoning to, and within, Cuba is a confusing business. The country is in the process of digitalizing services, but this is a piecemeal transition. Numbers and codes change frequently, especially in Havana.

If you're phoning from outside Cuba, dial the country code (**53**) and then the city code, losing the **0-** or **01-** from the prefix. Thus Havana is **+53-7**; Santiago is **+53-22**, Varadero **53-45** and Camagüey City **53-32**. However, this is not always the case and you sometimes have to retain the 0 or 1. It is not very helpful to say so, but it can be a process of trial and error.

Inside Cuba, it's even more complicated. For inter-provincial calls, all numbers except Havana start with 01 (e.g. Santiago 0122; Guantánamo province 0121, etc.). However, on some non-digital phones, you may have to drop the first "1" and you may only be able to call neighboring provinces.

For Havana all codes are 07.

In general, don't use the provincial code when phoning within a province.

However, there are certain provinces where you may have to do so.

In listings in this guide we have not included the international code (53), and we have kept to the general rules outlined above, but be aware that there may be differences and changes. If you're stuck, ask for help in a hotel or in an office of ETECSA, the Cuban state telephone company, although in the latter you will need to speak Spanish.

To make an international call, first dial the access code **119**, then the country code, area code and phone number. International operators speak English.

Time Zone

Cuba is on Eastern Standard Time (Daylight Saving applies during summer), which is GMT –5. When it's noon in Havana, it's 5pm in London, 6pm in Madrid and Rome, and 2pm in Buenos Aires.

Tipping

Taxi drivers, waiters and hotel staff should be tipped in CUCs – this is the only access to convertible currency that they get. Ten percent is usual for taxi drivers and restaurant staff. You should leave 1 CUC a day for a hotel chambermaid.

Toilets

The first thing to remember about toilets is that Cuban plumbing is dodgy so you must always throw paper in the bin provided, not into the bowl – even in hotels with smart new facilities. The second thing is to take your own toilet paper with you (this doesn't apply to hotels). There are very few public restrooms and those that do exist (at bus stations, for example) are best avoided, if possible. Restrooms in bars and restaurants are usually fairly decent, and in most places they don't question whether or not you are a customer, especially as you are expected to tip the attendant who sits outside and (sometimes) profers toilet paper.

Tourist Information

All hotels have a **tourism information desk**, where restaurant reservations can be made, sightseeing tours booked, etc. More complicated queries should be addressed to your guide (if you have one) or to your hotel public-relations manager (if they have one).

General tourist information offices

do not really exist in Cuba. **Infotur** is the only tourist-information service, with offices at José Martí Airport, Terminal 3 (tel: 07-641-6101; in Old Havana at Calle Obispo 521, between Bernaza and Villegas (tel: 07-866-3333) and on the corner of the Malecón and Calle G (tel: 07-836-0033).

Tour Agencies & Operators

There is a whole range of tourism enterprises whose services sometimes overlap and which concentrate on offering packages or other specific services, but they can give assistance in all areas, and most of them have improved greatly in recent years in both helpfulness and efficiency.

Amistur Cuba specializes in political tours for people wishing to see the revolutionary side of Cuba. They can be found on Paseo 406, between 17 and 19, Vedado. Tel: (07) 830-1220, (07) 833-4544; e-mail: amistur@ceniai.inf.cu.

Cubanacán administrates numerous hotels, promotes and arranges conventions, and organizes tours of all kinds, including health tourism, nature tourism and water-sports activities. Its main office is in Havana, at Calle 23 (La Rampa), 156 between O and P, Vedado, tel: (07) 833-4090; www.cubanacan.cu. In the UK, tel: 020-7536 8176

Cubamar specializes in ecotourism, youth activities, bicycle tours and other general sports. It also rents self-drive RVs and motor homes. The main office is at Calle 3, between 12 and Malecón, Vedado, Havana, tel: (07) 833-2523–4; fax: (07) 833-3111; e-mail: cubamarviajes@cubamarviajes.cu; www.cubamarviajes.cu.

Cubatur was for many years the only commercial subsidiary of the Ministry of Tourism (INTUR), the state umbrella organization for tourism. Now, Cubatur sells excursions through the tourism bureaux in most of Cuba's hotels and in their own offices, which can be found in most towns and resorts. Cubatur's headquarters and tourism office in Havana are at Calle F, 157, between calles 9 and Calzada, Vedado, tel: (07) 835-4155; e-mail: casamatriz@cubatur.cu; www.cubatur.cu.

Gaviota books hotel accommodations, organizes excursions, car rental, dive packages, and more. The main office is at Edificio La Marina, 3rd floor, Avenida del Puerto, 102, Old Havana, tel: (07) 66-6777; fax: (07) 33-2780; e-mail: gaviota@gaviota.gav.tur.cu; www.gaviota-grupo.com.

ACCOMMODATIONS ACTIVITIES A–Z LANGUAGE

Gran Caribe runs most of the island's luxury hotels, including the Hotel Nacional in Havana. Tel: (07) 204-9202; from the UK: 08715-504055; from Canada (toll-free: 800-984 2707; www.gran-caribe.com.

Habaguanex is part of the Havana City Historian's office. The company runs and promotes enterprises in Old Havana, and has a number of experienced multilingual guides attached to its own travel agency, called San Cristobal, at Calle Oficios 110 bajos, e/ Lamparilla and Amargura, Old Havana. Tel: (07) 861-9171/9172/ 4102; e-mail: ventas@viajessancristobal.cu; ww.habaguanex.com.

Havanatur arranges hotel accommodations, as well as excursions of all kinds. It has its own fleet of buses and a car rental agency, Havanautos. Its headquarters are in the Edificio Sierra Maestra, Calle 1a, between 2 and 0, Miramar, Tel: (07) 55-4082/55-4883; e-mail: havanatur.turandtravel@cimex.com; www.havanatur.cu.

Tour Agencies in the UK

A growing number of UK operators offer Cuba in their brochures:
Cox and Kings Travel,
Gordon House, 10 Greencoat Place, London SW1P 1PH.
tel: 020-7873 5000;
fax: 020-7630 6038;
www.coxandkings.co.uk
Cultural tours to Havana and tailor-made vacations.
First Choice Holidays,
First Choice House, Peel Cross Road, Salford, Manchester, M5 2AN.;
tel: 0870-850 3999;
www.firstchoice.co.uk.

All-inclusive to budget apartment accommodations in Varadero and Cayo Coco. Also tours taking in Havana, Trinidad and Viñales.
Gane & Marshall International,
7th Floor, Northway House,
1379 High Road, London N20 9LP.
tel: 020-8445 6000;
fax: 020-8445 6615;
www.ganeandmarshall.co.uk.
Tailor-made trips and self-drives.
Journey Latin America,
12–13 Heathfield Terrace, Chiswick, London W4 4JE.
tel: 020-8747 8315;
fax: 020-8742 1312.
12 St Anne's Square,
Manchester M2 7HW
tel: 0161-832 1441
ax: 0161-832 1551
www.journeylatinamerica.co.uk.
Cultural tours, tailor-made tours and twin-center vacations with other Latin American countries.
Kuoni Travel,
Kuoni House, Dorking,
Surrey RH5 4AZ.
tel: 01306-747002;
fax: 01306-740719.
www.kuoni.co.uk.
Offices throughout the UK.
Tours include Havana, Santiago and Camagüey. Packages to Varadero, Cayo Ensenachos and Cayo Coco.
Regent Holidays,
First Floor,
38–44 Gillingham Street
London SW1V 1HU.
tel: 0870-499 1311;
fax: 020 7821 4001;
www.regent-holidays.co.uk.
Regent arranges itineraries for independent travelers and for special-interest groups, plus cultural and general tours.
Saga Holidays,
The Saga Building, Enbrook Road,

BELOW: an all-inclusive resort, Guardalavaca.

Folkestone, Kent CT20 3SE.
tel: 0800-096 0078;
www.saga.co.uk.
Organizes cultural and general-interest tours.
South American Experience,
38–44 Gillingham Street, London SW1V 1HU.
tel: 0870-499 0683;
fax: 020-7821 4001;
www.southamericanexperience.co.uk.
Itineraries tailor-made to meet individual requirements.

V isas and Passports

All visitors entering Cuba must show a passport valid for at least six months beyond the date of your arrival in Cuba. In addition, visitors must have a **tourist card** *(tarjeta de turista)*, issued by the Cuban Consulate directly or, more commonly, through a travel agent. This will be valid for the length of your planned visit, but can be extended (once) up to the date shown on your return airplane ticket – as long as the total time you are in the country does not exceed 60 days. Immigration officials stamp your tourist card, not your passport. Do not lose it – you must show it when you leave the country.

Those planning to stay with a Cuban family must apply some time in advance for a **tourist visa**, while any commercial travelers must obtain a **business visa**. Regulations insists that travelers to Cuba must spend at least three nights in a pre-booked hotel. Officially, a *casa particular* counts, but in practice visitors can experience delays and searching questions at the airport. Ask at the local Cuban Consulate (or check with your travel agent) for more information.

Visas for US Citizens

These are handled by the Cuban Interests Section in Washington, DC. United States Treasury Department regulations prohibit US citizens from spending money in Cuba unless they qualify as journalists, researchers, businesspeople in specifically licensed sectors, or relatives of Cubans living on the island.

Americans who oppose their government's trade and travel blockade against Cuba regularly evade or purposely violate these restrictions, and some do so just out of curiosity: many fly in via Mexico or Jamaica. Although they could theoretically be prosecuted, they generally aren't.

A Dilemma

In most Cuban towns (Viñales is the big exception) you will be approached by people asking you for soap, moisturising cream, or pens. These are articles that are in short supply and/or can only be bought with *pesos convertibles*. It is difficult to know what the response should be. On one hand, it is cheap and easy to bring a small supply of these things with you and dole them out to people who have very little. On the other, it does encourage a culture in which Cubans look on tourists simply as suppliers of unobtainable goodies and pester them accordingly. Perhaps the best way to deal with this situation, if you would like to give things that could be useful but don't want to add to the problem, is to deliver things like pens and notebooks and soap directly to schools, where teachers can distribute them – or refuse them, if they choose.

Websites

www.cubagov.cu – official government site, general information in Spanish and English
www.cubasi.cu – general information about Cuba in Spanish, English and Italian
www.cubatravel.cu – Ministry of Tourism site. Information on accommodations, events, activities, etc. in Spanish and English
www.casaparticularcuba.org – useful site for booking *casas particulares*, in English.

What to Bring

Clothes

Casual, comfortable clothes are appropriate anywhere on the island, especially light cottons that can be put on and taken off in layers as the temperature changes. As far as many Cubans are concerned, the less you wear the better. Shorts and bathing suits are accepted at all seaside resorts, though more coverage is expected for dining out or visiting museums and galleries. Unless you're coming here for business you won't have much use for a suit and tie or a formal dress. You also don't want to stand out in a crowd by looking too smart and "dressed up.".

A waterproof jacket is optional – you can usually wait out a tropical shower; and if there is a real downpour, a waterproof jacket will be of minimal use – although an umbrella might be. Cubans often carry umbrellas for protection from the sun, and also whip them open at the first drop of rain.

You should take comfortable walking shoes and dark glasses for protection against the harsh tropical sunlight. Straw and cloth sunhats can be bought in any tourist store if you forget to bring one. If you are going to be traveling on long-distance buses bring a fleece or warm jersey. The air conditioning has only one setting – high.

Camera Film

You can buy color film in many tourist hotel stores, though it's tricky to track down slide film. Most types of video tape are also available. However, as a general rule, supplies of anything to do with normal or video cameras are variable in Cuba, and prices are almost always higher than those at home. It is always safer to bring important items with you.

Electrical Transformers and Adaptors

As already mentioned *(see Electricity)* you cannot be entirely sure of the voltage or the socket type you will encounter, so it is as well to come prepared.

Medical Supplies and Toiletries

Travelers to Cuba should bring their own medicines, vitamins, adhesive bandages, contraceptives, toothpaste, insect repellent, and suntan lotion. It's not a bad idea to bring a supply of toilet paper and tissues, as well.

Most of the larger hotels sell basic medicines at European prices. A wider range of drugs can be obtained from the Camilo Cienfuegos Hospital on Línea and L in Havana, or the International Pharmacy on Avenida 5ta in Miramar.

Emergency treatment is free, while follow-up treatment and medicines are payable in CUCs. Foreigners will be treated in a CUC-only hospital, and health costs at these hospitals are as high as in the US. You are strongly advised to take out **health insurance** before leaving home.

Women Travelers

Foreign women traveling alone may opt to visit Cuba on a package beach vacation, or a cultural tour, with Cuban specialists guiding and initiating most of the action. However, Cuba is not a difficult or dangerous place to travel as a single woman.

Cubans out in the hinterland may regard a foreign woman traveling alone as unusual, but they'll normally be friendly and helpful. Women are generally safer in Cuba than most places in the world. Although rape is uncommon in Cuba, foreign women should be aware that the Cuban definition of "rape" is not the same as in many other places; a woman who takes a man up to her hotel room or indulges in public heavy petting will not be taken seriously if she later claims rape.

Women can expect a lot of male attention: this may be in the form of whistling, hissing (this is not perceived as rude in Cuba), or comments whispered or shouted in the street. This can be annoying but it is rarely aggressive, and is just something a woman is expected to get used to in such a macho country – Cuban women receive similar attention. Ignore the perpetrators and they will normally leave you alone. Any kind of acknowledgement is likely to be taken as a come-on.

Weight and Measures

Officially, Cuba uses the metric system, but you'll find that goods offered at places that deal with mostly Cuban shoppers, such as farmers' markets, use imperial pounds *(libras)* – a hangover from the days when the USA provided almost all of Cuba's imports.

You may find the following conversion formulas useful:

Temperatures

To convert Centigrade into Fahrenheit, multiply by 1.8 and then add 32; for Fahrenheit to Centigrade, subtract 32 and multiply by 0.55.

Metric to Imperial

1 cm	=	0.39 inch
1 meter	=	3.28 ft
1 km	=	0.62 miles
1 gram	=	0.035 oz
1 kg	=	2.21 lbs
1 liter	=	0.22 Imp. gallons
1 liter	=	0.26 US gallons

Imperial to Metric

1 inch	=	2.54 cm
1 ft	=	0.30 meters
1 mile	=	1.61 km
1 oz	=	28.35 grams
1 lb	=	0.45 kg
1 Imp. gallon	=	4.55 liters
1 US gallon	=	3.79 liters

TRANSPORTATION · ACCOMMODATIONS · ACTIVITIES · A – Z · LANGUAGE

L ANGUAGE

UNDERSTANDING THE LANGUAGE

BASIC RULES

Spanish is the language of Cuba. Unlike English, Spanish is a phonetic language: words are pronounced exactly as they are spelled, which is why it is somewhat harder for Spaniards to learn English than vice versa (although Spanish distinguishes between the two genders, masculine and feminine, and the subjunctive verb form is an endless source of headaches for students). As a general rule, the accent falls on the second-to-last syllable, unless it is otherwise marked with an accent (´) or the word ends in D, L, R or Z.

Vowels in Spanish are always pronounced the same way. The double L (LL) is pronounced like the y in "yes", the double R is rolled. The H is silent in Spanish, whereas J (and G when it precedes an E or I) is pronounced like a guttural H (similar to the end sound of Scottish *loch*).

When addressing someone you are not familiar with, use the more formal "usted". The informal "tú" is reserved for relatives and friends. It is worth trying to master a few simple words and phrases, and it will be much appreciated. It will also make your stay more enjoyable, as the majority of Cubans do not speak English – except for staff in the smarter hotels, who are sometimes fluent; and waiters, who know enough English to understand what you want and tell you how much it will cost. There has been a recent emphasis on learning English, but during the years when the Soviet Union was Cuba's only friend, Russian was the only second language taught in many schools – and they are not finding this very useful now.

The following brief lexicon is Spanish as spoken in Spain, with a few Latin American amendments. A list of "Cubanisms" follows.

WORDS & PHRASES

Hello *Hola*
How are you? *¿Cómo está usted?*
How much is it? *¿Cuánto es?*
What is your name? *¿Cómo se llama usted?*
My name is... *Yo me llamo...*
Do you speak English? *¿Habla inglés?*
I am British/American *Yo soy británico(a)/norteamericano(a)*
Does anyone here speak English? *¿Hay alguien aquí que hable inglés?*
I don't understand *No comprendo*
Please speak more slowly *Hable más despacio, por favor*
Can you help me? *¿Me puede ayudar?*
I am looking for... *Estoy buscando*
Where is...? *¿Dónde está...?*
I'm sorry *Lo siento/Perdone*
I don't know *No lo se*
No problem *No hay problema*
Have a good day *Que tenga un buen día*
That's it *Ese es*
Here it is *Aquí está*
There it is *Allí está*
Let's go *Vámonos*
See you tomorrow *Hasta mañana*
See you soon *Hasta pronto*
At what time? *¿A qué hora?*
When? *¿Cuándo?*
What time is it? *¿Qué hora es?*
yes/no *sí/no*
please *por favor*
thank you (very much) *(muchas) gracias*
you're welcome *de nada*
excuse me *perdóneme*

hello *hola*
OK *bien*
goodbye *adiós*
good evening/night *buenas tardes/noches*
here *aquí*
there *allí*
today *hoy*
yesterday *ayer*
tomorrow *mañana (note: mañana also means "morning")*
pasado mañana *the day after tomorrow*
now *ahora*
later *después*
right away *ahora mismo*
this morning *esta mañana*
tomorrow morning *mañana por la mañana*
this afternoon *esta tarde*
this evening *esta tarde*
tonight *esta noche*
next week *la semana que viene*

Getting Around

I want to get off at... *Quiero bajarme en...*
Is there a bus to ...? *¿Hay un omnibús a ....?*
I'd like a taxi. *Quisiera un taxi.*
Please take me to... *Por favor, lléveme a...*
How much will it cost? *¿Cuánto va a costa el viaje?*
Keep the change. *Guarde el cambio.*
What street is this? *¿Qué calle es ésta?*
Which line do I take for...? *¿Qué línea tomo para...?*
How far is...? *¿A qué distancia está...?*
airport *aeropuerto*
customs *aduana*
train station *estación de tren*
bus station *estación de omnibuses*
bus *omnibús*

bus stop *parada de omnibús*
platform *andén*
ticket *tickete/boleto*
return ticket *boleto de ida y vuelta*
hitchhiking *autostop/la botella*
toilets *baños*
This is the hotel address *Ésta es la dirección del hotel*

At the Hotel

I'd like a (single/double) room
Quiero una habitación (sencilla/doble)
... with shower *con ducha*
... with bath and toilet *con baño*
... with a view *con vista*
Does that include breakfast?
¿Incluye desayuno?
May I see the room? *¿Puedo ver la habitación?*
washbasin *lavabo*
bed *cama*
key *llave*
elevator/lift *ascensor*
air conditioning *aire acondicionado*

Emergencies

Help! *¡Socorro!*
Stop! *¡Pare!/¡Alto!*
Go away! *¡Vayase!*

Numbers

0 *cero*
1 *uno*
2 *dos*
3 *tres*
4 *cuatro*
5 *cinco*
6 *seis*
7 *siete*
8 *ocho*
9 *nueve*
10 *diez*
11 *once*
12 *doce*
13 *trece*
14 *catorce*
15 *quince*
16 *dieciseis*
17 *diecisiete*
18 *dieciocho*
19 *diecinueve*
20 *veinte*
21 *veintiuno*
30 *treinta*
40 *cuarenta*
50 *cincuenta*
60 *sesenta*
70 *setenta*
80 *ochenta*
90 *noventa*
100 *cien*
200 *doscientos*
500 *quinientos*
1,000 *mil*
10,000 *diez mil*
1,000,000 *un millón*

Call a doctor *Llame a un médico*
Call an ambulance *Llame a una ambulancia*
Call the police *Llame a la policia*
Call the fire brigade *Llame a los bomberos*
Where is the nearest telephone?
¿Dónde está el teléfono más cercana?
Where is the nearest hospital?
¿Dónde está el hospital más cercana?
Where is the nearest police station?
¿Dónde está la estación de policia más cercana?
I am sick *Estoy enfermo*
I have lost my passport/purse (bag)
He perdido mi pasaporte/bolso
I want to report...
Querio denunciar..

On the Road

Where is the spare wheel? *¿Dónde está la rueda de repuesto?*
Where is the nearest garage?
¿Dónde está el taller más próximo?
Our car has broken down *Nuestro coche se ha averiado*
I want to have my car repaired
Quiero que reparen mi coche
It's not your right of way *Usted no tiene prioridad*
the road to... *la carretera a...*
left *izquierda*
right *derecha*
straight on *derecho/todo recto*
near *cerca*
far *lejos*
opposite *frente a*
beside *al lado de*
parking lot *aparcamiento*
over there *allí*
at the end *al final*
on foot *a pie*
by car *en carro/auto*
town map *plano de la ciudad*
road map *plano de carreteras*
street *calle*
square *plaza*
give way *ceda el paso*
exit *salida*
dead end *calle sin salida*
wrong way *dirección prohibida*
no parking *prohibido aparcar*
highway *autovía*
toll highway *autopista*
toll *peaje*
one-way street *una sola vía*
road closed *camino cerrado*
diversion *desvio*
speed limit
límite de velocidad
gas *gasolina*
gas station *gasolinera*
unleaded *sin plomo*
diesel *gasoil*
water *agua*
oil *aceite*

Dates and Seasons

Saying the Date

20 October 2003, *el veinte de octubre del dos mil tres* (no capital letters are used for days or months)

Days of the Week

Monday *lunes*
Tuesday *martes*
Wednesday *miércoles*
Thursday *jueves*
Friday *viernes*
Saturday *sábado*
Sunday *domingo*

Months

January *enero*
February *febrero*
March *marzo*
April *abril*
May *mayo*
June *junio*
July *julio*
August *agosto*
September *septiembre*
October *octubre*
November *noviembre*
December *diciembre*

Seasons

Spring *primavera*
Summer *verano*
Autumn *otoño*
Winter *invierno*

air *aire*
puncture *pinchazo*
bulb *bombilla*

On the Telephone

I would like a phonecard.
Quisiera una tarjeta de teléfono.
How do I make an outside call?
¿Cómo hago una llamada exterior?
I want to make an international (local) call *Quiero hacer una llamada internacional (local).*
What is the code for...? *¿Cuál es el código para...?*
I'd like an alarm call for 8 tomorrow morning
Quiero que me despierten a las ocho de la mañana
Hello? *¿Dígame?*
Who's calling? *¿Quién llama?*
Hold on, please
Un momento, por favor
I can't hear you *No le oigo*
Can you hear me? *¿Me oye?*
I would like to speak to... *Quisiera hablar con...*
He/she is not here *No está aquí.*
When will he/she be back? *¿A qué hora regresará?*
Will you tell him/her that I called?
¿Podría decirle que le llamé?

TRANSPORTATION

ACCOMMODATIONS

ACTIVITIES

A – Z

LANGUAGE

Speak more slowly, please.
¿Podría hablar más despacio?
Speak more loudly, please.
¿Podría hablar más fuerte?
Could you repeat that, please?
¿Me lo repite, por favor?
The line is busy *La línea está ocupada*
I must have dialed the wrong
number *Debo haber marcado un*
número equivocado

Banking

Where is the nearest bank? *¿Dónde*
está el banco más próximo?
Can I withdraw money on my
credit card here?
¿Puedo retirar dinero con mi tarjeta
de crédito aquí?
Where are the ATMs? *¿Dónde están*
los cajeros automáticos?

Shopping

I'd like to buy... *Quiero comprar...*
How much is it *¿Cuánto es?*
Do you accept credit cards?
¿Aceptan tarjetas?
I'm just looking
Sólo estoy mirando
Have you got...? *¿Tiene...?*
I'll take it *Me lo llevo*
I'll take this one/that one *Me llevo*
éste/ese
What size is it? *¿Qué talla es?*
size (clothes) *talla*
small *pequeño*
large *grande*
cheap *barato*
expensive *caro*
enough *suficiente/bastante*
too much *demasiado*
a piece *un trozo*
each *cada una/la pieza/*
la unidad
bill *la factura* (store), *la cuenta*
(restaurant)
bank *banco*
book store *librería*
pharmacy *farmacia*
hairdressers *peluquería*
post office *correos*

Food Shopping

In markets (*mercados* or, in Cuba,
agropecuarios) prices are usually
by the kilo, sometimes by *gramos*
(by the gram) or by *unidad* (by the
piece). Sometimes you will find
things sold by the *libra* (pound)
instead of by the kilo.

basket *cesta*
bag *bolsa*
bakery *panadería*
butcher's *carnicería*
cake store *pastelería*
fishmonger's *pescadería*
grocery *ultramarinos*
tobacconist *estanco*

Cuban Expressions

agropecuario **farmers' market**
asere **man (casual expression**
used in greeting)
bici-taxi **bicycle taxi**
bloqueo **the US embargo**
bohío **thatched house/hut**
camello **literally a camel but**
refers to strange two-part
buses in Havana
coche **cart**
coco-taxi **small, round yellow**
taxis
guagua **bus**
libreta **ration book**
mamey **mummy (used casually**
to women of any age). Also
the name of an orange-
fleshed fruit, a bit like a
sweet avocado
mojo **a garlicky sauce**
nylon **plastic bag**
organipónico **urban vegetable**
garden, allotment
Período Especial **Special Period**
– the tough years in the
1990s after the fall of the
Soviet Union.

Sightseeing

mountain *montaña*
hill *colina/loma*
valley *valle*
river *río*
lake *lago*
lookout *mirador*
city *ciudad*
small town, village *pueblo*
old town/quarter *casco antiguo*
monastery *monasterio*
convent *convento*
cathedral *catedral*
church *iglesia*
palace *palacio*
hospital *hospital*
town hall *ayuntamiento*
nave *nave*
statue *estatua*
fountain *fuente*
staircase *escalera*
tower *torre*
castle *castillo*
Iberian *ibérico*
Arabic *árabe*
museum *museo*
art gallery *galería de arte*
exhibition *exposición*
tourist information office *oficina de*
turismo
free *gratis*
open *abierto*
closed *cerrado*
every day *diario/todos los días*
all year *todo el año*
all day *todo el día*
swimming pool *piscina*
to book *reservar*

Dining Out

menu *la carta*
breakfast *desayuno*
lunch *comida*
dinner/supper *cena*
meal *comida*
first course *primer plato*
main course *plato principal*
made to order *hecho por encargo*
drink included *bebida incluida*
wine list *carta de vinos*
the bill *la cuenta*
fork *tenedor*
knife *cuchillo*
spoon *cuchara*
plate *plato*
glass *vaso*
wine glass *copa*
napkin *servilleta*
ashtray *cenicero*
waiter, please! *camarero, por favor*

Liquid Refreshment

coffee *café*
black *sólo*
with milk *con leche/cortado*
decaffeinated *descafeinado*
sugar *azúcar*
tea *té*
herbal tea *infusión*
milk *leche*
mineral water *agua mineral*
fizzy *con gas*
still *sin gas*
juice (fresh) *zumo/jugo (natural)*
cold *fresco/frío*
hot *caliente*
beer *cerveza*
bottled *en botella*
on tap *de barril*
soft drink *refresco*
diet drink *bebida "light"*
with ice *con hielo*
wine *vino*
red *tinto*
white *blanco*
rosé *rosado*
dry *seco*
sweet *dulce*
house wine *vino de la casa*
sparkling wine *vino espumoso*
Where is this wine from? *¿De dónde*
es este vino?
pitcher *jarra*
half liter *medio litro*
quarter liter *cuarto de litro*
cheers! *¡salud!*
hangover *resaca*

Menu Decoder

Breakfast and Snacks

pan **bread**
bollo **bun/roll**
mantequilla **butter**
mermelada/confitura **jam**
pimienta **pepper**
sal **salt**

azúcar **sugar**
huevos **eggs**
  cocidos **boiled, cooked**
  con beicon **with bacon**
  con jamón **with ham**
  escalfados **poached**
  fritos **fried**
  revueltos **scrambled**
  tortilla **omelet**
sandwich **sandwich**
tostada **toast**
yogur **yoghurt**

Main Courses

Meat/Carne/Lomo
buey **beef**
carne picada **minced meat**
cerdo **pork**
cabrito **kid**
chorizo **spicy sausage**
chuleta **chop**
cochinillo **roast pig**
conejo **rabbit**
cordero **lamb/mutton**
costilla **rib**
entrecot **beef rib steak**
filete **fillet steak**
jamón **ham**
jamón cocido **cooked ham**
jamón serrano **cured ham**
lengua **tongue**
morcilla **black pudding**
pierna **leg**
puerco **pork**
res **beef**
riñones **kidneys**
salchichón **sausage**
solomillo **sirloin steak**
ternera **veal or young beef**
a la brasa **charcoal grilled**
al horno **roast**
a la plancha **grilled**
asado **roast**
bien hecho **well done**
en salsa **in sauce**
en su punto **medium**
estofado **stew**
frito **fried**
pinchito **skewered meat**

poco hecho **rare**
relleno **stuffed**

Fowl/Aves
codorniz **quail**
faisán **pheasant**
pavo **turkey**
pato **duck**
perdiz **partridge**
pintada **guinea fowl**
pollo **chicken**

Fish/Pescado
anchoas **salted anchovies**
anguila **eel**
atún **tuna**
bacalao **salt cod**
besugo **red bream**
boquerones **fresh anchovies**
caballa **mackerel**
calamar **squid**
cangrejo **crab**
caracola **sea snail**
chopito **baby cuttlefish**
cigala **Dublin Bay prawn/scampi**
dorada **gilt-head bream**
gambas **shrimps/prawns**
jibia/sepia **cuttlefish**
langosta **lobster**
langostino **large prawn**
lenguado **sole**
lubina **sea bass**
mariscada **mixed shellfish**
mariscos **shellfish**
mejillón **mussels**
merluza **hake**
ostra **oyster**
peregrina **scallop**
pez espada **swordfish**
pulpo **octopus**
rape **monkfish**
rodaballo **turbot**
salmón **salmon**
salmonete **red mullet**
sardina **sardine**
trucha **trout**

Vegetables, Cereals and Salads
verduras **vegetables**
ajo **garlic**

alcachofa **artichoke**
apio **celery**
arroz **rice**
berenjena **eggplant/aubergine**
brocolí **broccoli**
calabacín **zuccini/courgette**
cebolla **onion**
champiñón **mushroom**
col **cabbage**
coliflor **cauliflower**
ensalada **salad**
espárrago **asparagus**
espinaca **spinach**
guisante **pea**
haba **broad bean**
judía **green bean**
lechuga **lettuce**
lenteja **lentil**
maíz **corn/maize**
menestra **cooked mixed vegetables**
patata **potato**
pepino **cucumber**
pimiento **pepper**
puerro **leek**
rábano **radish**
seta **wild mushroom**
tomate **tomato**
zanahoria **carrot**

Fruit and Desserts
fruta **fruta**
aguacate **avocado**
albaricoque **apricot**
cereza **cherry**
ciruela **plum**
frambuesa **raspberry**
fresa **strawberry**
granada **pomegranate**
higo **fig**
limón **lemon**
mandarina **tangerine**
manzana **apple**
melocotón **peach**
melón **melon**
naranja **orange**
pera **pear**
piña **pineapple**
plátano **banana**
pomelo **grapefruit**
sandía **watermelon**
uva **grape**
postre **dessert**
tarta **pie**
pastel **cake**
helado **ice cream**
natillas **custard**
queso **cheese**

Herbs and Spices
albahaca **basil**
cilantro **cilantro/coriander**
comino **cumin**
cúrcuma **turmeric**
hierbabuena **mint**
orégano **oregano**
perejil **parsley**
pimentón **paprika**
romero **rosemary**
salvia **sage**
tomillo **thyme**

BELOW: English words crop up in unexpected circumstances.

FURTHER READING

General

Before Night Falls: A Memoir by Reinaldo Arenas, Viking, New York (1993).
A Continent of Islands: Searching for the Caribbean Destiny by Mark Kurlansky, Addison-Wesley, New York (1992).
Cuba (photographs) by Adam Kufeld, W.W. Norton, New York (1994).
Cuba: A Journey by Jacobo Timerman, Picador, London (1994).
Cuba in Focus by Emily Hatchwell and Simon Calder, Latin America Bureau, London (1995).
Cuba: The Land, The History, The People, The Culture by Stephen Williams, Michael Friedman, New York (1994).
The Cubans: Voices of Change by Lynn Geldof, Bloomsbury Press, London (1992).
Driving Through Cuba: An East–West Journey by Carlos Gebler, Hamish Hamilton, London (1988).
The Early Diary of Anaïs Nin by Anaïs Nin, Harcourt Brace & Co., New York (1978–85).
The Exile: Cuba in the Heart of Miami by David Reef, Simon & Schuster, New York (1993).
Falling off the Map: Some Lonely Places of the World by Pico Iyer, Knopf, New York (1993).
Havana, Portrait of a City by Juliet Barclay, Cassell, London (1993).
Walker Evans: Havana – 1933 Pantheon, New York (1989).
Hemingway in Cuba by Norberto Fuentes and Lyle Stuart, Secaucus and L. Stuart, New Jersey (1984).
Into Cuba by Barry Lewis and Peter Marshall, Alfred van der Marck Editions, New York (1985).
Land of Miracles by Stephen Smith, Little Brown, London (1995).
Mea Cuba by Guillermo Cabrera Infante, Faber and Faber, London (1994).
Memories of a Cuban Kitchen by Mary Urrutia Randleman and Joan Schwartz, Macmillan, New York (1992).
Passing Through Havana by Felicia Rosshandler, St Martin's Press, New York (1984).
Portrait of Cuba by Wayne Smith, Turner Publishing, Atlanta (1991).

Six Days in Havana by James A. Michener and John Kings, University of Texas Press, Austin (1989).
A Taste of Cuba by Linette Creen, Dutton, New York (1991).
To Cuba and Back by Richard Henry Dana, Southern Illinois University Press, Carbondale (1966).
Trading with the Enemy: A Yankee Travels Through Castro's Cuba by Tom Miller, Atheneum, New York (1992).
When It's Cocktail Time in Cuba by Basil Woon, Horace Liveright, New York (1928).
With Hemingway: A Year in Key West and Cuba by Arnold Samuelson, Random House, New York (1984).

Feedback

We do our best to ensure the information in our books is as accurate and up-to-date as possible. The books are updated on a regular basis, using local contacts, who painstakingly add, amend, and correct as required. However, some mistakes and omissions are inevitable and we are ultimately reliant on our readers to put us in the picture.

We would welcome your feedback on any details related to your experiences using the book "on the road." Maybe we recommended a hotel that you liked (or another that you didn't), as well as interesting new attractions, or facts and figures you have found out about the country itself. The more details you can give us (particularly with regard to addresses, e-mails and telephone numbers), the better.

We will acknowledge all contributions, and we'll offer an Insight Guide to the best letters received.

Please write to us at:
Insight Guides
PO Box 7910
London SE1 1WE
United Kingdom
Or send e-mail to:
insight@apaguide.co.uk

I Wonder as I Wander: An Autobiographical Journey by Langston Hughes, Rinehart, New York (1956).

Fiction

Cecilia Valdés or **Angel Hill** by Cirilo Villaverde, translated by Helen Lane. OUP, New York. 19th-century novel about the children of white colonisers and their black slaves.
Cuba and the Night by Pico Iyer, Knopf, New York (1995). The protagonist is Cuba itself.
Dreaming in Cuban by Cristina García, Knopf (1992). A story of families divided across three generations by a Cuban-American writer.
Havana Bay by Martin Cruz Smith, Pan Books, UK (1999). The fourth in the Arkady Renko series of thrillers by the author best-known for *Gorky Park*.
The Old Man and the Sea by Ernest Hemingway, Scribner, New York (1952).
Our Man in Havana by Graham Greene, Viking, New York (1958).
The Mambo Kings Play Songs of Love by Oscar Hijuelos, Farrar, Straus & Giroux, New York (1989).
Patria o Muerte! The Great Zoo and Other Poems by Nicolás Guillén, Monthly Review Press, New York (1972).
The Voice of the Turtle edited by Peter Bush (1998). A collection of Cuban short stories translated into English.

Culture

Afrocuba by Pedro P. Sarduy and Jean Stubbs, Latin America Bureau, London (1993).
Los Negros Curros by Fernando Ortíz, Editorial de Ciencias Sociales, Havana (1986).
Salsa: Havana Heat, Bronx Beat by Hernando Calvo Ospina, Latin America Bureau, London (1995).
Santería from Africa to the New World by G. Brandon, Indiana University Press, Bloomington (1993).

Fidel Castro

Castro, the Blacks and Africa by Carlos Moore, Center for Afro-American Studies UCLA, Los Angeles (1988).
Castro's Cuba: Cuba's Fidel by Lee Lockwood, Macmillan, New York (1967).
Castro's Final Hour by Andres Oppenheimer, Simon & Schuster, New York (1992).
In Defense of Socialism by Fidel Castro, Pathfinder Press, New York (1989).
An Encounter with Fidel by Gianni Mina, Ocean Press, Melbourne (1991).
Fidel: A Critical Portrait by Tad Szulc, Morrow, New York (1986).
Fidel Castro by Robert E. Quirk, W.W. Norton, New York (1993).
Fidel Castro by John Gerassi, Doubleday, New York (1973).
Fidel Castro y la Revolución Cubana by Carlos Alberto Montaner, Plaza and Janes, Barcelona (1984).
Fidel Castro: Rebel Liberator or Dictator? by Jules Dubois, Bobbs-Merril, Indianapolis (1959).
Guerrilla Prince: The Untold Story of Fidel Castro by Georgie Anne Geyer, Little, Brown and Company, Boston (1991).
History Will Absolve Me by Fidel Castro, L. Stuart, New York (1961).
Papa and Fidel by Karl Alexander, Tom Doherty Associates, New York (1989).
Revolutionary Struggle 1947–1958: Selected Works of Fidel Castro by Fidel Castro, The M.I.T. Press, Cambridge (1972).
The Taming of Fidel Castro by Maurice Halpern, University of California Press, Berkeley (1981).

Politics and History

Baseball: The People's Game by Harold Seymore, Oxford University Press, New York (1990).
Baseball and the Cold War by Howard Senzel, Harcourt Brace Jovanovich, New York (1977).
Che: A Memoir by Fidel Castro, Ocean Press, Melbourne (1994).
Children of Che by Karen Wald, Ramparts Press, Palo Alto (1978).
Children of the Revolution by Jonathan Kozol, Delacorte Press, New York (1978).
Cuba Confidential: The Extraordinary History of Cuba, Its History and Its Exiles, by Ann Louise Bardach, Penguin Books, London (2004).
Cuba: A Short History, edited by Leslie Bethell, Cambridge University Press, Cambridge (1993).

Cuba after Communism by Eliana Cardosa and Ann Helwege, The M.I.T. Press, Cambridge (1993).
Cuba After the Cold War, edited by Carmelo Mesa-Lago, University of Pittsburgh Press, Pittsburgh (1993).
Cuba: Between Reform and Revolution by Louis A. Perez, Oxford University Press, New York (1988).
Cuba from Columbus to Castro by Jaime Suchlicki, Charles Scribner's Sons, New York (1974).
Cuba for Beginners by Rius, Pathfinder Press, New York (1970).
Cuba in the 1970s by Carmelo Mesa-Lago, University of New Mexico Press, Albuquerque (1974).
Cuba on the Brink by James G. Blight, Bruce J. Allyn and David A. Welch, Pantheon, New York (1993).
Cuba: Or the Pursuit of Freedom by Hugh Thomas, Eyre & Spottiswoode, London (1971).
Cuba: Order and Revolution by Jorge Dominguez, Harvard University Press, Cambridge (1978).
The Cuban Revolution by Jaime Suchlicki, University of Miami Press, Coral Gables (1968).
The Cuban Revolution: Origins, Course and Legacy by Marifeli Pérez Stable, Oxford University Press, New York (1993).
Cuba Roja: Cómo Viven los Cubanos con Fidel Castro by Román Orozco, Cambio 16, Madrid (1993).
Cuba vs the CIA by Robert E. Light and Carl Marzani, Marzani and Munsell, New York (1961).
In Cuba by Ernesto Cardenal, New Directions, New York (1974).
The Cuban Story by Herbert L. Matthews, George Braziller, New York (1961).
The Death of Che Guevara by Jay Cantor, Knopf, New York (1983).
Diary of the Cuban Revolution by Carlos Franqui, Viking, New York (1980).
The Historical Dictionary of Cuba by Suchlicki Jaime, Scarecrow Press, Metuchen (1988).
Khrushchev: A Biography by Roy Medvedev, Doubleday, New York (1984).
Lansky by Hank Messick, Putnam, New York (1971).
José Martí: Cuban Patriot by Richard Butler Gray, University of Florida Press, Gainesville (1962).
No Free Lunch: Food and Revolution in Cuba by M. Benjamin, J. Collins and M. Scott, Institute for Food and Development Policy, San Francisco (1984).
One Thousand Fearful Words for Fidel Castro by Lawrence Ferlin-ghetti, City Lights, San Francisco (1961).

Selected Works of Ernesto Guevara, edited by Rolando E. Bonachea and Nelson P. Valdes, The M.I.T. Press, Cambridge (1969).

Foreign Relations

Breaking with Moscow by Arkady Shevchenko, Knopf, New York (1985).
The Closest of Enemies by Wayne S. Smith, W.W. Norton, New York (1987).
Cuba in Transition: Options for US Policy by Gillian Gunn, Twentieth Century Fund Press, New York (1993).
The History of Guantánamo Bay by Marion Emerson Murphy, US Naval Base, Guantánamo Bay (1953).
Inside the Monster: Writings on the United States and American Imperialism by Jose Martí, Monthly Review Press, New York (1975).
The Soviet Union and Cuba Raymond W. Duncan, Praeger, New York (1985).
Thirteen Days: A Memoir of the Cuban Missile Crisis by Robert F. Kennedy, Norton, New York (1969).
Los Gusanos by John Sayles, HarperCollins, New York (1991).
The Missile Crisis by Elie Abel, Lippincott, Philadelphia (1966).

Other Insight Guides

In addition to this book, Cuba is also covered by an *Insight Pocket Guide* and an *Insight Compact Guide*.

Other Insight Guides which cover this region include *Insight Guide: Caribbean, Insight Guide: Haiti & Dominican Republic, Insight Guide: Bahamas, Insight Guide: Florida,* and *Insight Guide: Miami.*

Art & Photo Credits

Danny Aeberhard 16, 34R, 45, 70L, 154T, 225T, 261T, 263T, 265, 274T, 284, 289, 301BR
AFP/Getty Images 23L, 78, 123
akg-images 29T, 112R
Ulf Andersen/Getty Images 25L, 112L
AP/PA Photos 26/27, 83, 314B
Suzy Bennett/Alamy 1
Bettmann/Corbis 29BR, 44
Pam Barrett 6BL, 28TR & BL, 34L, 61, 161R, 178L, 201, 211, 295T, 300T, 301T, 302BL, 303, 306T, 315T, 316, 317T, 353, 355, 368
Trygve Bølstad/Panos Pictures 62
Camera Press/Gamma/2824
Federico Garcia Lorca 54L
M Chianura/Rex Features 72
Carlos B. Chils/Latinphoto 203T
Gerardo Churches/Contemporary Dance of Cuba 111
Cosmo Condina /Stock Connection/Rex Features 122
Corbis 43, 48
Roger Cracknell/Alamy 238
Cuban Film Institute/Kobal 40
c. Warner Br/Everett/Rex Features 113
Claudia Daut/Reuters/Corbis 22
Danita Delimont/Alamy 320/321
John Denham back flap top
Jean Du Boisberranger/hemis.fr 258
Adam Eastland/Pictures Colour Library 118
Alejandro Ernesto/epa/Corbis 82
Jure Erzen/WpN 14/15
Patrick Escudero/Hoa-Qui 126/127
Lydia Evans 18, 19, 20, 21L, 24, 25R, 81, 115
Barbara P. Fernandez/WpN 79
Focus on Sport/Getty Images 121B
Bertrand Gardel/hemis.fr 128/129
Glyn Genin/APA back cover left, 32, 89, 145T, 155T, 156T, 158, 162, 163, 165, 189, 190, 199, 202, 203, 204 & T, 210T, 219, 220, 221 & T, 223, 224, 231T, 232T, 236, 243, 244, 246BR & T, 251, 255, 264R, 269 & T, 275T, 285T, 287, 293, 295, 296, 301BL, 302BR & T, 305, 308, 313, 318L, 323, 325 & T, 326, 327 & T, 339
Getty Images/Altrendo 6CL
Getty Images/Robert Harding 130/131
Eduardo Gil 65, 71L, 178R, 187, 208, 226, 248/249, 255T, 324
Tria Giovan 245, 261, 310, 317BR
Jose Goitia/AFP/Getty Images 85
Jose Goitia/Corbis 31B
Michel Gotin/hemis.fr 329
Andreas M Gross back cover bottom
Corbin Gurkin/WpN 114
Emily Hatchwell 71R, 171T
Tobias Hauser/laif/Camera Press 299BL
Andre Huber/Latinphoto 96

Hulton Archive/Getty Images 55
Thomas Ives 64, 73, 266
Ivan Kashinsky/WpN 90
Glyn Kirk/Action Plus 124R
Lothar Kornblum/SIME-4Corners Images 227
Andrew Lepley/Redferns 100
Barry Lewis/Network 66, 328T
Pat Luethy/Latinphoto 292
Larry Luxner 218, 223T
Andy Lyons/Allsport/Getty 125
Reno Massola/Latinphoto 9B
Jenny Matthews/Network 334
Fred Mawer front flap bottom, back cover center, back flap bottom, 28T, 60, 156, 162T, 267, 283, 286, 288T, 311, 314T, 370
Miami Herald 52L, 53R, 62B, 85B
Mockford & Bonetti/APA 2/3, 4T, 6T & BR, 7T & B, 8BL, 9T, 17L & R, 21R, 30TR, 31T, 37L, 70R, 77R, 88, 91, 92/93, 94, 95, 107, 109L & R, 116, 121, 132, 133L & R, 136, 137L & R, 143, 144, 145, 147, 148, 149, 150T, 153 & T, 155, 159T, 160 & T, 168, 169, 171, 172, 173, 175R, 176 & T, 180, 182, 185T, 189, 193T, 194, 209L & R, 210, 226T, 229, 230, 232, 233 & T, 237, 239 & T, 240, 241, 242L & R, 243T, 247T, 250, 256T, 259, 260, 262 & T, 263, 264L, 270, 272T, 273, 276/277, 280, 281, 282 & T, 283T, 284T, 285, 288, 290 & T, 291, 297 & T, 298, 299BR, 300B, 304, 306, 307, 312, 315, 317L, 318R, 337, 350, 362
New York Times/eyevine 124L
North Wind Picture Archives/Alamy 33, 38, 42
Randy R. Pages/Latinphoto 332
Aldo Pavan/SIME-4Corners Images 299T
Tony Perrottet 36, 184T, 193, 195T, 196/197, 345
Jonathan Pile/Impact 119T
Christopher Pillitz/Getty Images 12/13
Polaris/eyevine 97
Popperfoto/Alamy 256BL
Karl-Heinz Raach/laif/Camera Press 154
Joe Raedle/Getty Images 225
David Redfern/Redferns 101
Richter Library, University of Miami 30TL, 41, 46, 50, 51
Silke Roetting/transit/Still Pictures 179
Adalberto Roque/AFP/Getty Images 106
RS/Keystone USA/Rex Features 119R
Philip Ryalls/Redferns 102
Neil E Schlecht 183
Erich Schlegel 31CL, 74
Wolfgang Schmidt/Das Fotoarchiv./Still Pictures 117

Alfonso Silva 8BR, 214/215, 228, 231, 319T
Sipa Press/Rex Features 30BR
Joe Skipper/Reuters/Corbis 313T
Michael Steele/Getty Images 120
Time & Life Pictures/Getty Image 53L
Topham Picturepoint 52R, 54R, 76, 77L
Agustin B. Torres/Latinphoto 98
Stefano Torrione/hemis.fr 150
Mireille Vautier back cover right, 67, 68, 69, 110, 143T, 175L, 254L & R
Francesco Venturi/Kea spine, front flap top, 35, 151
Joby Williams 3BR, 4B, 5, 23R, 68B, 75, 140, 141, 146 & T, 152, 157, 159, 170T, 173T, 174, 175T, 177, 181, 185, 186, 188, 191, 195, 198, 205, 206, 207 & T, 252, 253, 257, 271, 272, 274, 291T, 308T, 342, 358, 375
Marcus Wilson-Smith 252T, 330/331
Corrie Wingate 8T, 158T, 170, 222
World Illustrated/Photoshot 47
World Pictures/Photoshot 10/11, 80, 184B

PICTURE SPREADS

86/87: John Denham 86BR; Glyn Genin 86CR, 87CL; Eduardo Gil 87CR; Fred Mawer 86CL, 87BC; Tony Perrottet 87BL; Ray Roberts/Alamy 87TR; Mireille Vautier 86/87; Corrie Wingate 86BL.
104/105: Trygve Bølstad/Panos Pictures 104R; Naomi Peck 105TR; Rolando Pujol/South American Pictures 104B, 105TR; Emilio Jesús Reyer/Colección Museo di Guana bacoa 105BR; Mireille Vautier 105BL; Visual & Written SL/Alamy 105TL.
166/167: Glyn Genin/APA 167CL; J.L.D. Grande/AISA 166/167; Emily Hatchwell 166BL; Ismael R/ Phototeca 167TR; Nicolas Sapieha/ Kea 167CR; Hemis/Alamy 167B; Peter Woloszynski 166CR.
212/213: Danny Aeberhard 213BL; Jan Butchofsky Houser 212/213; Andreas M Gross 213CR; Barry Lewis/Alamy 213TR; Mockford & Bonetti/APA 212BL; Mireille Vautier 212BR, 213CL; Joby Williams 213BR.
234/235: AA World Travel Library/ Alamy 234TL; Glyn Genin/APA 235CL; imagebroker/Alamy 234/235; Dan McIntosh 234BL; Mockford & Bonetti/APA 235TR; Alfonso Silva 235BL & BR; Rob Walls/Alamy 234BR.

Map Production: Lovell Johns Ltd

© 2008 Apa Publications GmbH & Co. Verlag KG (Singapore branch)

Production: Linton Donaldson

INDEX

Numbers in italics refer to photographs